THE
SECOND
WORLD
WAR

A History

Combining New Selections

from the Greatest Chronicler of the War

and the Most Memorable Illustrations

by the Men Who Took Part in It

Volume II

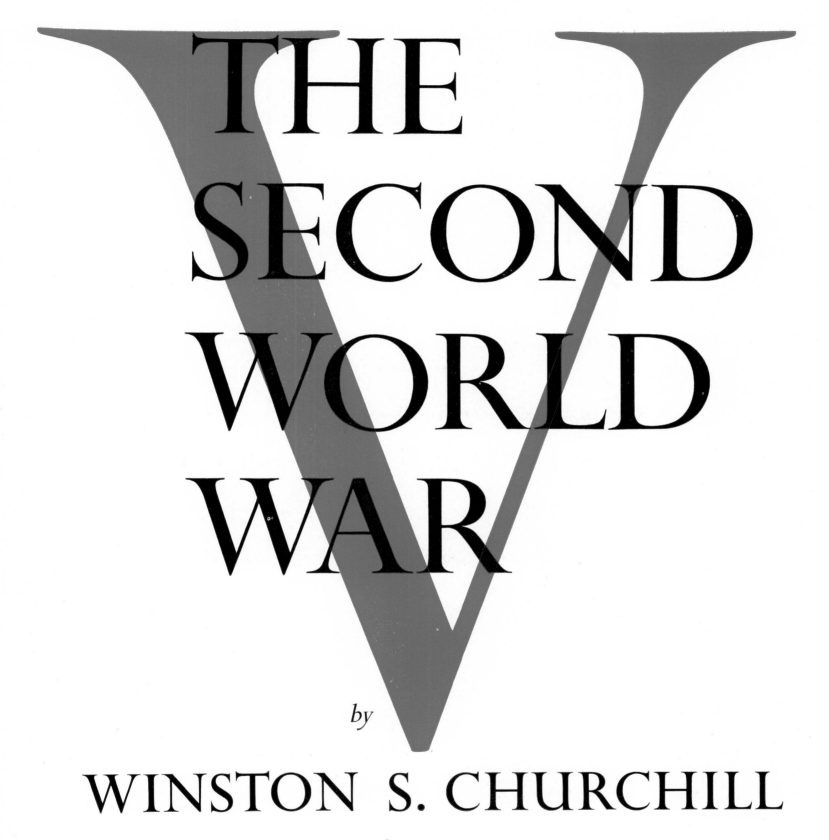

THE SECOND WORLD WAR

by

WINSTON S. CHURCHILL

and

The Editors of LIFE

TIME INCORPORATED   NEW YORK   1959

TIME INCORPORATED

Editor-in-Chief . . . . HENRY R. LUCE

Executive Assistant . . . ALBERT L. FURTH

President . . . . ROY E. LARSEN

Editorial Director . . . . . HEDLEY DONOVAN

LIFE MAGAZINE

Managing Editor EDWARD K. THOMPSON

Assistant Managing Editors PHILIP H. WOOTTON JR., GEORGE P. HUNT
HUGH MOFFETT

Art Director CHARLES TUDOR

Copy Editor JOSEPH KASTNER

Chief of Research MARIAN A. MACPHAIL

"The Second World War" was produced by the following editorial staff:

Editor NORMAN P. ROSS

Art Director RICHARD GANGEL

Associate Editors DENIS KELLY, ROBERT WERNICK

Chief Researcher BEATRICE T. DOBIE

Research Staff KATHLEEN HAMPTON, ELIZABETH HAWLEY
MARY H. MELVILLE, MARTHA R. WALLACE

Map Staff MARGARET BASSETT, DAVID BERGAMINI
ROSEMARY C. ALEXANDER

Art Associates ROBERT L. YOUNG, ARTHUR SOLIN
ALBERT J. DUNN

Copy Readers LINDA WOLFE, IDAMAE B. BROOKS
MARGUERITE SCHEIPS

Copy Assistants MARY JANE ENGLISH, CAROLYN MILLER

Picture Researcher BETTY DOYLE

Production Assistants GEORGE J. BLOODGOOD, JULIO DE LA TORRE

•

Publisher ANDREW HEISKELL

General Manager ROBERT T. ELSON

Business Manager for LIFE Books JAMES T. KERR

Production Manager ROBERT E. FOY

The text for this book was specially abridged by Denis Kelly from Sir Winston Churchill's six-volume memoirs entitled *The Second World War*, excerpts from which were published in LIFE from 1948 to 1953. The picture essays were written by Robert Wernick and the map captions by David Bergamini. The photographs and paintings were selected from the finest work of World War II made by both Allies and enemies. Many of these illustrations appeared in the weekly issues of LIFE during and after the war, while others are here published for the first time.

Working closely with the above staff were the following individuals and departments of LIFE: Ray Mackland, Picture Editor; Thomas N. Carmichael, Domestic Newsbureau Chief; George Caturani, Foreign Newsbureau Chief; Natalie Kosek, Picture Bureau Chief, and Doris O'Neil, Picture Library Chief.

Volume II

TABLE OF CONTENTS

A dying German soldier takes the bullet that ends his career of conquest in the East. He was photographed on the field of battle by a Russian frontline cameraman a split second after a Red Army sniper fired his rifle.

RUSSIA STRIKES BACK

The Thundering Battle Front

THROUGHOUT the early months of the year 1942 the Russians had by unrelenting pressure forced the enemy line back at many points. The Germans, unprepared for the rigours of winter campaigning, suffered great privations and heavy losses. When spring came Hitler issued a secret directive, dated April 5, with this preamble: "The winter campaign in Russia is nearing its close. The outstanding bravery and the self-sacrificing effort of our troops on the Eastern Front have achieved a great defensive success. The enemy suffered very severe losses in men and matériel. In an attempt to take advantage of what seemed to be initial successes, Russia during the course of the winter also expended the bulk of her reserves intended for future operations.

"As soon as weather and terrain conditions are favourable the superior German command and German forces must take the initiative once again to force the enemy to do our bidding. The objective is to wipe out the entire defence potential remaining to the Soviets and to cut them off as far as possible from their most important sources of supply."

He continued: "To give effect to this, it is intended to hold the central part of the front, in the north to bring about the fall of Leningrad, . . . and on the southern wing of the Army front to force a breakthrough into the Caucasus.

. . . To begin with, all available forces are to be combined for the main operations in the southern sector, the objective being to destroy the enemy before the Don in order to gain the oil region of the Caucasian area and to cross the Caucasus Mountains. . . . We must try to reach Stalingrad, or at least to subject this city to bombardment by our heavy weapons to such an extent that it is eliminated as an armament and traffic centre in the future."

As a preliminary to these main operations Sevastopol was to be captured by Manstein's Eleventh Army and the Russians ejected from the Crimea. The Southern Army Group, under Field-Marshal von Bock, was given very large forces for its task. There were a hundred divisions, grouped into five Armies, of which nearly sixty divisions were German, including eight armoured divisions; the rest were Romanian, Italian, or Hungarian. Of a total of 2,750 German aircraft on the Eastern Front, 1,500 were detailed to support the southern operations.

It was probably intended to open this great campaign at the end of May, but the Russians struck first. On May 12 Marshal Timoshenko launched a heavy attack on and south of Kharkov, making a deep bulge in the German line. But his southern flank was vulnerable, and a series of German counterassaults forced him to give up all the ground he had gained. This "spoiling" attack, though it cost the Russians heavy casualties, probably caused a month's delay in plans; if so the time gained proved invaluable later.

While this battle was still in progress the German Eleventh Army opened its assault on Sevastopol. The great fortress fell after a month of siege and hard fighting.

In order to free the way for the southeasterly drive to the Caucasus, Rostov had to be taken and the Russians cleared from within the bend of the Lower Don. The first thrusts, on May 28, were from north of Kursk and Belgorod. By July 7 the former had reached the outskirts of Rostov, but could not capture it. The long defensive flank from Orel to Voronezh was left to be guarded largely by Hungarians, while the German 4th Panzer Army drove down the western bank of the Don. A later thrust broke through the Russian defences before Izyum and joined the southerly drive. Finally, a third attack from Stalino swept round to reach the Lower Don above Rostov. All this went very much according to plan, though not so swiftly as had been hoped. Russian resistance was strong, but the several penetrations of their line by armoured and motorised troops enforced a general withdrawal, much harassed by the enemy, to behind the river Don.

After three weeks the first phase was virtually over and Hitler then gave his orders for the next. The Southern Army Group was now divided into Army Group A, commanded by List, and Army Group B, under Bock. Hitler's directive of July 23 gave them their tasks. Army Group A was to capture the entire eastern shore of the Black Sea. After the capture of the Maikop oil fields a mobile force was to take Grozny. "Subsequently the Baku area is to be captured by an advance along the Caspian Sea." Army Group B, having established a defensive flank along the river Don, was to advance on Stalingrad, "smash the enemy forces being assembled there, and occupy the city." Mobile forces were to proceed down the Volga to Astrakhan.

Local operations by the Central Army Group were to take place in order to prevent the Russians withdrawing troops from that front, and in the north Leningrad was to be captured in early September. For this purpose Hitler ordered five divisions of the Eleventh Army, released by the capture of Sevastopol, to join the Northern Army Group, an improvident weakening of his major attack. They arrived in time not to attack, but to defend a German line sagging under

Occupied Russia (*blue area*), at height of German invasion, reached to gates of Moscow and Stalingrad. Aided by new supply lines Russians (*black*) retook grey area before Moscow in winter of 1941-42. German supply line (*center*) extended 1,600 miles.

Russian assault. The drive of the German Army Group A to reach the Caucasus was led by Kleist's First Panzer Army of fifteen divisions. Once across the Don they made much headway against little opposition. They reached Maikop on August 9, to find that the oil fields were thoroughly destroyed. Another column took Mozdok on August 25, but was held on the river Terek and failed to reach the Grozny oil fields. Those of Baku, the greatest of them all, were still 300 miles away. On the shore of the Black Sea, Novorossisk was taken on September 10, and the Russian Black Sea Fleet, which had sheltered there when Sevastopol fell, sailed to Tuapse, where they remained. Hitler's orders to seize the entire Black Sea littoral could not be carried out. In the centre the Germans reached the foothills of the Caucasus, but no farther. Russian resistance, reinforced by fresh troops sent by railway along the western shore of the Caspian, was everywhere firm. Kleist, weakened by diversions for the Stalingrad effort, struggled on till November. He took Nalchik on November 2. Winter conditions then intervened. His bolt was shot.

On the front of Army Group B worse than failure befell. The lure of Stalingrad fascinated Hitler; its very name was a challenge. The city was important both as a centre of industry and as an ominous strong point on the defensive flank protecting his main thrust to the Caucasus. It now became a magnet drawing to itself the supreme effort of the German Army and Air Force.

The deflection southward of the Fourth Panzer Army to help Army Group A in its crossing of the Don also had serious consequences. It delayed the drive on Stalingrad, and by the time this army turned east again the Russian forces that had withdrawn across the river were reorganising. Resistance grew daily stiffer. It was not till September 15 that after heavy fighting between the Don and the Volga, the outskirts of Stalingrad were reached. The battering-ram attacks of the next month made some progress at the cost of terrible slaughter. Nothing could overcome the Russians, fighting with passionate devotion amid the ruins of their city.

The German generals, long uneasy, had good cause for their anxiety. After three months of fighting the main objectives of the campaign, the Caucasus, Stalingrad, and Leningrad, were still in Russian hands. Casualties had been very heavy and replacements insufficient. Hitler, instead of sending fresh contingents forward to replace losses, was forming them into new and untrained divisions. In military opinion it was high time to call a halt, but "the Carpeteater" would not listen. At the end of September Halder, Hitler's Chief of Staff, finally resisted his master, and was dismissed. Hitler scourged his armies on.

By the middle of October the German position had markedly worsened. The frontage of Army Group B stretched over 700 miles. General Paulus's Sixth Army had expended its efforts at Stalingrad, and now lay exhausted with its flanks thinly protected by allies of dubious quality. Winter was near, when the Russians would surely make their counterstroke. If the Don front could not be held the safety of the armies on the Caucasus front would be undermined. But Hitler would not countenance any suggestion of withdrawal. On November 19, 1942 the Russians delivered their long and valiantly prepared encircling assault, striking both north and south of Stalingrad against the weakly defended German flanks. Four days later the Russian pincers met and the Sixth German Army was trapped between the Don and the Volga. Paulus proposed to break out. Hitler ordered him to hold his ground. As the days passed his army was compressed into an ever-lessening space. On December 12, in bitter weather, General Manstein made a supreme effort to break through the Russian cordon from the southwest and relieve the besieged Sixth Army. He pierced the Russian line to a depth of forty miles, but there he was stopped, still fifty miles from Stalingrad. A new Russian offensive from the north threatened his flank and forced him into a retreat which spread to all the German southern front, including the Caucasus, and ended only when it was back behind Rostov-on-the-Don.

There was now no hope for further succour for Paulus. He and his army held out for seven more terrible weeks, but their doom was certain. The tremendous drama unfolded. Great efforts were made to supply him from the air, but little got through, and at the expense of heavy losses in aircraft. The cold was intense; food and ammunition were scarce, and an outbreak of typhus added to the miseries of his men. On January 8 he rejected an ultimatum to surrender, and next day the last phase began with violent Russian attacks from the west. The Germans fought strongly, so that only five miles were gained in as many days. But at last they began to crack, and by January 17 the

Russians were within ten miles of Stalingrad itself. Paulus threw into the fight every man who could bear arms, but it was no use. On January 22 the Russians surged forward again, until the Germans were thrown back on the outskirts of the city they had tried in vain to take. Here the remains of a once-great army were pinned in an oblong only four miles deep by eight long. Under intense artillery fire and air bombardment the survivors defended themselves in violent street-fighting, but their plight was hopeless, and as the Russians pressed forward exhausted units began to surrender wholesale. Paulus and his staff were captured on January 31, and on February 2 Marshal Voronov reported that all resistance had ceased and that 90,000 prisoners had been taken. These were the survivors of twenty-one German and one Romanian divisions.

This crushing disaster to the German arms ended Hitler's prodigious effort to conquer Russia by force of arms, and destroy Communism by an equally odious form of totalitarian tyranny.

Victory, however, made Stalin no more genial. If he could have come to Casablanca the three Allies might have worked out a common plan face to face. But this was not to be, and discussions were pursued by telegram. We told him of our military decisions, and on my return home, with the President's authority, I had sent him an additional explanation of our plans, namely, to liberate Tunisia in April, capture Sicily, and push all our preparations to the limit for crossing the Channel in August or September.

"... It is evident," he replied promptly, "that, contrary to your previous calculations, the end of operations in Tunis is expected in April instead of February. I hardly need to tell you how disappointing is such a delay. ... It is [also] evident from your message that the establishment of the Second Front, in particular in France, is envisaged only in August-September."

Nevertheless the spring of 1943 marked the turning point of the war on the Eastern Front. Even before the German Army at Stalingrad had been overwhelmed the mounting Russian tide had swept the enemy back all along the line. The German army of the Caucasus was skilfully withdrawn, half of it to Rostov; the rest formed strong bridgeheads at Novorossisk and in the Kuban peninsula. The Russians pressed the enemy from the Don and back beyond the Donets River, the starting line of Hitler's

Resurgent Russia in 1943 had regained 60 percent of ground occupied by Germans. Red Army (*black*) outflanked Germans (*blue*) at Stalingrad, advanced to new line (*center*), checked German counterattack at Kursk, then pushed on past Dnieper in fall.

315

offensive of the previous summer. Farther north again the Germans lost ground, until they were more than 250 miles from Moscow. The investment of Leningrad was broken. The Germans and their satellites suffered immense losses in men and matériel. The ground gained in the past year was taken from them. They were no longer superior to the Russians on land. In the air they had now to reckon with the growing power of the British and American Air Forces, operating both from Britain and in Africa.

After the spring thaw both sides gathered themselves for a momentous struggle. The Russians, both on land and in the air, had now the upper hand, and the Germans can have had few hopes of ultimate victory. Nevertheless they got their blow in first. The Russian salient at Kursk projected dangerously into the German front, and it was decided to pinch it out by simultaneous attacks from north and south. This was foreseen by the Russians, who had had full warning and were ready. In consequence, when the attack started on July 5 the Germans met an enemy strongly installed in well-prepared defences. The northern attack made some ground, but at the end of a fortnight it had been thrown back. In the south success at first was greater and the Germans bit fifteen miles into the Russian lines. Then major counterattacks began, and by July 23 the Russian line was fully restored. The German offensive had completely failed. They gained no advantages to make up for their heavy losses, and the new "Tiger" tanks, on which they had counted for success, had been mauled by the Russian artillery.

THE German Army had already been depleted by its previous campaigns in Russia and diluted by inclusion of its second-rate allies. A great part of its strength had been massed against Kursk at the expense of other sectors of the thousand-mile active front. Now, when the Russian blows began to fall, it was unable to parry them. While the Kursk battle was still raging and the German reserves had been deeply committed the first blow came on July 12 against the German salient around Orel. After intense artillery preparation the main Russian attack fell on the northern face of the salient, with subsidiary onslaughts in the east. Deep penetrations were soon made, and although the defenders fought stoutly and bravely their strong points were in succession outflanked, surrounded, and reduced. Their counterattacks were repulsed, and under the weight of superior numbers and matériel they were crushed and overborne. Orel fell on August 5, and by the 18th the whole salient to a depth of fifty miles had been cut out.

The second major Russian offensive opened on August 3, while the Orel attack was still at its height. This time it was the German salient around Kharkov that suffered. Kharkov was an important centre of communications, and barred the way to the Ukraine and the Donets industrial basin. Its defences had been prepared with more than usual thoroughness. Again the major attacks fell on the northern face of the salient, one being directed due south against Kharkov itself, another thrusting southwestward so as to threaten the whole German rear. Within forty-eight hours both of these had bitten deep, in places up to thirty miles, and Belgorod had been taken. By August 11 Kharkov was threatened on three sides, a further attack from the east having been launched, while fifty miles to the northwest the Russians were advancing fast. On that day Hitler ordered that Kharkov was to be held at all costs. The German garrison stood to fight it out, and it was not till the 23rd that the whole town was in Russian hands.

THESE three immense battles of Kursk, Orel and Kharkov, all within a space of two months, marked the ruin of the German army on the Eastern Front. Everywhere they had been outfought and overwhelmed. The Russian plan, vast though it was, never outran their resources. And it was not only on land that the Russians proved their new superiority. In the air about 2,500 German aircraft were opposed by at least twice as many Russian planes, whose efficiency had been much improved. The German Air Force at this period of the war was at the peak of its strength, numbering about 6,000 aircraft in all. That less than half could be spared to support this crucial campaign is proof enough of the value to Russia of our operations in the Mediterranean and of the growing Allied bomber effort based on Britain. In fighter aircraft especially the Germans felt the pinch. Although already inferior on the Eastern Front, in September they had to weaken it still more in order to defend themselves in the West, where by the winter nearly three-quarters of the total German fighter strength was deployed. The swift and overlapping Russian blows gave the Germans no opportunity to make the best use of their air resources. Air units were frequently moved from one battle area to another in order to meet a fresh crisis, and wherever they went, leaving a gap behind them, they found the Russian planes in overmastering strength.

In September the Germans were in retreat along the whole of their southern front, from opposite Moscow to the Black Sea. The Russians swung forward in full pursuit. At the northern hinge a Russian thrust from Vyazma took Smolensk on September 25. No doubt the Germans hoped to stand on the Dnieper, the next great river line, but by early October the Russians were across it north of Kiev, and to the south at Pereyaslav and Kremenchug. Farther south again Dnepropetrovsk was taken on October 25. Only near the mouth of the river were the Germans still on the western bank of the Dnieper; all the rest had gone. The land approach to the Crimea, at Perekop, was captured by the Red Army, and the retreat of the strong German garrison in the Crimea was cut off. Kiev, outflanked on either side, fell on November 6, with many prisoners, and the Russians, driving forward, reached Korosten and Zhitomir. But a strong armoured counterattack on their flank drove them back, and the Germans recaptured the two towns. Here the front stabilised for the time being. In the north the Russians took Gomel at the end of November, and they crossed the upper reaches of the Dnieper on each side of Mogilev.

By December, after a three months' pursuit, the German armies in Central and South Russia had been thrust back more than 200 miles, and, failing to hold the Dnieper River line, lay open and vulnerable to a winter campaign in which, as they knew from bitter experience, their opponents excelled. Such was the grand Russian story of 1943.

Russian women by the hundreds dig an antitank ditch in the improvised defense system that was to stop the Germans in front of Moscow

THE INDOMITABLE

Soviet Triumphs
on the Snows

In December 1941, while the Nazi radio was still blaring fanfares of victory, winter in Russia arrived with a paralyzing violence. Frost and blizzards immobilized German trucks and tanks. Frostbitten Wehrmacht soldiers—shivering in their summer uniforms and whatever warmer clothes they could loot from burned-out villages—were beaten back and often surrounded by fresh, Siberian-trained Soviet soldiers, well equipped for winter warfare. This was two months after Hitler's announcement that "this enemy is already broken and will never rise again."

Winter was grim for the Russians too. A million people died of cold and hunger in besieged Leningrad, and other millions suffered fearful hardships while rebuilding Russia's war industry in Siberia. But Russia was a tougher nut than Hitler ever dreamed of cracking. The iron brace of the Communist dictatorship held firm, and the Russian masses made heroic sacrifices in the defense of their homeland.

All through the winter the German front sagged and split badly. It was probably saved from complete collapse only by Hitler's insistence that his armies stand and fight where they were. They succeeded then, but their very success sowed the seed for later trouble: Hitler became convinced that an order to stand at all costs was the way to stop the Russian. Next winter, with catastrophic results, he repeated that order at Stalingrad (*pages 320-321*).

Crossing snow fields (*below*), mobile Russian teams of camouflaged ski troops and tanks pulling infantry on sledges slip through an undefended sector of the long front to strike at the German rear.

Hunting mines, Russians push detectors across a field studded with antitank obstacles. Camouflage uniforms for snow fighting were plentiful in the Red Army; the Germans had neglected to bring any.

318

Cutting wire as they advance under fire, Russian sappers make a path for assault troops. The appalling winter made it difficult for the Germans even to erect flimsy wire obstructions like this: it took high

explosives to help dig post holes in ground frozen to a depth of five feet. Guns mired in the fall rains had frozen so stubbornly into the ground that they were torn to pieces when tractors tried to pull them out.

Capturing Germans, Soviet infantrymen cover four enemy soldiers floundering across the snow. German discipline was superlative in the early stages of the war and the Russians took few prisoners.

Victory in the Ruins of Stalingrad

For five months charge and countercharge, barrage and bombing succeeded one another in the heap of rubble that was once the great industrial city of Stalingrad (*below*). The city was one of the two chief goals of Hitler's 1942 campaign in Russia, the other being the oil wells of the Caucasus. One army actually got to the Caucasus but its attack petered out short of its objective. Another, the Sixth, reached the outskirts of Stalingrad in mid-September

and at frightful cost occupied all of the city except for a few blocks along the Volga. Hitler was so fascinated by Stalingrad—apparently more for its name than for its strategic value—that he refused to pay any attention to the increasing dangers of its position. It was located at the end of a long vulnerable salient, one side of which was held by unenthusiastic Romanian troops while the other was bounded by a 190-mile stretch of steppe protected by almost no troops at all. In November the Russians came charging in on both sides. Hitler told the Sixth Army to die rather than retreat—and die it did, after a long agony in which more than 100,000 men were killed in battle or by the Russian winter. When the last of the 90,000 survivors surrendered on February 2, a period of national mourning was decreed in Germany. From that day onward, the advances in Russia were made by Russians (*next page*).

Charging Russians, recalling cavalry sweeps of another age, race across the steppes of southwest Russia. Cavalry units like this found it easy to exploit the big gaps which the Germans necessarily left along their immense front. Since it was easier to find grass for horses than oil for tanks, cavalry was even better than armored units for swooping down on German communications and supply depots far in the rear.

Surrendering Germans come up out of their foxholes in a Russian forest clearing. Many captured officers, including the general at Stalingrad, Friedrich von Paulus, turned against Hitler and made anti-Nazi propaganda broadcasts to Germany. For most prisoners, surrender meant little relief from the hardships of the front: more than a million of the 3.5 million men captured in Russia never came home.

On Guadalcanal, where U.S. Marines took the first chip out of Japan's swollen empire, Japanese bones, bullet-shattered American helmets and abandoned gas masks around an empty dugout scar the jungle floor with rust and rot.

14

COMMAND OF THE SEAS

The Defeat of the U-Boats

WE have now reached the turning point of the Second World War. The entry of the United States into the struggle after the Japanese assault on Pearl Harbor made it certain that the cause of Freedom would not be cast away. The aggressors, both in Europe and Asia, had been driven to the defensive. Stalingrad in February 1943 marked the turn of the tide in Russia. By May all German and Italian forces in the African continent had been killed or captured. The American victories in the Coral Sea and at Midway a year before had stopped Japanese expansion in the Pacific Ocean. Australia and New Zealand were freed from the threat of invasion, and the leaders of Japan were already conscious that their onslaught had passed its zenith. Hitler had still to pay the full penalty of his fatal error in trying to conquer Russia by invasion. He had still to squander the immense remaining strength of Germany in many theatres not vital to the main result. Soon the German nation was to be alone in Europe, surrounded by an infuriated world.

But between survival and victory there are many stages. Over two years of intense and bloody fighting lay before us all. Henceforward however the danger was not Destruction, but Stalemate. The Americans' armies had to mature and their vast construction of shipping to become effective before the full power of the Great Republic could be hurled into the struggle, and the Western Allies could never strike home at Hitler's Europe, and thus bring the war to a decisive end, unless another major favourable change came to pass. Anglo-American "maritime power," a modern term expressing the combined strength of naval and air forces properly woven together, became supreme on and under the surface of the seas and the oceans during the year 1943. Without this no amphibious operations on the enormous scale required to liberate Europe would have been possible. Soviet Russia would have been left to face Hitler's whole remaining strength while most of Europe lay in his grip.

The singlehanded British struggle against the U-boats, the magnetic mines, and the surface raiders in the first two and a half years of the war has already been described. The long awaited supreme event of the American alliance, which arose from the Japanese attack on Pearl Harbor, seemed at first to have increased our perils at sea. In 1940 and 1941 we lost four million tons of merchant shipping a year. In 1942, after the United States was our Ally, this figure nearly doubled, and the U-boats sank ships faster than the Allies could build them. During 1943, thanks to the immense shipbuilding programme of the United States, the new tonnage at last surpassed losses at sea from all causes, and the second quarter saw, for the

325

first time, U-boat losses exceed their rate of replacement. The time was presently to come when more U-boats would be sunk in the Atlantic than merchant ships. But before this lay a long and bitter conflict.

The Battle of the Atlantic was the dominating factor all through the war. Never for one moment could we forget that everything happening elsewhere, on land, at sea, or in the air, depended ultimately on its outcome, and amid all other cares we viewed its changing fortunes day by day with hope or apprehension. The tale of hard and unremitting toil, often under conditions of acute discomfort and frustration and always in the presence of unseen danger, is lighted by incident and drama. But for the individual sailor or airman there were few moments of exhilarating action to break the monotony of an endless succession of anxious, uneventful days. Dire crisis might at any moment flash upon the scene with brilliant fortune or glare with mortal tragedy. Many gallant actions and incredible feats of endurance are recorded, but the deeds of those who perished will never be known.

In April 1943 we could see the balance turn. The U-boat packs were kept underwater and harried continually, while the air and surface escort of the convoys coped with the attackers. We were now strong enough to form independent flotilla groups to act like cavalry divisions, apart from all escort duties. This I had long desired to see. Two hundred and thirty-five U-boats, the greatest number the Germans ever achieved, were in action. But their crews were beginning to waver. They could never feel safe. Their attacks, even when conditions were favourable, were no longer pressed home, and our Atlantic losses fell by nearly 300,000 tons. In May alone forty U-boats perished in the ocean. The German Admiralty watched their charts with strained attention, and at the end of the month Admiral Doenitz recalled the remnants of his fleet to rest or to fight in less hazardous waters. By June the sinkings fell to the lowest figure since the United States had entered the war. The convoys came through intact, the supply line was safe, the decisive battle had been fought and won.

Our armies could now be launched across the sea against the underbelly of Hitler's Europe. The extirpation of Axis power in North Africa opened to our convoys the direct route to Egypt, India, and Australia, protected from Gibraltar to Suez by sea and air forces working from the newly won bases along the route. The long haul round the Cape, which had cost us so dear in time, effort, and tonnage, would soon be ended. The saving of an average of forty-five days for each convoy to the Middle East increased magnificently at one stroke the fertility of our shipping.

As the defeat of the U-boats affected all subsequent events we must here carry the story forward. For a time they dispersed over the remote wastes of the South Atlantic and Indian Oceans, where our defences were relatively weak but we presented fewer targets. Our air offensive in the Bay of Biscay continued to gather strength. In July thirty-seven U-boats were sunk, mostly by air attack, and of these nearly half perished in the Bay. In the last three months of the year fifty-three were destroyed while we lost only forty-seven merchant ships.

Throughout a stormy autumn the U-boats struggled vainly, and with small results, to retrieve their ascendency in the North Atlantic. Although in the face of the harsh facts Admiral Doenitz was forced to recoil, he continued to maintain as many U-boats at sea as ever. But their attack was blunted and they seldom tried to cut through our defences. He did not however despair. "The enemy," he declared in January 1944, "has succeeded in gaining the advantage in defence. The day will come when I shall offer Churchill a first-rate submarine war. The submarine weapon has not been broken by the setbacks of 1943. On the contrary, it has become stronger. In 1944, which will be a successful but a hard year, we shall smash Britain's supply [line] with a new submarine weapon."

This confidence was not wholly unfounded. A gigantic effort was being made in Germany to develop a new type of U-boat which could move more quickly underwater and travel much farther. At the same time many of the older boats were withdrawn so that they could be fitted with the "snorkel" and work in British coastal waters. This new device enabled them to recharge their batteries while submerged with only a small tube for the intake of air remaining above the surface. Their chances of eluding detection from the air were thus improved, and it soon became evident that the snorkel-fitted boats were intended to dispute the passage of the English Channel whenever the Allied invasion was launched.

Guadalcanal and New Guinea

WHILE British sea power was deployed mainly in the Atlantic and the Mediterranean, the United States was bearing almost alone the whole burden of the war against Japan. In the immense ocean spaces from India to the western coast of America itself we could give little support except with slender Australian and New Zealand naval forces. Our depleted Eastern Fleet, now based in East Africa, could do no more for a time than protect our convoys. In the Pacific however the balance had turned. The naval superiority of the United States was re-established, and the Japanese, while trying to consolidate their gains in the East Indies, had nothing to spare for incursions into the Indian Ocean. Much had happened in the Pacific since the Battles of the Coral Sea and Midway in the summer of 1942. Admiral Nimitz, with his headquarters at Pearl Harbor, controlled the North, Central, and South Pacific. General MacArthur, who had reached Australia from the Philippines in March 1942, commanded the Southwest Pacific, extending from the China coast to Australia, and including the Philippines, the Bismarck Archipelago, New Guinea, all the east coast of Australia, and the Solomon Islands.

The Imperial Japanese Navy, deeply conscious of defeat in the Central Pacific, turned once more to the Southwest. Here, more remote from the main sources of American power, they hoped to renew their triumphant advance.

Their first thrust, towards Port Moresby, in New Guinea, having been foiled by the Battle of the Coral Sea, the enemy resolved to attack by land across the Owen Stanley Mountains. Thus began the struggle for New Guinea. Simultaneously they determined to seize the Solomon Islands. They already held the small island of Tulagi, and could quickly set about the construction of an air base in the neighbouring island of Guadalcanal. With both Port Moresby and Guadalcanal in their possession they hoped the Coral Sea would become a Japanese lake, bordering upon northeastern Australia. From Guadalcanal Japanese airmen could reach out towards other and still more distant island groups along the main line of sea communications between America and New Zealand. American and Australian resistance to these two assaults form an admirable example of bold inter-Service action resting on maritime power.

The Solomon Islands became the objective of both sides, and Admiral King in Washington had long planned their occupation. On the 4th of July, 1942, air reconnaissance disclosed that the enemy were already constructing an airfield on Guadalcanal. Admiral Ghormley, commanding the South Pacific area, without waiting to perfect his plans, struck on August 7 with the 1st Marine Division, already in New Zealand. The uncompleted Japanese air base was quickly captured and the battle for Guadalcanal began. It was to last six months.

From their main Fleet base in the Carolines and from Rabaul the Japanese were able to maintain greatly superior naval and air forces in these waters. The Japanese commander in Rabaul at once sent a strong force of cruisers and destroyers to Guadalcanal. In the early hours of August 9, aided by heavy rain squalls, the Japanese surprised the Allied naval forces guarding the approach to the landing place and almost annihilated them. In about forty minutes they sank three American heavy cruisers and the Australian cruiser *Canberra*, while receiving themselves only minor damage. Had the Japanese admiral followed up this remarkable success he could have swept through the strait to the eastward and destroyed the American transports, which were still discharging their troops and stores. Like other Japanese commanders before and after him in this war, he missed his opportunity and withdrew.

The American commander could however no longer support the landing. After unloading all that he could he retired, leaving his 16,000 Marines ashore alone on a hostile island without air cover and exposed to reinforced land attack. This was indeed a grim moment. But the United States Marines were undaunted. In spite of ceaseless air

attack they held and improved their position, while a supply service by sea was improvised and the captured airfield was brought into use. From this moment fighters and dive bombers manned by the Marines worked from Guadalcanal itself and gave instant relief.

The Japanese now sought a decision at sea. On August 24 an inconclusive action was fought to the north of the Solomons. Enemy transports approaching Guadalcanal were driven off by air attack. On August 31 the aircraft carrier *Saratoga* was damaged by a submarine, and a fortnight later the carrier *Wasp*, of Mediterranean repute, was sunk. Both sides built up their strength. Early in October, in another night engagement, a strong force of Japanese cruisers was beaten off, one being sunk; but two enemy battleships bombarded the airfield, and presently landed 4,500 reinforcements at a stroke. Another crisis was at hand.

Admiral Nimitz and General MacArthur urged, not unnaturally, that priority be given to the Pacific theatre at the expense of European operations, and Admiral King gave them powerful support at Washington. But the descent in North Africa ("Torch") was dominant, and the major strategy prevailed. The climax of the battle on land now came. For ten days from October 19, 1942, the Marines in close jungle fighting held all their positions and beat the Japanese to a standstill. In another fleet action, principally fought by aircraft north of the Solomons, the carrier *Hornet*, which had replaced the *Wasp*, was sunk. The carrier *Enterprise*, and the battleship

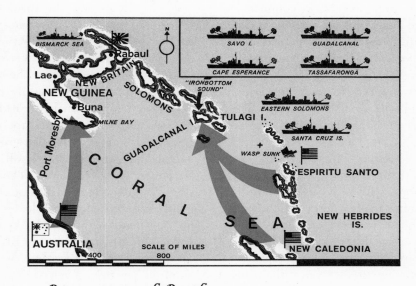

Reconquest of Pacific from Japanese began with Allied landings (*blue arrows*) by Americans on Guadalcanal and by Australians and Americans on southern tip of New Guinea. Struggle for islands led to seven fierce naval actions located and identified above.

South Dakota, and two cruisers were damaged. The Japanese had two carriers disabled. Admiral Halsey, who had succeeded Admiral Ghormley, and who found himself for the moment without any carriers, now appealed through Admiral Nimitz for one or more British carriers. Although we had little knowledge of American Pacific plans, we realised that an intense crisis had arisen in the Solomons. It was obvious that no carriers could reach the scene for many weeks. I earnestly desired to help in this heroic struggle, but with the main naval responsibility for landing the Anglo-American Army in Northwest Africa upon us we could make no immediate proposal. It was not until December that the strain and climax of "Torch" lessened. I then sent the President a full account of our carrier position and made the best offer in our power.

". . . The hazards of 'Torch' are not yet ended," I cabled, "as our build-up of shore-based aircraft will not enable the withdrawal for some time of the two carriers now employed on 'Torch.' Knowing however how urgently you require a reinforcement of carriers in the

Pacific, we are prepared to take a risk now and come to a decision as to what we can give you. Our carrier strength consists of four long-endurance armoured fleet carriers. We are prepared to withdraw *Illustrious* from the Eastern Fleet, and . . . *Victorious* from the Home Fleet and to send you both *Victorious* and *Illustrious* if you can allow [your] *Ranger* [a smaller carrier] to join the Home Fleet. In view of the vital importance of the Atlantic communications, the necessity of supporting the North Russian convoys, the possible appearance of *Graf Zeppelin* at the end of the year, and the present condition of *Indomitable* and *Formidable* we could not release both *Victorious* and *Illustrious* without the addition of *Ranger* to the Home Fleet.

"I am much in favour of sending you two carriers rather than one if this can be managed, as this will not only give you increased strength, but would allow the two ships to work as a tactical unit, which would appear to be necessary, as neither ship carries sufficient aircraft to operate singly. I would propose to send Admiral Lyster, who is known to a good many of your officers, in command. Both ships should proceed to Pearl Harbor, arriving about the end of December, to adjust their complement of aircraft. If you are in favour of this exchange Pound will settle details with King."

Admiral King was however unwilling to spare the *Ranger*, and in consequence we could only send the *Victorious*. She left the Home Fleet for Pearl Harbor in December.

MEANWHILE in November a series of sea and air fights which eventually proved decisive began around the Solomons, with heavy losses on both sides. On the night of November 13, in a fierce action, two United States cruisers and four destroyers were lost, with both the American admirals engaged. On the Japanese side a battleship and two destroyers were sunk. Eleven Japanese transports, with strong supporting forces, were at the same time moving towards Guadalcanal. In the thirty-six hours of ceaseless fighting which followed, a second Japanese battleship, a cruiser, three destroyers, and above all seven transports filled with troops, were sunk, at the cost to the Americans of only one more destroyer.

The Japanese at this point lost confidence in the venture. Ever-increasing American reinforcements began to arrive, and the glorious Marines were relieved by the Army. The conflict continued without pause, but the enemy made no further bid for victory. On January 4, 1943, Imperial Headquarters in Tokyo ordered the evacuation of Guadalcanal, which was accomplished without serious loss. On February 9 Admiral Halsey was able at last to report that the island had been conquered.

This episode marked the end of the Japanese offensive surge. In six major naval engagements and many lesser encounters two American carriers, seven cruisers, and fourteen destroyers had been sunk, besides the Australian cruiser *Canberra*. The Japanese losses were one carrier, two battleships, four cruisers, and eleven destroyers. The loss of life on both sides was severe, on land, at sea, and in the air. "For us who were there," writes an American eyewitness, Admiral Samuel Eliot Morison, whose moving account I have followed, "Guadalcanal is not a name but an emotion, recalling desperate fights in the air, furious night naval battles, frantic work at supply or construction, savage fighting in the sodden jungle, nights broken by screaming bombs and deafening explosions of naval shells." Long may the tale be told in the great Republic.

The tide of war had also turned in New Guinea. The Japanese overland advance began on July 22, 1942, from the north coast towards Port Moresby, which was guarded by two brigades of the 7th Australian Division back from the Middle East. The Owen Stanley Mountains, rising to over 13,000 feet, form the spine of the New Guinea land mass. Through these a foot track traverses the passes and the virgin jungle. A single Australian Militia Battalion fought a stubborn delaying action, and it was not until the middle of September that the five Japanese battalions employed approached Port Moresby. Here, at the Imita Ridge, the enemy advance was stayed.

WHILE all this was in progress 2,000 Japanese Marines landed from the sea and tried on August 26 to take the three airstrips being built near Milne Bay, at the southernmost tip of the great island. After a fortnight's intense fighting along the seashore more than half of the invaders were killed and the rest dispersed. The Japanese were thenceforth thrown on to the defensive in New Guinea. By trying to take both New Guinea and Guadalcanal they had lost their chance of winning either. They now had to retreat over the mountain track under close Australian ground and air pursuit. Disease and hunger took a heavy toll. The American-Australian air power grew constantly. The United States 32nd Division was flown in. The Japanese convoys carrying reinforcements suffered enormous losses. Ten thousand desperate fighting men, with their backs to the sea, held the final perimeter at Buna. It was not till the third week of January 1943 that the last resistance was overcome. Only a few hundred Japanese survived. More than 15,000 had been killed or perished from starvation and disease. By February the southeastern end of New Guinea, as well as Guadalcanal, was firmly in Allied hands. A Japanese convoy of twelve transports, escorted by ten warships, on its way to reinforce their important outpost at Lae was detected in the Bismarck Sea. It was attacked from the air on March 2 and 3, and both transports and escort, carrying about 15,000 men, were destroyed.

† † †

By June 1943 the prospect in the Pacific was encouraging. The last Japanese thrusts had been hurled back and the enemy was now everywhere on the defensive. They were compelled to reinforce by costly processes the positions they still held in New Guinea, especially the garrisons of Salamaua and Lae, and to build a series of supporting airfields along the coast. The American movement towards the Philippines began to be defined. General MacArthur was working steadily westward along the north coast of New Guinea, and Admiral Halsey was slowly advancing along the island chain of the Solomons towards Rabaul. Behind all towered up the now rapidly rising strength of the United States. The eighteen months which had passed since Pearl Harbor had revealed to the rulers of Japan some of the facts and proportions they had ignored.

In the hot, matted jungle near the American airfield on Guadalcanal, a column of Marines slogs wearily down a trail leading to the battlefield

ISLAND WARFARE

Half a Year of Hell on Guadalcanal

On August 7, 1942, the U.S. 1st Marine Division went ashore on Guadalcanal, an island of so little interest to the world that no accurate map of it existed. Thrown into panic, the enemy garrison fled to the jungle, leaving its provisions behind—fortunately for the Marines who might otherwise have starved. For on the second night of the invasion they were left stranded by the Allied naval disaster in the Battle of Savo Island, and no reinforcements or sizeable amount of supplies got through to them for 38 days.

The Marines' first task was to finish the airfield the Japanese had begun to build, but because their bulldozers never got unloaded from the transports that had fled Guadalcanal after the naval battle, they were forced to do the work by hand. Meanwhile, they had to struggle for existence and fight off the Japanese through the dark, soggy jungles that cover most of the rough surface of Guadalcanal. They also had to bear daily air raids, nightly shellings from the sea, constant patrols and battles in the dense tangle of the rain forest, malarial mosquitoes, dengue, dysentery and skins ulcerated with jungle rot. The fighting went on

for six months, both sides pouring in reserves to plug up or to widen this first breach in the vast perimeter of Japanese conquest in the Pacific.

Supplies for Guadalcanal were brought in over hundreds of miles of dangerous waters, and the effort strained both the U.S. and the Japanese navies. American ships generally arrived in the daytime—when they could get air cover from the Guadalcanal airfield—and withdrew at dusk. Then the Japanese—who were better trained in night fighting—took over with their "Tokyo Express," a shuttle service of fast ships which brought reinforcements down from the north and shelled the airfield on their way back. These goings and comings erupted into numerous naval battles in which so many ships were sunk that the waters north of Guadalcanal acquired the nickname "Ironbottom Sound."

Finally, in February of 1943, the Japanese had to give up. In three night operations which totally escaped the notice of the American troops, they evacuated all 11,700 of their surviving soldiers—and left the first of their thousands of conquered islands securely in American hands.

Defeated Japanese sprawl dead on the beach in front of a coconut grove on the north shore of Guadalcanal after one of the many costly failures to break through the Marine perimeter around the airfield.

Victorious Marines (*opposite*), weary after months of battle and exposure to tropical disease, take their first rest in a long time after their place in the line has been taken by a U.S. Army division.

Shell-shattered palms (*left*), splintered by weeks of bombardment, overlook a G.I. washing in one of the leech-filled streams, whose waters were described by soldiers as "tasting of dead Jap."

Abandoned transport provides a protected backwater for Americans swimming on the conquered Guadalcanal coast. This was the *Kinugawa Maru,* one of the four transports driven ashore on November 14, during the great naval battle of Guadalcanal. All the transports were wrecked by strafing carrier planes, and the 2,000 soldiers who got off them went into the jungle with little but the clothes on their backs.

Disaster on the Way to Guadalcanal

A howling inferno in the middle of a soft and beautiful sky and an untroubled tropic sea'' is the artist's description of the explosion that destroyed the U.S.S. *Wasp* on September 15, 1942 when it was torpedoed by a submarine which had slipped up undetected. This painting is by Tom Lea, who saw the disaster from the deck of the *Hornet* while the two carriers were guarding a convoy headed for Guadalcanal.

335

The Last Hours of the 'Hornet'

A bomb explodes deep in the bowels of the carrier U.S.S. *Hornet*, peeling back the deck on which these men were standing. Planes from Japanese carriers hit the big *Hornet* with bombs and torpedoes and turned the ship into a derelict so useless that the U.S. Navy was forced to sink her a day later. She was the biggest casualty in the indecisive Battle of the Santa Cruz Islands, about 400 miles southeast of Guadalcanal.

The guns blaze on the *Hornet* (*opposite*) as a Japanese dive bomber gets through the barrage for a suicide crash. The plane bounced off the signal bridge and went through the flight deck before exploding.

An American dies on the bloodstained deck of the *Hornet* as two medical corpsmen work on him in vain. He was one of 111 killed. The other 875 crewmen and all the carrier's planes were saved.

A Flier's Fight for His Carrier

High above the Hornet, Lieutenant A. C. Emerson, his F4F Wildcat ripped by Japanese machine-gun bullets, bites his tongue as he guns his fighter toward the Japanese bombers attacking his dying ship. Emerson—here painted by his artist friend Tom Lea—was a Pacific veteran who had seen three other American carriers go down in battle. He was to be killed three months later, fighting in the Solomons.

Another Island, Another Jungle

While the Marines were painfully securing Guadalcanal, General MacArthur was sending an Australian-American Army through even more forbidding country on the first step of his drive back to the Philippines. Into the thick primitive jungles of New Guinea, soldiers went stumbling and sweating under the weight of modern weapons. It took them six months to pry about 15,000 Japanese one by one out of their sturdy bunkers—made of coconut logs and sand-filled oil drums—at Buna, Gona and Sanananda. By January 1943, at a cost of 8,600 battle casualties and at least as many cases of tropical disease, the Allies had won a new base for further advances into more island jungle ahead.

Wary jungle fighter comes down the trail toward Buna. Air transport enabled Allied troops to skip much rough country, but the final blow at the Japanese had to be delivered through jungle like this.

Ambushed Americans (*opposite*) lie on a beach in northern New Guinea. They had fought their way out of the jungle and were heading past wrecked landing barges when a hidden machine gun killed them.

Fogbound Diversion
in the Aleutians

At the other end of the Pacific from the stifling jungles of Guadalcanal and New Guinea, other American fighting men were plunged into the fog and frost of a strategic blind alley in the Aleutians. There, in a vain effort to lure the American Navy away from Midway, the Japanese, in June of 1942, had landed troops on the inhospitable islands of Attu and Kiska. Once there, they had no place to go and dug themselves into the barren mountains and spongy muskeg valleys. U.S. strategists, mistaking this for the first stage of an enemy assault on Alaska and the Pacific northwest, mounted a major expedition to retake these uninviting pieces of American soil.

Attu was invaded first. The U.S. Army 7th Division —which had been trained in California deserts—was put ashore on the freezing island in thick fog on May 11, 1943. The terrain, the weather, and the fierce opposition of the 2,600-man Japanese garrison held them back for 20 days. Then, beaten at last, the Japanese who had not been killed in battle blew themselves up with hand grenades.

Two months later, a big American fleet sailed to Kiska, shelled it for several days and landed 34,000 troops, armed to the teeth. They discovered that the Japanese had slipped away unobserved in the fog, leaving behind three dogs.

Falling on Attu (*left*), an American soldier slides to an icy grave after being hit by enemy fire while trying to cross a mountain slope. U.S. battle casualties on Attu were 600 dead and 1,200 wounded.

Landing on Adak, American bombers come in from a raid on Japanese-held Kiska. Later, the Aleutians became a base for raids on Japan's northern outposts. But airfields were hard to build on the boggy soil, and were closed in most of the time by the weather. Wisps of fog could turn into impenetrable pea soup in a few minutes and williwaw winds of more than 100 miles an hour might start blowing at any time.

H-Hour for the invasion of southern Europe sounds before dawn on July 10 as tense American soldiers leave their transports for the assault boats that will take them to the Sicilian shore, where naval bombardment provides a beacon fire.

15

THE INVASION OF ITALY

The 'Trident' Conference

THE reasons which led me to hasten to Washington in May 1943, once the decision in Africa was certain, were serious. What should we do with our victory? Were its fruits to be gathered only in the Tunisian tip, or should we drive Italy out of the war and bring Turkey in on our side? These were fateful questions, which could only be answered by a personal conference with the President. Second only to these were the plans for action in the Indian theatre. I was conscious of serious divergences beneath the surface which, if not adjusted, would lead to grave difficulties and feeble action during the rest of the year. I was resolved to have a conference on the highest possible level.

The doctors did not want me to fly at the great height required in a bomber, and it was therefore decided to go by sea. We left London on the night of May 4, and went aboard the *Queen Mary* in the Clyde on the following day. The ship had been admirably fitted up to meet all our needs. The whole delegation was accommodated on the main deck, which was sealed off from the rest of the ship. Offices, conference rooms, and of course the Map Room, stood ready for immediate use. From the moment we got on board our work went forward ceaselessly. The conference, which I had christened "Trident," was to last at least a fortnight, and was intended to cover every aspect of the war. Our party had therefore to be a large one. There was much to be settled among ourselves before we reached Washington, and now we were all under one deck. The Joint Planning and Intelligence Staffs were in almost continuous session. The Chiefs of Staff met daily, and sometimes twice a day. I adhered to my usual practice of giving them my thoughts each morning in the shape of minutes and directives, and I generally had a discussion with them each afternoon or evening. These processes of probing, sifting, and arguing continued throughout the voyage, and grave decisions were reached in measured steps.

Upon the operations which we thought should be undertaken in Europe, following the victory in Africa, we were in complete agreement. It had been decided at Casablanca to attack Sicily, and all preparations were far advanced. The British Chiefs of Staff were convinced that an attack upon the mainland of Italy should follow, or even overlap, the capture of Sicily. They proposed seizing a bridgehead on the toe of Italy, to be followed by a further assault on the heel as prelude to an advance on Naples. A paper setting out these views and the arguments which led up to them was prepared on board ship and handed to the American Chiefs of Staff as a basis for discussion on our arrival in Washington. On May 11 we arrived off Staten Island. Harry Hopkins was there to meet us, and we immediately entrained for Washington. The President was on the platform to greet me, and whisked me off to my old rooms at the White House. The next afternoon, May 12, at 2:30 p.m., we all met in his oval study to survey and lay out our work at the conference.

In the days that followed, many grave strategic issues were thrashed out by our Combined Staffs and their experts. At first the differences seemed insuperable and it looked like a hopeless breach. During this period leakages from high American officers were made to Democratic and Republican senators, leading to a debate in the Senate. By patience and perseverance our difficulties were gradually overcome. The fact that the President and I were living side by side seeing each other at all hours, that we were known to be in close agreement, and that the President intended to decide himself on the ultimate issues—all this, together with the priceless work of Hopkins, exercised throughout a mollifying and also a dominating influence on the course of Staff discussions. After a serious crisis of opinions, side by side with the most agreeable personal relations between the professional men, an almost complete agreement was reached about invading Sicily.

But although so much had gone well, I was extremely concerned that no definite recommendations had been made by the Combined Staffs to follow up the conquest of Sicily by the invasion of Italy. I knew that the American Staff's mind had been turned to Sardinia. They thought that this should be the sole remaining objective for the mighty forces which were gathered in the Mediterranean during the whole of the rest of 1943. On every ground, military and political, I deplored this prospect. The Russians were fighting every day on their enormous front, and their blood flowed in a torrent. Were we then to keep over a million and a half fine troops, and all their terrific air and naval power, idle for nearly a year?

The President had not seemed ready to press his advisers to become more precise about invading Italy, but as this was the main purpose for which I had crossed the Atlantic I could not let the matter rest. Hopkins said to me privately, "If you wish to carry your point you will have to stay here another week, and even then there is no certainty." I was deeply distressed at this, and on May 25 appealed personally to the President to let General Marshall come to Algiers with me. I explained to the conference that I should feel awkward in discussing these matters with General Eisenhower without the presence of a United States representative on the highest level. If decisions were taken it might subsequently be thought

Routes into Europe opened up by Allies' African victories are shown by blue arrows. Eisenhower wanted to seize Sardinia as threat to France and Italy. Churchill preferred assault via Sicily into Italy to gain air bases and ties (*blue links*) with Balkan partisans.

that I had exerted an undue influence. I was accordingly very gratified to hear that General Marshall would accompany me, and I was sure that it would now be possible to arrange for a report to be sent back to the Combined Chiefs of Staff for their consideration.

Early the next day, General Marshall, the C.I.G.S., Ismay, and the rest of my party took off from the Potomac River in a flying boat. On alighting at Gibraltar at about 5 p.m., we were met by the Governor. It was too late to continue our journey to Algiers that night, and he conveyed us to the Convent, where he resides, the nuns having been removed two centuries ago.

We did not leave Gibraltar for Algiers until the following afternoon. There was therefore an opportunity to show General Marshall the famous Rock, and we all made a few hours' pilgrimage, and inspected the new distillery which assured the fortress a permanent supply of fresh water, and various important guns, some hospitals, and also a large number of troops. I finally went below to see the Governor's special pet, a new gallery cut deep into the rock, with its battery of eight quick-firing guns commanding the isthmus and the neutral ground between Britain and Spain. An immense amount of work had been put into this. It certainly seemed, as we walked along, that whatever perils Gibraltar might have to fear, attack from the mainland was no longer one of them. The Governor's pride in his achievement was shared by his British visitors. It was not until we said good-bye upon the flying boat that General Marshall somewhat hesitatingly observed, "I admired your gallery, but we had one like it at Corregidor. The Japanese fired their artillery at the rock several hundred feet above it, and in two or three days blocked it off with an immense bank of rubble." I was grateful to him for his warning, but the poor Governor seemed thunderstruck and all the smiles vanished from his face.

I have no more pleasant memories of the war than the eight days in Algiers and Tunis. I telegraphed to Eden to come out and join me so as to make sure we saw eye to eye on the meeting we had arranged between Giraud and de Gaulle, and all our other business.

I was determined to obtain before leaving Africa the decision to invade Italy should Sicily be taken. Brooke and I imparted our views to General Alexander, Admiral Andrew Cunningham, and Air Marshal Tedder, and later to Montgomery. All these leading figures in the recent battles were inclined to action on the greatest scale, and saw in the conquest of Italy the natural fruition of our whole series of victories from Alamein onwards. We had however to procure the agreement of our Ally. Eisenhower was very reserved. He listened to all our arguments, and I am sure agreed with their purpose. But Marshall remained up till almost the last moment silent or cryptic.

The circumstances of our meeting were favourable to the British. We had three times as many troops, four times as many warships, and almost as many aeroplanes available for actual operations as the Americans. We had since Alamein, not to speak of the earlier years, lost in the Mediterranean eight times as many men and three times as many ships as our Allies. But what ensured for these potent facts the fairest and most attentive consideration with the American leaders was that notwithstanding our immense preponderance of strength we had continued to accept General Eisenhower's Supreme Command and to preserve for the whole campaign the character of a United States operation. The American chiefs do not like to be outdone in generosity. No people respond more spontaneously to fair play. If you treat Americans well they always want to treat you better. Nevertheless I consider that the argument which convinced the Americans was on its merits overwhelming.

We held our first meeting at General Eisenhower's villa in Algiers at five o'clock on May 29, and although much lay in the balance, I was well satisfied with the opening discussion. The desire of all the leaders to go forward on the boldest lines was clear, and I felt myself that the reservations made on account of the unknowable would be settled by events in accordance with my hopes.

We met again on the afternoon of May 31. Mr. Eden arrived in time to be present. I tried to clinch matters, and said my heart lay in an invasion of Southern Italy, but the fortunes of battle might necessitate a different course. At any rate, the alternative between Southern Italy and Sardinia involved the difference between a glorious campaign and a mere convenience.

GENERAL Marshall was in no way hostile to these ideas, but did not wish for a clear-cut decision to be taken at this moment. It would be better to decide what to do after we had started the attack on Sicily. He felt it would be necessary to know something of the German reactions in order to determine whether there would be real resistance in Southern Italy; whether the Germans would withdraw to the Po, and, for example, whether they could organise and handle the Italians with any finesse; what preparations had been made in Sardinia, Corsica, or in the Balkans; what readjustments they would make on the Russian front. He, General Eisenhower, and the Combined Chiefs of Staff were fully aware of my feelings about invading Italy, but their only desire was to select the "Post-Sicily" alternative which would give the best results. I said that I very passionately wanted to see Italy out of the way and Rome in our possession. I could not endure to see a great army standing idle when it might be engaged in striking Italy out of the war. Parliament and the people would become impatient if the Army were not active, and I was willing to take almost desperate steps in order to prevent such a calamity.

An incident now occurred which, as it relates to matters which have become the subject of misunderstandings and controversy after the war, must be related. Mr. Eden, at my request, commented on the Turkish situation, and said that knocking Italy out of the war would go a long way towards bringing the Turks in. They would become much more friendly "when our troops had reached the Balkan area." Anthony Eden and I were in full agreement on war policy, but I feared that the turn of his phrase might mislead our American friends. The British record states, "The Prime Minister intervened to observe emphatically that he was not advocating sending an army into the Balkans now or in the near future." Mr. Eden agreed that it would not be necessary to put an army into the Balkans, since the Turks would begin to show favourable reactions as soon as we were able to constitute an immediate threat to the Balkans.

ON the two following days we travelled by plane and car to some beautiful places rendered historic by the battles of a month before. General Marshall went on a brief American tour of his own, and then travelled with Alexander and myself, meeting all the commanders and seeing stirring sights of troops. The sense of victory was in the air. The whole of North Africa was cleared of the enemy. A quarter of a million prisoners were cooped in our cages. Everyone was very proud and delighted. There is no doubt that people like winning very much. I addressed many thousand soldiers at Carthage in the ruins of an immense amphitheatre. Certainly the hour and setting lent themselves to oratory. I have no idea what I said, but the whole audience clapped and cheered as doubtless their predecessors of two thousand years ago had done as they watched gladiatorial combats.

I felt that great advances had been made in our discussions and that everybody wanted to go for Italy. I therefore, in summing up at our last meeting on June 3, stated the conclusions in a most moderate form and paid my tribute to General Eisenhower.

Eden and I flew home together by Gibraltar. As my presence in North Africa had been fully reported, the Germans were exceptionally vigilant, and this led to a tragedy which much distressed me. The regular commercial aircraft was about to start from the Lisbon airfield when a thickset man smoking a cigar walked up and was thought to be a passenger on it. The German agents therefore signalled that I was on board. Although these passenger planes had plied unmolested for many months between Portugal and England, a German war plane was instantly ordered out, and the defenceless aircraft was ruthlessly shot down. Thirteen passengers perished, and among them the well-known British actor Leslie Howard, whose grace and gifts are still preserved for us by the records of the many delightful films in which he took part. The brutality of the Germans was only matched by the stupidity of their agents. It is difficult to understand how anyone could imagine that with all the resources of Great Britain at my disposal I should have booked a passage in an unarmed and unescorted plane from Lisbon and flown home in broad daylight. We of course made a wide loop out by night from Gibraltar into the ocean, and arrived home without incident. It was a painful shock to me to learn what had happened to others in the inscrutable workings of Fate.

The Fall of Mussolini

"USKY," as the capture of Sicily was called in our code names, was an undertaking of the first magnitude. Although eclipsed by events in Normandy, its importance and its difficulties should not be underrated. The landing was based on the experience gained in North Africa, and those who planned "Overlord" learned much from "Husky." In the initial assault nearly 3,000 ships and landing craft took part, carrying between them 160,000 men, 14,000 vehicles, 600 tanks, and 1,800 guns. These forces had to be collected, trained, equipped, and eventually embarked, with all the vast impedimenta of amphibious warfare, at widely dispersed bases throughout the Mediterranean, in Great Britain, and in the United States. In spite of anxieties all went forward smoothly and proved a remarkable example of joint Staff work. Alexander was to command the 15th Army Group, consisting of the Seventh United States Army under General George Patton and the Eighth British Army under Montgomery. Air Chief Marshal Tedder commanded the Allied Air Force, and Admiral Cunningham the Allied naval forces. The whole was under the overall command of General Eisenhower.

Intense air attack upon the island began on July 3 with the bombing of airfields both there and in Sardinia, which made many unusable. Two of the four train ferries operating across the Strait of Messina were sunk. By the time our convoys were approaching the island air superiority was firmly established, and Axis warships and aircraft made no serious effort to interfere with the sea-borne assault. By our cover plans the enemy were kept in doubt until the last moment where our stroke would fall. Our naval movements and military preparations in Egypt suggested an expedition to Greece. Since Tunis fell, the Germans had in fact sent more planes to the Mediterranean, but the additional squadrons had gone, not indeed to Sicily, but to the Eastern Mediterranean, Northwest Italy, and Sardinia. July 10 was the appointed day. On the morning of July 9 the great armadas from east and west were converging south of Malta, and it was time for all to steam for the beaches of Sicily. On my way to Chequers, where I was to await the result, I spent an hour in the Admiralty War Room. The map covered an entire wall, and showed the enormous convoys, escorts, and supporting detachments moving towards their assault beaches. This was the greatest amphibious operation so far attempted in history. But all depended on the weather.

The morning was fine, but by noon a fresh and unseasonable northwest wind sprang up. During the afternoon the wind increased, and by evening there was a heavy swell, which threatened to make landings hazardous, particularly on the western beaches in the American sector. The landing craft convoys plunging northward from Malta and from many African ports between Bizerte and Benghazi were having a rough voyage.

Arrangements had been made for postponing the landing in case of necessity, but a decision would have to be taken not later than midday. Watching anxiously from the Admiralty, the First Sea Lord inquired by signal about the weather conditions. Admiral Cunningham replied at 8 p.m., "Weather not favourable, but operation proceeding." Many ships arrived late, but fortunately no great harm resulted. The bad weather helped to give us surprise. Admiral Cunningham continues: "The very efficient cover plan and deceptive routeing of convoys played their part. In addition the vigilance of the enemy was undoubtedly relaxed owing to the unfavourable phase of the moon. Finally came this wind, dangerously close at the time to making some, if not all, of the landings impracticable. These apparently unfavourable factors had actually the effect of making the weary Italians, who had been alert for many nights, turn thankfully in their beds, saying, 'To-night at any rate they can't come.' BUT THEY CAME."

The airborne forces met hard fortune. More than one third of the gliders carrying our 1st Air Landing Brigade were cast off too early by their American towing aircraft and many of the men they carried were drowned. The rest were scattered over southeastern Sicily, and only twelve gliders arrived at the important bridge which was their aim. Out of eight officers and sixty-five men who seized and held it until help came twelve hours later only nineteen survived. This was a forlorn feat of arms. On the American front the air landings were also too widely dispersed, but the many small parties creating damage and confusion inland worried the Italian coastal divisions.

The sea-borne landings, under continuous fighter protection, were everywhere highly successful. Twelve airfields were soon in our hands, and by July 18 there were only twenty-five serviceable German aircraft in the island. Masses of planes, more than half of them German, were left behind destroyed or damaged. The enemy, once they had recovered from the initial surprise, had fought stubbornly. The difficulties of the ground were great. The roads were narrow, and cross-country movement was often impossible except for men on foot. Nevertheless, once we were safely ashore and our Air Forces were operating from captured airfields the issue was never in doubt. Contrary to our earlier hopes, the bulk of the Germans successfully withdrew across the Strait of Messina, but after thirty-eight days of fighting General Alexander telegraphed: "By 10:00 a.m. this morning, August 17, 1943, the last German soldier was flung out of Sicily and the whole island is now in our hands."

MUSSOLINI had now to bear the brunt of the military disasters into which he had, after so many years of rule, led his country. He had exercised almost absolute control and could not cast the burden on the Monarchy, Parliamentary institutions, the Fascist Party, or the General Staff. All fell on him. Now that the feeling that the war was lost spread throughout well-informed circles in Italy the blame fell upon the man who had so imperiously thrust the nation on to the wrong and the losing side. These convictions formed and spread widely during the early months of 1943. The lonely dictator sat at the summit of power, while military defeat and Italian slaughter in Russia, Tunis, and Sicily were the evident prelude to direct invasion of the Italian homeland.

In vain he made changes among the politicians and generals. In February General Ambrosio had succeeded Cavallero as Chief of the Italian General Staff. Ambrosio, together with the Duke of Acquarone, the Minister of Court, were personal advisers of the King and had the confidence of the Royal circle. For months they had been hoping to overthrow the Duce and put an end to the Fascist regime. But Mussolini still dwelt in the European scene as if he were a principal factor. He was affronted when his new military chief proposed the immediate withdrawal of the Italian divisions from the Balkans. These forces he regarded as the counterpoise to German predominance in Europe. He did not realise that defeats abroad and internal demoralisation had robbed him of his former status as Hitler's ally. He still cherished the illusion of power and consequence when the reality had gone. Thus he resisted Ambrosio's formidable request. So durable however was the impression of his authority and the fear of his personal action in extremity that there was prolonged hesitation throughout all the forces of Italian society

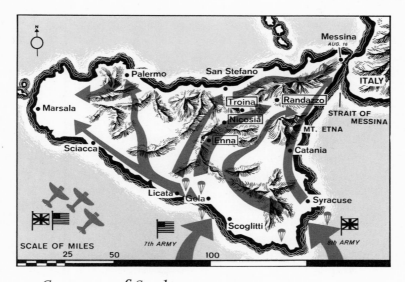

Conquest of Sicily proceeded from American beachhead at Licata and British beachhead at Syracuse. Supporting parachutists were dropped inaccurately, some landing in the sea left and right. Drives inland (*red arrows*) met less opposition in west than in east.

about how to oust him. Who would "bell the cat"? Thus the spring had passed, with invasion by a mighty foe, possessing superior power, drawing ever nearer.

The climax had now come. Since February the taciturn, cautious-minded, constitutional King had been in contact with Marshal Badoglio, who had been dismissed after the Greek disasters in 1940. He found in him at length a figure to whom he might entrust the conduct of the State. A definite plan was made. It was resolved that Mussolini should be arrested on July 26, and General Ambrosio agreed to find the agents and create the situation for this stroke. The General was aided unwittingly by elements in the Fascist Old Guard, who sought a new revival of the party, by which, in many cases, they would not be the losers. They saw in the summoning of the highest party organ, the Fascist Grand Council, which had not met since 1939, the means of confronting the Duce with an ultimatum. On July 13 they called on Mussolini and induced him to convene a formal session of the Council on July 24. The two movements appear to have been separate and independent, but their close coincidence in date is significant.

On July 19, accompanied by General Ambrosio, Mussolini left by air to meet Hitler at a villa at Feltre, near Rimini. All preparations had been made to entertain the Fuehrer for at least two days, but he left the same afternoon. "The meeting," says Mussolini, "was, as usual,

cordial, but the entourage and the attitude of the higher Air Force officers and of the troops was chilly." The Fuehrer held forth lengthily upon the need for a supreme effort. The new secret weapons, he said, would be ready for use against England by the winter. Italy must be defended, "so that Sicily may become for the enemy what Stalingrad was for us." The Italians must produce both the manpower and the organisation. Germany could not provide the reinforcements and equipment asked for by Italy owing to the pressure on the Russian front.

Ambrosio urged his chief to tell Hitler plainly that Italy could not continue in the war. It is not clear what advantage would have come from this, but the fact that Mussolini seemed almost dumbstruck finally decided Ambrosio and the other Italian generals present that no further leadership could be expected from him.

In the midst of Hitler's discourse on the situation an agitated Italian official entered the room with the news, "At this moment Rome is undergoing violent enemy air bombardment." Apart from a promise of some German reinforcements for Sicily, Mussolini returned to Rome without anything to show. As he approached he flew into a huge black cloud of smoke rising from hundreds of wagons on fire in the Littoria railway station. He had an audience of the King, whom he found "frowning and nervous." "A tense situation," said the King. "We cannot go on much longer. Sicily has gone west now. The Germans will double-cross us. The discipline of the troops has broken down. . . ." Mussolini answered, according to the records, that he hoped to disengage Italy from the Axis alliance by September 15. The date shows how far he was out of contact with reality.

The chief actor in the final drama now appeared on the scene. Count Dino Grandi, veteran Fascist, former Foreign Minister and Ambassador to Britain, a man of strong personal determination, who had hated the Italian declaration of war upon Britain, but had hitherto submitted to the force of events, arrived in Rome to take the lead at the meeting of the Grand Council. He called on his old leader on the 22nd of July, and told him brutally that he intended to propose the formation of a National Government and the restoration to the King of the supreme command of the armed forces.

At 5 p.m. on the 24th the Grand Council met. Care appears to have been taken by the Chief of Police that they should not be disturbed by violence. Mussolini's musketeers, his personal bodyguard, were relieved of their duty to guard the Palazzo Venezia, which was also filled with armed police. The Duce unfolded his case, and the Council, who were all dressed in their black Fascist uniform, took up the discussion. Mussolini ended: "War is always a party war—a war of the party which desires it; it is always one man's war—the war of the man who declared it. If to-day this is called Mussolini's war, the war in 1859 could have been called Cavour's war. This is the moment to tighten the reins and assume the necessary responsibility. I shall have no difficulty in replacing men, in turning the screw, in bringing forces to bear not yet engaged, in the name of our country, whose territorial integrity is to-day being violated.''

GRANDI then moved a resolution calling upon the Crown to assume more power and upon the King to emerge from obscurity and assume his responsibilities. He delivered what Mussolini describes as "a violent philippic, the speech of a man who was at last giving vent to a long-cherished rancour." The contacts between members of the Grand Council and the Court became evident. Mussolini's son-in-law, Ciano, supported Grandi. Everyone present was now conscious that a political convulsion impended. The debate continued till midnight, when Scorza, secretary of the Fascist Party, proposed adjourning till next day. But Grandi leaped to his feet, shouting, "No, I am against the proposal. We have started this business and we must finish it this very night!" It was after two o'clock in the morning when the voting took place. Nineteen replied "Yes" to Grandi's motion and seven "No." Two abstained. Mussolini rose. "You have provoked a crisis of the regime. So much the worse. The session is closed." The party secretary was about to give the salute to the Duce when Mussolini checked him with a gesture, saying, "No, you are excused." They all went away in silence. None slept at home.

Meanwhile the arrest of Mussolini was being quietly arranged. The key telephone exchanges, the police headquarters, and the offices of the Ministry of the Interior were quietly and unobtrusively taken over. A small force of military police was posted out of sight near the Royal villa.

Mussolini spent the morning of Sunday, July 25, in his office, and visited some quarters in Rome which had suffered by bombing. He asked to see the King, and was granted an audience at five o'clock. On reaching the Royal abode he noticed that there were everywhere reinforcements of Carabinieri. The King, in Marshal's uniform, stood in the doorway. The two men entered the drawing room. The King said, "My dear Duce, it's no longer any good. Italy has gone to bits. Army morale is at rock-bottom. The soldiers don't want to fight any more. . . . The Grand Council's vote is terrific—nineteen votes for Grandi's motion, and among them four holders of the Order of the Annunciation! . . . At this moment you are the most hated man in Italy. You can no longer count on more than one friend. You have one friend left, and I am he. That is why I tell you that you need have no fears for your personal safety, for which I will ensure protection. I have been thinking that the man for the job now is Marshal Badoglio. . . ."

Mussolini replied, "You are taking an extremely grave decision. A crisis at this moment would mean making the people think that peace was in sight, once the man who

declared war had been dismissed. The blow to the Army's morale would be serious. The crisis would be considered as a triumph for the Churchill-Stalin set-up, especially for Stalin. I realise the people's hatred. I had no difficulty in recognising it last night in the midst of the Grand Council. One can't govern for such a long time and impose so many sacrifices without provoking resentments. In any case, I wish good luck to the man who takes the situation in hand." The King accompanied Mussolini to the door. "His face," says Mussolini, "was livid and he looked smaller than ever, almost dwarfish. He shook my hand and went in again. I descended the few steps and went towards my car. Suddenly a Carabinieri captain stopped me and said, 'His Majesty has charged me with the protection of your person.' I was continuing towards my car when the captain said to me, pointing to a motor ambulance standing near by, 'No. We must get in there.' I got into the ambulance, together with my secretary. A lieutenant, three Carabinieri, and two police agents in plain clothes got in as well as the captain, and placed themselves by the door armed with machine guns. When the door was closed the ambulance drove off at top speed. I still thought that all this was being done, as the King had said, in order to protect my person."

Later that afternoon Badoglio was charged by the King to form a new Cabinet of Service chiefs and civil servants, and in the evening the Marshal broadcast the news to the world. Two days later the Duce was taken on Marshal Badoglio's order to be interned on the island of Ponza.

THUS ended Mussolini's twenty-one years' dictatorship in Italy, during which he had raised the Italian people from the Bolshevism into which they might have sunk in 1919 to a position in Europe such as Italy had never held before. A new impulse had been given to the national life. The Italian Empire in North Africa was built. Many important public works in Italy were completed. In 1935 the Duce had by his will power overcome the League of Nations—"Fifty nations led by one"—and was able to complete his conquest of Abyssinia. His regime was far too costly for the Italian people to bear, but there is no doubt that it appealed during its period of success to very great numbers of Italians. He was, as I had addressed him at the time of the fall of France, "the Italian lawgiver." The alternative to his rule might well have been a Communist Italy, which would have brought perils and misfortunes of a different character both upon the Italian people and upon Europe.

His fatal mistake was the declaration of war on France and Great Britain following Hitler's victories in June 1940. Had he not done this he could well have maintained Italy in a balancing position, courted and rewarded by both sides and deriving an unusual wealth and prosperity from the struggles of other countries. Even when the issue of the war became certain Mussolini would have been welcomed by the Allies. He had much to give to shorten its course. He could have timed his moment to declare war on Hitler with art and care. Instead he took the wrong turning. He never understood the strength of Britain, nor the long-enduring qualities of Island resistance and sea power. Thus he marched to ruin. His great roads will remain a monument to his personal power and long reign.

Synthetic Harbours

PROSPECTS of victory in Sicily, the Italian situation, and the progress of the war had made me feel the need in July for a new meeting with the President and for another Anglo-American Conference. It was Roosevelt who suggested that Quebec should be the scene. Mr. Mackenzie King welcomed the proposal, and nothing could have been more agreeable to us. No more fitting or splendid setting for a meeting of those who guided the war policy of the Western world could have been chosen at this cardinal moment than the ancient citadel of Quebec, at the gateway of Canada, overlooking the mighty St. Lawrence River. The President, while gladly accepting Canadian hospitality, did not feel it possible that Canada should be formally a member of the Conference, as he apprehended similar demands by Brazil and other American partners in the United Nations. We also had to think of the claims of Australia and the other Dominions. This delicate question was solved and surmounted by the broadminded outlook of the Canadian Prime Minister and Government. I for my part was determined that we and the United States should have the Conference to ourselves, in view of all the vital business we had in common. A triple meeting of the heads of the three major Powers was a main object of the future; now it must be for Britain and the United States alone. We assigned to it the name "Quadrant."

I left London for the Clyde, where the *Queen Mary* awaited us, on the night of August 4, in a train which carried the very heavy staffs we needed. We were, I suppose, over 200, besides about fifty Royal Marine orderlies. The scope of the Conference comprised not only the Mediterranean campaign, now at its first climax, but even more the preparations for the cross-Channel design of 1944, the whole conduct of the war in the Indian theatre, and our share in the struggle against Japan. For the Channel crossing we took with us three officers sent by Lieut.-General F. E. Morgan, Chief of Staff to the Supreme Allied Commander, yet to be finally chosen, who with his combined Anglo-American staff had completed our joint outline plan. As the whole of our affairs in the Indian and Far Eastern theatres were under examination I brought with me General Wavell's Director of Military Operations, who had flown specially from India.

I also took with me a young Brigadier named Wingate, who had already made his mark as a leader of irregulars in Abyssinia, and had greatly distinguished himself in the jungle fighting in Burma. These new brilliant exploits won him, in some circles of the Army in which he served, the title of "the Clive of Burma." I had heard much of all this, and knew also how the Zionists had sought him as a future Commander-in-Chief of any Israelite army that might be formed. I had him summoned home in order that I might have a look at him before I left for Quebec. I was about to dine alone on the night of August 4 at Downing Street when the news that he had arrived by air and was actually in the house was brought to me. I immediately asked him to join me at dinner. We had not talked for half an hour before I felt myself in the presence of a man of the highest quality.

He plunged at once into his theme of how the Japanese could be mastered in jungle warfare by long-range penetration groups landed by air behind the enemy lines. This interested me greatly. I wished to hear much more about it, and also to let him tell his tale to the Chiefs of Staff.

I decided at once to take him with me on the voyage. I told him our train would leave at ten. It was then nearly nine. Wingate had arrived just as he was after three days' flight from the actual front, and with no clothes but what he stood up in. He was of course quite ready to go, but expressed regret that he would not be able to see his wife, who was in Scotland and had not even heard of his arrival. However, the resources of my Private Office were equal to the occasion. Mrs. Wingate was aroused at her home by the police and taken to Edinburgh in order to join our train on its way through and to go with us to Quebec. She had no idea of what it was all about until, in the early hours of the morning, she actually met her husband on a platform at Waverley Station. They had a very happy voyage together.

As I knew how much the President liked meeting young, heroic figures, I had also invited Wing-Commander Guy Gibson, fresh from leading the attack which had destroyed the Möhne and Eder Dams. A special type of mine had been invented for their destruction, but it had to be dropped at night from a height of no more than sixty feet. After months of continuous and concentrated practice sixteen Lancasters of No. 617 Squadron of the Royal Air Force attacked on the night of May 16. Half were lost, but Gibson had stayed to the end, circling under fierce fire over the target to direct his squadron.

My wife came with me, and my daughter Mary, now a subaltern in an antiaircraft battery, was my aide-de-camp. We sailed on August 5, this time for Halifax, in Nova Scotia, instead of New York.

THE *Queen Mary* drove on through the waves, and we lived in the utmost comfort on board her, with a diet of prewar times. As usual on these voyages, we worked all day long. Our large cipher staff, with attendant cruisers to dispatch outgoing messages, kept us in touch with events from hour to hour. Each day I studied with the Chiefs of Staff the various aspects of the problems we were to discuss with our American friends. The most important of these was of course "Overlord."

One morning on our voyage, at my request, Brigadier K. G. McLean, with two other officers from General Morgan's staff, came to me as I lay in my bed in the spacious cabin, and, after they had set up a large-scale map, explained in a tense and cogent tale the plan which had been prepared for the cross-Channel descent upon France. The reader is perhaps familiar with all the arguments of 1941 and 1942 upon this burning question in all its variants, but this was the first time that I had heard the whole coherent plan presented in precise detail both of numbers and tonnage as the result of prolonged study by officers of both nations. The choice narrowed to the Pas-de-Calais or Normandy. The former gave us the best air cover, but here the defences were the most formidable, and although it promised a shorter sea voyage this advantage was only apparent. While Dover and Folkestone are much closer to Calais and Boulogne than the Isle of Wight is to Normandy, their harbours were far too small to support an invasion. Most of our ships would have had to sail from ports along the whole south coast of England and from the Thames estuary, and so cross a lot of salt water in any case. General Morgan and his advisers recommended the Normandy coast, which from the first had been advocated by Mountbatten. There can be no doubt now that this decision was sound. Normandy gave us the greatest hope. The defences were not so strong as in the Pas-de-Calais. The seas and beaches were on the whole suitable, and were to some extent sheltered from the westerly gales by the Cotentin peninsula. The hinterland favoured the rapid deployment of very large forces, and was sufficiently remote from the main strength of the enemy. The port of Cherbourg could be isolated and captured early in the operation. Brest could be outflanked and taken later on.

All the coast between Le Havre and Cherbourg was of course defended with concrete forts and pillboxes, but as there was no harbour capable of sustaining a large army

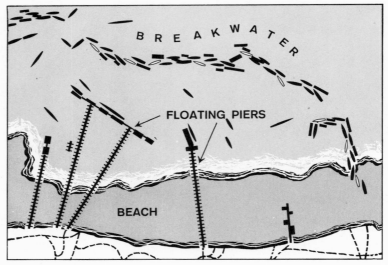

Improvised port for supplying an army which has landed on an open beach is shown in diagram as planned by Allies. Breakwater, formed by ships sunk in shallow water, protects floating piers from action of ocean so that cargo ships can unload even in rough weather.

in this fifty-mile half-moon of sandy beaches it was thought that the Germans would not assemble large forces in immediate support of the sea front. Their High Command had no doubt said to themselves, "This is a good sector for raids up to ten or twenty thousand men, but unless Cherbourg is taken in working order no army in any way equal to the task of an invasion can be landed or supplied. It is a coast for a raid, but not for wider operations." If only there were harbours which could nourish great armies, here was the front on which to strike.

I was, of course, well abreast of all the thought about landing craft and tank landing craft. I had also long been a partisan of piers with their heads floating out in the sea. Much work had since been done on them, following a minute which in the course of our discussions I had issued to Lord Louis Mountbatten, the Chief of Combined Operations, as long ago as May 30, 1942:

"They *must* float up and down with the tide. The anchor problem must be mastered. The ships must have a side-flap cut in them, and a drawbridge long enough to overreach the moorings of the piers. Let me have the best solution worked out. Don't argue the matter. The difficulties will argue for themselves."

Thought later moved to the creation of a large area of sheltered water protected by a breakwater which would be

based on blockships brought to the scene by their own power and then sunk in a prearranged position. This idea had originated with Commodore J. Hughes-Hallett in June 1943, while he was serving as Naval Chief of Staff in General Morgan's organisation. Imagination, contrivance, and experiment had been ceaseless, and now in August 1943 there was a complete project for making two full-scale temporary harbours which could be towed over and brought into action within a few days of the original landing. These synthetic harbours were called "Mulberries," a code name which certainly did not reveal their character or purpose.

The whole project was majestic. On the beaches themselves would be the great piers, with their seaward ends afloat and sheltered. At these piers our coasters and landing craft would be able to discharge at all states of the tide. To protect them against the wanton winds and waves the breakwaters would be spread in a great arc to seaward, enclosing a large area of sheltered water. Thus sheltered our deep-draught ships could lie at anchor and discharge, and all types of landing craft could ply freely to and from the beaches. These breakwaters would be composed of immense sunken concrete structures known as "Phoenix" and blockships known as "Gooseberries." In the First World War I had contemplated similar structures which might have been used to create artificial harbours for a landing in the Helgoland Bight. Now they were to form a principal part of the great plan.

Further discussions on succeeding days led into more technical detail. The Channel tides have a play of more than twenty feet, with corresponding scours along the beaches. The weather is always uncertain, and winds and gales may whip up in a few hours irresistible forces against frail human structures. The fools or knaves who had chalked "Second Front Now" on our walls for the past two years had not had their minds burdened by such problems. I had long pondered upon them.

I was now convinced of the enormous advantages of attacking the Havre-Cherbourg sector, provided these unexpected harbours could be brought into being from the first and thus render possible the landing and sustained advance of armies of a million rising to two million men, with all their immense modern equipment and impedimenta. This would mean being able to unload at least 12,000 tons a day.

Three dominating assumptions were made by the framers of the plan and the British Chiefs of Staff. With these I was in entire agreement, and, as will be seen later, they were approved by the Americans and accepted by the Russians. "1. That there must be a substantial reduction in the strength of the German fighter aircraft in Northwest Europe before the assault took place.

"2. That there should be not more than twelve mobile German divisions in Northern France at the time the operation was launched, and that it must not be possible for the Germans to build up more than fifteen divisions in the succeeding two months.

"3. That the problem of beach maintenance of large forces in the tidal waters of the English Channel over a prolonged period must be overcome. To ensure this it was essential that we should be able to construct at least two effective synthetic harbours."

I was very well satisfied with the prospect of having the whole of this story presented to the President with my full support. At least it would convince the American authorities that we were not insincere about "Overlord" and had not grudged thought or time in preparation. I arranged to assemble in Quebec the best experts in such matters from London and Washington. Together they could pool resources and find the best answers to the many technical problems.

I ALSO had many discussions with the Chiefs of Staff on our affairs in the Indian and Far Eastern theatres. We had none too good a tale to tell. A division had advanced at the end of 1942 down the Arakan coast of Burma to recapture the port of Akyab. Though strengthened until a complete corps was engaged, the operation had failed, and our troops were forced back.

Although there was much to be said in explanation, I felt that the whole question of the British High Command against Japan must come under review. New methods and new men were needed. I had long felt that it was a bad arrangement for the Commander-in-Chief of India to command the operations in Burma in addition to his other far-reaching responsibilities. It seemed to me that the vigorous prosecution of large-scale operations against the Japanese in Southeast Asia necessitated the creation of a separate Supreme Allied Command. The Chiefs of Staff were in complete agreement, and prepared a memorandum on these lines for discussion with their American colleagues in Quebec. There remained the question of the commander of this new theatre, and we were in no doubt that he should be British. Of the various names that were put forward, I was sure in my own mind that Admiral Mountbatten had superior qualifications for this great command, and I determined to make this proposal to the President at the first opportunity. The appointment of an officer of the substantive rank of Captain R.N. to the Supreme Command of one of the main theatres of the war was an unusual step; but, having carefully prepared the ground beforehand, I was not surprised when the President cordially agreed.

It is astonishing how quickly a voyage can pass if one has enough to do to occupy every waking minute. I had looked forward to an interval of rest and a change from the perpetual clatter of the war. But as we approached our destination the holiday seemed to be over before it had begun.

Halifax was reached on August 9. The great ship drew in to the landing jetty and we went straight to our train. In spite of all precautions about secrecy, large crowds were assembled. As my wife and I sat in our saloon at the end of the train the people gathered round and gave us welcome. Before we started I made them sing *The Maple Leaf* and *O Canada!* I feared they did not know *Rule, Britannia*, though I am sure they would have enjoyed it if we had had a band. After about twenty minutes of handshakings, photographs, and autographs we left for Quebec. On August 17 the President and Harry Hopkins arrived and Eden and Brendan Bracken flew in from England. As the delegations gathered, news of Italian peace moves came out to us, and it was under the impression of Italy's approaching surrender that our talks were held.

The first plenary session was held on August 19. Highest strategic priority "as a prerequisite to 'Overlord' " was given to the combined bomber offensive against Germany. The lengthy discussions upon Operation "Overlord" were then summarised in the light of the combined planning in London by General Morgan. The Chiefs of Staff now reported as follows:

"This operation will be the primary United States-British ground and air effort against the Axis in Europe. Target date, May 1, 1944. . . .

"As between Operation 'Overlord' and operations in the Mediterranean, where there is a shortage of resources, available resources will be distributed and employed with the main object of ensuring the success of 'Overlord.' Operations in the Mediterranean theatre will be carried out with the forces allotted at 'Trident' [the previous Conference at Washington in May], except in so far as these may be varied by decision of the Combined Chiefs of Staff. . . ."

These paragraphs produced some discussion at our meeting. I pointed out that the success of "Overlord" depended on certain conditions being fulfilled in regard to relative strength. I emphasised that I strongly favoured "Overlord" in 1944, though I had not been in favour of trying to attack Brest or Cherbourg in 1942 or 1943. The objections which I had to the cross-Channel operation were however now removed. I thought that every effort should be made to add at least 25 per cent to the first assault. This would mean finding more landing craft. There were still nine months to go, and much could be done in that time. The beaches selected were good, and it would be better if at the same time a landing were to be made on the inside beaches of the Cotentin peninsula. "Above all," I said, "the initial lodgment must be strong."

AS the United States had the African command, it had been earlier agreed between the President and me that the commander of "Overlord" should be British, and I proposed for this purpose, with the President's agreement, General Alan Brooke, the Chief of the Imperial General Staff, who, it may be remembered, had commanded a corps in the decisive battle on the road to Dunkerque, with both Alexander and Montgomery as his subordinates. I had informed General Brooke of this intention early in 1943. This operation was to begin with equal British and American forces, and as it was to be based on Great Britain it seemed right to make such an arrangement. However, as the year advanced and the immense plan of the invasion began to take shape I became increasingly impressed with the very great preponderance of American troops that would be employed after the original landing with equal numbers had been successful, and now at Quebec I myself took the initiative of proposing to the President that an American commander should be appointed for the expedition to France. He was gratified at this suggestion, and I dare say his mind had been moving that way. We therefore agreed that an American officer should command "Overlord" and that the Mediterranean should be entrusted to a British commander, the actual date of the change being dependent upon the progress of the war. I informed General Brooke, who had my entire confidence, of this change, and of the reasons for it. He bore the great disappointment with soldierly dignity.

As for the Far East, the main dispute between the British and American Chiefs of Staff was on the issue that Britain demanded a full and fair place in the war against Japan from the moment when Germany was beaten. She demanded a share of the airfields, a share of the bases for the Royal Navy, and a proper assignment of duties to whatever divisions she could transport to the Far East after the Hitler business was finished. My friends on the Chiefs of Staff Committee had been pressed by me to fight this point to the utmost limit, because at this stage in the war what I most feared was that American critics would say, "England, having taken all she could from us to help her beat Hitler, stands out of the war against Japan and will leave us in the lurch." However, at the Quebec Conference this impression was effectively removed. No decision was reached on the actual operations to be undertaken, though it was decided that the main effort should be put into offensive operations with the object of "establishing land communications with China and improving and securing the air route." In the "overall strategic concept" of the Japan war, plans were to be made to bring about the defeat of Japan within twelve months after the collapse of Germany.

Finally there was the Mediterranean scene. On August 10 Eisenhower held a meeting of his commanders to select from a variety of proposals the means by which the campaign should be carried into Italy. He had to take special account of the enemy dispositions at that time. Eight of the sixteen German divisions in Italy were in the north under Rommel, two were near Rome, and six were farther south under Kesselring. These might be reinforced from another twenty which had been withdrawn from the Russian front to refit in France. Nothing we might gather for a long time could equal such strength, but the British and Americans had command of sea and air, and also the initiative. The assault upon which all minds were now set was a daring enterprise. It was hoped to gain the ports of Naples and Taranto, whose combined facilities were proportioned to the scale of the armies we must use. The early capture of airfields was a prime aim. Those near Rome were as yet beyond our reach, but there was an important group at Foggia adaptable for heavy bombers, and our tactical air forces sought others in the heel of Italy and at Montecorvino, near Salerno.

† † †

General Eisenhower decided to begin the assault in early September by an attack across the Strait of Messina, with subsidiary descents on the Calabrian coast. This would be the prelude to the capture of Naples (Operation "Avalanche") by a British and an American army corps landing on the good beaches in the Gulf of Salerno. This was at the extreme range of fighter cover from the captured Sicilian airfields. As soon as possible after the landings the Allied forces would drive north to capture Naples.

The Combined Chiefs of Staff advised the President and me to accept this plan, and to authorise the seizure of Sardinia and Corsica in second priority. We did so with alacrity; indeed, it was exactly what I had hoped and striven for. Later it was proposed to land an airborne division to capture the airfields south of Rome. This also we accepted. The circumstances in which this feature was cancelled will be recounted in due course.

The Italian Surrender

THE Quebec Conference ended on August 24, and our notable colleagues departed and dispersed. They flew off in every direction like the fragments of a shell. After all the study and argument there was a general desire for a few days' rest. One of my Canadian friends, Colonel Clarke, who had been attached to me by the Dominion Government during the proceedings, owned a ranch about seventy-five miles away amid the mountains and pine forests from which the newspapers get their pulp to guide us on life's journey. Here lay the Lake of the Snows, an enormous dammed-up expanse of water reported to be full of the largest trout. Brooke and Portal were ardent and expert anglers, and a plan had been made among other plans at the Conference for them to see what they could do. I promised to join them later if I could, but I had undertaken to deliver a broadcast on the 31st, and this hung overhead like a vulture in the sky. I remained for a few days in the Citadel, pacing the ramparts for an hour each afternoon, and brooding over the glorious panorama of the St. Lawrence and all the tales of Wolfe and Quebec. I had promised to drive through the city, and I had a lovely welcome from all its people. I attended a meeting of the Canadian Cabinet, and told them all that they did not already know about the Conference and the war. I had the honour to be sworn a Privy Counsellor of the Dominion Cabinet. This compliment was paid me at the instance of my old friend of forty years' standing and trusted colleague, Mr. Mackenzie King.

There was so much to say and not to say in the broadcast that I could not think of anything, so my mind turned constantly to the Lake of the Snows, of which glittering reports had already come in from those who were there. I thought I might combine fishing by day with preparing the broadcast after dark. I resolved to take Colonel Clarke at his word, and set out with my wife by car. I had noticed that Admiral Pound had not gone with the other two

Chiefs of Staff to the lake, and I suggested that he should come with us now. His Staff officer said that he had a lot of cleaning up to do after the Conference. I had been surprised by the subdued part he had taken in the far-ranging naval discussions, but when he said he could not come fishing I had a fear that all was not well. We had worked together in the closest comradeship from the first days of the war. I knew his worth and courage. I also knew that at home he would get up at four or five in the morning for a few hours' fishing before returning to the Admiralty whenever he saw the slightest chance. However, he kept to his quarters and I did not see him before starting.

WE had a wonderful all-day drive up the river valley, and after sleeping at a resthouse on the way my wife and I reached the spacious log cabin on the lake. Brooke and Portal were leaving the next day. It was just as well. They had caught a hundred fish apiece each day, and had only to continue at this rate to lower the level of the lake appreciably. My wife and I sallied forth in separate boats for several hours, and though we are neither of us experts we certainly caught a lot of fine fish. We were sometimes given rods with three separate hooks, and I once caught three fish at the same time. I do not know whether this was fair. We did not run at all short of fresh trout at the excellent meals. The President had wanted to come himself, but other duties claimed him. I sent the biggest fish I caught to him at Hyde Park. The broadcast made progress, but original composition is more exhausting than either arguing or fishing.

We returned to Quebec for the night of the 29th. I attended another meeting of the Canadian Cabinet, and at the right time on the 31st, before leaving for Washington, I spoke to the Canadian people and to the Allied world. Next day I reached the White House. The President and I sat talking after dinner in his study, and Admiral Pound came to see us upon a naval point. The President asked him several questions about the general aspects of the war, and I was pained to see that my trusted naval friend had lost the outstanding matter-of-fact precision which characterised him. Both the President and I were sure he was very ill. Next morning Pound came to see me in my big bed-sitting-room and said abruptly, "Prime Minister, I have come to resign. I have had a stroke and my right side is largely paralysed. I thought it would pass off, but it gets worse every day and I am no longer fit for duty." I at once accepted the First Sea Lord's resignation, and expressed my profound sympathy for his breakdown in health. I told him he was relieved at that moment from all responsibility, and urged him to rest for a few days and then come home with me in the *Renown*. He was completely master of himself, and his whole manner was instinct with dignity. As soon as he left the room I cabled to the Admiralty placing Vice-Admiral Syfret in responsible charge from that moment pending the appointment of a new First Sea Lord.

Throughout the talks at Quebec events had been marching forward in Italy. The President and I had directed during these critical days the course of secret armistice negotiations with the Badoglio Government, and had also been following anxiously and closely the military arrangements for a landing on Italian soil. I deliberately prolonged my stay in the United States in order to be in close contact with our American friends at this crucial moment in Italian affairs. On the day of my arrival in Washington the first definite and official news was received that Badoglio had agreed to capitulate to the Allies, and on September 3 in an olive grove near Syracuse, General Castellano signed the military terms of the surrender of Italy. Before dawn on the same day the British Eighth Army crossed the Strait of Messina to enter the Italian mainland.

It now remained to co-ordinate the terms of the Italian surrender with our military strategy. The American General Taylor, of the 82nd Airborne Division, was sent to Rome on September 7. His secret mission was to arrange with the Italian General Staff for the airfields around the capital to be seized during the night of the 9th. But the situation had radically changed since General Castellano had asked for Allied protection. The Germans had powerful forces at hand, and appeared to be in possession of the airfields. The Italian Army was demoralised and short of ammunition. Divided counsels seethed around Badoglio. Taylor demanded to see him. Everything hung in the balance. The Italian leaders feared that any announcement of the surrender, which had already been signed, would lead to the immediate German occupation of Rome and the end of the Badoglio Government. At two o'clock on the morning of September 8 General Taylor saw Badoglio, who, since the airfields were lost, begged for delay in broadcasting the armistice terms. He had in fact already telegraphed to Algiers that the security of the Rome airfields could not be guaranteed. The Allied air descent was therefore cancelled.

Eisenhower now had to make a quick decision. The attack on Salerno was due to be launched within less than twenty-four hours. He refused Badoglio's request and at 6 p.m. broadcast the announcement of the armistice, followed by the text of the declaration, which Marshal Badoglio himself announced about an hour later from Rome. The surrender of Italy had been completed.

DURING the night of September 8–9 German forces began the encirclement of Rome. Badoglio and the Royal Family installed themselves in a state of siege in the building of the Ministry of War. There were hasty discussions in an atmosphere of mounting tension and panic. In the small hours a convoy of five vehicles passed through the eastern gates of Rome on the road to the Adriatic port of Pescara. Here two corvettes took on board the party, which contained the Italian Royal Family, together with Badoglio and his Government and senior officials. They reached Brindisi in the early morning of September 10, when the essential services of an anti-Fascist Italian Government were rapidly set up on territory occupied by Allied forces.

After the departure of the fugitives the veteran Marshal Caviglia, the victor of Vittorio Veneto in the First World War, arrived in Rome to take upon himself the responsibility of negotiating with the German forces closing in round the city. Scattered fighting was already taking place at the gates. Certain regular units of the Italian Army and Partisan bands of Roman citizens engaged the Germans on the outskirts. On September 11 opposition ceased with the signature of a military truce, and the Nazi divisions were free to move throughout the city.

Meanwhile, after dark on September 8, in accordance with Allied instructions, the main body of the Italian Fleet left Genoa and Spezia on a daring voyage of surrender to Malta, unprotected either by Allied or Italian aircraft. Next morning when steaming down the west coast of Sardinia it was attacked by German aircraft from bases in France. The flagship *Roma* was hit, and blew up with heavy loss of life, including the Commander-in-Chief, Admiral Berga-mini. The battleship *Italia* was also damaged. Leaving some light craft to rescue survivors, the rest of the Fleet continued its painful journey. On the 10th they were met at sea by British forces, including the *Warspite* and *Valiant*, which had so often sought them under different circumstances, and they were escorted to Malta. From Taranto a squadron including two battleships had also sailed on the 9th, and on the morning of the 11th Admiral Cunningham informed the Admiralty that "the Italian battle fleet now lies at anchor under the guns of the fortress of Malta."

On the whole, therefore, things had so far gone very smoothly for the Allies. After crossing the Strait of Messina the Eighth Army had encountered practically no opposition. Reggio was speedily taken, and the advance began along the narrow and hilly roads of Calabria. "The Germans," cabled Alexander on September 6, "are fighting their rear-guard action more by demolitions than by fire. . . . While in Reggio this morning there was not a warning sound to be heard or a hostile plane to be seen. On the contrary, on this lovely summer day naval craft of all types were plying backwards and forwards between Sicily and the mainland, carrying men, stores, and munitions. In its lively setting it was . . . like a regatta in peacetime. . . ." There was little fighting, but the advance was severely delayed by the physical difficulties of the country, demolitions carried out by the enemy, and his small but skilfully handled rear guard.

But on the night of the 8th Alexander sent me his "Zip" message. It had been planned that I and those of our party who had not already flown to England should go home by sea, and the *Renown* awaited us at Halifax. I broke the train journey to say good-bye to the President, and was thus with him at Hyde Park when the Battle of Salerno began. I resumed my train journey on the night of the 12th, to reach Halifax on the morning of the 14th. The various reports which reached me on the journey, as well as the newspapers, made me deeply anxious. Evidently a most critical and protracted struggle was in progress. My concern was all the greater because I had always strongly pressed for this landing, and felt a special responsibility for its success.

Surprise, violence, and speed are the essence of all amphibious landings. After the first twenty-four hours the advantage of sea power in striking where you will may well have vanished. Where there were ten men there are soon ten thousand. My mind travelled back over the years. I thought of General Stopford waiting nearly three days on the beach at Suvla Bay in 1915 while Mustafa Kemal marched two Turkish divisions from the lines at Bulair to the hitherto undefended battlefield. I had had a more recent experience when General Auchinleck had remained at his headquarters in Cairo surveying orthodoxly from the summit the wide and varied sphere of his command, while the battle, upon which everything hung, was being decided against him in the Desert. I had the greatest confidence in Alexander, but all the same I passed a painful day while our train rumbled forward through the pleasant lands of Nova Scotia. At length I wrote out the following message for Alexander, feeling sure he would not resent it. It was not sent till after I had sailed: "I hope you are watching above all the Battle of 'Avalanche,' which dominates everything. None of the commanders engaged has fought a large-scale battle before. The Battle of Suvla Bay was lost because Ian Hamilton was advised by his Chief of Staff to remain at a remote central point where he would know everything. Had he been on the spot he could have saved the show. At this distance and with time lags I cannot pretend to judge, but I feel it my duty to set before you this experience of mine from the past. *Nothing* should be denied which will nourish the decisive battle for Naples. . . ."

His answer was prompt and comforting. He was already at Salerno. "Many thanks," he replied, "for your offer of help. Everything possible is being done to make 'Avalanche' a success. Its fate will be decided in the next few days."

I was also relieved to learn that Admiral Cunningham had not hesitated to hazard his battleships close inshore in support of the Army. On the 14th he sent up the *Warspite* and *Valiant*, which had just arrived at Malta conducting to surrender the main body of the Italian Fleet. Next day they were in action, and their accurate air-directed bombardment with heavy guns impressed both friend and foe and greatly contributed to the defeat of the enemy.

It was a relief to board the *Renown*. The splendid ship lay alongside the quay. Admiral Pound was already on board, having come through direct from Washington. He bore himself as erect as ever, and no one looking at him would

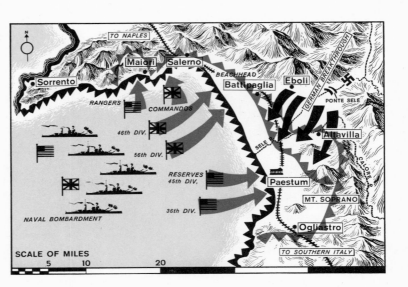

Salerno landing by Allies (*red arrows*) was made in teeth of German shore defenses (*black line*). After hard fighting on Sele River and at classic temple at Paestum, Allies drove to outer red line, then fell back to inner line in face of German counterattacks (*black arrows*).

have dreamed that he was stricken. I invited him to join us at my table on the homeward voyage, but he said he would prefer to take his meals in his cabin with his staff officer. He died on October 21, Trafalgar Day. He had been a true comrade to me, both at the Admiralty and on the Chiefs of Staff Committee. He was succeeded as First Sea Lord by Admiral Sir Andrew Cunningham.

While we zigzagged our way across the ocean a remarkable stroke was made upon Taranto, for which not only Alexander but Admiral Cunningham, on whom fell the brunt of execution, deserve the highest credit for well-run risks. This first-class port was capable of serving a whole army. The Italian surrender seemed to Alexander to justify daring. There were no transport aircraft to lift the British 1st Airborne Division, nor any ordinary shipping to carry it by sea. Six thousand of these picked men were embarked on British warships, and on September 9, the day of the landing on Salerno beaches, the Royal Navy steamed boldly into Taranto harbour and deposited the troops ashore, unopposed. One of our cruisers which struck a mine and sank was our only naval loss.

All the time the Battle of Salerno went on. The telegrams flowed in. Alexander was kind enough to keep me fully informed, and his vivid messages can be read in their relation to the whole event. For three critical days the issue hung in the balance, but after bitter fighting, in which we suffered moments of grave hazard, the Germans failed to throw us back into the sea. Kesselring realised he could not succeed. Pivoting his right on the high ground above Salerno, he began to swing his whole line back. The Eighth Army, spurred on by Montgomery, joined hands with the hard-pressed Fifth. The British X Corps, with the United States VI Corps on their right, drove back the enemy's rear guards around Vesuvius, marched past the ruins of Pompeii and Herculaneum, and entered Naples on October 1. We had won.

Deadlock in the Mediterranean

A FEW days after my return from Halifax I sent General Eisenhower a telegram which should be borne in mind in reading my account of the autumn and winter. The second paragraph sought to establish the proportion of effort, especially where bottlenecks were concerned, which should be devoted to our various enterprises. These proportions should not be overlooked by those who wish to understand the controversies with which this chapter deals. War presents the problem of the correct employment of available means, and cannot be epitomised as "One thing at a time."

"As I have been pressing for action in several directions," I cabled, "I feel I ought to place before you the priorities which I assign in my own mind to these several desirable objectives.

"2. Four-fifths of our effort should be the build-up of Italy. One-tenth should be our making sure of Corsica (which will soon finish) and in the Adriatic. The remaining tenth should be concentrated on Rhodes. This of course applies to the limiting factors only. These, I presume, are mainly landing craft, assault shipping and light naval craft.

"3. I send this as a rough guide to my thought only because I do not want you to feel I am pressing for everything in all directions without understanding how grim are your limitations."

Eisenhower replied the next day: "We are examining resources carefully to give Mid-East necessary support in this project, and feel sure that we can meet minimum requirements of Mid-East. When Montgomery can get the bulk of his forces forward to support the right of the Fifth Army things will begin to move more rapidly on the Naples front. As is always the case following the early stages of a combined operation, we have been badly stretched both tactically and administratively. We are all working hard to improve the situation and you will have the good news before long."

This answer did not refer as specifically as I had hoped to what I deemed the all-important part of my message, namely, the small proportion of troops required for subsidiary enterprises, and of these there were indeed many.

The surrender of Italy gave us the chance of gaining important prizes in the Aegean at very small cost and effort. The Italian garrisons obeyed the orders of the King and Marshal Badoglio, and would come over to our side if we could reach them before they were overawed and disarmed by the Germans in the islands. These were much inferior in numbers, but it is probable that for some time past they had been suspicious of their allies' fidelity and had their plans laid. Rhodes, Léros, and Kos were island fortresses which had long been for us strategic objectives of a high order in the secondary sphere, and their occupation had been specifically approved by the Combined Chiefs of Staff in their final summary of the Quebec decisions on September 10. Rhodes was the key to the group, because it had good airfields from which we could defend any other islands we might occupy and complete our naval control of these waters. Moreover, the British air forces in Egypt and Cyrenaica could guard Egypt just as well, or even better, if some of them moved forward to Rhodes. It seemed to me a rebuff to fortune not to pick up these treasures. The command of the Aegean by air and by sea was within our reach. The effect of this might be decisive upon Turkey, at that time deeply moved by the Italian collapse. If we could use the Aegean and the Dardanelles the naval short cut to Russia was established. There would be no more need for the perilous and costly Arctic convoys, or the long and wearisome supply line through the Persian Gulf.

General Wilson was eager for action, and plans and preparations for the capture of Rhodes had been perfected in the Middle East Command over several months. In August the 8th Indian Division had been trained and rehearsed in the operation, and was made ready to sail on September 1. But the American pressure to disperse our trained assault shipping from the Mediterranean, either westward for the preparations for a still remote "Overload" or to the Indian theatre, was very strong. Agreements made before the Italian collapse and appropriate to a totally different situation were rigorously invoked, at least at the secondary level, and on August 26, in pursuance of a minor decision at the Washington Conference in the previous May, the Combined Chiefs of Staff ordered the dispatch to the Far East, for an operation against the coast of Burma, of the shipping that could have transported the division to Rhodes. Thus Wilson's well-conceived plans for rapid action in the Dodecanese were harshly upset. He had sent with great promptitude small parties by sea and air to a number of other islands, but once Rhodes was denied to us our gains throughout the Aegean became precarious. Only a powerful use of air forces could give us what we needed. It would have taken very little of their time had there been accord. General Eisenhower and his Allied staff seemed unaware of what lay at our finger tips, although we had voluntarily placed all our considerable resources entirely in their hands.

We have since learnt how deeply the Germans were alarmed at the deadly threat which they expected us to develop on their southeastern flank. At a conference at the Fuehrer's headquarters on September 24 both the Army and the Navy representatives strongly urged the evacuation of Crete and other islands in the Aegean while there was still time. They pointed out that these advanced bases had been seized for offensive operations in the Eastern Mediterranean, but that now the situation was entirely changed. They stressed the need to avoid the loss of troops and matériel which would be of decisive importance for the defence of the continent. Hitler overruled them. He insisted that he could not order evacuation, particularly of Crete and the Dodecanese, because of the political repercussions which would follow. He said, "The attitude of our allies in the southeast and Turkey's attitude is determined solely by their confidence in our strength. Abandonment of the islands would create a most unfavourable impression." In this decision to fight for the Aegean islands he was justified by events. Hitler gained large profits in a subsidiary theatre at small cost to the main strategic position. In standing fast in the Balkans he was wrong. In standing fast in the Aegean he was right.

For a time our affairs prospered in the outlying small islands. By the end of September Kos, Léros, and Sámos were occupied by a battalion each, and detachments occupied a number of other islands. Italian garrisons, where encountered, were friendly enough, but their vaunted coast and antiaircraft defences were found to be in poor shape,

Action in Aegean to open new route to Russia (*dotted blue arrow*) began with British seizure (*solid blue*) of Sámos, Léros and Kos but ended with the Germans (*black*) recapturing the islands.

and the transport of our own heavier weapons and vehicles was hardly possible with the shipping at our disposal.

On September 22 Wilson reported his minimum and modest needs for a new attempt on Rhodes. Using the 10th Indian Division and part of an armoured brigade, he required only naval escorts and bombarding forces, three LSTs (Landing Ship, Tanks), a few motor transport ships, a hospital ship, and enough transport aircraft to lift one parachute battalion. I was greatly troubled at our inability to support these operations, and cabled for help to General Eisenhower. The small aids needed seemed very little to ask from our American friends. The concessions which they had made to my unceasing pressure during the last three months had been rewarded by astounding success. The landing craft for a single division, a few days' assistance from the main Allied Air Force, and Rhodes would be ours. The Germans, having now regripped the situation, had moved many of their planes to the Aegean to frustrate the very purpose which I had in mind. On October 7 I also laid the issue before the President in its full scope, but was pained to receive a telegram which practically amounted to a refusal, and left me, already committed, with his and the American Chiefs of Staff's approval, to face the impending blow. The negative forces which hitherto had been so narrowly overcome had indeed resumed their control. Mr. Roosevelt said:

"I do not want to force diversions on Eisenhower which limit the prospects for the early successful development of the Italian operations to a secure line north of Rome.

"I am opposed to any diversion which will in Eisenhower's opinion jeopardise the security of his current situation in Italy, the build-up of which is exceedingly slow, considering the well-known characteristics of his opponent, who enjoys a marked superiority in ground troops and Panzer divisions.

"It is my opinion that no diversion of forces or equipment should prejudice 'Overlord' as planned. The American Chiefs of Staff agree. I am transmitting a copy of this message to Eisenhower."

I noticed in particular the sentence "It is my opinion that no diversion of forces or equipment should prejudice 'Overlord' as planned." To pretend that the delay of six weeks in the return of nine landing craft for "Overlord" out of over 500 involved, which would in any case have had six months in hand, would compromise the main operation of May 1944 was to reject all sense of proportion. On October 8, I therefore made a further earnest appeal. Looking back upon the far-reaching favourable results which had followed from my journey with General Marshall to Algiers in June, from which the whole of our good fortune had sprung, I thought I might ask for the same procedure, and I made all preparations to fly at once to Tunis, where the Commanders-in-Chief were now assembling in conference.

But Mr. Roosevelt's reply quenched my last hopes. He thought my attendance would be inappropriate. I accordingly cancelled my proposed flight. At the critical moment of the conference information was received that Hitler had decided to reinforce his army in Italy and fight a main battle south of Rome. This tipped the scales against the small reinforcement required for the attack on Rhodes.

Although I could understand, in the altered situation, how the opinion of the generals engaged in our Italian campaign had been affected, I remained—and remain—in my heart unconvinced that the capture of Rhodes could not have been fitted in. Nevertheless, with one of the sharpest pangs I suffered in the war I submitted. If one has to submit it is wasteful not to do so with the best grace possible. When so many grave issues were pending I could not risk any jar in my personal relations with the President. I therefore took advantage of the news from Italy to accept what I thought, and think, to have been an improvident decision.

Nothing was gained by all of this over-caution. The capture of Rome proved to be eight months distant. Twenty times the quantity of shipping that would have helped to take Rhodes in a fortnight was employed throughout the autumn and winter to move the Anglo-American heavy bomber bases from Africa to Italy. Rhodes remained a thorn in our side. Turkey, witnessing the extraordinary inertia of the Allies near her shores, became much less forthcoming, and denied us her airfields. The American Staff had enforced their view; the price had now to be paid by the British. Kos fell to the Germans on October 3. Although we strove to maintain our position in Léros the fate of our small force there was also virtually sealed. The garrison was brought up to the strength of a brigade—three fine battalions of British infantry who had undergone the whole siege and famine of Malta and were still regaining their physical weight and strength. The Admiralty did their best, and General Eisenhower dispatched two groups of long-range fighters to the Middle East as a temporary measure. There they soon made their presence felt. But on October 11 they were withdrawn. Early on November 12, German troops came ashore on Léros, and in the afternoon 600 parachutists cut the defense in two. With little air support of their own and heavily attacked by enemy aircraft,

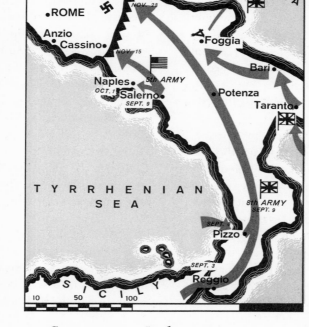

Campaign in Italy began well with Allied landings (*blue*) at Reggio, Taranto and Salerno but bogged down at German line (*black*) above Naples. Allies used Foggia air base to bomb Balkan oil fields.

the battalions fought on till the evening of the 16th, when, exhausted, they could fight no more. Thus this fine brigade of troops fell into enemy power. All our hopes in the Aegean were for the time being ended. We tried at once to evacuate the small garrisons in the other islands, and to rescue survivors from Léros. Over a thousand British and Greek troops were brought off, as well as many friendly Italians and German prisoners, but our naval losses were again severe. Six destroyers and two submarines were sunk by aircraft or mine and four cruisers and four destroyers damaged. These trials were shared by the Greek Navy, which played a gallant part throughout.

I have recounted the painful episodes of Rhodes and Léros in some detail. They constitute, happily on a small scale, the most acute difference I ever had with General Eisenhower. For many months, in the face of endless resistances, I had cleared the way for his successful campaign in Italy. Instead of only gaining Sardinia, we had now established a large group of armies on the Italian mainland. Corsica was a bonus in our hands. We had drawn an important part of the German reserves away from other theatres. And the Italian people and Government had come over to our side. Italy had declared war on Germany. Their Fleet was added to our own. Mussolini was a fugitive. The liberation of Rome seemed not far distant. Nineteen German divisions, abandoned by their Italian comrades, lay scattered through the Balkans, in which we had not used a thousand officers and men. The date for "Overlord" had not been decisively affected.

I had been instrumental in finding from the British and Imperial forces in Egypt four first-class divisions over and above those which had been deemed possible. We had aided General Eisenhower's Anglo-American Staff upon their victorious career, and we had also furnished them with substantial unexpected resources, without which disaster might well have occurred. I was grieved that the small requests I had made for strategic purposes almost as high as those already achieved should have been so obdurately resisted and rejected. Of course, when you are winning a war almost everything that happens can be claimed to be right and wise. It would however have been easy, but for pedantic denials in the minor sphere, to have added to our side the control of the Aegean, and very likely the accession of Turkey, to all the fruits of the Italian campaign.

At the same time, on Kesselring's advice, Hitler changed his mind about his Italian strategy. Till then he had meant to withdraw his forces behind Rome and hold only northern

Italy. Now he ordered them to fight as far south as possible. The line selected, the so-called "Winterstellung," ran behind the river Sangro, on the Adriatic side, across the mountainous spine of Italy, to the mouth of the Garigliano River on the west. The natural features of the country, its steep mountains and swift rivers, made this position, several miles in depth, immensely strong. After a year of almost continuous retreat in Africa, Sicily, and Italy the German troops were glad to turn about and fight. They now had nineteen divisions in Italy, and the Allies the equivalent of thirteen.

LARGE reinforcements and much consolidation were required to hold our rapid and brilliant conquests. All this put a strain on our shipping. The first probing efforts at the German line met with little success. Our men had been fighting hard for two months, the weather was shocking, and the troops needed rest and re-grouping. Bridgeheads were thrown across the river, but the main enemy defences lay on high ground beyond. Bad weather, with rain, mud, and swollen rivers, postponed the Eighth Army attack until November 28, but then it made good progress. After a week of heavy fighting we were established ten miles beyond the Sangro. But the enemy still held firm, and more reinforcements came to them from northern Italy. Some more ground was gained during the month of December, but no vital objectives were taken, and winter weather brought active operations to a close.

The U.S. Fifth Army (which included the British X Corps), under General Clark, struggled on up the road towards Cassino, and attacked the foremost defences of the German main positions. The enemy were strongly posted on mountains overlooking the road on either side. The formidable Monte Cassino massif to the west was attacked and finally cleared after a tough struggle. But it was not till the beginning of the New Year that the Fifth Army was fully aligned along the river Garigliano and its tributary, the Rapido, where it then faced the heights of Cassino and the famous monastery.

Thus the position in Italy was changed greatly to our disadvantage. The Germans were strongly reinforced and ordered to resist instead of to withdraw. The Allies, on the contrary, were sending eight of their best divisions from Italy and the Mediterranean back to England for the "Overlord" cross-Channel attack in 1944. The four extra divisions I was gathering or had sent did not repair the loss. A deadlock supervened, and was not relieved during eight months of severe fighting.

Nevertheless, in spite of these disappointments, the Italian campaign had attracted to itself twenty good German divisions. For reasons which are evident I had called it the Third Front. If the enemy garrisons kept in the Balkans for fear of attack there are added, nearly forty divisions were retained facing the Allies in the Mediterranean. Our Second Front, Northwest Europe, had not yet flared into battle, but its existence was real. About thirty Nazi divisions was the least number ever opposite it, and this rose to sixty as the invasion loomed closer. The Anglo-American strategic bombing from Britain forced the enemy to divert great numbers of men and masses of matériel to defend their homeland. These were not negligible contributions to the Russians on what they had every right to call the First Front.

I must end this chapter with a summary. In this period in the war all the great strategic combinations of the Western Powers were restricted and distorted by the shortage of tank landing craft for the transport, not so much of tanks, but of vehicles of all kinds. The letters "LST" (Landing Ship, Tanks) are burnt in upon the minds of all those who dealt with military affairs in this period. We had invaded Italy in strong force. We had an army there which, if not supported, might be entirely cast away, giving Hitler the greatest triumph he had had since the fall of France. On the other hand, there could be no question of our not making the "Overlord" attack in 1944. The utmost I asked for was an easement, if necessary, of two months—i.e., from some time in May 1944 to some time in July. This would meet the problem of the landing craft. Instead of their having to return to England in the late autumn of 1943 before the winter gales, they could go in the early spring of 1944. If however the May date were insisted upon pedantically, and interpreted as May 1, the peril to the Allied Army in Italy seemed beyond remedy. If some of the landing craft earmarked for "Overlord" were allowed to stay in the Mediterranean over the winter there would be no difficulty in making a success of the Italian campaign. There were masses of troops not in action in the Mediterranean: three or four French divisions, two or three American divisions, at least four (including the Poles) British or British-controlled divisions. The one thing that stood between these and effective operation in Italy was the LSTs, and the main thing that stood between us and the LSTs was the insistence upon an early date for their return to Britain.

THE reader of this narrative must not be misled into thinking (a) that I wanted to abandon "Overlord," (b) that I wanted to deprive "Overlord" of vital forces, or (c) that I contemplated a campaign by armies operating in the Balkan Peninsula. These are legends. Never had such a wish entered my mind. Give me an easement of six weeks or two months from May 1 in the date of "Overlord" and I could for several months use the landing craft in the Mediterranean in order to bring really effective forces to bear in Italy, and thus not only take and liberate Rome but draw off German divisions from either or both the Russian and Normandy fronts. All these matters had been discussed in Washington without regard to the limited character of the issues with which my argument was concerned.

As we shall see presently, in the end everything that I asked for was done. The landing craft not only were made available for upkeep in the Mediterranean; they were even allowed a further latitude for the sake of the Anzio operation in January. This is no way prevented the successful launching of "Overlord" on June 6 with adequate forces. What happened however was that the long fight about trying to get these small easements and to prevent the scrapping of one vast front in order to conform to a rigid date upon the other led to prolonged, unsatisfactory operations in Italy.

On a sandbar off Sicily, assault troops climb down a bomb-shattered LST while others wait to be taken off the ramp by amphibious ducks

THE AXIS SPLITS

First Invasion
of European Soil

The U.S. soldiers painted below by Mitchell Jamieson are bringing equipment ashore and evacuating wounded on Gela beach in Sicily. There, on July 10, 1943, they could look in all directions and see nothing but evidence of Allied power sweeping into Europe. Ahead were airborne troops dropped around bridges and road junctions. Behind was an invasion fleet of 1,400 ships, of which just a handful were

lost to enemy action. In the air the Luftwaffe could sneak in only a few raiders. For over a hundred miles around the southeast tip of the island British and American armies were landing, generally having had more interference from rough water than from the enemy. For the coastal guards—generally Sicilians because Mussolini thought they would fight like lions for their homeland—took one look at the armada off their shores and decamped. German tanks tried to break up the landings, but were stopped by naval gunfire.

The progress of the Sicilian campaign did not live up to its brilliant beginning. A mere three German divisions held up the two Allied armies for 38 days and then withdrew successfully back across the sea to the Italian mainland with their tanks and artillery, their fighting power intact.

Hard Slow Advance through Sicily

In a hillside foxhole, an American soldier sends a message by portable radio in northeast Sicily, where stubborn fighting by the American Seventh Army cracked the last-ditch German defense line.

In a smoking street in Messina, a reconnaissance patrol goes looking for snipers left behind when the Germans gave up their last toe hold on the island and slipped across the narrow strait to Italy. German defensive tactics were most efficient, and small forces posted in the rubble of wrecked towns or in narrow mountain defiles often held up the Allied advance long enough for the main German forces to get away.

Friendly Greetings from a Former Foe

The troops were not long ashore in Sicily before they learned that this particular enemy territory had no hard feelings against them. Like most of the Italian people, the Sicilians were tired of the war, sick of Mussolini's rantings, angry at German bullying. As the troops pushed forward through the acrid dust of the searing Sicilian summer, the roads were lined with people waving greetings, shouting *Bravo Americano!* or *Viva l'Inghilterra!* depending on the nationality of the invaders. Sicilians offered watermelons to slake the soldiers' thirst and little embroidered cushions to make their foxholes more comfortable. Every village had its quota of men who had lived in Pittsburgh or Brooklyn and hundreds of families asked for news of relatives serving in the American army.

The shock of Sicily brought Mussolini and his Fascist dictatorship down, and two months later, on September 8, the first of Hitler's allies was the first of the Axis powers to capitulate. In a false dawn of hope the Italian people came out to celebrate. On that day, Allied ships sailing to the invasion of the mainland at Salerno saw towns brilliantly lit while the population danced in the squares to celebrate what they thought was the end of the war. Both troops and civilians were unaware that the Germans had guns zeroed in on the beaches at Salerno and were prepared to make a bitter fight for every rocky yard of Italian soil.

Friendly exchange passes between an American and a grocer's wife doing her washing in the town of Agrigento. This soldier was a cowboy in civilian life, and the grocer's family called him Tom Mix.

Heroes' welcome greets American troops—some of them already a little bored with their triumphal progress—as they roll through Monreale, near Palermo, in the amphibious vehicles that put them ashore

on the southern coast a week or so earlier. At this stage of the campaign, General George Patton's Seventh Army was scooping up the western half of Sicily with only token resistance from the disintegrating Italian army, a good part of which was changing into civilian clothes and merging with the local population. Chief obstacle to the speed of the American advance was the mass of cheering Sicilians who clogged the narrow roads.

The ruins of Cassino, where the Germans stalled the Allies for almost four months, look down on a German corpse and heaps of graveyard bones churned up—like everything else in and near the town—by the fury of the bombs.

16

CLOSING THE RING

Tehran: The Opening

I HAD hardly got home after my visits to the Citadel, the White House, and Hyde Park during the Quebec Conference in August and September 1943 when I turned to the theme of a meeting of the three heads of Governments which logically followed upon the Anglo-American conversations. In principle there was general agreement that this was urgent and imperative, but no one who did not live through it can measure the worries and complications which attended the fixing of the time, place, and conditions of this, the first conference of what were then called the Big Three.

Several serious aspects of the impending Conference absorbed my mind. The selection of a Supreme Commander for "Overlord," our cross-Channel entry into Europe in 1944, was urgent. This of course affected in the most direct manner the military conduct of the war, and raised a number of personal issues of importance and delicacy. At the Quebec Conference I had agreed with the President that "Overlord" should fall to an American officer, and had so informed General Brooke, to whom I had previously offered the task. I understood from Mr. Roosevelt that he would choose General Marshall, and this was entirely satisfactory to us. However, in the interval between Quebec and our meeting in Cairo I became conscious that the President had not finally made up his mind about Marshall.

None of the other arrangements could of course be made before the command decision had been taken. Meanwhile rumour became rife in the American Press, and there was the prospect of Parliamentary reactions in London.

I also thought it most important that the British and American Staffs, and above them the President and I, should reach a general agreement on the policy of "Overlord" and its impingement on the Mediterranean theatre. The whole armed strength overseas of our two countries was involved, and the British forces were to be equal at the outset of "Overlord," twice as strong as the Americans in Italy, and three times as numerous in the rest of the Mediterranean. Surely we ought to reach some solid understanding between us before inviting the Soviet representatives, either political or military, to join us.

The President appeared to favour the idea, but not the timing. There was emerging a strong current of opinion in American Government circles which seemed to wish to win Russian confidence even at the expense of co-ordinating the Anglo-American war effort. I on the other hand felt it of the utmost importance that we should meet the Russians with a clear and united view both on the outstanding problems of "Overlord" and upon the question of the High Commands. I wished the proceedings to take three stages: first, a broad Anglo-American agreement at Cairo;

secondly, a Supreme Conference between the three heads of the Governments of the three major Powers at Tehran; and, thirdly, on returning to Cairo, the discussion of what was purely Anglo-American business about the war in the Indian theatre and the Indian Ocean, which was certainly urgent. I did not want the short time we had at our disposal to be absorbed in what were after all comparatively minor matters, when the decision involving the course of the whole war demanded at least provisional settlement.

Mr. Roosevelt agreed to come to Cairo first, but he wanted Molotov to come as well and also the Chinese. Nothing, however, would induce Stalin to compromise his relations with the Japanese by entering a four-Power conference with their three enemies. All question of Soviet representatives coming to Cairo was thus negatived. This was in itself a great relief. It was obtained however at a serious inconvenience and subsequent cost.

On the afternoon of November 12, I sailed in the *Renown* from Plymouth with my personal staff on a journey which was to keep me from England for more than two months. After calling at Algiers and Malta, we reached Alexandria on the morning of the 21st. I flew at once to the desert landing ground near the Pyramids. Here Mr. Casey had placed at my disposal the agreeable villa he was using. We lay in a broad expanse of Kasserine woods, thickly dotted with the luxurious abodes and gardens of the cosmopolitan Cairo magnates. Generalissimo Chiang Kai-shek and Madame had already been ensconced half a mile away. The President was to occupy the spacious villa of the American Ambassador Kirk, about three miles down the road to Cairo. I went to the rough desert airfield to welcome him when he arrived in the "Sacred Cow" next morning, and we drove to his villa together.

The Staffs congregated rapidly. The headquarters of the Conference and the venue of all the British and American Chiefs of Staff was at the Mena House Hotel, opposite the Pyramids, and I was but half a mile away. The whole place bristled with troops and antiaircraft guns, and the strictest cordons guarded all approaches. Everyone set to work at once at their various levels upon the immense mass of business which had to be decided or adjusted.

What we had apprehended from Chiang Kai-shek's presence now in fact occurred. The talks of the British and American Staffs were sadly distracted by the Chinese story, which was lengthy, complicated, and minor. Moreover, as will be seen, the President, who took an exaggerated view of the Indian-Chinese sphere, was soon closeted in long conferences with the Generalissimo. All hope of persuading Chiang and his wife to go and see the Pyramids and enjoy themselves till we returned from Tehran fell to the ground, with the result that Chinese business occupied first instead of last place at Cairo.

The President, in spite of my arguments, gave the Chinese the promise of a considerable amphibious operation

---

16 Oct 43

Prime Minister
to Minister of War Transport

I am glad you are taking steps to improve the position [about bus queues]. In the London Passenger Transport Board region about 5,500,000 bus journeys are made daily. An extra minute wasted per journey every day is equivalent to 10,000 persons working a nine-hour day over the year in this area alone.

---

across the Bay of Bengal within the next few months. This would have cramped "Overlord" for landing and tank landing craft, which had now become the bottleneck, far more than any of my Turkey and Aegean projects. It would also have hampered grievously the immense operations we were carrying out in Italy. On November 29 I wrote to the British Chiefs of Staff: "The Prime Minister wishes to put on record the fact that he specifically refused the Generalissimo's request that we should undertake an amphibious operation simultaneously with the land operations in Burma." It was not until we returned from Tehran to Cairo that I at length prevailed upon the President to retract his promise. Even so, many complications arose. Of this more anon.

I of course took occasion to visit the Generalissimo at his villa, where he and his wife were suitably installed. This was the first time I had met Chiang Kai-shek. I was impressed by his calm, reserved, and efficient personality. At this moment he stood at the height of his power and fame. To American eyes he was one of the dominant forces in the world. He was the champion of "the New Asia." He was most certainly a steadfast defender of China against Japanese invasion. He was a strong anti-Communist. The accepted belief in American circles was that he would be the head of the great Fourth Power in the world after the victory had been won. All these views and values have since been cast aside by many of those who held them. I, who did not in those days share the excessive estimates of Chiang Kai-shek's power or of the future helpfulness of China, may record the fact that the Generalissimo is still serving the same causes which at this time had gained him such wide renown. He has however since been beaten by the Communists in his own country, which is a very bad thing to be. I had a very pleasant conversation with Madame Chiang Kai-shek, and found her to be a most remarkable and charming personality. The President had us all photographed together at one of our meetings at his villa, and although both the Generalissimo and his wife are now regarded as wicked and corrupt reactionaries by many of their former admirers I am glad to keep this as a souvenir.

On November 24 a meeting of our Combined Chiefs of Staff was held by the President, without the presence of the Chinese delegation, to discuss operations in Europe and the Mediterranean. We sought to survey the relations of the two theatres and to exchange our views before going on to Tehran. The President opened upon the effect on "Overlord" of any possible action we could take in the meantime in the Mediterranean, including the problem of Turkey's entry into the war.

When I spoke I said "Overlord" remained top of the bill, but this operation should not be such a tyrant as to rule out every other activity in the Mediterranean; for example, a little flexibility in the employment of landing craft ought to be conceded. General Alexander had asked that the date of their leaving for "Overlord" should be deferred from mid-December to mid-January. Eighty additional LSTs had been ordered to be built in Britain and Canada. We should try to do even better than this. The points which were at issue between the American and British Staffs would probably be found to affect no more than a tenth of our common resources, apart from the Pacific. Surely some degree of elasticity could be arranged. Nevertheless I wished to remove any idea that we had weakened, cooled, or were trying to get out of "Overlord." We were in it up to the hilt. I said, in summing up, that the programme I advocated was to try to take Rome in January and Rhodes in February; to renew supplies to the Yugoslavs, settle the Command arrangements, and to open the Aegean, subject to the outcome of an approach to Turkey; in the meantime all preparations for "Overlord" to go ahead full steam within the framework of the foregoing policy for the Mediterranean.

MR. Eden now joined us from England, whither he had flown after his discussions in Moscow. His arrival was a great help to me. On the way back from the Moscow Conference he and General Ismay had met the Turkish Foreign Minister and other Turks. Mr. Eden pointed out to them that we had urgent need of air bases in the southwest of Anatolia. He explained that our military situation at Léros and Sámos was precarious, owing to German air superiority. Both places had since been lost. Mr. Eden also dwelt on the advantages that would be derived from Turkey's entry into the war. In the first place, it would oblige the Bulgarians to concentrate their forces on the frontier, and thus compel the Germans to replace Bulgarian troops in Greece and Yugoslavia to the extent of some ten divisions. Secondly, it would be possible to attack the one target which might be decisive—the Romanian oil wells at Ploesti. Thirdly, Turkish chrome would be cut off from Germany. Finally, there was the moral advantage. Turkey's entry into the war might well hasten the process of disintegration in Germany and among her satellites.

By all this argument the Turkish delegation were unmoved. They said, in effect, that the granting of bases in Anatolia would amount to intervention in the war, and that if they intervened in the war there was nothing to prevent a German retaliation on Istanbul, Ankara, and Smyrna. They refused to be comforted by the assurances that we would give them sufficient fighters to deal with any air attack that the Germans could launch and that the Germans were so stretched everywhere that they had no divisions available to attack Turkey. The only result of the discussions was that the Turkish delegation promised to report to their Government. Considering what had been happening under their eyes in the Aegean, the Turks can hardly be blamed for their caution.

Finally, there was the issue of the High Commands. Neither the President nor any of his immediate circle referred to the matter in any way on the occasions, formal and informal but always friendly, when we came into contact. I therefore rested under the impression that General Marshall would command "Overlord," that General Eisenhower would succeed him in Washington, and that

it would fall to me, representing His Majesty's Government, to choose the Mediterranean commander, who at that time I had no doubt would be Alexander, already waging the war in Italy. Here the issue rested till we returned to Cairo.

There have been many misleading accounts of the line I took, with the full agreement of the British Chiefs of Staff, at the Triple Conference at Tehran. It has become a legend in America that I strove to prevent the cross-Channel enterprise called "Overlord," and that I tried vainly to lure the Allies into some mass invasion of the Balkans, or a large-scale campaign in the Eastern Mediterranean, which would effectively kill it. Much of this nonsense has already in previous chapters been exposed and refuted, but it may be worth while to set forth what it was I actually sought, and what, in a very large measure, I got. In spite of a cold and a sore throat, Moran with sprays and ceaseless care enabled me to say what I had to say—which was a lot.

"Overlord," now planned in great detail, should be launched in May or June, or at the latest in the opening days of July 1944. The troops and all the ships to carry them still had first priority. Secondly, the great Anglo-American army in action in Italy must be nourished to achieve the capture of Rome and advance to secure the airfields north of the capital, from which the air attack on southern Germany became possible. After these were gained there should be no advance in Italy beyond the Pisa-Rimini line—i.e., we should not extend our front into the broader part of the Italian peninsula. These operations, if resisted by the enemy, would attract and hold very large German forces, would give the Italians the chance to "work their passage," and keep the flame of war burning continually upon the hostile front.

I was not opposed at this time to a landing in the south of France, along the Riviera, with Marseille and Toulon as objectives, and thereafter an Anglo-American advance northward up the Rhône valley in aid of the main invasion across the Channel. Alternatively, I preferred a right-handed movement from the north of Italy, using the Istrian peninsula and the Ljubljana gap, towards Vienna. I was delighted when the President suggested this, and tried, as will be seen, to engage him in it. If the Germans then resisted we should attract many of their divisions from the Russian or Channel fronts. If we were not resisted we should liberate at little cost enormous and invaluable regions. I was sure we should be resisted, and thus help "Overlord" in a decisive manner.

MY third request was that the Eastern Mediterranean, with all the prizes that it afforded, should not be neglected, provided no strength which could be applied across the Channel should be absorbed. In all this I adhered to the proportions which I had mentioned to General Eisenhower two months earlier—namely, four-fifths in Italy, one-tenth in Corsica and the Adriatic, and one-tenth in the Eastern Mediterranean. From this I never varied—not an inch in a year.

We were all agreed, British, Russians, and Americans, upon the first two, involving nine-tenths of our available strength. All I had to plead was the effective use of one-tenth of our strength in the Eastern Mediterranean. Simpletons will argue, "Would it not have been much better to centre all upon the decisive operation and dismiss all other opportunities as wasteful diversions?'' But this ignores the governing facts. All the available shipping in the Western Hemisphere was already committed to the last ton to the preparation of ''Overlord'' and the maintenance of our front in Italy. Even if more shipping had been found it could not have been used, because the programmes of disembarkation filled to the utmost limit all the ports and camps involved.

As for the Eastern Mediterranean, nothing was needed that could be applied elsewhere. The Air Force massed for the defence of Egypt could equally well or better discharge its duty if used from a forward frontier. All the troops, two or three divisions at the outside, were already in that theatre, and there were no ships, except local vessels, to carry them to the larger scenes. To get the active, vigorous use of these forces, who otherwise would be mere lookers-on, might inflict grave injury upon the enemy. If Rhodes were taken the whole Aegean could be dominated by our Air Force and direct sea contact established with Turkey. If, on the other hand, Turkey could be persuaded to enter the war, or to strain her neutrality by lending us the airfields we had built for her, we could equally dominate the Aegean and it would not be necessary to capture Rhodes. Either way it would work.

And of course the prize was Turkey. If we could gain Turkey it would be possible without the subtraction of a single man, ship, or aircraft from the main and decisive battles to dominate the Black Sea with submarines and light naval forces, and to give a right hand to Russia and carry supplies to her armies by a route far less costly, far more swift, and far more abundant than either the Arctic or the Persian Gulf. This was the triple theme which I pressed upon the President and Stalin on every occasion, not hesitating to repeat the arguments remorselessly. I could have gained Stalin, but the President was oppressed by the prejudices of his military advisers and drifted to and fro in the argument, with the result that the whole of these subsidiary but gleaming opportunities were cast aside unused. Our American friends were comforted in their obstinacy by the reflection that ''at any rate we have stopped Churchill entangling us in the Balkans.'' No such idea had ever crossed my mind. I regard the failure to use otherwise unemployable forces to bring Turkey into the war and dominate the Aegean as an error in war direction which cannot be excused by the fact that in spite of it victory was won.

The first plenary meeting was held at the Soviet Embassy on Sunday, November 28, at 4 p.m. The conference room

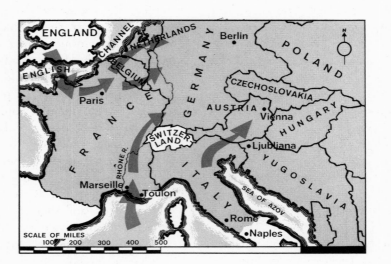

Strategic alternatives for attacking Germany are shown by arrows as they were discussed at Tehran. The Big Three agreed on landing in northern France. For a subsidiary offensive, Roosevelt backed landing in south of France, Churchill a drive into Austria.

was spacious and handsome, and we seated ourselves at a large round table. I had with me Eden, Dill, and the three Chiefs of Staff, and Ismay. The President had Harry Hopkins, Admiral Leahy, Admiral King, and two other officers. General Marshall and General Arnold were not present: ''They had misunderstood the time of the meeting,'' says Hopkins' biographer, ''and had gone off on a sight-seeing tour round Tehran.'' I had my admirable interpreter of the previous year, Major Birse. Pavlov again performed this service for the Soviets, and Mr. Bohlen, a new figure, for the United States. Molotov and Marshal Voroshilov alone accompanied Stalin. He and I sat almost opposite one another. The discussion on this first day came to a crucial point. The record says: ''Marshal Stalin addressed the following questions to the Prime Minister:

''*Question:* Am I right in thinking that the invasion of France is to be undertaken by thirty-five divisions? *Answer:* Yes. Particularly strong divisions.

''*Question:* Is it intended that this operation should be carried out by the forces now in Italy? *Answer:* No. Seven divisions are in process of being, or have already been, withdrawn from Italy and North Africa to take part in 'Overlord.' These seven divisions are required to make up the thirty-five divisions you mentioned in your first question. After they have been withdrawn about twenty-two divisions will be left in the Mediterranean for Italy or other objectives. Some of these could be used either for an operation against Southern France or for moving from the head of the Adriatic towards the Danube. Both these operations will be timed in conformity with 'Overlord.' Meanwhile it should not be difficult to spare two or three divisions to take the islands in the Aegean.''

The formal conferences were interspersed with what may be thought to be even more important talks between Roosevelt, Stalin, and myself at luncheons and dinners. Here there were very few things that could not be said and received in good humour. On this night the President was our host for dinner. We were a party of ten or eleven, including the interpreters, and conversation soon became general and serious.

After dinner, when we were strolling about the room, I led Stalin to a sofa and suggested that we talk for a little on what was to happen after the war was won. He assented, and we sat down. Eden joined us. ''Let us,'' said the Marshal, ''first consider the worst that might happen.'' He thought that Germany had every possibility of recovering from this war, and might start a new one within a comparatively short time. He feared the revival of German nationalism. After Versailles peace had seemed assured, but Germany had recovered very quickly. We must therefore establish a strong body to prevent Germany starting a new war. He was convinced that she would recover. When I asked, "How soon?" Stalin replied, "Within fifteen to twenty years." I said that the world must be made safe for at least fifty years. If it was only for fifteen to twenty years then we should have betrayed our soldiers.

Stalin thought that we should consider restraints on Germany's manufacturing capacity. The Germans were an able people, very industrious and resourceful, and they would recover quickly. I replied that there would have to be certain measures of control. I would forbid them all aviation, civil and military, and I would forbid the General Staff system. "Would you," asked Stalin, "also forbid the existence of watchmakers' and furniture factories for making parts of shells? The Germans produced toy rifles which were used for teaching hundreds of thousands of men how to shoot."

"Nothing," I said, "is final. The world rolls on. We have now learnt something. Our duty is to make the world safe for at least fifty years by German disarmament, by preventing rearmament, by supervision of German factories, by forbidding all aviation, and by territorial changes of a far-reaching character. It all comes back to the question whether Great Britain, the United States, and the U.S.S.R. can keep a close friendship and supervise Germany in their mutual interest. We ought not to be afraid to give orders as soon as we see any danger."

"There was control after the last war," said Stalin, "but it failed." "We were inexperienced then," I replied. "The last war was not to the same extent a national war, and Russia was not a party at the Peace Conference. It will be different this time." I had a feeling that Prussia should be isolated and reduced, that Bavaria, Austria, and Hungary might form a broad, peaceful, unaggressive confederation. I thought Prussia should be dealt with more sternly than the other parts of the Reich, which might thus be influenced against throwing in their lot with her. It must be remembered that these were wartime moods. "All very good, but insufficient," was Stalin's comment.

RUSSIA, I continued, would have her Army, Great Britain and the United States their Navies and Air Forces. In addition, all three Powers would have their other resources. All would be strongly armed, and must not assume any obligation to disarm. "We are the trustees for the peace of the world. If we fail there will be perhaps a hundred years of chaos. If we are strong we can carry out our trusteeship. There is more," I went on, "than merely keeping the peace. The three Powers should guide the future of the world. I do not want to enforce any system on other nations. I ask for freedom and for the right of all nations to develop as they like. We three must remain friends in order to ensure happy homes in all countries."

Stalin asked again what was to happen to Germany. I replied that I was not against the toilers in Germany, but only against the leaders and against dangerous combinations. He said that there were many toilers in the German divisions who fought under orders. When he asked German prisoners who came from the labouring classes (such is the record, but he probably meant "Communist Party") why they fought for Hitler they replied that they were carrying out orders. He shot such prisoners.

I then suggested we should discuss the Polish question. He agreed and invited me to begin. I said that we had declared war on account of Poland. Poland was therefore important to us. Nothing was more important than the security of the Russian western frontier. But I had given no pledges about frontiers. I wanted heart-to-heart talks with the Russians about this. When Marshal Stalin felt like telling us what he thought about it the matter should be discussed and we could reach some agreement, and the Marshal should tell me what was necessary for the defence of the western frontiers of Russia. After this war in Europe, which might end in 1944, Russia would be overwhelmingly strong and the Soviet Union would have a great responsibility in any decision she took with regard to Poland. Personally I thought Poland might move westward, like soldiers taking two steps "left close." If Poland trod on some German toes that could not be helped, but there must be a strong Poland. Poland was an instrument needed in the orchestra of Europe.

STALIN said the Polish people had their culture and their language, which must exist. They could not be extirpated. "Are we to try," I asked, "to draw frontier lines?" "Yes," he replied. I then said, "I have no power from Parliament, nor, I believe, has the President, to define any frontier lines. But we might now, in Tehran, see if the three heads of Governments, working in agreement, could form some sort of policy which we could recommend to the Poles and advise them to accept."

Stalin asked whether this was possible without Polish participation. I said "Yes," and that when this was all informally agreed between ourselves we could go to the Poles later. Mr. Eden here remarked that he had been much struck by Stalin's statement that afternoon that the Poles could go as far west as the Oder. He saw hope in that and was much encouraged. Stalin asked whether we thought he was going to swallow Poland up. Eden said he did not know how much the Russians were going to eat. How much could they leave undigested? Stalin said the Russians did not want anything belonging to other people, although they might have a bite at Germany. Eden said that what Poland lost in the east she might gain in the west. Stalin replied that possibly she might, but he did not know. I then demonstrated with the help of three matches my idea of Poland moving westward. This pleased Stalin, and on this note our group parted for the moment.

† † †

The morning of the 29th was occupied by a conference of the British, Soviet, and American military chiefs. As I knew that Stalin and Roosevelt had already had a private conversation, and were in fact staying at the same Embassy, I suggested that the President and I might lunch together before the second plenary meeting that afternoon. Roosevelt however declined, and sent Harriman to me to explain that he did not want Stalin to know that he and I were meeting privately. I was surprised at this, for I thought we all three should treat each other with equal confidence. The President after luncheon had a further interview with Stalin and Molotov, at which many important matters were discussed, including particularly Mr. Roosevelt's plan for the government of the postwar world. This should be carried out by the "Four Policemen," namely, the U.S.S.R., the United States, Great Britain, and China. Stalin did not react favourably to this. He said the "Four Policemen" would not be welcomed by the small nations of Europe. He did not believe that China would be very powerful when the war ended, and even if she were, European States would resent having China as an enforcement authority for themselves. In this the Soviet leader certainly showed himself more prescient and possessed of a truer sense of values than the President.

When Stalin proposed as an alternative that there should be one committee for Europe and another for the Far East —the European committee to consist of Britain, Russia, the United States, and possibly one other European nation —the President replied that this was somewhat similar to my idea of regional committees, one for Europe, one for the Far East, and one for the Americas. He does not seem to have made it clear that I also contemplated a Supreme United Nations Council, of which the three regional committees would be the components. As I was not informed till much later of what had taken place I was not able to correct this erroneous presentation.

Before our second plenary session began at four o'clock I presented, by the King's command, the Sword of Honour which His Majesty had had specially designed and wrought to commemorate the glorious defence of Stalingrad. The larger outer hall was filled with Russian officers and soldiers. When, after a few sentences of explanation, I handed the splendid weapon to Stalin he raised it in a most impressive gesture to his lips and kissed the scabbard. He then passed it to Voroshilov, who dropped it. It was carried from the room in great solemnity escorted by a Russian guard of honour. As this procession moved away I saw the President sitting at the side of the room, obviously stirred by the ceremony. We then moved to the conference chamber and took our seats again at the round table, this time with all the Chiefs of Staff, who now reported the result of their morning's labours.

In the discussions which followed I reminded Stalin of the three conditions on which the success of "Overlord" depended. First, there must be a satisfactory reduction in the strength of the German fighter force in Northwest Europe between now and the assault. Secondly, German reserves in France and the Low Countries must not be more on the day of the assault than about twelve full-strength first-quality mobile divisions. Thirdly, it must not be possible for the Germans to transfer from other fronts more than fifteen first-quality divisions during the first sixty days of the operation. To obtain these conditions we should have to hold as many Germans as possible in Italy and Yugoslavia. If Turkey entered the war, this would be an added help, but not an essential condition. The Germans now in Italy had for the most part come from France. If we slackened off our pressure in Italy they would go back again. We must continue to engage the enemy on the only front where at present we could fight them. If we engaged them as fiercely as possible during the winter months in the Mediterranean this would make the best possible contribution towards creating the conditions needed for a successful "Overlord."

Stalin asked what would happen if there were thirteen or fourteen mobile divisions in France and more than fifteen available from other fronts. Would this rule out "Overlord"? I said, "No, certainly not."

Before we separated Stalin looked at me across the table and said, "I wish to pose a very direct question to the Prime Minister about 'Overlord.' Do the Prime Minister and the British Staff really believe in 'Overlord'?" I replied, "Provided the conditions previously stated for 'Overlord' are established when the time comes, it will be our stern duty to hurl across the Channel against the Germans every sinew of our strength." On this we separated.

Tehran: Crux and Conclusions

NOVEMBER 30 was for me a crowded and memorable day. It was my sixty-ninth birthday, and was passed almost entirely in transacting some of the most important business with which I have ever been concerned. The fact that the President was in private contact with Marshal Stalin and dwelling at the Soviet Embassy, and that he had avoided ever seeing me alone since we left Cairo, in spite of our hitherto intimate relations and the way in which our vital affairs were interwoven, led me to seek a direct personal interview with Stalin. I felt that the Russian leader was not deriving a true impression of the British attitude. The false idea was forming in his mind that, to put it shortly, "Churchill and the British Staffs mean to stop 'Overlord' if they can, because they want to invade the Balkans instead." It was my duty to remove this double misconception.

The exact date of "Overlord" depended upon the movements of a comparatively small number of landing craft. These landing craft were not required for any operation in the Balkans. The President had committed us to an operation against the Japanese in the Bay of Bengal. If this were cancelled there would be enough landing craft for all I wanted, namely, the amphibious power to land against opposition two divisions at a time on the coasts of Italy or Southern France, and also to carry out "Overlord" as planned in May. I had agreed with the President that May should be the month, and he had, for his part, given up the specific date of May 1. This would give me the time I needed.

If I could persuade the President to obtain relief from his promise to Chiang Kai-shek and drop the Bay of Bengal plan, which had never been mentioned in our Tehran conferences, there would be enough landing craft both for the Mediterranean and for a punctual "Overlord." In the event the great landings began on June 6, but this date was decided much later on, not by any requirements of mine, but by the moon and the weather. I also succeeded when we returned to Cairo, as will be seen, in persuading the President to abandon the enterprise in the Bay of Bengal. I therefore consider that I got what I deemed imperative. But this was far from certain at Tehran on this November morning. I was determined that Stalin should know the main facts. I did not feel entitled to tell him that the President and I had agreed upon May for "Overlord." I knew that Roosevelt wanted to tell him this himself at our luncheon which was to follow my conversation with the Marshal.

The following is founded upon the record made by Major Birse, my trusted interpreter, of my private talk with Stalin.

I BEGAN by reminding the Marshal that I was half American and had a great affection for the American people. What I was going to say was not to be understood as disparaging to the Americans, and I would be perfectly loyal towards them, but there were things which it was better to say outright between two persons.

We had a preponderance of troops over the Americans in the Mediterranean. There were two or three times more British troops than American there. That was why I was anxious that the armies in the Mediterranean should not be hamstrung if it could be avoided. I wanted to use them all the time. In Italy there were some thirteen to fourteen divisions, of which nine or ten were British. There were two armies, the Fifth Anglo-American Army, and the Eighth Army, which was entirely British.

The choice had been represented as keeping to the date of "Overlord" or pressing on with the operations in the Mediterranean. But that was not the whole story. The Americans wanted me to undertake an amphibious operation in the Bay of Bengal against the Japanese in March. I was not keen about it. If we had the landing craft needed for the Bay of Bengal in the Mediterranean we should have enough to do all we wanted there and still be able to keep to an early date for "Overlord." It was not a choice between the Mediterranean and the date of "Overlord," but between the Bay of Bengal and the date of "Overlord." However, the Americans had pinned us down to a date for "Overlord" and operations in the Mediterranean had suffered in the last two months. Our army in Italy was somewhat disheartened by the removal of seven divisions. We had sent home three divisions, and the Americans were sending four of theirs, all in preparation for "Overlord." That was why we had not been able to take full advantage of the Italian collapse. But it also proved the earnestness of our preparations for "Overlord." Stalin said that was good.

I then turned to the question of landing craft, and explained once again how and why they were the bottleneck. We had plenty of troops in the Mediterranean, even after the removal of the seven divisions, and there would be an adequate invading British and American army in the United Kingdom. All turned on landing craft. When Stalin had made his momentous announcement two days before about Russia's coming into the war against Japan after Hitler's surrender I had immediately suggested to the Americans that they might find more landing craft for the operations we had been asked to carry out in the Indian Ocean, or that they might send some landing craft from the Pacific to help the first lift of "Overlord." In that case there might be enough for all. But the Americans were very touchy about the Pacific. I had pointed out to them that Japan would be beaten much sooner if Russia joined in the war against her, and that they could therefore afford to give us more help.

The issue between myself and the Americans was in fact a very narrow one. It was not that I was in any way lukewarm about "Overlord." I wanted to get what I needed for the Mediterranean and at the same time keep to the date for "Overlord." The details had to be hammered out between the Staffs, and I had hoped that this might be done in Cairo. Unfortunately Chiang Kai-shek had been there and Chinese questions had taken up nearly all the time. But I was sure that in the end enough landing craft would be found for all.

Now about "Overlord." The British would have ready by the date fixed in May or June nearly sixteen divisions, with their corps troops, landing craft troops, antiaircraft, and services, a total of slightly over half a million men. These would consist of some of our best troops, including battle-trained men from the Mediterranean. In addition the British would have all that was needed from the Royal Navy to handle transportation and to protect the Army, and there would be the metropolitan Air Forces of about 4,000 first-line British aircraft in continuous action. The American import of troops was now beginning. Up till now they had sent mainly air troops and stores for the Army, but in the next four or five months I thought 150,000 men or more would come every month, making a total of seven to eight hundred thousand men by May. The defeat of the submarines in the Atlantic had made this movement possible. I was in favour of launching the operation in the South of France about the same time as "Overlord" or at whatever moment was found correct. We should be holding enemy troops in Italy, and of the twenty-two or twenty-three divisions in the Mediterranean as many as possible would go to the South of France and the rest would remain in Italy.

A GREAT battle was impending in Italy. General Alexander had about half a million men under him. There were thirteen or fourteen Allied divisions against nine to ten German. The weather had been bad and bridges had been swept away, but in December we intended to push on, with General Montgomery leading the Eighth Army. An amphibious landing would be made near the Tiber. At the same time the Fifth Army would be fiercely engaged holding the enemy. It might turn into a miniature Stalingrad. We did not intend to push into the wide part of Italy, but to hold the narrow leg.

Stalin said he must warn me that the Red Army was depending on the success of our invasion of Northern France. If there were no operations in May 1944 then the Red Army would think that there would be no operations at all that year. The weather would be bad and there would be transport difficulties. If the operation did not take place he did not want the Red Army to be disappointed. Disappointment could only create bad feeling. If there was no big change in the European war in 1944 it would be very difficult for the Russians to carry on. They were war-weary. He feared that a feeling of isolation might develop in his troops. That was why he had tried to find out whether "Overlord" would be undertaken on time as promised. If not, he would have to take steps to prevent bad feeling in the Red Army. It was most important.

I said "Overlord" would certainly take place, provided the enemy did not bring into France larger forces than the Americans and British could gather there. If the Germans had thirty to forty divisions in France I did not think the force we were going to put across the Channel would be able to hold on. I was not afraid of going on shore, but of what would happen on the thirtieth, fortieth, or fiftieth day. However, if the Red Army engaged the enemy and we held them in Italy, and possibly the Turks came into the war, then I thought we could win.

Stalin said that the first steps of "Overlord" would have a good effect on the Red Army, and if he knew that it was going to take place in May or June he could already prepare blows against Germany. The spring was the best time. March and April were both months of slackness, in which he could concentrate his troops and matériel, and in May and June he could attack. Germany would have no troops for France. The transfer of German divisions to the east was continuing. The Germans were afraid for their Eastern Front, because it had no Channel which had to be crossed and there was no France to be entered. The Germans were afraid of the Red Army advance. The Red Army would advance if it saw that help was coming from the Allies. He asked when "Overlord" would begin.

I said that I could not disclose the date for "Overlord" without the President's agreement, but the answer would be given at lunchtime, and I thought he would be satisfied.

After a short interval Stalin and I separately proceeded to the President's quarters for the luncheon of "Three Only" (with our interpreters) to which he had invited us. Roosevelt then told him that we were both agreed that "Overlord" should be launched during the month of May. Stalin was evidently greatly pleased and relieved by this solemn and direct engagement which we both made. The conversation turned on lighter subjects, and the only part of which I have a record was the question of Russia's outlet upon the seas and oceans. I had always thought it was a wrong thing, capable of breeding disastrous quarrels, that a mighty land mass like the Russian Empire, with its population of nearly two hundred millions, should be denied during the winter months all effective access to the broad waters.

After a brief interval the third plenary session began as before in the Russian Embassy at four o'clock. There was a full attendance and we numbered nearly thirty. General Brooke then announced that, after sitting in combined session, the United States and British Chiefs of Staff had recommended us to launch "Overlord" in May,

---

24 Oct 43

PRIME MINISTER TO BRIGADIER HOLLIS

This paper about directives to Supreme Commanders looks very simple from a distance and appeals to the American sense of logic. However, in practice it is found not sufficient for a Government to give a general a directive to beat the enemy and wait to see what happens. The matter is much more complicated. The general may well be below the level of his task, and has often been found so. A definite measure of guidance and control is required from the Staffs and from the high Government authorities. It would not be in accordance with the British view that any such element should be ruled out.

"in conjunction with a supporting operation against the South of France, on the largest scale permitted by the landing craft available at that time."

Stalin said he understood the importance of the decision and the difficulties inherent in carrying it out. The danger period for "Overlord" would be at the time of deployment from the landings. At this point the Germans might transfer troops from the east in order to create the maximum difficulties for "Overlord." In order to prevent any movement from the east of any considerable German forces he undertook to organise a large-scale Russian offensive in May. I asked if there would be any difficulty in the three Staffs concerting cover plans. Stalin explained that the Russians had made considerable use of deception by means of dummy tanks, aircraft, and airfields. Radio deception had also proved effective. He was entirely agreeable to the Staffs collaborating with the object of devising joint cover and deception schemes. "In wartime," I said, "truth is so precious that she should always be attended by a bodyguard of lies." Stalin and his comrades greatly appreciated this remark when it was translated, and upon this note our formal conference ended gaily.

Hitherto we had assembled for our conferences or meals in the Soviet Embassy. I had claimed however that I should be the host at the third dinner, which should be held in the British Legation. This could not well be disputed. Great Britain and I myself both came first alphabetically, and in seniority I was four or five years older than Roosevelt or Stalin. We were by centuries the longest established of the three Governments; I might have added, but did not, that we had been the longest in the war; and, finally, November 30 was my birthday. These arguments, particularly the last one, were conclusive, and all preparations were made by our Minister for a dinner of nearly forty persons, including not only the political and military chiefs but some of their higher staffs. The Soviet Political Police, the N.K.V.D., insisted on searching the British Legation from top to bottom, looking behind every door and under every cushion, before Stalin appeared; and about fifty armed Russian policemen, under their own General, posted themselves near all the doors and windows. The American Security men were also much in evidence. Everything however passed off agreeably. Stalin, arriving under heavy guard, was in the best of tempers, and the President, from his wheeled chair, beamed on us all in pleasure and good will.

This was a memorable occasion in my life. On my right sat the President of the United States, on my left the master of Russia. Together we controlled a large preponderance of the naval and three-quarters of all the air forces in the world, and could direct armies of nearly twenty millions of men, engaged in the most terrible of wars that had yet occurred in human history. I could not help rejoicing at the long way we had come on the road to victory since the summer of 1940, when we had been alone, and, apart from the Navy and the Air, practically unarmed, against the triumphant and unbroken might of Germany and Italy, with almost all Europe and its resources in their grasp. Mr. Roosevelt gave me for a birthday present a beautiful Persian porcelain vase, which, although it was broken into fragments on the homeward journey, has been marvellously reconstructed and is one of my treasures.

DURING dinner I had a most pleasant conversation with both my august guests. Stalin repeated the question he had posed at the Conference, "Who will command 'Overlord'?" I said that the President had not yet finally made up his mind, but that I was almost certain it would be General Marshall, who sat opposite us at no great distance, and that was how it had stood hitherto. He was evidently very pleased at this. He then spoke about General Brooke. He thought that he did not like the Russians. He had been very abrupt and rough with them at our first Moscow meeting in August 1942. I reassured him, remarking that military men were apt to be blunt and hard-cut when dealing with war problems with their professional colleagues. Stalin said that he liked them all the better for that. He gazed at Brooke intently across the room.

When the time came I proposed the health of our illustrious guests, and the President proposed my health and wished me many happy returns of the day. He was followed by Stalin, who spoke in a similar strain.

Many informal toasts were then proposed, according to the Russian custom, which is certainly very well suited to banquets of this kind. Hopkins made a speech couched in a happy vein, in the course of which he said that he had made "a very long and thorough study of the British Constitution, which is unwritten, and of the War Cabinet, whose authority and composition are not specifically defined." As the result of this study, he said, "I have learnt that the provisions of the British Constitution and the powers of the War Cabinet are just whatever Winston Churchill wants them to be at any given moment." This caused general laughter.

The reader of this tale will know how little foundation there was in this jocular assertion. It is true that I received a measure of loyal support in the direction of the war from Parliament and my Cabinet colleagues which may well be unprecedented, and that there were very few large issues upon which I was overruled; but it was with some pride that I reminded my two great comrades on more than one occasion that I was the only one of our trinity who could at any moment be dismissed from power by the vote of a House of Commons freely elected on universal franchise, or could be controlled from day to day by the opinion of a War Cabinet representing all parties in the State. The President's term of office was fixed, and his powers not only as President but as Commander-in-Chief were almost absolute under the Constitution of the United States. Stalin appeared to be, and at this moment certainly was, all-powerful in Soviet Russia. They could order; I had to convince and to persuade. I was glad

that this should be so. The process was laborious, but I had no reason to complain of the way in which it worked.

As the dinner proceeded there were many speeches, and most of the principal figures, including Molotov and General Marshall, made their contribution. But the speech which stands out in my memory came from General Alan Brooke. I quote the account he was good enough to write for me some years later.

"Half-way through the dinner," he says, "the President very kindly proposed my health, referring to the time when my father had visited his father at Hyde Park. Just as he was finishing, and I was thinking what an easy time I should have replying to such kind words, Stalin got up and said he would finish the toast. He then proceeded to imply that I had failed to show real feelings of friendship towards the Red Army, that I was lacking in a true appreciation of its fine qualities, and that he hoped in future that I should be able to show greater comradeship towards the soldiers of the Red Army!

"I was very much surprised by these accusations, as I could not think what they were based on. I had however seen enough of Stalin by then to know that if I sat down under these insults I should lose any respect he might ever have had for me, and that he would continue such attacks in the future.

"I therefore rose to thank the President most profusely for his very kind expressions, and then turned to Stalin in approximately the following words:

" 'Now, Marshal, may I deal with your toast. I am surprised that you should have found it necessary to raise accusations against me that are entirely unfounded. You will remember that this morning while we were discussing cover plans Mr. Churchill said that "in war truth must have an escort of lies." You will also remember that you yourself told us that in all your great offensives your real intentions were always kept concealed from the outer world. You told us that all your dummy tanks and dummy aeroplanes were always massed on those fronts that were of an immediate interest, while your true intentions were covered by a cloak of complete secrecy.

" 'Well, Marshal, you have been misled by dummy tanks and dummy aeroplanes, and you have failed to observe those feelings of true friendship which I have for the Red Army, nor have you seen the feelings of genuine comradeship which I bear towards all its members.' "

AS this was translated by Pavlov, sentence by sentence, to Stalin I watched his expression carefully. It was inscrutable. But at the end he turned to me and said with evident relish, "I like that man. He rings true. I must have a talk with him afterwards."

At length we moved into the antechamber, and here everyone moved about in changing groups. I felt that there was a greater sense of solidarity and good-comradeship than we had ever reached before in the Grand Alliance. I had not invited Randolph and Sarah to the dinner, though they came in while my birthday toast was being proposed, but now Stalin singled them out and greeted them most warmly, and of course the President knew them well.

As I moved around I saw Stalin in a small circle face to face with "Brookie," as I called him. The General's account continues: "As we walked out of the room the Prime Minister told me that he had felt somewhat nervous as to what I should say next when I had referred to 'truth' and 'lies.' He comforted me however by telling me that my reply to the toast had had the right effect on Stalin. I therefore decided to return to the attack in the anteroom. I went up to Stalin and told him how surprised I was, and grieved, that he should have found it necessary to raise such accusations against me in his toast. He replied at once through Pavlov, 'The best friendships are those founded on misunderstandings,' and he shook me warmly by the hand."

It seemed to me that all the clouds had passed away, and in fact Stalin's confidence in my friend was established on a foundation of respect and good will which was never shaken while we all worked together.

It must have been after two in the morning when we finally separated. The Marshal resigned himself to his escort and departed, and the President was conveyed to his quarters in the Soviet Embassy. I went to bed tired out but content, feeling sure that nothing but good had been done. It certainly was a happy birthday for me.

ON December 1st our long and hard discussions at Tehran reached their end. The military conclusions governed in the main the future of the war. The cross-Channel invasion was fixed for May, subject naturally to tides and the moon. It was to be aided by a renewed major Russian offensive. At first sight I liked the proposed descent upon the French southern shore by part of the Allied Armies in Italy. The project had not been examined in detail, but the fact that both the Americans and the Russians favoured it made it easier to secure the landing craft necessary for the success of our Italian campaign and the capture of Rome, without which it would have been a failure. I was of course more attracted by the President's alternative suggestion of a right-handed move from Italy by Istria and Trieste, with ultimate designs for reaching Vienna through the Ljubljana gap. All this lay five or six months ahead. There would be plenty of time to make a final choice as the general war shaped itself, if only the life of our armies in Italy was not paralysed by depriving them of their modest requirements in landing craft. Many amphibious or semiamphibious schemes were open. I expected that the sea-borne operations in the Bay of Bengal would be abandoned, and this, as the next chapter will show, proved correct. I was glad to feel that several important options were still preserved. Our strong efforts were to be renewed to bring Turkey into the war, with all that might accompany this in the Aegean, and follow from it in the Black Sea. In this we were to be disappointed. Surveying the whole military scene, as we separated in an atmosphere of friendship and unity of immediate purpose, I personally was well content.

The political aspects were at once more remote and speculative. Obviously they depended upon the results of the great battles yet to be fought, and after that upon the mood of each of the Allies when victory was gained. It would not have been right at Tehran for the Western democracies to found their plans upon suspicions of the Russian attitude in the hour of triumph and when all her dangers were removed. Stalin's promise to enter the war against Japan as soon as Hitler was overthrown and his armies defeated was of the highest importance. The hope of the future lay in the most speedy ending of the war and the establishment of a World Instrument to prevent another war, founded upon the combined strength of the three Great Powers, whose leaders had joined hands in friendship around the table.

We had procured a mitigation for Finland, which on the whole is operative to-day. The frontiers of the new Poland had been broadly outlined both in the east and in the west. The "Curzon Line," subject to interpretation in the east, and the line of the Oder, in the west, seemed to afford a true and lasting home for the Polish nation after all its sufferings. At the time the question between the Eastern and Western Neisse, which flow together to form the Oder River, had not arisen. When in July 1945 it arose in a violent form and under totally different conditions at the Potsdam Conference I at once declared that Great Britain adhered only to the eastern tributary. And this is still my position.

The supreme question of the treatment to be accorded to Germany by the victors could at this milestone only be the subject of "a preliminary survey of a vast political problem," and, as Stalin described it, "certainly very preliminary." It must be remembered that we were in the midst of a fearful struggle with the mighty Nazi Power. All the hazards of war lay around us, and all its passions of comradeship among Allies, of retribution upon the common foe, dominated our minds. The President's tentative projects for the partition of Germany into five self-governing states and two territories, of vital consequence, under the United Nations, were of course far more acceptable to Stalin than the proposal which I made for the isolation of Prussia and the constitution of a Danubian Confederation, or of a South Germany and also a Danubian Confederation. This was only my personal view. But I do not at all repent having put it forward in the circumstances which lay about us at Tehran.

WE all deeply feared the might of a united Germany. Prussia had a great history of her own. It would be possible, I thought, to make a stern but honourable peace with her, and at the same time to re-create in modern forms what had been in general outline the Austro-Hungarian Empire, of which it has been well said, "If it did not exist it would have to be invented." Here would be a great area in which not only peace but friendship might reign at a far earlier date than in any other solution. Thus a United Europe might be formed in which all the victors and vanquished might find a sure foundation for the life and freedom of all their tormented millions.

I do not feel any break in the continuity of my thought in this immense sphere. But vast and disastrous changes have fallen upon us in the realm of fact. The Polish frontiers exist only in name, and Poland lies quivering in the Russian-Communist grip. Germany has indeed been partitioned, but only by a hideous division into zones of military occupation. About this tragedy it can only be said IT CANNOT LAST.

Carthage and Marrakech

ON December 2 I got back to Cairo from Tehran, and was once more installed in the villa near the Pyramids. The President arrived the same evening, and we resumed our intimate discussions on the whole scene of the war and on the results of our talks with Stalin. Meanwhile the Combined Chiefs of Staff, who had refreshed themselves by a visit to Jerusalem on their way back from Tehran, were to carry forward their discussions on all their great business the next day. Admiral Mountbatten had returned to India, whence he had submitted the revised plan he had been instructed to make for an amphibious attack on the Andaman Islands (Operation "Buccaneer"). This would absorb the vitally needed landing craft already sent to him from the Mediterranean. I wished to make a final attempt to win the Americans to the alternative enterprise against Rhodes.

The next evening I dined again with the President. Eden was with me. We remained at the table until after midnight, still discussing our points of difference. I shared the views of our Chiefs of Staff, who were much worried by the promise which the President had made to Chiang Kai-shek before Tehran to launch an early attack across the Bay of Bengal. This would have swept away my hopes and plans of taking Rhodes, on which I believed the entry of Turkey into the war largely depended. But Mr. Roosevelt's heart was set upon it. When our Chiefs of Staff raised it in the military conferences the United States Staffs simply declined to discuss the matter. The President, they said, had taken his decision and they had no choice but to obey.

On the afternoon of December 4 we held our first plenary meeting since Tehran, but made little headway. The President began by saying that he must leave on December 6, and that all reports should be ready for the final agreement of both parties by the evening of Sunday, December 5. Apart from the question of the entry of Turkey into the war, the only outstanding point seemed to be the comparatively small one of the use to be made of a score of landing craft and their equipment. It was unthinkable that one could be beaten by a petty item like that, and he felt bound to say that the detail *must* be disposed of.

I said that I did not wish to leave the Conference in any doubt that the British delegation viewed our early dispersal with great apprehension. There were still many questions of first-class importance to be settled. Two decisive events had taken place in the last few days. In the first place, Stalin had voluntarily proclaimed that the Soviet would declare war on Japan the moment Germany was defeated. This would give us better bases than we could ever find in China, and made it all the more important that we should concentrate on making "Overlord" a success. It would be necessary for the Staffs to examine how this new fact would affect operations in the Pacific and Southeast Asia.

The second event of first-class importance was the decision to cross the Channel during May. I myself would have preferred a July date, but I was determined nevertheless to do all in my power to make a May date a complete success. It was a task transcending all others. A million Americans were to be thrown in eventually, and five or six hundred thousand British. Terrific battles were to be expected, on a scale far greater than anything that we had experienced before. In order to give "Overlord" the greatest chance, it was thought necessary that the descent on the Riviera (code-named "Anvil") should be as strong as possible. It seemed to me that the crisis for the invading armies would come at about the thirtieth day, and it was essential that every possible step should be taken by action elsewhere to prevent the Germans from concentrating a superior force against our beachheads. As soon as the "Overlord" and "Anvil" forces got into the same zone they would come under the same commander.

The President, in summing up the discussion, asked whether he was correct in thinking that there was general agreement on the following points:

"(a) Nothing should be done to hinder 'Overlord.'

"(b) Nothing should be done to hinder 'Anvil.'

"(c) By hook or by crook we should scrape up sufficient landing craft to operate in the Eastern Mediterranean if Turkey came into the war.

"(d) Admiral Mountbatten should be told to go ahead and do his best [in the Bay of Bengal] with what had already been allocated to him."

On this last point I suggested that it might be necessary to withdraw resources from Mountbatten in order to strengthen "Overlord" and "Anvil." The President said that he could not agree. We had a moral obligation to do something for China, and he would not be prepared to forgo the amphibious operation except for some very good and readily apparent reason. I replied that this "very good reason" might be provided by our supreme adventure in France. At present the "Overlord" assault was only on a three-division basis, whereas we had put nine divisions ashore in Sicily on the first day. The main operation was at present on a very narrow margin.

REVERTING to the Riviera attack, I expressed the view that it should be planned on the basis of an assault force of at least two divisions. This would provide enough landing craft to do the outflanking operations in Italy, and also, if Turkey came into the war soon, to capture Rhodes. I then pointed out that operations in Southeast Asia must be judged in their relation to the predominating importance of "Overlord." I said that I was surprised at the demands for taking the Andamans which had reached me from Admiral Mountbatten. In the face of Stalin's promise that Russia would come into the war, operations in the Southeast Asia Command had lost a good deal of their value, while, on the other hand, their cost had been put up to a prohibitive extent.

The discussion continued on whether or not to persist in the Andamans project. The President resisted the British wish to drop it. No conclusion was reached, except that the Chiefs of Staff were directed to go into details.

On December 5 we met again, and the report of the Combined Staffs on operations in the European theatre was read out by the President and agreed. Everything was now narrowed down to the Far Eastern operation. Rhodes had receded in the picture, and I concentrated on getting the landing craft for "Anvil" and the Mediterranean. A new factor had presented itself. The estimates of the Southeast Asia Command of the force needed to storm the Andamans had been startling. The President said that 14,000 should be sufficient. Anyhow, the 50,000 men proposed certainly broke the back of the Andamans expedition so far as this meeting was concerned. It was agreed for the moment that Mountbatten should be asked what amphibious operations he could undertake on a smaller scale, on the assumption that most of the landing craft and assault shipping were withdrawn from Southeast Asia during the next few weeks. Thus we parted, leaving Mr. Roosevelt much distressed.

Before anything further could be done the deadlock in Cairo was broken. In the afternoon the President, in consultation with his advisers, decided to abandon the Andaman Islands plan. He sent me a laconic private message: " 'Buccaneer' is off." General Ismay reminds me that when I told him the welcome news cryptically on the telephone that the President had changed his mind and was so informing Chiang Kai-shek I said, "He is a better man that ruleth his spirit than he that taketh a city." We all met together at 7:30 p.m. the next evening to go over the final report of the Conference. The Southern France assault operation was formally approved, and the President read out his signal to Generalissimo Chiang Kai-shek, informing him of the decision to abandon the Andamans plan.

One of the main purposes of our Cairo meeting had been to resume talks with the Turkish leaders. I had telegraphed President Inönü on December 1 from Tehran suggesting that he should join the President and myself in Cairo. It was arranged that Vyshinsky should also be present. These conversations arose out of the meeting between Mr. Eden and the Turkish Foreign Minister in Cairo at the beginning of November on the former's journey home from Moscow. The Turks now came again to Cairo on the 4th of December, and the following evening I entertained the Turkish President to dinner. My guest, however, displayed great caution, and in subsequent meetings showed to what extent his advisers were still impressed by the German military machine. I pressed the case hard. With Italy out of the war the advantages of Turkey's entry were manifestly increased and her risks lessened.

The Turks soon departed to report to their Parliament. It was agreed that in the meantime British specialists should be assembled to implement the first stages of establishing an Allied force in Turkey. And there the matter rested. By the time Christmas arrived I was becoming resigned to Turkish neutrality.

In all our many talks at Cairo the President never referred to the vital and urgent issue of the command of

---

25 Feb 44

PRIME MINISTER TO FOREIGN SECRETARY

We "invade" all countries with whom we are at war.

2. We "enter" all subjugated Allied lands we wish to "liberate."

3. With regard to a country like Italy, with whose Government we have signed an armistice, we "invaded" in the first instance, but, in view of the Italian co-operation, we must consider all further advances by us in Italy to be in the nature of "liberation."

"Overlord," and I was under the impression that our original arrangement and agreement held good. But on the day before his departure from Cairo he told me his final decision. We were driving in his motorcar from Cairo to the Pyramids. He then said, almost casually, that he could not spare General Marshall, whose great influence at the head of military affairs and of the war direction, under the President, was invaluable, and indispensable to the successful conduct of the war. He therefore proposed to nominate Eisenhower to "Overlord," and asked me for my opinion. I said it was for him to decide, but that we had also the warmest regard for General Eisenhower, and would trust our fortunes to his direction with hearty good will.

Up to this time I had thought Eisenhower was to go to Washington as Military Chief of Staff, while Marshall commanded "Overlord." Eisenhower had heard of this too, and was very unhappy at the prospect of leaving the Mediterranean for Washington. Now it was all settled: Eisenhower for "Overlord," Marshall to stay at Washington, and a British commander for the Mediterranean.

The full story of the President's long delay and hesitations and of his final decision is referred to by Mr. Hopkins' biographer, who says that Roosevelt made the decision on Sunday, the 5th of December, "against the almost impassioned advice of Hopkins and Stimson, against the known preference of both Stalin and Churchill, against his own proclaimed inclination." Then Mr. Sherwood quotes the following extract from a note which he had from General Marshall after the war. "If I recall," said Marshall, "the President stated, in completing our conversation, 'I feel I could not sleep at night with you out of the country.' " There can be little doubt that the President felt that the command only of "Overlord" was not sufficient to justify General Marshall's departure from Washington.

At last our labours were finished. I gave a dinner at the villa to the Combined Chiefs of Staff, Mr. Eden, Mr. Casey, and one or two others. I remember being struck by the optimism which prevailed in high Service circles. The idea was mooted that Hitler would not be strong enough to face the spring campaign, and might collapse even before "Overlord" was launched in the summer. I was so much impressed by the current of opinion that I asked everybody to give his view in succession round the table. All the professional authorities were inclined to think that the German collapse was imminent. The three politicians present took the opposite view. Of course, on these vast matters on which so many lives depend there is always a great deal of guesswork. So much is unknown and immeasurable. Who can tell how weak the enemy may be behind his flaming fronts and brazen mask? At what moment will his will power break? At what moment will he be beaten down?

The President had found no time for sight-seeing, but I could not bear his leaving without seeing the Sphinx.

One day after tea I said, "You must come now." We motored there forthwith, and examined this wonder of the world from every angle. Roosevelt and I gazed at her for some minutes in silence as the evening shadows fell. She told us nothing and maintained her inscrutable smile. There was no use waiting longer. On December 7, I bade farewell to my great friend when he flew off from the airfield beyond the Pyramids.

I HAD not been at all well during this journey and Conference, and as it drew to its close I became conscious of being very tired. For instance, I noticed that I no longer dried myself after my bath, but lay on the bed wrapped in my towel till I dried naturally. A little after midnight on December 11, my personal party and I left in our aircraft for Tunis. I had planned to spend one night there at General Eisenhower's villa, and to fly next day to Alexander's and then Montgomery's headquarters in Italy, where the weather was reported to be absolutely vile and all advances were fitful.

Morning saw us over the Tunis airfields. We were directed by a signal not to land where we had been told, and were shifted to another field some forty miles away. We all got out, and they began to unload the luggage. It would be an hour before motorcars could come, and then a long drive. As I sat on my official boxes near the machines I certainly did feel completely worn out. Now however came a telephone message from General Eisenhower, who was waiting at the first airfield, that we had been wrongly transferred and that landing was quite possible there. So we scrambled back into our plane, and in ten minutes were with him, quite close to his villa. Ike, always the soul of hospitality, had waited two hours with imperturbable good humour. I got into his car, and after we had driven for a little while I said, "I am afraid I shall have to stay with you longer than I had planned. I am completely at the end of my tether, and I cannot go on to the front until I have recovered some strength." All that day I slept, and the next day came fever and symptoms at the base of my lung which were adjudged to portend pneumonia. So here I was at this pregnant moment on the broad of my back amid the ruins of ancient Carthage.

When the X-ray photographs showed that there was a shadow on one of my lungs I found that everything had been diagnosed and foreseen by Lord Moran. Dr. Bedford and other high medical authorities in the Mediterranean and excellent nurses arrived from all quarters as if by magic. The admirable M and B, from which I did not suffer any inconvenience, was used at the earliest moment, and after a week's fever the intruders were repulsed. Although Moran records that he judged that the issue was at one time in doubt, I did not share his view. I did not feel so ill in this attack as I had the previous February. The M and B, which I also called Moran and Bedford, did the work most effectively. There is no doubt that pneumonia is a very different illness from what it was before this marvelous drug was discovered. I did not at any time relinquish my part in the direction of affairs, and there was not the slightest delay in giving the decisions which were required from me.

My immediate task, as British Minister of Defence responsible to the War Cabinet, was to propose a British Supreme Commander for the Mediterranean. This post we confided to General Wilson, it being also settled that General Alexander should command the whole campaign in Italy, as he had done under General Eisenhower. It was also arranged that General Devers, of the U.S. Army, should become General Wilson's Deputy in the Mediterranean, and Air Chief Marshal Tedder General Eisenhower's Deputy in "Overlord," and that Montgomery should actually command the whole cross-Channel invasion force until such time as the Supreme Commander could transfer his headquarters to France and assume the direct operational control. All this was carried out with the utmost smoothness in perfect agreement by the President and by me, with Cabinet approval, and worked in good comradeship and friendship by all concerned.

But the days passed in much discomfort. Fever flickered in and out. I lived on my theme of the war, and it was like being transported out of oneself. The doctors tried to keep the work away from my bedside, but I defied them. They all kept on saying, "Don't work, don't worry," to such an extent that I decided to read a novel. I had long ago read Jane Austen's *Sense and Sensibility*, and now I thought I would have *Pride and Prejudice*. Sarah read it to me beautifully from the foot of the bed. I had always thought it would be better than its rival. What calm lives they had, those people! No worries about the French Revolution, or the crashing struggle of the Napoleonic wars. Only manners controlling natural passion so far as they could, together with cultured explanations of any mischances. All this seemed to go very well with M and B.

One morning Sarah was absent from her chair at the foot of my bed, and I was about to ask for my box of telegrams in the prohibited hours when in she walked with her mother. I had no idea that my wife was flying out from England to join me. She had hurried to the airport to fly in a two-engined Dakota. The weather was bad, but Lord Beaverbrook was vigilant. He got to the airport first, and stopped her flight until a four-engined plane could be procured. (I always think it better to have four engines when flying long distances across the sea.) Now she had arrived after a very rough journey in an unheated plane in midwinter. Jock Colville had escorted her, and was a welcome addition to my hard-pressed personal staff, through whom so much business was being directed. "My love to Clemmie," cabled the President. "I feel relieved that she is with you as your superior officer."

AS I lay prostrate I felt we were at one of the climaxes of the war. The mounting of "Overlord" was the greatest event and duty in the world. But must we sabotage everything we could have in Italy, where the main strength overseas of our country was involved? Were we to leave it a stagnant pool from which we had drawn every fish we wanted? As I saw the problem, the campaign in Italy, in which a million or more of our British, British-controlled, and Allied troops were engaged, was the faithful and indispensable comrade and counterpart of the main cross-Channel operation. Here the American clear-cut, logical, large-scale, mass production style of thought was formidable. In life people have first to be taught "Concentrate on essentials." This is no doubt the first step out of confusion and fatuity; but it is only the first step. The second stage in war is a general harmony of war effort by making everything fit together, and every scrap of fighting strength play its full part all the time. I was sure that a vigorous campaign in Italy during the first half of 1944 would be the greatest help to the supreme operation of crossing the Channel, on which all minds were set and all engagements made. But every item which any Staff officer could claim as "essential" or "vital," to use these hard-worked words, had to be argued out as if it carried with it the success or failure of our main purpose. Twenty or a dozen vehicle landing craft had to be fought for as if the major issue turned upon them.

THE case seemed to be brutally simple. All the ships we had would be used to carry to England everything the United States could produce in arms and men. Surely the enormous forces we could not possibly move by sea from the Italian theatre should play their part. Either they would gain Italy easily and immediately bite upon the German inner front, or they would draw large German forces from the front which we were to attack across the Channel in the last days of May, or the early days of June, as the moon and the tides prescribed.

The deadlock on the eighty-mile front from sea to sea to which our armies in Italy had been brought by the stubborn German resistance had already led General Eisenhower to contemplate an amphibious flanking attack. He had planned to land with one division south of the Tiber and make a dart for Rome, in conjunction with an attack by the main armies. The arrest of these armies and the distance of the landing point from them made everyone feel that more than one division was required. I had of course always been a partisan of the "end run," as the Americans call it, or "cat-claw," which was my term. I had never succeeded in getting this manoeuvre open to sea power included in any of our Desert advances. In Sicily however General Patton had twice used the command of the sea flank as he advanced along the northern coast of the island with great effect. Both at Carthage and at Marrakech I was near enough to the scene of action to convene meetings of all the Chief Commanders.

There was a great deal of professional support. General Eisenhower was already committed in principle, though his new appointment to the command of "Overlord" now gave him a different sense of values and a new horizon. Alexander, Deputy Supreme Commander and commanding the armies in Italy, thought the operation right and necessary; Bedell Smith was ardent and helpful in every direction. This was also true of Admiral John Cunningham, who held all the naval cards, and of Air Marshal Tedder. I had therefore a powerful array of Mediterranean authorities. Moreover, I felt sure the British Chiefs of Staff would like the plan, and that with their agreement I could obtain the approval of the War Cabinet. When you cannot give orders, hard and lengthy toils must be faced.

I began my effort on December 19, when the C.I.G.S. arrived at Carthage to see me on his way home from Montgomery's headquarters in Italy. We had hoped to go there together, but my illness had prevented me. We had a full discussion, and I found that General Brooke had by a separate route of thought arrived at the same conclusion as I had. We agreed on the policy, and also that while I should deal with the commanders on the spot he would do his best to overcome all difficulties at home. He then left by air for London. The Chiefs of Staff had evidently been thinking on the same lines, and, after hearing his account, telegraphed on the 22nd: "We are in full agreement with you that the present stagnation cannot be allowed to continue. . . . The solution, as you say, clearly lies in making use of our amphibious power to strike round on the enemy's flank and open up the way for a rapid advance on Rome. . . . We think the aim should be to provide a lift for at least two divisions. . . ." After explaining that the new plan would involve giving up both the capture of Rhodes and also a minor amphibious operation on the Arakan coast of Burma, they ended: "If you approve the above line of thought we propose to take the matter up with the Combined Chiefs of Staff with a view to action being taken on these lines at once."

This led to a hard scrutiny of our resources. Some landing craft for the cancelled operation against the Andamans were on their way to the Mediterranean across the Indian Ocean. Others were due to return home for "Overlord." All were in extreme demand.

The whole morning of Christmas Day I held a conference at Carthage. Eisenhower, Alexander, Bedell Smith, General Wilson, Tedder, Admiral John Cunningham, and other high officers were present. The only one not there was General Mark Clark, of the Fifth Army. This was an oversight which I regret, as it was to his army that the operation was eventually entrusted and he ought to have had the background in his mind. We were all agreed that nothing less than a two-division lift would suffice. At this time I contemplated an assault by two British divisions from the Eighth Army, in which Montgomery was about to be succeeded by General Leese. I thought the amphibious operation involved potential mortal risks to the landed forces, and I preferred to run them with British troops, because it was to Britain that I was responsible. Moreover, the striking force would then have been homogeneous instead of half and half.

EVERYTHING turned on landing craft, which held for some weeks all our strategy in the tightest ligature. What with the rigid date prescribed for "Overlord" and the movement, repair, and refitting of less than a hundred of these small vessels, all plans were in a strait jacket. We escaped, though mauled, from this predicament. But I must also admit that I was so much occupied in fighting for the principle that I did not succeed in getting, and indeed did not dare to demand, the necessary weight and volume for the "cat-claw." Actually there were enough LSTs for the operation as planned, and in my opinion, if the extravagant demands of the military machine had been reduced, we could, without prejudice to any other pledge or commitment, have flung ashore south of the Tiber a still larger force with full mobility. However, the issue was fought out in terms of routine Army requirements and the exact dates when LSTs could be free for "Overlord," making of course all allowances for their return home in winter

Biscay weather, and with the time margins for their refits stated at their maximum. If I had asked for a three-division lift I should not have got anything. How often in life must one be content with what one can get! Still, it would be better to do it right.

At the close of our discussion I sent the following to the President, and a similar telegram home. I was careful to state the root fact bluntly.

". . . Having kept fifty-six LSTs in the Mediterranean so long, it would seem irrational to remove them for the very week when they can render decisive service. What, also, could be more dangerous than to let the Italian battle stagnate and fester on for another three months? We cannot afford to go forward leaving a vast half-finished job behind us. It therefore seemed to those present that every effort should be made to bring off Anzio on a two-division basis around January 20, and orders have been issued to Alexander to prepare accordingly. If this opportunity is not grasped we must expect the ruin of the Mediterranean campaign of 1944. I earnestly hope therefore that you may agree to the three weeks' delay in return of the fifty-six landing craft, and that all the authorities will be instructed to make sure that the May 'Overlord' is not prejudiced thereby."

Lord Moran thought it possible for me to leave Carthage after Christmas, but insisted that I must have three weeks' convalescence somewhere. And where could be better than the lovely villa at Marrakech, where the President and I had stayed after Casablanca a year before? All plans had been made during the past few days. I was to be the guest of the United States Army at Marrakech. It was also thought that I had been long enough at Carthage to be located. Small vessels had ceaselessly to patrol the bay in front of the villa in case some U-boat turned up for a surprise raid. There might also be a long-range air attack. I had my own protection in a battalion of the Coldstream Guards. I was too ill, or too busy, to be consulted about all this, but I saw in my beloved Marrakech a haven where I could regain my strength. As I was leaving the door a telegram was put in my hand, giving the fateful news of the sinking of the *Scharnhorst*. I dictated a message to Stalin. A very cordial reply came a few days later, ending "I shake your hand firmly."

Outside the villa a magnificent guard of the Coldstream was drawn up. I had not realised how much I had been weakened by my illness. I found it quite a difficulty to walk along the ranks and climb into the motorcar. The flight at 6,000 feet had been planned on the weather forecast that the skies would be clear. However, as we sailed on and the uplands of Tunisia began to rise about us I saw a lot of large fleecy and presently blackish clouds gathering around, and after a couple of hours we were more often in mist than in sunlight. I have always had a great objection to what are called "stuffed clouds"—*i.e.*, clouds with mountains inside them—and flying an intricate route through the various

valleys before us in order to keep under 6,000 feet seemed to me an unfair proposition for the others in the plane. I therefore sent for the pilot and told him to fly at least 2,000 feet above the highest mountain within a hundred miles of his route. Lord Moran agreed. Oxygen was brought by a skilled administrator, specially provided for the journey. We sailed up into the blue. I got along all right, and we made a perfect landing at about four o'clock on the Marrakech airfield. Our second plane, which had adhered strictly to its instructions, had a very severe and dangerous flight through the various gorges and passes, many of which were traversed with only fleeting glimpses of the towering mountains. At this low height the weather was by no means good. The plane arrived safely an hour behind us with one of its doors blown off and nearly everybody very sick. I was sorry indeed they should have been put to so much discomfort and risk on my account. They could have flown it all out safely and comfortably under blue skies at twelve or even eleven thousand feet.

Nothing could exceed the comfort, and even luxury, of my new abode, or the kindness of everyone concerned. But one thing rose above all others in my mind —what answer would the President give to my telegram? When I thought of the dull, dead-weight resistance, taking no account of timing and proportion, that I had encountered about all our Mediterranean projects I awaited the answer with deep anxiety. What I asked for was a hazardous enterprise on the Italian coast, and a possible delay of three weeks from May 1—four if the moon phase was to be observed—in the date of the Channel crossing. I had gained the agreement of the Commanders on the spot. The British Chiefs of Staff had always agreed in principle, and were now satisfied in detail. But what would the Americans say to a four weeks' postponement of "Overlord?" However, when one is thoroughly tired out the blessing of sleep is not usually denied.

It was with joy, not, I confess, unmingled with surprise, that on December 28 I received a telegram from Mr. Roosevelt agreeing to delay the departure of the fifty-six LSTs "on the basis that 'Overlord' remains the paramount operation and will be carried out on the date agreed to at Cairo and Tehran." "I thank God," I replied, "for this fine decision, which engages us once again in wholehearted unity upon a great enterprise. . . ."

Great efforts had indeed been made by the Staffs at home, and especially by the Admiralty, to accomplish the "cat-claw," and I hastened to congratulate them. The President's telegram was a marvel. I was sure that I owed it not only to his good will but to Marshall's balance of mind, to Eisenhower's loyalty to the show he was about to quit, and Bedell Smith's active, knowledgeable, fact-armed diplomacy. On the same day Alexander sent us his plan. After conferring with General Mark Clark and General Brian Robertson, he had decided to use an American and a British

---

30 Dec 43

PRIME MINISTER TO PRESIDENT ROOSEVELT

I have now received from my brother Jack full accounts of the Christmas tree [you sent me] at Chequers. All my grandchildren were there. . . . The sun is shining to-day, but nothing did me the same good as your telegram showing how easily our minds work together on the grimly simple issues of this vast war.

I received on the same day congratulations on my recovery from Franco and Tito. So what?

---

division. Armour, paratroops, and Commandos would be on a fifty-fifty basis, and the whole would be under an American corps commander. The attack would go in about January 20. Ten days beforehand he would launch a big offensive against Cassino to draw off the German reserves. The forward plunge of the main armies would follow. I was well content. So far so good.

Physical weakness oppressed me at Marrakech following my illness at Carthage. All my painting tackle had been sent out, but I could not face it. I could hardly walk at all. Even tottering from the motorcar to a picnic luncheon in lovely weather amid the foothills of the Atlas was limited to eighty or a hundred yards. I passed eighteen hours out of the twenty-four prone. I never remember such extreme fatigue and weakness in body. On the other hand, every temptation, inducement, exhortation, and to some extent compulsion, to relax and lie down presented itself in the most seductive form. The Taylor villa was a perfect haven, lacking nothing that comfort could require or luxury suggest. I was utterly tired out, and here was the most attractive bed of repose, not only offered by gracious hosts, but enjoined by Lord Moran, the President, and the War Cabinet. However, events continued to offer an irresistible distraction.

I determined to be at home before the shock of Anzio occurred. On January 14 therefore we all flew in beautiful weather to Gibraltar, where the *King George V* awaited me. On the 15th she made her way out of Algeciras Bay wide into the Atlantic, and thence to Plymouth. After a restful voyage we were welcomed by the War Cabinet and Chiefs of Staff, who really seemed quite glad to see me back. I had been more than two months away from England, and they had been through a lot of worry on account both of my illness and my activities. It was indeed a homecoming, and I felt deeply grateful to all these trusty friends and fellow workers.

Anzio and Rome

RETROSPECT is now inevitable if the Italian setting is to be understood. After the surrender in September 1943, the organisation of resistance to the Germans fell by default into the hands of an underground Committee of Liberation in Rome, and linked with the mounting activity of Partisan bands which now began activities throughout the peninsula. The members of this committee were politicians driven from power by Mussolini in the early 1920s or representatives of groups hostile to Fascist rule. Over all hung the menace of a recrudescence of the hard core of Fascism in the hour of defeat. The Germans certainly did their best to promote it.

Mussolini had been interned on the island of Ponza, and later at La Maddalena, off the coast of Sardinia. Fearing a German *coup de main*, Badoglio had at the end of August moved his former master to a small mountain resort high in the Abruzzi, in Central Italy. In the haste of the flight from Rome no precise instructions were given to the police agents and Carabinieri guarding the fallen Dictator. On the morning of Sunday, September 12, ninety German parachutists landed by glider near the hotel where Mussolini was confined. He was removed, without casualties, in a light German aircraft, and carried to yet another meeting in Munich with Hitler.

During the succeeding days the two men debated how to extend the life of Italian Fascism in those parts of Italy still occupied by the German troops. On the 15th the Duce announced that he had reassumed the leadership of Fascism and that a new Republican-Fascist Party, purged and uplifted from traitorous elements, would rebuild a faithful Government in the North. For a moment it seemed that the old system, now dressed up in a pseudo-revolutionary garb, might flare again into life. The results disappointed the Germans, but there was to be no turning back. Mussolini's half-hearted "Hundred Days" began. At the end of September he set up his headquarters on the shores of Lake Garda. This pitiful shadow Government is known as the "Republic of Salò." Here the squalid tragedy was played out. The dictator and lawgiver of Italy for more than twenty years dwelt with his mistress in the hands of his German masters, ruled by their will, and cut off from the outside world by carefully chosen German guards and doctors.

The Italian surrender caught their armies in the Balkans completely unawares, and many troops were trapped in desperate positions between local guerrilla forces and the vengeful Germans. There were savage reprisals. The Italian garrison of Corfu, over 7,000 strong, were almost annihilated by their former allies. The Italian troops of the island of Cephalonia held out until September 22. Many of the survivors were shot, and the rest deported. Some of the garrisons of the Aegean islands managed to escape in small parties to Egypt. In Albania, on the Dalmatian coast, and inside Yugoslavia a number of detachments joined the Partisans. More often they were taken off to forced labour and their officers executed. In Montenegro the greater part of two Italian divisions were formed by Tito into the "Garibaldi Divisions," which suffered heavy losses by the end of the war. In the Balkans and Aegean the Italian armies lost nearly 40,000 men after the announcement of the armistice on September 8, not including those who died in deportation camps.

Italy herself was plunged into the horrors of civil war. Officers and men of the Italian Army stationed in the German-occupied North, and Patriots from the towns and countryside began to form Partisan units and to operate against the Germans and against their compatriots who still adhered to the Duce. Contacts were made with the Allied armies south of Rome and with the Badoglio Government. In these months the network of Italian resistance to the German occupation was created in a cruel atmosphere of civil strife, assassinations, and executions. The insurgent movement in Central and Northern Italy here as elsewhere in occupied Europe convulsed all classes of the people.

Not the least of their achievements was the succour and support given to our prisoners of war trapped by the armistice in camps in Northern Italy. Out of about 80,000 of these men, conspicuously clothed in battle dress, and in the main with little knowledge of the language or geography of the country, at least 10,000, mostly helped by the local population with civilian clothes, were guided to safety, thanks to the risks taken by members of the Italian Resistance and the simple people of the countryside.

The bitterness and confusion were heightened in the New Year. Mussolini's phantom republic now came under mounting pressure from the Germans. The governing circles around Badoglio in the south were assailed by intrigues in Italy and despised by public opinion in Britain and the United States. Mussolini was the first to react. When he arrived in Munich after his rescue by the Germans he found there his daughter Edda and her husband, Count Ciano. These two had fled from Rome at the time of the surrender, and although Ciano had voted against his father-in-law at the fateful meeting of the Grand Council, he hoped, thanks to the influence of his wife, for a reconciliation. During these days in Munich this in fact happened. This aroused the indignation of Hitler, who had already placed the Ciano family under house arrest on their arrival. The reluctance of the Duce to punish the traitors to Fascism, and particularly Count Ciano, was perhaps the main reason why Hitler formed such a low opinion of his colleague at this critical time.

It was not until the declining strength of the Republic of Salò had fallen far, and the impatience of its German masters had sharpened, that Mussolini agreed to let loose a wave of calculated vengeance. All those leaders of the old Fascist regime who had voted against him in July and who could be caught in German-occupied Italy were brought to trial at the end of 1943, in the medieval fortress at Verona. Among them was Ciano. Without exception they received the death sentence. In spite of the entreaties and threats of Edda, the Duce could not relent. In January 1944 the group, which included not only Ciano but also the seventy-eight-year-old Marshal de Bono, a colleague in the march on Rome, were taken out to die a traitor's death—to be shot in the back tied to a chair. They all died bravely.

The end of Ciano was in keeping with all the elements of Renaissance tragedy. Mussolini's submission to Hitler's vengeful demands brought him only shame, and the miserable neo-Fascist republic dragged on by Lake Garda—a relic of the Broken Axis.

WE had spent the first weeks of January in intensive preparations for Operation "Shingle," as Anzio was called in our codes, and in preliminary operations by the Fifth Army to draw the enemy's attention and reserves away from the beachhead. Fighting was bitter, for the Germans clearly meant to prevent us from breaking into the Gustav Line, which, with Cassino as its central feature, was the rearmost position of their deep defensive zone. In these rocky mountains a great fortified system had been created, with lavish use of concrete and steel. From their observation posts on the heights the enemy could direct their guns on all movements in the valleys below. Our troops made great efforts which, though gaining little ground, had the desired effect on the enemy. It distracted their attention from the approaching threat to their vulnerable seaward flank and caused them to bring up three good divisions from reserve to restore the situation.

By the afternoon of the 21st the convoys for Anzio were well out to sea, covered by our aircraft. The weather was well suited to a concealed approach. Our heavy attacks on enemy airfields, and especially at Perugia, the German air reconnaissance base, kept many of their aircraft grounded, and it was with tense, but I trust suppressed, excitement that I awaited the outcome of this considerable stroke. Presently I learned that the VI Corps, consisting of the 3rd United States and 1st British Divisions under the American General Lucas, had landed on the Anzio beaches at 2 a.m. on the 22nd. There was very little opposition and practically no casualties. By midnight 36,000 men and over 3,000 vehicles were ashore. "We appear," signalled Alexander, who was on the spot, "to have got almost complete surprise. I have stressed the importance of strong-hitting mobile patrols being boldly pushed out to gain contact with the enemy, but so far have not received reports of their activities." I was in full agreement with this, and replied: "Thank you for all your messages. Am very glad you are pegging out claims rather than digging in beachheads."

BUT now came disaster, and the ruin in its prime purpose of the enterprise. General Lucas confined himself to occupying his beachhead and having many vehicles and equipment brought ashore. General Penney, commanding the British 1st Division, was anxious to push inland. His reserve brigade was however held back with the corps. Minor probing attacks toward Cisterna and Campoleone occupied most of the 22nd and 23rd. No general attempt to advance was made by the commander of the expedition. By the evening of the 23rd the whole of the two divisions and their attached troops, including two British Commandos, United States Rangers, and parachutists, had been landed, with masses of impedimenta. The defences of the beachhead were growing and multiplying, but the opportunity for which great exertions had been made was gone.

Kesselring reacted quickly to his critical situation. The bulk of his reserves were already committed against us on the Cassino front, but he pulled in whatever units were available, and in forty-eight hours the equivalent of about two divisions was assembled to resist our further advance. On the 27th serious news arrived. The Guards Brigade had gone forward, but they were still about a mile and a half short of Campoleone, and the Americans were still south of Cisterna. Alexander said that neither he nor General Clark was satisfied with the speed of the advance, and that Clark was going to the beachhead at once. I replied: "I am glad to learn that Clark is going to visit the beachhead. It would be unpleasant if your troops were sealed off there and the main army could not advance up from the south." This however was exactly what was going to happen.

Meanwhile our attacks on the Cassino positions continued. The threat to his flank did not weaken Kesselring's determination to withstand our assaults. And the German resolve was made crystal-clear by an order from Hitler captured on the 24th: "The Gustav Line must be held at all costs for the sake of the political consequences which would follow a completely successful defence. The Fuehrer expects the bitterest struggle for every yard."

He was certainly obeyed. At first we made good progress. We crossed the river Rapido above Cassino town and attacked southwards against Monastery Hill; but the Germans had reinforced and held on fanatically, and by early February our strength was expended. A New Zealand Corps of three divisions was brought over from the Adriatic, and on February 15 our second major attack began with the bombing of the monastery itself. The height on which the monastery stood surveyed the junction of the rivers Rapido and Liri and was the pivot of the whole German defence. It had already proved itself a formidable, strongly defended obstacle. Its steep sides, swept by fire, were crowned by the famous building, which several times in previous wars had been pillaged, destroyed, and rebuilt. There is controversy about whether it should have been destroyed once again. The monastery did not contain German troops, but the enemy fortifications were hardly separated from the building itself. It dominated the whole battlefield, and naturally General Freyberg, the Corps Commander concerned, wished to have it heavily bombarded from the air before launching the infantry attack. The Army Commander, General Mark Clark, unwillingly sought and obtained permission from General Alexander, who accepted the responsibility. On February 15 therefore, after the monks had been given full warning, over 450 tons of bombs were dropped and heavy damage was done. The great outer walls and gateway still stood. The result was not good. The Germans had now every excuse for making whatever use they could of the rubble of the ruins, and this gave them even better opportunities for defence than when the building was intact.

It fell to the 4th Indian Division, which had recently relieved the Americans on the ridges north of the monastery, to make the attack. On two successive nights they tried in vain to seize a knoll that lay between their position and Monastery Hill. On the night of February 18 a third attempt was made. The fighting was desperate, and all our men who reached the knoll were killed. Later, that night a brigade bypassed the knoll and moved directly at the monastery, only to encounter a concealed ravine heavily mined and covered by enemy machine guns at shortest range. Here they lost heavily and were stopped. While this fierce conflict was raging on the heights above them the New Zealand Division succeeded in crossing

the river Rapido; but they were counterattacked by tanks before their bridgehead was secure and forced back again. The direct attack on Cassino had failed.

We must now return to the beachhead. By January 30 the 1st U.S. Armoured Division had landed at Anzio and the 45th U.S. Division was on its way. All this had to be done over the difficult beaches or through the tiny fishing port. "The situation as it now stands," signalled Admiral John Cunningham, "bears little relation to the lightning thrust by two or three divisions envisaged at Marrakech, but you may rest assured that no effort will be spared by the Navies to provide the sinews of victory." This promise, as will be seen, was amply redeemed.

On the same day the VI Corps made its first attack in strength. Some ground was gained, but on February 3 the enemy launched a counterstroke which drove in the salient of the British 1st Division. And this was clearly only a prelude to harder things to come. In the words of General Wilson's report, "the perimeter was sealed off and our forces therein . . . are not capable of advancing." Though General Lucas had achieved surprise he had failed to take advantage of it. All this was a great disappointment at home and in the United States. I did not of course know what orders had been given to General Lucas, but it is a root principle to push out and join issue with the enemy, and it would seem that his judgment was against it from the beginning. As I said at the time, I had hoped that we were hurling a wild cat on to the shore, but all we had got was a stranded whale. We were apparently still stronger than the Germans in fighting power. The ease with which they moved their pieces about on the board and the rapidity with which they adjusted the perilous gaps they had to make on their southern front was most impressive. It all seemed to give us very adverse data for "Overlord."

The expected major effort to drive us back into the sea opened on the 16th when the enemy employed over four divisions, supported by 450 guns, in a direct thrust southwards from Campoleone. Hitler's special order of the day was read out to the troops before the attack. He demanded that our beachhead "abscess" be eliminated in three days. The attack fell at an awkward moment, as the 45th U.S. and 56th British Divisions, transferred from the Cassino front, were just relieving our gallant 1st Division, who soon found themselves in full action again. A deep, dangerous wedge was driven into our line, which was forced back here to the original beachhead. All hung in the balance. No further retreat was possible. Even a short advance would have given the enemy the power to use not merely their

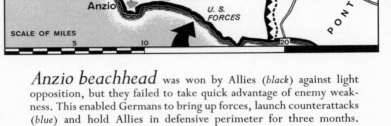

Anzio beachhead was won by Allies (*black*) against light opposition, but they failed to take quick advantage of enemy weakness. This enabled Germans to bring up forces, launch counterattacks (*blue*) and hold Allies in defensive perimeter for three months.

long-range guns in harassing fire upon the landing stages and shipping, but to put down a proper field artillery barrage upon all intakes or departures. I had no illusions about the issue. It was life or death.

But fortune, hitherto baffling, rewarded the desperate valour of the British and American armies. Before Hitler's stipulated three days the German attack was stopped. Then their own salient was counterattacked in flank and cut out under fire from all our artillery and bombardment by every aircraft we could fly. The fighting was intense, losses on both sides were heavy, but the deadly battle was won.

ONE more attempt was made by Hitler—for his was the will power at work—at the end of February. The 3rd U.S. Division, on the eastern flank, was attacked by three German divisions. These were weakened and shaken by their previous failure. The Americans held stubbornly, and the attack was broken in a day, when the Germans had suffered more than 2,500 casualties. On March 1 Kesselring accepted his failure. He had frustrated the Anzio expedition. He could not destroy it.

I cabled to the President: "I must send you my warmest congratulations on the grand fighting of your troops, particularly the United States 3rd Division, in the Anzio beachhead. I am always deeply moved to think of our men fighting side by side in so many fierce battles and of the inspiring additions to our history which these famous episodes will make. Of course I have been very anxious about the beachhead, where we have so little ground to give. The stakes are very high on both sides now, and the suspense is long-drawn. I feel sure we shall win both here and at Cassino."

† † †

At the beginning of March the weather brought about a deadlock. Napoleon's fifth element—mud—bogged down both sides. We could not break the main front at Cassino, and the Germans had equally failed to drive us into the sea at Anzio. In numbers there was little to choose between the two combatants. By now we had twenty divisions in Italy, but both Americans and French had had very heavy losses. The enemy had eighteen or nineteen divisions south of Rome, and five more in Northern Italy, but they too were tired and worn.

There could be no hope now of a break-out from the Anzio beachhead and also no prospect of an early link-up between our two separated forces until the Cassino front was broken. The prime need therefore was to make the beachhead really firm, to relieve and reinforce the troops, and to pack in stores to withstand a virtual siege and nourish a subsequent sortie. Time was short, since many of the landing craft must soon leave for "Overlord." Their move had so far been rightly postponed, but no further delay was possible. The Navies put all their strength into the effort, with admirable results. The previous average daily tonnage landed had been 3,000; in the first ten days of March this was more than doubled.

But although Anzio was now no longer an anxiety the campaign in Italy as a whole had dragged. We had hoped that by this time the Germans would have been driven north of Rome and that a substantial part of our armies would have been set free for a strong landing on the French Riviera coast to help "Overlord," the main cross-Channel invasion. This operation, "Anvil," had been agreed in principle at Tehran. It was soon to become a cause of contention between ourselves and our American Allies. The campaign in Italy had obviously to be carried forward a long way before this issue arose, and the immediate need was to break the deadlock on the Cassino front. Preparations for the third Battle of Cassino were begun soon after the February failure, but the bad weather then delayed it until March 15.

This time Cassino town was the primary objective. After a heavy bombardment, in which nearly 1,000 tons of bombs and 1,200 tons of shells were expended, our infantry advanced. "It seemed to me inconceivable," said Alexander, "that any troops should be left alive after eight hours of such terrific hammering." But they were.

The 1st German Parachute Division, probably the toughest fighters in all their Army, fought it out amid the heaps of rubble with the New Zealanders and Indians. By nightfall the greater part of the town was in our hands, while the 4th Indian Division, coming down from the north, made equally good progress and next day were two-thirds of the way up Monastery Hill. Then the battle swung against us. Our tanks could not cross the large craters made by the bombardment and follow up the infantry assault. Nearly two days passed before they could help. The enemy filtered in reinforcements. The weather broke in storm and rain. The struggle in the ruins of Cassino town continued until the 23rd, with hard fighting in attacks and counterattacks. The New Zealanders and the Indians could do no more. We had however established a firm bridgehead over the river Rapido, which, with a deep bulge made across the lower Garigliano in January, was of great value when the final, successful battle came. Here and at the Anzio bridgehead we had pinned down in Central Italy nearly twenty good German divisions. Many of them might have gone to France.

SUCH is the story of the struggle of Anzio; a story of high opportunity and shattered hopes, of skilful inception on our part and swift recovery by the enemy, of valour shared by both. We now know that early in January the German High Command had intended to transfer five of their best divisions from Italy to Northwest Europe. Kesselring protested that in such an event he could no longer carry out his orders to fight south of Rome and he would have to withdraw. Just as the argument was at its height the Anzio landing took place. The High Command dropped the idea, and instead of the Italian front contributing forces to Northwest Europe the reverse took place. We knew nothing of all these changes of plan at the time, but it proves that the aggressive action of our armies in Italy, and specifically the Anzio stroke, made its full contribution towards the success of "Overlord."

Deadlock at Anzio and Cassino now imposed a halt in the Allied advance in Italy which lasted for nearly two months. Our troops had to be rested and regrouped. Most of the Eighth Army had to be brought over from the Adriatic side and the two armies concentrated for the next assault. In the meantime General Wilson used all his air power to impede and injure the enemy, who, like us, were using the pause for reorganising and replenishing themselves for further battle.

The Allied Air joined in attacking enemy land communications in the hope that these could be kept cut and their troops forced to withdraw for lack of supplies. This operation, optimistically called "Strangle," aimed at blocking the three main railway lines from Northern Italy, the principal targets being bridges, viaducts, and other bottlenecks. They tried to starve the Germans out. The effort lasted more than six weeks, and did great damage. Railway movement was consistently stopped far north of Rome, but it failed to attain all we hoped. By working their coastal shipping to the utmost, transferring loads to motor transport, and making full use of the hours of darkness the enemy contrived to maintain themselves. But they could not build enough reserve stocks for protracted and heavy fighting, and in the severe land battles at the end of May they were much weakened. The junction of our separated armies and the capture of Rome took place more rapidly than we had forecast. The German Air Force suffered severely and in early May it could muster only a bare 700 planes against our thousand combat aircraft.

By then General Clark, of the Fifth Army, had over seven divisions, four of them French, on the front from the sea to the river Liri; thence the Eighth Army, now under General Leese, continued the line through Cassino into the mountains with the equivalent of nearly twelve. In all the Allies mustered over twenty-eight divisions, of which the equivalent of only three remained in the Adriatic sector.

Opposed to them were twenty-three German divisions, but our deception arrangements had puzzled Kesselring so well that they were widely spread. Between Cassino and the sea, where our main blows were to fall, there were only four, and reserves were scattered and at a distance. Our attack came unexpectedly. The Germans were carrying out reliefs opposite the British front, and one of their Army Commanders had planned to go on leave.

THE great offensive began at 11 p.m. on May 11, 1944, when the artillery of both our armies, 2,000 guns, opened a violent fire, reinforced at dawn by the full weight of the Tactical Air Force. After much heavy fighting the enemy began to weaken. On the morning of May 18 Cassino town was finally cleared by the 4th British Division, and the Poles triumphantly hoisted their red and white standard over the ruins of the monastery. Kesselring had been sending down reinforcements as fast as he could muster them, but they were arriving piecemeal, only to be thrown into the battle to check the flood of the Allied advance. By the 25th the Germans were in full retreat and hotly pursued on the whole of the Eighth Army front.

Six divisions under the American General Truscott, who had succeeded General Lucas, had been packed into the Anzio beachhead and burst forth with the simultaneous onslaught of the Eighth Army. After two days of stiff fighting they captured Cisterna and gained contact with the U.S. II Corps. At long last our forces were reunited, and we began to reap the harvest from our winter sowing. General Truscott quickly took advantage of the breach he had made at Cisterna. Under General Clark's orders,

he dispatched three divisions, one of them armoured, to Velletri and the Alban Hills, but only one, the 3rd U.S. Division, towards Valmontone, where they would cut the most important escape route of the enemy farther south. This was not in accord with Alexander's instructions, which put Valmontone as the primary objective.

". . . The glory of this battle, already great," I cabled to Alexander, "will be measured, not by the capture of Rome or the juncture with the bridgehead, but by the number of German divisions cut off. I am sure you will have revolved all this in your mind, and perhaps you have already acted in this way. Nevertheless I feel I ought to tell you that it is the cop that counts."

BUT the Hermann Goering Division and elements of others, delayed though they were by our damaging attacks from the air, got to Valmontone first. The single American division sent by General Mark Clark was stopped short of it and the escape road remained open. That was very unfortunate.

The enemy in the south were in full retreat, and the Allied Air did its utmost to impede movement and break up concentrations. Obstinate rear guards frequently checked our pursuing forces, and their retirement did not degenerate into a rout. The II U.S. Corps moved on Priverno, the French to Ceccano, while the Canadian Corps and British XIII Corps advanced up the valley to Frosinone and the X Corps up the road to Avezzano. The three American divisions dispatched from the Anzio breach towards Velletri and the Alban Hills, later reinforced by a fourth, the 36th, met very stiff resistance, and for three days could make no ground. They got ready to renew the attack on Valmontone, which Kesselring had been reinforcing with any troops he could find that were fit to fight. However, a brilliant stroke by the 36th U.S. Division must have disconcerted him. They had been fighting hard at the southwest corner of the Alban Hills. On the night of May 30 they found that the Germans had left a commanding height unguarded. Their infantry moved forward in close columns and occupied their key points. Within twenty-four hours the whole 36th Division was firmly established and the last German defence line south of Rome penetrated.

The success of the 36th U.S. Division did not bear immediate fruit. The enemy hung on desperately both in the Alban Hills and at Valmontone, although the retreat of most of their army had now been deflected northwards towards Avezzano and Arsoli, where they were hunted by the X and XIII British Corps and the aircraft of the Tactical Air Force. Unhappily, the mountainous country stopped us using our great strength in armour, which otherwise could have been employed to much advantage.

On June 2 the II U.S. Corps captured Valmontone and drove westwards. That night German resistance broke, and next day the VI U.S. Corps in the Alban Hills, with the British 1st and 5th Divisions on its left, pressed on towards Rome. The II American Corps led them by a short head. They found the bridges mostly intact, and at 7:15 p.m. on June 4 the head of their 88th Division entered the Piazza Venezia, in the heart of the capital. From many quarters came messages of warm congratulation. I even got a pat from the Bear.

Bound for Anzio, a platoon of Americans meets on shipboard to study reconnaissance photos of the Italian beach it is preparing to storm

MUD AND BLOOD

The Push up Italy over Hill and Plain

As the boats were quietly moving in to one of the Salerno beaches before dawn on September 9, 1943, the first noise the troops heard from shore was a German loudspeaker which blared, "Come on in and give up. We have you covered." They didn't give up, but for months they were to live and die in an uneasy world where the enemy did, as a matter of fact, keep them covered most of the time.

Having rooted the stubborn foe out of a valley, the Allied infantrymen would climb the slippery slope beyond. And once they got to the top of the slope, they found the Germans still looking down their throats—for the mountains got higher as they went north from Naples.

Four and a half months after Salerno, the Allies tried to change the style of the campaign by a landing behind the German lines. But when they came ashore at Anzio things got no better. The beachhead was comfortably flat but miserably small and every square inch of it could be fired on by enemy artillery in the surrounding hills.

LIFE Photographer Robert Capa was with the infantrymen through most of the crises of the Italian campaign as well as the daily undramatic round of skirmishes and lonely deaths, bored waiting and aimless sloshing through the mud. The pictures here and on pages 392-393 are a faithful record of life on this waterlogged and often forgotten front where men could find slim satisfaction in knowing they had drawn almost half a million German soldiers from the crucial battles yet to come on the beaches of Normandy.

On guard by their antiaircraft gun, American artillerymen— their helmets still marked for easy identification in the night landings —stand in deep grass in a position defending the beachhead at Anzio.

On the attack, four infantrymen (*below*) rise from foxholes in a flowery field near Anzio to advance past a farmhouse from which the Germans have fled, and on toward the smoking wreck of an enemy tank.

In a gully a blinded soldier gets a guiding hand from a buddy. Casualties in the six British and American divisions which were packed into the narrow beachhead for almost four months totalled over 22,000.

The Waiting and the Fighting

A quick bite is snatched from captured German rations by American soldiers on the first day of the Anzio operation when the almost unopposed landings gave a rare chance to sit unhelmeted in the sun.

The long wait for something to happen—while the generals make up their minds where and how the battle is to be fought—finds these troops slouched in a dugout a few miles inland from the beachhead.

Deafening mortar (*opposite*) causes its crew to flinch from blast. This was overlooking the Liri River valley, where the Allied armies coming up the Italian boot from Salerno were held back for four months.

Freezing march over miles of mountain roads takes a Canadian-U.S. battalion off to another in the succession of heights whose skillful defense by the Germans led to the long stalemate at Cassino (*next page*).

393

Mark of the Bombs
on Monte Cassino

The flames and wreckage of Cassino in these pictures summarize a winter of blundering frustration. Here, from January through March, the Allies made three futile tries to ram their way through the German lines to Rome.

Drenched by freezing rains, under constant fire by a well dug-in enemy, Allied troops tended to ascribe their repulse in early February to German use of the massive monastery of Monte Cassino, brooding high above the battlefield. Willing eyes manufactured "irrefutable evidence" that snipers and artillery observers were in the buildings, whereupon 254 bombers wrecked the monastery.

With Germans now strongly posted in the rubble, the attackers were no better off. So one month later the air forces were called in again to break the deadlock by annihilating the town of Cassino with a 475-plane raid. About half the bombers hit the target (others blew up French Corps headquarters 12 miles away) and wrecked every building in town. The Germans, however, were not in the buildings but in tunnels underneath. Repulsed again, the ground troops had to dig deeper into the mud and rubble and go on looking up at the heights of Monte Cassino until May 17, when the Germans were finally taken from the rear.

Flaming monastery (*left*) pours smoke over the mountain battlefield. The monks and several hundred refugees who had crowded into its walls were warned by leaflets but many could not get out in time.

Silent ruins of Cassino are what the Allies found when the Germans withdrew in May. In the foreground is one of the rain-filled bomb craters which had to be bridged before tanks could enter the town.

A Skirmish
on a Mountain Road

In the middle of May, while the Allies were gnawing at the last German defense line before Rome, a column of French troops was chasing the enemy past a village west of Cassino. There it had to swing around a clump of wrecked German vehicles. German gunners on the next hill were expecting it and had their mortars zeroed in on the spot.

A whine overhead, and the shells came down. A tank disintegrated with a flash and a roar as its ammunition exploded. There were more hits, the wounded screamed and the unhurt scrambled frantically back to the shelter of the stone houses in the village. A chaplain ran up through the shellbursts and helped bleeding men out of their burning jeeps. Medical corpsmen came up to join him while infantry worked its way painfully down the rocky slopes and rooted out the Germans who had caused the damage.

This brief skirmish—witnessed and recorded here by LIFE Photographer George Silk—was part of the daily action by which the French army, resuscitated in Africa and armed by the U.S., redeemed its reputation. Eager to wipe out the shame of 1940, the French gave the decisive punch which broke the stalemate in Italy and opened the way for the Allied liberation of Rome (*pages 398-399*).

Taking cover behind a disabled truck (*left*), the column of French soldiers pulls over to the side of the road when German fire starts sweeping its way along the dusty mountain road to the village of Esperia.

Hit at the roadside by a hundred shells in a few minutes, tanks and jeeps of the ambushed French column lie abandoned by all except soldiers too badly burned to scramble for safety in the village.

Evacuating casualties, French soldiers and medics put a wounded man in temporary shelter under a wrecked jeep (*top*) and then carry him on a stretcher (*bottom*) down to the first aid station.

All Roads Lead at Last to Rome

Defeated German, haggard after days of fighting, holds a white flag as he gives up, and is liberated of a package of cigarettes by soldiers of the U.S. 3rd Division, on their way from Anzio to Rome.

Victorious American (opposite), a young soldier of Italian descent and the latest in the line of conquerors who have been dwarfed by the monuments of Rome, takes it easy on the Campidoglio steps.

A crippled B-17, one of a vast American formation of bombers returning to England from a raid on Germany, drops flares to signal it has wounded
men on board, for whom an ambulance already waits in readiness by the runway.

17

THE WAR
IN THE AIR

The Unseen Struggle

D URING the human struggle in the year 1940 between the British and German Air Forces, between pilot and pilot, between antiaircraft batteries and aircraft, between ruthless bombing and the fortitude of the British people, another conflict was going on step by step, month by month. This was a secret war, whose battles were lost or won unknown to the public; and only with difficulty is it comprehended, even now, by those outside the small high scientific circles concerned. No such warfare had ever been waged by mortal men. The terms in which it could be recorded or talked about were unintelligible to ordinary folk. Yet if we had not mastered its profound meaning and used its mysteries even while we saw them only in the glimpse, all the efforts, all the prowess of the fighting airmen, all the bravery and sacrifices of the people, would have been in vain. Unless British science had proved superior to German, and unless its strange, sinister resources had been effectively brought to bear on the struggle for survival, we might well have been defeated, and, being defeated, destroyed.

A wit wrote ten years ago: "The leaders of thought have reached the horizons of human reason, but all the wires are down, and they can only communicate with us by unintelligible signals." Yet upon the discerning of these signals, and upon the taking of right and timely action on the impressions received, depended our national fate and much else. I knew nothing about science, but I knew something of scientists, and had had much practice as a Minister in handling things I did not understand. I had, at any rate, an acute military perception of what would help and what would hurt, of what would cure and of what would kill. My four years' work upon the Air Defence Research Committee before 1939 had made me familiar with the outlines of radar problems. I therefore immersed myself so far as my faculties allowed in this Wizard War, and strove to make sure that all that counted came without obstruction or neglect at least to the threshold of action.

There were no doubt greater scientists than Frederick Lindemann, though his credentials and genius command respect. But he had two qualifications of vital consequence to me. First he was my trusted friend and confidant of twenty years. Together we had watched the advance and onset of world disaster. Together we had done our best to sound the alarm. And now we were in it, and I had the power to guide and arm our effort. How could I have the knowledge?

Here came the second of his qualities. Lindemann could decipher the signals from the experts on the far horizons and explain to me in lucid, homely terms what the issues were. There are only twenty-four hours in the day, of which at least seven must be spent in sleep and three in eating and relaxation. Anyone in my position would have been ruined if he had attempted to dive into depths which not even a lifetime of study could plumb. What I had now to grasp were the practical results, and just as Lindemann gave me his view for all it was worth in this field, so I made sure by turning on my power-relay that some at least of these terrible and incomprehensible truths emerged in executive decisions.

PROGRESS in every branch of radar was constant and unceasing during 1939, but even so the Battle of Britain, from July to September 1940, was, as I have described, fought mainly by eye and ear. I comforted myself at first in these months with the hope that the fogs and mist and cloud which accompany the British winter and shroud the Island with a mantle would at least give a great measure of protection against accurate bombing by day and still more in darkness.

For some time the German bombers had navigated largely by radio beacons. Scores of these were planted like light-houses in various parts of the Continent, each with its own call-sign, and the Germans, using ordinary directional wireless, could fix their position by the angles from which any two of these transmissions came. To counter this we soon installed a number of stations which we called "Meacons." These picked up the German signals, amplified them, and sent them out again from somewhere in England. The result was that the Germans, trying to home on their beams, were often led astray, and a number of hostile aircraft were lost in this manner. Certainly one German bomber landed voluntarily in Devonshire, thinking it was France.

However, in June 1940 I received a painful shock. Professor Lindemann reported to me that he believed the Germans were preparing a device by means of which they would be able to bomb by day or night whatever the weather. It now appeared that the Germans had developed a radio beam which, like an invisible searchlight, would guide the bombers with considerable precision to their target. The beacon beckoned to the pilot, the beam pointed to the target. They might not hit a particular factory, but they could certainly hit a city or town. No longer therefore had we only to fear the moonlight nights, in which our fighters could see at any rate as well as the enemy, but we must even expect the heaviest attacks to be delivered in cloud and fog.

Lindemann told me also that there was a way of bending the beam if we acted at once, but that I must see some of the scientists, particularly the Deputy Director of Intelligence Research at the Air Ministry, Dr. R. W. Jones, a former pupil of his at Oxford. Accordingly, with anxious mind, I convened on June 21 a special meeting in the Cabinet Room, at which about fifteen persons were present, including Sir Henry Tizard and various Air Force commanders. A few minutes late, a youngish man—who, as I afterwards learned, had thought his sudden summons to the Cabinet Room must be a practical joke—hurried in and took his seat at the bottom of the table. According to plan, I invited him to open the discussion.

For some months, he told us, hints had been coming from all sorts of sources on the Continent that the Germans had some novel mode of night bombing on which they placed great hopes. In some way it seemed to be linked with the code word "Knickebein," which our Intelligence had several times mentioned without being able to explain. At first it had been thought that the enemy had got agents to plant beacons in our cities on which their bombers could home; but this idea had proved untenable. Some weeks before two or three curious squat towers had been photographed in odd positions near the hostile coast. They did not seem the right shape for any known form of radio or radar. Nor were they in places which could be explained on any such hypothesis. Recently a German bomber had been shot down with apparatus which seemed more elaborate than was required for night landing by the ordinary Lorenz beam, which appeared to be the only known use for which it might be intended. For this and various other reasons, which he wove together into a cumulative argument, it looked as if the Germans might be planning to navigate and bomb on some sort of system of beams. A few days before, under cross-examination on these lines, a German pilot had broken down and admitted that he had heard that something of the sort was in the wind. Such was the gist of Dr. Jones's tale.

For twenty minutes or more he spoke in quiet tones, unrolling his chain of circumstantial evidence, the like of which for its convincing fascination was never surpassed by tales of Sherlock Holmes or Monsieur Lecoq. As I listened the *Ingoldsby Legends* jingled in my mind:

> But now one Mr. Jones
> Comes forth and depones
> That, fifteen years since, he had heard certain groans
> On his way to Stone Henge (to examine the stones
> Described in a work of the late Sir John Soane's),
> That he'd followed the moans,
> And led by their tones,
> Found a Raven a-picking a Drummer-boy's bones!

When Dr. Jones had finished there was a general air of incredulity. One high authority asked why the Germans should use a beam, assuming that such a thing was possible, when they had at their disposal all the ordinary facilities of navigation. Above 20,000 feet the stars were nearly always visible. All our own pilots were laboriously trained in navigation, and it was thought they found their way about very well. Others round the table appeared concerned.

I WILL now explain in the kind of terms which I personally can understand how the German beam worked and how we twisted it. Like the searchlight beam, the radio beam cannot be made very sharp; it tends to spread; but if what is called the "split beam" method is used considerable accuracy can be obtained. Let us imagine two searchlight beams parallel to one another, both flickering in such a way that the left-hand beam comes on exactly when the right-hand beam goes out, and vice versa. If an attacking aircraft was exactly in the centre between the two beams, the pilot's course would be continuously illuminated, but if it got, say, a little bit to the right, nearer the centre of the right-hand beam, this would become the stronger and the pilot would observe the flickering light, which was no guide. By keeping in the position where he avoided the flickerings he would be flying exactly down the middle, where the light from both beams is equal. And this middle path would guide him to the target. Two split beams from two stations could be arranged to cross over any town in the Midlands or Southern England. The German airman had only to fly along one beam until he detected the second, and then to drop his bombs. Q.E.D.!

This was the principle of the split beam and the celebrated Knickebein apparatus, upon which Goering founded his hopes, and the Luftwaffe were taught to believe that the bombing of English cities could be maintained in spite of cloud, fog, and darkness, and with all the immunity, alike from guns and intercepting fighters, which these gave to the attacker. With their logical minds and deliberate large-scale planning, the German High Air Command staked their fortunes in this sphere on a device which, like the magnetic mine, they thought would do us in. Therefore they did not trouble to train the ordinary bomber pilots, as ours had been trained, in the difficult art of navigation. A far simpler and surer method, lending itself to drill and large numbers, producing results wholesale by irresistible science, attracted alike their minds and their nature. The German pilots followed the beam as the German people followed the Fuehrer. They had nothing else to follow.

But, duly forewarned, and acting on the instant, the simple British had the answer. By erecting the proper stations in good time in our own country we could jam the beam. This would of course have been almost immediately realised by the enemy. There was another and superior alternative. We could put a repeating device in such a position that it strengthened the signal from one half of the split beam and not from the other. Thus the hostile pilot, trying to fly so that the signals from both halves of the split beam were equal, would be deflected from the true course. The cataract of bombs which would have shattered, or at least tormented, a city would fall fifteen or twenty miles away in an open field. Being master, and not having to argue too much, once I was convinced about the principles of this queer and deadly game I gave all the necessary orders that very day in June for the existence of the beam to be assumed, and for all countermeasures to receive absolute priority. The slightest reluctance or deviation in carrying out this policy was to be reported to me. With so much going on I did not trouble the Cabinet, or even the Chiefs of Staff. If I had encountered any serious obstruction I should of course have appealed and told a long story to these friendly tribunals. This however was not necessary, as in this limited and at that time almost occult circle obedience was forthcoming with alacrity, and on the fringes all obstructions could be swept away.

About August 23 the first new Knickebein stations, near Dieppe and Cherbourg, were trained on Birmingham, and a large-scale night offensive began. We had of course our "teething troubles" to get through; but within a few days the Knickebein beams were deflected or jammed, and for the next two months, the critical months of September and October, the German bombers wandered around England bombing by guesswork, or else being actually led astray.

THE German air crews soon suspected that their beams were being mauled. There is a story that during these two months nobody had the courage to tell Goering that his beams were twisted or jammed. In his ignorance he pledged himself that this was impossible. Special lectures and warnings were delivered to the German Air Force, assuring them that the beam was infallible, and that anyone who cast doubt on it would be at once thrown out. We suffered, as has been described, heavily under the Blitz, and almost anyone could hit London anyhow. Of course there would in any case have been much inaccuracy, but the whole German system of bombing was so much disturbed by our countermeasures, added to the normal percentage of error, that not more than one-fifth of their bombs fell within the target areas. We must regard this as the equivalent of a considerable victory, because even the fifth part of the German bombing, which we got, was quite enough for our comfort and occupation.

The Battle of the Beams

THE Germans, after internal conflicts, at last revised their methods. It happened, fortunately for them, that one of their formations, Kampf Gruppe 100, was using a special beam of its own. It called its equipment the "X apparatus," a name of mystery which, when we came across it, threw up an intriguing challenge to our Intelligence. By the middle of September we had found out enough about it to design countermeasures, but this particular jamming equipment could not be produced for a further two months. In consequence Kampf Gruppe 100 could still bomb with accuracy. The enemy hastily formed a pathfinder group from it, which they used to raise fires in the target area by incendiary bombs, and these became the guide for the rest of the de-Knickebeined Luftwaffe.

Coventry, on November 14–15, 1940, was the first target attacked by the new method. Although our new jamming had now started, a technical error prevented it from becoming effective for another few months. Even so our knowledge of the beams was helpful. From the settings of the hostile beams and the times at which they played we could forecast the target and the time, route and height of attack. Our night fighters had, alas! at this date neither the numbers nor the equipment to make much use of the information. It was nevertheless invaluable to our fire fighting and other Civil Defence services. These could often be concentrated in the threatened area and special warnings given to the population before the attack started. Presently our countermeasures improved and caught up with the attack. Meanwhile decoy fires, code-named "Starfish," on a very large scale were lighted by us with the right timing in suitable open places to lead the main attack astray, and these sometimes achieved remarkable results.

By the beginning of 1941 we had mastered the "X apparatus"; but the Germans were also thinking hard, and about this time they brought in a new aid called the "Y apparatus." Whereas the two earlier systems had both used cross beams over the target, the new system used only one beam, together with a special method of range-finding by radio, by which the aircraft could be told how far it was along the beam. When it reached the correct distance it dropped its bombs. By good fortune and the genius and devotion of all concerned, we had divined the exact method of working the ''Y apparatus'' some months before the Germans were able to use it in operations, and by the time they were ready to make it their pathfinder we had the power to render it useless. On the very first night when the Germans committed themselves to the ''Y apparatus'' our new countermeasures came into action against them. The success of our efforts was manifest from the acrimonious remarks heard passing between the pathfinding aircraft and their controlling ground stations by our listening instruments. The faith of the enemy air crews in their new device was thus shattered at the outset, and after many failures the method was abandoned. The bombing of Dublin on the night of May 30, 1941, may well have been an unforeseen and unintended result of our interference with ''Y.''

General Martini, the German chief in this sphere, has since the war admitted that he had not realised soon enough that the ''high-frequency war'' had begun, and that he underrated the British Intelligence and countermeasures organisation. Our exploitation of the strategic mistakes which he made in the Battle of the Beams diverted enormous numbers of bombs from our cities during a period when all other means of defence had either failed or were still in their childhood. These were however very rapidly improving under the pressure of potentially mortal attack.

Since the beginning of the war we had brought into active production a form of airborne radar called A.I., on which the Air Defence Research Committee had fruitfully laboured from 1938 onwards, and with which it was hoped to detect and close on enemy bombers. This apparatus was too large and too complicated for a pilot to operate himself. It was therefore installed in two-seater Blenheims, and later in Beaufighters, in which the observer operated the radar, and directed his pilot until the enemy aircraft became visible and could be fired on—usually at night about a hundred yards away. I had called this device in its early days ''the Smeller,'' and longed for its arrival in action. This was inevitably a slow process. However, it began. A widespread method of ground-control interception grew up and came into use. The British pilots, with their terrible eight-gun batteries, in which cannon-guns were soon to play their part, began to close—no longer by chance but by system—upon the almost defenceless German bombers.

The enemy's use of the beams now became a positive advantage to us. They gave clear warning of the time and direction of the attacks, and enabled the night-fighter squadrons in the areas affected and all their apparatus to come into action at full force and in good time, and all the anti-aircraft batteries concerned to be fully manned and directed by their own intricate science, of which more later. During March and April the steadily rising rate of loss of German bombers had become a cause of serious concern to the German war chiefs. The ''erasing'' of British cities had not been found so easy as Hitler had imagined. It was with relief that the German Air Force received their orders in May to break off the night attacks on Great Britain and to prepare for action in another theatre.

Thus the three main attempts to conquer Britain after the fall of France were successively defeated or prevented. The first was the decisive defeat of the German Air Force in the Battle of Britain during July, August, and September. Instead of destroying the British Air Force and the stations and air factories on which it relied for its life and future, the enemy themselves, in spite of their preponderance in numbers, sustained losses which they could not bear. Our second victory followed from our first. The German failure to gain command of the air prevented the cross-Channel invasion. The prowess of our fighter pilots, and the excellence of the organisation which sustained them, had in fact rendered the same service—under conditions indescribably different—as Drake and his brave little ships and hardy mariners had done 350 years before, when, the Spanish Armada being broken and dispersed, the Duke of Parma's powerful army waited helplessly in the Low Countries for the means of crossing the Narrow Seas.

The third ordeal was the indiscriminate night bombing of our cities in mass attacks. This was broken by the continued devotion and skill of our fighter pilots, by the fortitude and endurance of the mass of the people, and notably by the Londoners, who, together with the civil organisations which upheld them, bore the brunt. But these noble efforts in the high air and the flaming streets would have been in vain if British science and British brains had not played the ever-memorable and decisive part which this narrative records.

There is a useful German saying, ''The trees do not grow up to the sky.'' Nevertheless we had every reason to expect that the air attack on Britain would continue in an indefinite crescendo. Until Hitler actually invaded Russia we had no right to suppose it would die away and stop. We therefore strove with might and main to improve the measures and devices by which we had hitherto survived and to find new ones. The highest priority was assigned to all forms of radar study and application. Scientists and technicians were engaged and organised on a very large scale. Labour and material was made available to the fullest extent. Other methods of striking down the hostile bomber were sought tirelessly, and for many months to come these efforts were spurred by repeated, costly, and bloody raids upon our ports and cities.

I will mention three developments in which, at Lindemann's prompting and in the light of what we had studied

---

12 Nov 40

PRIME MINISTER

TO SIR EDWARD BRIDGES AND GENERAL ISMAY

The Prime Minister has noticed that the habit of private secretaries and others of addressing each other by their Christian names about matters of an official character is increasing, and ought to be stopped. The use of Christian names in inter-departmental correspondence should be confined to brief explanatory covering notes or to purely personal and private explanations. It is hard enough to follow people by their surnames.

---

together on the Air Defence Research Committee of pre-war years, I took special interest and used my authority. These were, first, the massed discharge of rockets, as a reinforcement of our antiaircraft batteries; secondly, the laying of aerial mine curtains in the path of a raiding force by means of bombs with long wires descending by parachutes; thirdly, the search for fuses so sensitive that they did not need to hit their target, but would be set off by merely passing near an aircraft. Of these three methods, on which we toiled with large expenditure of our resources, some brief account must now be given.

None of these methods could come to fruition in 1940. At least a year stood between us and practical relief. By the time we were ready to go into action with our new apparatus and methods the enemy attack they were designed to meet came suddenly to an end, and for nearly three years we enjoyed almost complete immunity from it. Critics have therefore been disposed to underrate the value of these efforts, which could only be proved by major trial, and in any case in no way obstructed other developments in the same sphere.

BY itself, beam-distortion was not enough. Once having hit the correct target, it was easy for the German bombers, unless they were confused by our "Starfish" decoy fires, to return again to the glow of the fires they had lit the night before. Somehow they must be clawed down. For this we developed two new devices, rockets and aerial mines. By fitting our antiaircraft batteries with radar it was possible to predict the position of an enemy aircraft accurately enough, provided it continued to fly in a straight line at the same speed, but this is hardly what experienced pilots do. Of course they zigzagged or "weaved," and this meant that in the twenty or thirty seconds between firing the gun and the explosion of the shell they might well be half a mile or so from the predicted point.

A wide yet intense burst of fire round the predicted point was an answer. Combinations of a hundred guns would have been excellent, if the guns could have been produced and the batteries manned and all put in the right place at the right time. This was beyond human power to achieve. But a very simple, cheap alternative was available in the rocket, or, as it had been called for secrecy, the Unrotated Projectile (U.P.). Even before the war Dr. Crow, in the days of the Air Defence Research Committee, had developed 2-inch and 3-inch rockets which could reach almost as high as our antiaircraft guns. The 3-inch rocket carried a much more powerful warhead than a 3-inch shell. It was not so accurate. On the other hand, rocket projectors had the inestimable advantage that they could be made very quickly and easily in enormous numbers without burdening our hard-driven gun factories.

Thousands of these U.P. projectors were made, and some millions of rounds of ammunition. An officer of great distinction, General Sir Frederick Pile, who was in command of our antiaircraft ground defences throughout the war, and who was singularly free from the distaste for novel devices so often found in professional soldiers, welcomed this accession to his strength. He formed these weapons into huge batteries of ninety-six projectors each,

manned largely by the Home Guard, which could produce a concentrated volume of fire far beyond the power of antiaircraft artillery.

I worked in increasing intimacy throughout the war with General Pile, and always found him ingenious and serviceable in the highest degree. He was at his best not only in these days of expansion, when his command rose to a peak of over 300,000 men and women and 2,400 guns, apart from the rockets, but also in the period which followed after the air attack on Britain had been beaten off. Here was a time when his task was to liberate the largest possible numbers of men from static defence by batteries, and, without diminishing the potential firepower, to substitute the largest proportion of women and Home Guard for Regulars and technicians. But this is a story which must be told in its proper place.

The task of General Pile's command was not merely helped by the work of our scientists; as the battle developed their aid was the foundation on which all stood. In the daylight attacks of the Battle of Britain the guns had accounted for 296 enemy aircraft, and probably destroyed or damaged seventy-four more. But the night raids gave them new problems which with their existing equipment of only searchlights and sound locators could not be surmounted. In four months from October 1 only about seventy aircraft were destroyed. Radar came to the rescue. The first of these sets for directing gunfire was used in October, 1940, and Mr. Ernest Bevin and I spent most of the night watching them. The searchlight beams were not fitted till December. However, much training and experience were needed in their use, and many modifications and refinements in the sets themselves were found necessary. Great efforts were made in all this wide field, and the spring of 1941 brought a full reward.

During the attacks on London in the first two weeks of May—the last of the German offensive—over seventy aircraft were destroyed, or more than the four winter months had yielded. Of course in the meanwhile the number of guns had grown. In December there had been 1,400 heavy guns and 650 light; in May there were 1,687 heavy guns and 790 light, with about forty rocket batteries. But the great increase in the effectiveness of our gun defences was due in its origin to the new inventions and technical improvements which the scientists put into the soldiers' hands, and of which the soldiers made such good use.

BY the middle of 1941, when at last the rocket batteries had begun to come into service in substantial numbers, air attack was much diminished, so that they had few chances of proving themselves. But when they did come into action the number of rounds needed to bring down an aircraft was little more than that required by the enormously more costly and scanty antiaircraft guns, of which we were so short. The rockets were good in themselves, and also an addition to our other means of defence.

Shells or rockets alike are of course only effective if they reach the right spot and explode at the right moment. Efforts were therefore made to produce aerial mines suspended on long wires floating down on parachutes which could be laid in the path of the enemy air squadrons. It was impossible to pack these into shells. But a rocket, with much thinner walls, has more room. A certain amount of 3-inch rocket ammunition which could lay an aerial mine field on wires 700 feet long at heights up to 20,000 feet was made and held ready for use against mass attacks on London. The advantage of such mine fields over shell fire is of course that they remain lethal for anything up to a minute. For wherever the wing hits the wire it pulls up the mine until it reaches the plane and explodes. There is thus no need for exact fuse-setting, as is the case with ordinary antiaircraft shells.

Aerial mines could of course be placed in position by rockets laid by aircraft, or simply raised on small balloons. The last method was ardently supported by the Admiralty. In fact however the rockets were never brought into action on any considerable scale. By the time they were manufactured in large numbers mass attacks by bombers had ceased. Nevertheless it was surprising and fortunate that the Germans did not develop this counter to our mass-bombing raids in the last three years of the war. Even a few mine-laying aircraft would have been able to lay and maintain a mine field over any German city, which would have taken a toll of our bombers the more deadly as numbers grew.

There was another important aspect. In 1940 the dive bomber seemed to be a deadly threat to our ships and key factories. One might think that aircraft diving on a ship would be easy to shoot down, as the gunner can aim straight at them without making allowance for their motion. But an aeroplane end on is a very small target, and a contact fuse will work only in the rare event of a direct hit. To set a time fuse so that the shell explodes at the exact moment when it is passing the aircraft is almost impossible. An error in timing of one-tenth of a second causes a miss of many hundreds of feet. It therefore seemed worthwhile to try to make a fuse which could detonate automatically when the projectile passed near to the target, whether it actually hit it or not.

As there is little space in the head of a shell the roomier head of the 3-inch rocket was attractive. While I was still at the Admiralty in 1940 we had pressed this idea. Photoelectric (P.E.) cells were used which produced an electrical impulse whenever there was a change of light, such as the shade of the enemy plane. By February 1940 we had a model which I took to the Cabinet and showed my colleagues after one of our meetings. When a matchbox was thrown past the fuse it winked perceptibly with its demonstration lamp. The cluster of Ministers who gathered round were powerfully impressed. But there is a long road between a grimacing model and an armed, mass-produced robot. We worked hard at the production of the so-called P.E. fuses, but here again by the time they were ready in any quantity our danger and their hour had for the moment passed.

ATTEMPTS were made in 1941 to design a similar proximity fuse, using a tiny radar set arranged to explode the warhead when the projectile passed near the aircraft. Successful preliminary experiments and trials were made in England. We imparted our knowledge to the Americans who succeeded not only in perfecting the instrument but in reducing its size so much that the whole thing could be put into the head not merely of a rocket but of a shell. These so-called "Proximity Fuses," made in the United States, were used in great numbers in the last year of the war, and proved potent against the small unmanned aircraft (V-1) with which we were assailed in 1944, and also in the Pacific against Japanese aircraft.

The final phase of the "Wizard War" was of course the radar developments and inventions required for our counterattack upon Germany. These suggested themselves to some extent from our own experiences and defensive efforts. The part they played has still to be described. In September 1940 we had nearly nine long months ahead of us of heavy battering and suffering before the tide was to turn. It may be claimed that while struggling, not without success, against the perils of the hour we bent our thoughts steadily upon the future, when better times might come.

The Radar Counterattack

DURING the winter of 1941 our Intelligence suspected that the Germans were using a new radar apparatus for giving the direction and range of our planes to their antiaircraft guns. This apparatus was believed to look like a large electric bowl heater. Our secret agents, our listening devices and air photographs, soon found out that a chain of stations stretched along the northern coast of Europe, and that one of them, probably containing the new equipment, was established at Bruneval, on Cap d'Antifer, not far from Le Havre. On December 3, 1941, a squadron leader of the Photographic Reconnaissance Unit happened to visit our Intelligence Centre and learnt of our suspicions. On his own initiative he flew over next day and spotted the apparatus. On December 5 he made another sortie and took a brilliant and successful photograph.

Our scientists found that it was exactly what they had expected. Although the station was at the top of a 400-foot cliff, a shelving beach near by provided a possible landing place, and a Commando raid was planned accordingly. On the night of February 27, 1942, in the snow and darkness, a detachment of paratroops dropped at midnight behind the German station on the cliff summit, and held the defenders at bay. With them went a carefully briefed party of sappers and an R.A.F. radio mechanic, with instructions to remove as much of the equipment as they could, sketch and photograph the rest, and if possible capture one of the German operators.

In all this they succeeded, although a hitch in the timetable cut down their working period from half an hour to barely ten minutes. Most of the equipment was found, dismantled under fire, and carried to the beach. Here the Navy was waiting and took the party off. We thus became the possessors of vital portions of a key piece of equipment in the German radar defences and gathered information which greatly helped our air offensive. Supplemented by a rapidly increasing network of agents who were specially briefed in radar intelligence, and by friendly neutrals who brought back information from the occupied countries, our knowledge of the German defences grew all through 1942. In speaking of "agents" and "friendly neutrals" it would be fair to single out the Belgians for special mention. In 1942 they provided about 80 per cent of all "agent" information on this subject, including a vital map, stolen from the German officer commanding searchlight and radar equipment for the more northerly of the two sectors of the German night-fighter line in Belgium. It was this map, in conjunction with other information, which enabled our experts to unravel the system of the German air defence. By the end of the year we knew not only how the hostile system worked, but how to cope with it.

One detail however was still missing, and not to be discovered for many months. Towards the end of the year Professor Lindemann, now Lord Cherwell, told me that the Germans had fitted their night fighters with a new kind of radar set. Little was known about it except that it was called "Lichtenstein" and was designed for hunting our bombers. It was imperative to find out more about it before the start of our air offensive.

On the night of December 2, 1942, an aircraft of 192 Squadron was presented as a decoy. It was attacked many times by an enemy night fighter radiating the Lichtenstein transmissions. Nearly all the crew were hit. The special operator listening to the radiations was severely wounded in the head, but continued to observe with accuracy. The wireless operator, though badly injured, was parachuted out of the aircraft over Ramsgate, and survived with the precious observations. The rest of the crew flew the plane out to sea and alighted on the water because the machine was too badly damaged to land on an airfield. They were rescued by a boat from Deal. The gap in our knowledge of the German night defences was closed.

LATE in 1940 Lord Cherwell had begun to raise doubts in my mind about the accuracy of our bombing, and in 1941 I authorised his Statistical Department to make an investigation at Bomber Headquarters. The results confirmed our fears. We learnt that although Bomber Command believed they had found the target, two-thirds of the crews actually failed to strike within five miles of it. The air photographs showed how little damage was being done. It also appeared that the crews knew this, and were discouraged by the poor results of so much hazard. Unless we could improve on this there did not seem much use in continuing night bombing.

Several methods had been proposed to guide bombers to their targets by radio aids, but until we recognised how inaccurate our bombing was there seemed no reason to embark on such complications. Now attention was focused on them. We had developed a device called "Gee," by which radio pulses were sent out simultaneously from three stations far apart in England. By exact timing of their arrival at an aircraft it could fix its position within a mile. This was an improvement, and we began to use it on a large scale about ten days after the Bruneval raid. With its aid we struck at most of the Ruhr, but it could not reach deep enough into Germany. Lübeck and Rostock were also bombed at this time, but not by "Gee." Another device on similar lines called "Oboe" was much more accurate. But since it involved flying for a considerable time in a straight line the bombers were exposed to great dangers from antiaircraft fire. And, as with "Gee," the radio waves for which it was designed were too short to curve round the earth's surface; hence it could only be used up to distances at which the aircraft was above the horizon— say 200 miles at 25,000 feet. This limited seriously the regions we could attack. Something better was needed.

Since 1941, when the idea had been shown to be feasible, Lindemann had argued that a radar set mounted in the aircraft itself could throw on to a screen in the cockpit a map of the ground over which it flew. If the bomber navigated with the aid of "Gee" or other methods to within say fifty miles of the target it could then switch on this apparatus and drop its bombs through cloud or haze without possibility of jamming or interference. Distance would not matter, as the plane would carry its radar eye with it wherever it went and the eye could see in the dark.

THIS device, which afterwards became well known by the code name H_2S, encountered many obstacles, and I was for some time warned from several quarters that it could not be achieved. But I persisted in pressing the theme, and eventually it worked well. Special ultra-short waves were used. The shorter the wave the clearer the picture became on the aircraft's screen. The transmitting machine for these microwaves, as they were called, was entirely a British invention, and it revolutionised the Radio war both on land and at sea. It was not until it fell into German hands that they were able to copy it.

Early in 1943 the equipment was ready for operations. It was issued to the pathfinder group which, copying the German example of Kampf Gruppe 100, we had formed some months earlier. Success was immediate. Nor did its usefulness stop at bombing on land. For some time our planes had had airborne radar, called A.S.V., for detecting surface vessels. But in the autumn of 1942 the Germans had begun to fit their U-boats with special receivers for detecting the signals which it sent out. They could thus dive in time to avoid attack. As a result Coastal Command successes in sinking U-boats declined and our losses in merchant shipping increased. H_2S was adapted for use in the A.S.V. role with striking advantage, and made a definite contribution to the final defeat of the U-boats.

To anticipate the story, our air offensive in 1943 started well, and the accuracy of the "Oboe" attacks worried the Germans considerably. The news that we were hitting individual factories on cloudy nights in the Ruhr reached Hitler at his headquarters in Russia. He immediately sent for Goering and General Martini, Director-General of Signals of the Luftwaffe. After haranguing them he stated that it was a scandal that the British could achieve this feat and the Germans could not. Martini replied that the Germans were not only able to do it, but had done it in the Blitz with the "X" and "Y" beam systems. The Fuehrer said he would not be convinced by words, and demanded a demonstration. At the cost of considerable effort this was arranged. In the meantime Bomber Command, guided by "Oboe," had wrought great damage in the Ruhr.

Hitler's 'Secret Weapon'

SEVERAL years before the war the Germans had begun the development of rockets and pilotless aircraft, and had built an experimental station to carry out this work on the Baltic coast at Peenemünde. This activity was of course a closely guarded secret. Nevertheless they were not able entirely to conceal what was going on, and already in the autumn of 1939 references to long-range weapons of various kinds began to appear in our Intelligence reports. During the early years of the war rumours on this subject and scraps of information, often contradictory, reached us from various quarters.

In the spring of 1943 the position was reviewed by the Chiefs of Staff, as a result of which on the 15th of April General Ismay sent me the following minute: "The Chiefs of Staff are of the opinion that no time should be lost in establishing the facts, and, if the evidence proves reliable, in devising countermeasures. They feel this is a case where investigation directed by one man who could call on such scientific and Intelligence advisers as might be appropriate would give the best and quickest results. They therefore suggest that you should appoint an individual who should be charged with the task forthwith. They suggest for your consideration the name of Mr. Duncan Sandys, who, they think, would be very suitable if he could be made available. . . ."

Mr. Sandys had served in an antiaircraft unit in Norway in the early days of the war. Later he had suffered crippling disablement to both his feet in a motor accident when commanding the first experimental rocket regiment. He had joined the Government in July 1941 as Financial Secretary at the War Office, and afterwards as Under-Secretary at the Ministry of Supply. In both these offices he had had considerable responsibility for the general direction of weapon development, and had consequently been brought into close contact with the Chiefs of Staff Committee. As he was my son-in-law I was naturally glad that the Chiefs of Staff should wish to give him this important work, though I had in no way suggested it.

Hitler was meanwhile intent upon the plan. Accompanied by some of his principal adherents of Cabinet level, he inspected Peenemünde about the beginning of June 1943. We were at this time better informed about rocket missiles than about pilotless aircraft. Both methods were in full preparation on a large scale, and Peenemünde was the summit of all research and experiment. No decisive progress had been made by the Germans toward the atomic bomb. "Heavy water" gave little encouragement, but in pilotless aircraft and the rockets Hitler and his advisers saw a means of delivering a new and possibly decisive attack upon England and the rupturing of the Anglo-American plans for a major cross-Channel return to the Continent. The Fuehrer was comforted by all he learned at Peenemünde, and he hurled the utmost German effort into this new and perhaps last hope.

About June 10 he told his assembled military leaders that the Germans had only to hold out. By the end of 1943 London would be levelled to the ground and Britain forced to capitulate. October 20 was fixed as zero day for rocket attacks to begin. It is said that Hitler personally ordered the construction of 30,000 rockets for that day. This, if true, shows the absurd ideas on which he lived. The German Minister of Munitions, Dr. Speer, said that each V-2 (our name for the rocket; pilotless aircraft were called V-1) required about as many man-hours to make as six fighters. Hitler's demand was therefore for the equivalent of 180,000 fighters to be made in four months. This was ridiculous; but the production of both weapons was given first priority and 1,500 skilled workers were transferred from antiaircraft and artillery production to the task.

On June 28 Sandys reported that aerial photographs of Peenemünde showed large rockets alongside the firing point which might have a range of about 90 to 130 miles, and on July 9 he told us that in addition to their plans for a rocket attack on London there was also evidence that the Germans intended to use pilotless aircraft and very long-range guns. Two excavations of a suspicious character had been detected—at Watten, near St. Omer, and at Bruneval, near Fécamp.

When all these facts and reports were brought before the Defence Committee many differences of opinion arose concerning them. Among the scientists and technical officers opinions varied deeply and sharply on the question whether the new form of attack on the Island would be by rocket bombs or by pilotless aircraft. At first the rocket was favourite, but its backers weakened their case by what turned out to be vastly exaggerated estimates of the size and destructive power of the missile. Confronted with these, those responsible for home security faced the possibility not only of evacuating children, expectant mothers, and other selected persons from London, but even a wholesale evacuation of the capital itself.

THE Minister for Home Security was profoundly disquieted by the reports he studied, and always presented the danger in its most serious aspect. It was certainly his special duty to make sure that the danger was not underrated. Lord Cherwell, on the other hand, did not believe that even if giant rockets could be made it would pay the Germans to make them. As he had maintained from the very beginning, he insisted that they would get far better results at much smaller cost by using pilotless aircraft. Even if they used rockets with warheads of ten or twenty tons, as had been forecast, but which he did not believe was possible, he did not think the destruction in Britain would approach the figures which were produced. Listening to the discussions, which were frequent over many months, between him and Mr. Herbert Morrison, it might have seemed at times that the two protagonists were divided as to whether the attack by self-propelled weapons would be annihilating or comparatively unimportant. Actually the issue, as is usual, was not in the realm of "Yes or No," but in that of "More or Less."

These discussions had caused no delay or indecision in our actions. An attack on Peenemünde was difficult, but imperative, and on the night of August 17 Air Marshal Harris, Chief of Bomber Command, struck with 571 heavy bombers. The buildings were scattered along a narrow strip of coast and protected by a smoke screen. They could neither be reached by radio-navigation beams from the United Kingdom nor sufficiently identified by the apparatus carried in our planes. It was therefore necessary to bomb by moonlight, although the German night fighters were close at hand and it was too far to send our own.

The crews were ordered to bomb from 8,000 feet, much below their usual height, and were told by Air Marshal Harris that if the operation failed on the first night it would have to be repeated on the next night, and on all suitable nights thereafter, regardless of casualties and regardless of the fact that the enemy would obviously do everything possible to increase his defences after the first attack. At the same time everything was done to guide our airmen and deceive the foe. Pathfinders flew ahead to mark the route and straggling installations. A master bomber circled the target, assessing results and instructing our planes by radio-telephone. The

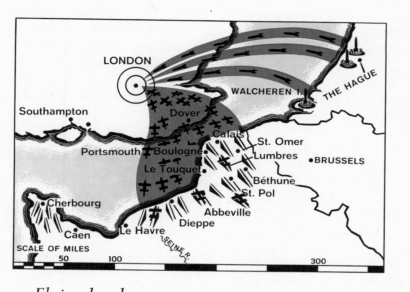

Flying bombs of two kinds were launched on southeast England in 1944. V-1s—pilotless planes—came from France (*center*). Later V-2s—rockets—came from Netherlands (*right*). Other ramps near Cherbourg (*left*) were captured by Allies before being used.

route taken was almost the same as in previous raids on Berlin, and a small force of Mosquitoes was sent over the capital to mislead the enemy.

The weather was worse than expected and landmarks were difficult to find, but it cleared towards Rügen Island and many crews punctually started their time and distance runs. There was more cloud over the target and the smoke screen was working, but, says Harris, "the very careful planning of the attack ensured a good concentration of bombs on all the aiming points." The enemy was at first deceived by the feint on Berlin, but not for long enough. Most of our force got away, but the German fighters caught them during their return, and in the bright moonlight forty of our bombers were shot down.

The results were of capital importance. Although the physical damage was much less than was supposed, the raid had a far-reaching influence on events. All the constructional drawings just completed for issue to the workshops were burned, and the start of large-scale manufacture was considerably delayed. The parent factory at Peenemünde was hit, and the fear of attacks on factories producing the rocket elsewhere led the Germans to concentrate manufacture in underground works in the Harz Mountains. All these changes caused serious delays in perfecting and producing the weapon.

They also decided to shift their experimental activities to an establishment in Poland beyond the range of our

bombers. There our Polish agents kept vigilant watch, and in the middle of January 1944 the new weapon was tried. They soon discovered its range and line of fire, but of course the rockets came down many miles apart from each other. German patrols always raced to where they fell and collected the fragments, but one day a rocket fell on the bank of the river Bug and did not explode. The Poles got there first, rolled it into the river, waited till the Germans had given up the search, and then salvaged and dismantled it under cover of darkness. This dangerous task accomplished, a Polish engineer was picked up by a Royal Air Force Dakota on the night of July 25, 1944, and flown to England with many technical documents and more than 100 lbs. of essential parts of the new weapon. The gallant man returned to Poland, and was later caught by the Gestapo and executed in Warsaw on August 13, 1944.

The attack on Peenemünde, for which such sacrifices were made, had therefore played an important and definite part in the general progress of the war. But for this raid and the subsequent attacks on the launching points in France, Hitler's bombardment of London by rockets might well have started early in 1944. In fact it was delayed until September. By that time the prepared launching sites in Northern France had been overrun by General Montgomery's forces. In consequence the projectiles had to be fired from improvised positions in Holland, nearly twice as far away from London, and with much less accuracy. By the autumn German communications became so congested by battle needs that the transport of rockets to the firing point could no longer secure high priority.

In his book, *Crusade in Europe*, General Eisenhower goes so far as to say: "It seemed likely that if the German had succeeded in perfecting and using these new weapons six months earlier than he did our invasion of Europe would have proved exceedingly difficult, perhaps impossible. I feel sure that if they had succeeded in using these weapons over a six-month period, and particularly if they had made the Portsmouth-Southampton area one of their principal targets, 'Overlord' might have been written off."

This is an overstatement. The average error of both these weapons was over ten miles. Even if the Germans had been able to maintain a rate of fire of 120 a day and if none whatever had been shot down the effect would have been the equivalent of only two or three one-ton bombs to a square mile per week. However, it shows that the military commanders considered it necessary to eliminate the menace of the "V" weapons, not only to protect civilian life, but also to prevent interference with our offensive operations.

In the early autumn of 1943 it became certain that the Germans were planning to attack us not only with rockets but also with pilotless aircraft. It was observed that in Northern France a large number of groups of curiously shaped structures were being erected. All were laid out after the same fashion, and most of them appeared to be directed on London. Each included one or more buildings shaped rather like a ski. We later discovered from air photographs that there were structures similar to these in the neighbourhood of Peenemünde, and one of the photographs revealed a minute aircraft close to an inclined ramp. From this it was deduced that the so-called "ski sites" in Northern France were probably designed to store, fill, and launch small unmanned aircraft or flying bombs.

British and American Air Forces accordingly bombed them. This was so effective that at the end of April aerial reconnaissance indicated that the enemy was giving up work on them. But our satisfaction was short-lived, for it was discovered that he was building instead modified sites which were much less elaborate and more carefully camouflaged and therefore harder to find and to hit. Wherever found these new sites were bombed. Many were destroyed, but about forty escaped damage or detection. It was from these that the attack was ultimately launched in June.

Nearly fifteen months passed between the minute which the Chiefs of Staffs sent me in April 1943 and the actual attack in June 1944. Not a day was wasted. No care was lacking. Preparations involving many months to perfect were set on foot on a large and costly scale in good time. When at length the blow fell upon us we were able to ward it off, albeit with heavy loss in life and much damage to property, but without any effective hindrance to our war-making capacity or to the operations in France. The whole story may stand as an example of the efficiency of our governing machine, and of the foresight and vigilance of all connected with it.

The Mounting Air Offensive

IT was not till 1943 that we possessed sufficient and suitable aircraft for striking heavy and continuous blows, and in the same year the bombers of the American Eighth Air Force joined in our strategic air offensive. Ever since 1940 I had encouraged the expansion of our bomber strength. The difficulties were numerous. Production lagged behind forecasts; other theatres of war and the campaign against the U-boats made heavy demands; and when the Americans came into the war their output was of course at first largely diverted to their own needs. Although growth in numbers had been slow, our new four-engined planes carried a far heavier weight of bombs. In the opening months of 1942 the average load per aircraft was 2,800 lbs.; by the end of that year it was 4,400 lbs.; during 1943 it rose to 7,500 lbs.

Both we and the Germans had found that bombers, even in close formation, could not penetrate an efficient fighter defence in daylight without overheavy casualties. Like the enemy we had had to turn to night attacks. We were too confident at first about the accuracy of our bombing, and our attempts in the winter of 1940–41 to destroy German oil plants, paramount but small targets, proved a failure. In the spring of 1941 Bomber Command was called to join in the Battle of the Atlantic, and not till July was the offensive against Germany resumed. The targets now chosen were industrial cities and their railway centres, especially the Ruhr, and Hamburg, Bremen, Hannover, Frankfurt, and Stuttgart. However, neither our means nor our methods sufficed. Our losses mounted, and during the winter months we had to reduce our effort.

In February 1942 "Gee," the new position-finder already described, was brought into use, and with its help the Ruhr became our primary goal. Under the vigorous leadership of Air Marshal Harris dramatic results were achieved. His operations included fire-raising attacks on Lübeck and on Rostock, the thousand-bomber assault on Cologne in May, and the daylight attack on the submarine Diesel engine works at Augsburg, when Squadron-Leader Nettleton won the Victoria Cross. In August the Pathfinder Force was formed, under Air Commodore Bennett. Radar aids were playing a growing part in navigation and target-finding, and it was a wise measure to entrust the scarce and complicated apparatus to specialists whose duty was to find the way and point the target to others.

Although accurate night bombing, denied so long, thus came gradually into being, the bomber offensive of 1942 did not lower Germany's war production or civilian morale. The strength of her economy had been under-estimated. Productive capacity and labour were drawn extensively from the occupied countries, and German armament production seems to have actually increased. Under the iron discipline imposed by Goebbels, who was in charge of relief measures, civilian morale stood firm and local disasters were prevented from having a national effect.

But the German leaders had become deeply alarmed and were forced on to the defensive in the air. German aircraft production was increasingly devoted to fighters rather than bombers. This was the beginning of defeat for the Luftwaffe, and a turning point in our struggle for the air supremacy which we gained in 1944, without which we could not have won the war. Second only in importance to this moral victory over the minds of Hitler and his air commanders was the dangerous Third Air Front created for Germany in the West, to the advantage of the Russians, and of ourselves in the Mediterranean.

Thus we come to the year 1943, when the Americans joined in the bombing of Axis Europe. They had different ideas about method. Whereas we had adopted and were now bringing to efficiency our night-bombing technique, they were convinced that their heavily armed Fortress bombers in close formation could penetrate deeply into Germany by daylight without fighter escort. I was doubtful whether this was a practicable system. At Casablanca I discussed my misgivings with General Eaker, commanding the U.S. Air Forces in England, and withdrew my opposition. The Casablanca directive, issued to the British and

American Bomber Commands in the United Kingdom on February 4, 1943, gave them their task in the following general terms: ". . . . Your primary objectives . . . will . . . be in the following priority: (*a*) German submarine yards; (*b*) the German aircraft industry; (*c*) transportation; (*d*) oil plants; (*e*) other targets in enemy war industry."

General Eaker, with the American Eighth Air Force, aimed at destroying six groups of targets by daylight precision bombing. He did not receive the reinforcements for which he had asked, but made many gallant and costly attacks. Air Marshal Harris, bombing only at night, concentrated from March to July mainly on the Ruhr, beginning on the night of March 5 with the heavily defended town of Essen. Eight Mosquitoes dropped target indicators, using the blind-bombing device of "Oboe"; then twenty-two heavy bombers of the Pathfinder Force further illuminated the target for an intense attack by 392 aircraft. Essen was severely damaged for the first time in the war.

As the power and activities of Bomber Command developed Goebbels became more and more despairing of the outcome, and his diaries bitterly reproach the Luftwaffe for its failure to stop the British bombers. Speer, the most capable of German Ministers of Production, in an address to Gauleiters in June 1943, referred to the serious losses in production of coal and iron and crankshafts, and to the decision to double the antiaircraft defences of the Ruhr and draft in 100,000 men for repair duties.

While the British were at last succeeding in wrecking the Ruhr munitions centres the American Fortresses were meeting with serious opposition from German dayfighters, and General Eaker soon realised that if his plan was to succeed he must first defeat the German Air Force. In the greatly improved state of the U-boat war a change in the priorities of targets was accepted by the Combined Chiefs of Staff. In a directive known as "Point-blank," issued on June 10, 1943, they amended the Casablanca decisions so as to give first emphasis to the attack on the German fighter forces and the German aircraft industry.

ON July 24–25 the very heavy British attacks on Hamburg began. Hamburg was beyond the range of "Oboe," and the fullest use was made of the blind-bombing device of H_2S, which was carried in the aeroplane and did not depend on signals from home. This instrument gave an outline of the main ground features on a screen in the aircraft which resembled a television screen of to-day. The picture was particularly good where the land was broken up by water, as it is in the dock area of Hamburg. Bomber Command had been gaining experience of H_2S since its first use in January, and for the assault on Hamburg an additional device called "Window," which we had long held in reserve, was used for the first time. This simply consisted of strips of metallised paper dropped by the bombers. A cloud of such strips, tuned to the German wavelength and weighing only a few pounds, looked like an aircraft on the enemy's radar screens, and thus made it very difficult for either their night fighters to be guided to our bombers or for the antiaircraft guns and searchlights to be aimed at them.

The four attacks against Hamburg from July 24 to August 3 caused greater destruction than had ever been suffered by so large a city in so short a time. The second attack delivered such a concentration of incendiary bombs mixed with high explosive that there arose a fire tornado which raged through the city with a terrifying howl and defied all human countermeasures. The Air Battle of Hamburg has been described by many Germans as "the great catastrophe."

Speer himself admitted after the war that he had calculated that if similar attacks had been delivered in quick succession against six other major German cities it would have led to a breakdown of war production. Germany was saved from this fate in 1943 partly because H_2S was found to be difficult to use, even for area bombing, if there were no prominent water features within the target, and partly because of the resolute defence put up by Germany's ever-resourceful night fighters.

OUR third great air onslaught of 1943 was upon Berlin. It lasted from November 1943 to March 1944. If this great industrial centre could have been paralysed like Hamburg, German war production as well as morale might have been given a mortal blow. Bomber Command pressed home its attacks with undaunted courage and determination in the face of fearful difficulties. The weather was appalling, and most of the bombing had to rely on the radar eye of H_2S.

The night photographs taken by the bombers at the moment of bomb release showed nothing but clouds. The same disappointment befell the daylight flights over Berlin of the Photographic Reconnaissance Unit. We knew from the admissions of the Germans themselves that great destruction was being caused, but we could not judge the relative success of our sixteen major attacks by comparing the photographic evidence of each. Indeed we had to wait until March 1944 to obtain photographs clear enough for the damage to be assessed. It fell short of what had been achieved at Hamburg.

Meanwhile the U.S. Eighth Air Force in its assault on the enemy's fighter forces and aircraft industry in accordance with the new "Point-blank" directive was enduring increasing losses at the hands of the German day fighters, which met them with mounting strength and efficiency. The culmination was reached on October 14, 1943. In their attack on the ball-bearing plants at Schweinfurt, which were vital to the German aircraft industry, the Americans had sixty of their large Fortress aircraft destroyed out of 291. It was thereafter accepted that unescorted daylight bombers could not gain air superiority over Germany, and their offensive was suspended until long-range fighters could be produced to cover them in sufficient strength.

Something very like a dispute arose upon whether British Bomber Command should attack Schweinfurt by their own methods. In the end it was decided that the attack should be made by both Air Forces in daylight and in darkness. The British and the American Eighth Air Force, aided at last by the long-range fighters for which they had waited a long time, attacked with 266 bombers by daylight on February 24, 1944, and on the same night Bomber Command sent 734 aircraft. Here was a really combined offensive directed towards the common aim. But unfortunately, the service discussions had lasted so long that the tremendous attack was robbed of much of its effectiveness. Warned by the American daylight attack four months earlier, Speer had dispersed Schweinfurt's industry.

Prolonged and obstinate technical argument on the policy of night or day bombing, and generous rivalry in trying out the opposing theories with the utmost sacrifice and heroism by both the British and American Air Forces, reached its climax after the last attack on Berlin. On March 30–31, 1944, out of 795 aircraft dispatched by British Bomber Command against Nürnberg ninety-four did not return. This was our heaviest loss in one raid, and caused Bomber Command to re-examine its tactics before launching further deep-penetration attacks by night into Germany. This was proof of the power which the enemy's night fighter force, now strengthened by the best crews from other vital fronts, had developed under our relentless offensive. But by forcing the enemy to concentrate his strength on defending inner Germany the Western Allies gained the complete air superiority which they needed for the approaching cross-Channel invasion.

During this time the Americans were intent on bringing their Fortress bombers into action by day as soon as they could be protected by fighters of sufficiently long range to seek out and destroy the enemy's fighters in the air or go down and attack them on their airfields. After long delay this vital need was met. First the Thunderbolt, then the Lightning, and then finally the Mustang gave them day fighters which had auxiliary fuel tanks and a radius of action which was increased from 475 miles to 850. On February 23, 1944, there began a week of concentrated bomber attacks by day on the German aircraft industry. The American long-range fighters at last mastered the enemy's and the day bombers delivered precision attacks without undue interference or loss.

This was a turning point in the air war against Germany. From now onwards the U.S. Eighth Air Force was able to bomb targets in Germany by day with high accuracy and ever-increasing freedom. Germany, through her loss of air superiority by day, exposed her vitals to our strategic offensive. The German night fighters, with the cream of their pilots, remained formidable till the end of the war; but this, by lowering the standard of the day fighters, aided the new developments in the American Air Force, and in 1944 daylight air superiority over Germany was gained. By April new measures of deception and new tactics to confuse

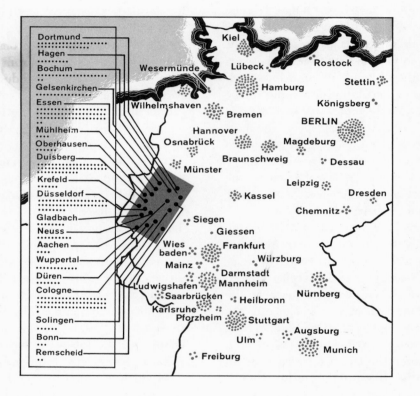

Bombing of Germany by Allies is shown in dots, each of which represents 500 tons of explosives. The industrial Ruhr and Rhineland (*brown rectangle*) took the worst drubbing, but bombing was hardest on civilians, of whom 7.5 million were made homeless.

the enemy's defences enabled the British to resume full-scale night offensives against German cities. The U.S. Eighth Air Force, having got the measure of the enemy's day fighters, was ready to complete this offensive "round the clock." Such was the position at the advent of "Overlord."

It is difficult to say to what extent German war economy and armaments production had so far been damaged by the Anglo-American bomber offensive. Bomber Command's three great area battles of 1943—the Ruhr, Hamburg, and Berlin—had created widespread havoc and caused consternation and alarm throughout Germany, and especially in the minds of the German leaders. But they were able to use factories and forced labour from the occupied countries, and under the brilliant control of Speer these were mobilised with extraordinary speed and efficiency. The morale of the people in the bombed cities, though severely shaken, was not allowed to degenerate into any nation-wide panic.

In reports submitted to Hitler, which must of course be taken with reserve, it was claimed that in fact German armament production was doubled in 1942. Remembering our own loss of output under much less severe bombing, this assertion is difficult to credit. The Germans admitted that production was almost stationary in 1943, and this is evidence of the increasing power of Bomber Command. In the spring of 1944 the Allied strategic bombers were required for "Overlord," and the weight of attack on Germany itself was inevitably reduced. But by now we were the masters in the air. The bitterness of the struggle had thrown a greater strain on the Luftwaffe than it was able to bear. By being forced to concentrate on building fighters it had lost all power of strategic counterattack by bombing back at us. Unbalanced and exhausted, it was henceforth unable to defend either itself or Germany from our grievous blows. For our air superiority, which by the end of 1944 was to become air supremacy, full tribute must be paid to the U.S. Eighth Air Force, once it gained its long-range fighters.

This chapter has been dominated by technical matters. The British and United States rival themes of air attack by night or day have been shown under the hard test of results. The intricacies of radar and all its variants have been presented, I trust, in a form intelligible to the lay reader. But it would be wrong to end without paying our tribute of respect and admiration to the officers and men who fought and died in this fearful battle of the air, the like of which had never before been known, or even with any precision imagined. The moral tests to which the crew of a bomber were subjected reached the extreme limits of human valour and sacrifice. Here chance was carried to its most extreme and violent degree above all else. There was a rule that no one should go on more than thirty raids without a break. But many who entered on their last dozen wild adventures felt that the odds against them were increasing. How can one be lucky thirty times running in a world of averages and machinery? Detective-Constable McSweeney, one of the Scotland Yard officers who looked after me in the early days of the war, was determined to fight in a bomber. I saw him several times during his training and his fighting. One day, gay and jaunty as ever, but with a thoughtful look, he said, "My next will be my twenty-ninth." It was his last. Not only our hearts and admiration but our minds in strong comprehension of these ordeals must go out to these heroic men, whose duty to their country and their cause sustained them in superhuman trials. I have mentioned facts like "the Americans had sixty of their large Fortress aircraft destroyed out of 291," and on another occasion "out of 795 aircraft dispatched by British Bomber Command against Nürnberg ninety-four did not return." The American Flying Fortresses carried a crew of ten men, and the British night bombers seven. Here we have each time six or seven hundred of these skilled, highly trained warriors lost in an hour. This was indeed ordeal by fire. In the British and American bombing of Germany and Italy during the Second World War the casualties were over 140,000 and in the period with which this chapter deals there were more British and American air-crew casualties than there were killed and wounded in the great operation of crossing the Channel. They never flinched or failed. It is to their devotion that in no small measure we owe our victory. Let us give them our salute.

The Pilotless Bombardment

THE long-studied assault on England by unmanned missiles now began. The target was Greater London. For more than a year we had argued among ourselves about the character and scale of the attack, and every preparation which our wits could devise and our resources permit had been made in good time.

In the early hours of June 13, 1944, exactly a week after D-Day, four pilotless aircraft crossed our coast. They were the premature result of a German order, sent urgently on D-Day in reaction to our successes in Normandy. One reached Bethnal Green, where it killed six people and injured nine; the others caused no casualties. Nothing further happened until late on June 15, when the Germans started their campaign of "Retaliation" (Vergeltung) in earnest. More than 200 of the missiles came against us within twenty-four hours, and over 3,000 were to follow in the next five weeks.

The flying bomb, as we came to call it, was named V-1 by Hitler, since he hoped—with some reason—that it was only the first of a series of terror weapons which German research would provide. To Londoners the new weapon was soon known as the "doodle-bug," or "buzz bomb," from the strident sound of its engine, which was a jet of new and ingenious design. The bomb flew at speeds up to 400 miles an hour, and at heights around 3,000 feet, and it carried about a ton of explosive. It was steered by a magnetic compass, and its range was governed by a small propeller, which was driven round by the passage of the bomb through the air. When the propeller had revolved a number of times which corresponded to the distance of London from the launching site the controls of the missile were tripped to make it dive to earth. The blast damage of these weapons was all the more vicious because the bomb usually exploded before penetrating the ground.

This new form of attack imposed upon the people of London a burden perhaps even heavier than the air raids of 1940 and 1941. Suspense and strain were more prolonged. Dawn brought no relief, and cloud no comfort. The man going home in the evening never knew what he would find; his wife, alone all day or with the children, could not be certain of his safe return. The blind, impersonal nature of the missile made the individual on the ground feel helpless. There was little that he could do, no human enemy that he could see shot down.

My daughter Mary was still serving in the Hyde Park Antiaircraft Battery. On the morning of Sunday, June 18, when I was at Chequers, Mrs. Churchill told me she would pay the battery a visit. She found it in action. One bomb had passed over it and demolished a house in the Bayswater Road. While my wife and daughter were standing together on the grass they saw a tiny black object dive out of the clouds, which looked as if it would fall very near Downing Street. My car had gone to collect the letters, and the driver was astonished to see all the passers-by in Parliament Square fall flat on their faces. There was a dull explosion nearby and everyone went on their business.

The bomb had fallen on the Guards Chapel at Wellington Barracks quite close to Buckingham Palace. A special service for which a large number of members of the Brigade, active and retired, had gathered was going on. There was a direct hit. The whole building was demolished in a second, and nearly 200 Guardsmen, including many distinguished officers, and their relations and friends were left killed or maimed under the ruins. This was a tragic event. I was still in bed working at my boxes when my wife returned. "The battery has been in action," she said, "and the Guards Chapel is destroyed."

I gave directions at once that the Commons should retire again to the Church House, whose modern steel structure offered somewhat more protection than the Palace of Westminster. This involved a lot of messages and rearrangements. We had a brief interlude in Secret Session, and a Member indignantly asked, "Why have we come back here?" Before I could reply another Member intervened. "If the honorable gentleman will walk a few hundred yards to Birdcage Walk he will see the reason.'' There was a long silence and the matter dropped.

As the days passed, every borough in London was hit. About 750,000 houses were damaged, 23,000 of them beyond repair. But although London was the worst sufferer the casualties and the damage spread well outside its bounds. Parts of Sussex and Kent, popularly known as ''Bomb Alley'' because they lay on the line of route, paid a heavy toll; and bombs, although all were aimed at Tower Bridge, fell far and wide over the countryside from Hampshire to Suffolk. One landed near my home at Westerham, killing, by a cruel mischance, twenty-two homeless children and five grown-ups collected in a refuge made for them in the woods.

OUR Intelligence had accurately foretold six months before how the missiles would perform, but we had not found it easy to prepare fighter and gun defences of adequate quality. Hitler had in fact believed, from trials he had witnessed of a captured Spitfire against a flying bomb, that our fighters would be useless. Our timely warning enabled us to disappoint him, but only by a narrow margin. Our fastest fighters, specially stripped and with added power, could barely overtake the speediest missiles. Many bombs did not fly as fast as their makers intended, but even so it was often difficult for our fighters to catch them in time. To make things worse, the enemy fired the bombs in salvoes, in the hope of saturating our defences. Our normal procedure of ''scrambling'' was too slow, and so the fighters had to fly standing patrols, finding and chasing their quarry with the help of instructions and running commentaries from radar stations and Observer Corps posts on the ground. The flying bombs were much smaller than normal aircraft, and so they were difficult either to see or hit. There were poor chances of a ''kill'' from much more than 300 yards; but it was dangerous to open fire from less than 200 yards, because the exploding bomb might destroy the attacking fighter.

The red flame of their exhausts made the bombs easier to see in the dark, and during the first two nights our antiaircraft batteries in London fired on them and claimed to have brought many down. This tended to serve the enemy's purpose, since some of the missiles might otherwise have fallen in open country beyond the capital. Firing in the Metropolitan area was therefore stopped, and by June 21 the guns had moved to an advanced line on the North Downs. Many of the bombs flew at heights which we at first thought would be awkward for the guns, rather too low for the heavies and too high for the others; but fortunately it proved possible to use the heavies against lower targets than we had previously thought.

We had realised of course that some bombs would escape both fighters and guns, and these we tried to parry by a vast balloon barrage deployed to the south and southeast of London. In the course of the campaign the barrage did in fact catch 232 bombs, each of which would almost inevitably have fallen somewhere in the London area.

''We shall not,'' I said in the House of Commons, ''allow the battle operations in Normandy nor the attacks we are making against special targets in Germany to suffer. They come first, and we must fit our own domestic arrangements into the general scheme of war operations. It may be a comfort to some to feel that they are sharing in no small degree the perils of our soldiers overseas.''

We now know that Hitler had thought that the new weapon would be ''decisive'' in fashioning his own distorted version of peace. Even his military advisers, who were less obsessed than their master, hoped that London's agony would cause some of our armies to be diverted to a disastrous landing in the Pas-de-Calais in an attempt to capture the launching sites. But neither London nor the Government flinched, and I had been able to assure General Eisenhower on June 18 that we would bear the ordeal to the end, asking for no change in his strategy in France.

Our bombing attacks on launching sites went on for a time, but it was clear before the end of June that these were now poor targets. Bomber Command, anxious to share more effectively in relieving London, sought better ones; and they were soon found. The main storage depots for the flying bombs in France now lay in a few large natural caverns around Paris, long exploited by French mushroom growers. One of these caverns, at St.-Leu-d'Esserent, in the Oise valley, was rated by the Germans to store 2,000 bombs, and it had supplied 70 per cent of all the bombs fired in June. Early in July it was largely destroyed by Bomber Command, using some of their heaviest bombs to crush the roof in. Another, rated to hold 1,000, was smashed by American bombers. We know that at least 300 flying bombs were irretrievably buried in this one cavern. London was spared all these, and the Germans were forced to use bombs of a type which they had previously condemned as unsatisfactory.

Our bombers did not achieve their success without loss. Of all our forces they were the earliest engaged against the flying bombs. They had attacked research centres and factories in Germany, and launching sites and supply depots in France. By the end of the campaign nearly 2,000 airmen of British and Allied bombers had died in London's defence.

AT the headquarters of Air Defence of Great Britain much thought had been given to the roles of fighters and guns. Our dispositions had seemed sensible: fighters ranging out over the sea and most of Kent and Sussex, where the bombs were dispersed, and guns concentrated in a belt nearer London, where the bombs drew into a more compact front as they approached their target. This seemed to give each method of defence its best chance, and it was no surprise that in the first few weeks of the campaign, as indeed in all other campaigns previously, the fighters had much more success than the guns.

By the second week of July however General Pile, the General Officer commanding Antiaircraft Command, and some discerning experts came to the conclusion that the guns could do very much better without undue prejudice to the success of the fighters if the batteries were moved on to the coast. Their radar for fire control would have more scope, and it would be safer to use the proximity-fused shells which were now arriving from America. These shells, which were designed to explode as they passed near the target, were dangerous to use over land, since if they missed the target badly they did not explode until they fell to earth. We had not been sure if the guns could use their radar on the coast, owing to the danger of enemy jamming, but so good had been our Intelligence, and so accurate our bombing, that by D-Day we had put all the German jamming stations out of action. It was nevertheless a grave decision to uproot the enormous Anti-aircraft organisation from the North Downs and to redeploy it on the coast, knowing that this might spoil the success of the fighters.

The new deployment of our weapons was a vast undertaking, and it was executed with the most praiseworthy speed. Nearly 400 heavy and 600 Bofors guns had to be moved and re-sited. Three thousand miles of telephone cable were laid. Twenty-three thousand men and women were moved, and the vehicles of Antiaircraft Command travelled over 2,750,000 miles in a week. In four days the move to the coast was completed.

The whole vast operation was decided upon and carried out on their own responsibility by Air Marshal Hill, who commanded the Air Defence of Great Britain, and General Pile, with the approval of Duncan Sandys. For a few days after the re-deployment our combined defences caught far fewer bombs, mainly because the fighters were much hampered by the new restrictions on their movement. But this setback did not last long. The guns soon got their grip, and the results improved rapidly. With the new radar and predicting equipment, and above all with the new proximity fuses, all of which we had asked for from America six months before, the performance of the gunners exceeded all our hopes. By the end of August not more than one bomb in seven got through to the London area. The record "bag" was on August 28, when ninety-four bombs approached our coast and all but four were destroyed. The balloons caught two, the fighters twenty-three, and the guns sixty-five. The V-1 had been mastered.

The Germans, who keenly watched the performance of our guns from across the Channel, were completely bewildered by the success of our artillery. They had still not solved the mystery when their launching sites were overwhelmed in the first week of September by the victorious and rapid advance of the British and the Canadian armies from Normandy to Antwerp. Although the Germans thereafter irritated us from time to time with flying bombs launched from aircraft, and with a few long-range bombs from Holland, the threat was thenceforward insignificant. In all about 8,000 bombs were launched against London, and about 2,400 of these got through. Our total civilian casualties were 6,184 killed and 17,981 seriously injured. These figures, however, do not tell the whole

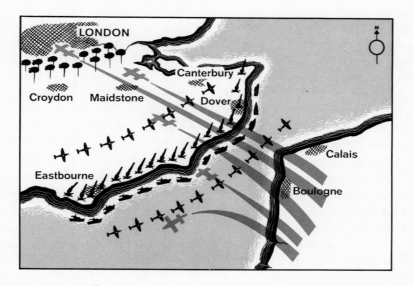

V-1 defense by British consisted of planes attacking flying bombs over Channel and inland, A.A. guns shooting them down over the coast and balloons snaring them in air near London. Of some 8,000 bombs released in 1944, only 30% penetrated this defense.

story. Many people, though wounded, did not have to stay in hospital, and their sufferings have gone unrecorded.

A second threat drew near. This was the long-range rocket, or V-2, with which we had been so preoccupied twelve months before. The Germans however had found it difficult to perfect, and in the meantime it had been overtaken by the flying bomb. But almost as soon as the bombs began to hit us the signs appeared that a rocket assault was also approaching. The weight of the rocket and its war head became subjects of high dispute. Certain early but doubtful Intelligence reports had suggested war heads of five to ten tons, and these were seized upon by those of our experts who believed on other grounds that such weights were reasonable. Some believed that the rocket would weight eighty tons, with a ten-ton war head. Lord Cherwell, now strongly vindicated in his stand for the flying bomb in June 1943, even before there were any indications from Intelligence, was very doubtful whether we should ever see the rocket in operation at all, and certainly not the monster of eighty tons. Between the extremes there were a few Intelligence reports which suggested a much lighter rocket than eighty tons; but, with all the controversy, anxiety remained acute.

We knew that work was continuing at Peenemünde, and sparse reports from the Continent renewed our concern about the scale and imminence of the attack. On July 18 Dr. Jones informed us that there might well be a thousand rockets already in existence. On July 27 the Cabinet considered proposals by Mr. Herbert Morrison, Home Secretary and Minister of Home Security, which would have involved evacuating about a million people from London.

Every effort was made to complete the remaining gaps in our knowledge about the size, performance, and characteristics of the rocket. Fragmentary evidence from many sources was pieced together by our Intelligence services. From this it was deduced that the rocket weighed twelve tons, with a one-ton war head. This light weight explained many things that had puzzled us, such as the absence of elaborate launching arrangements. These calculations were confirmed when the Royal Aircraft Establishment had the opportunity to examine the wreckage of an actual rocket. It came into our hands as the result of a lucky and freak error in the trials at Peenemünde on June 13, and according to a prisoner the explanation was as follows. For some time the Germans had been using glider bombs against our shipping. These were launched from aircraft and guided to the target by radio. It was now decided to see whether a rocket could be steered in the same way. An expert operator was obtained, and placed in a good position to watch the missile from the start. The Peenemünde experimenters were well accustomed to seeing a rocket rise, and it had not occurred to them that the glider-bomb expert would be surprised by the spectacle. But surprised he was, so much so that he forgot his own part in the procedure. In his astonishment he pushed the control lever well off to the left and held it there. The rocket obediently kept turning to the left, and by the time the operator had pulled himself together it was out of control range and heading for Sweden. There it fell. We soon heard about it, and after some negotiations the remains were brought to Farnborough, where our experts sorted out the battered fragments with noteworthy success.

THE rocket was an impressive technical achievement. Its thrust was developed in a jet from the combustion of alcohol and liquid oxygen, nearly four tons of the former and five of the latter being consumed in about a minute. To force these fuels into the jet chamber at the required rate needed a special pump of nearly a thousand horsepower. The pump in its turn was worked by a turbine driven by hydrogen peroxide. The rocket was controlled by gyroscopes or by radio signals operating on large graphite vanes placed behind the jet to deflect the exhaust gases and so steer the rocket. The rocket first rose vertically for six miles or so, and automatic controls then turned it over to climb with increasing speed at about forty-five degrees. When the speed was sufficient for the desired range further controls cut off the fuels from the jet, and the missile then flew in a gigantic parabola, reaching a height of about fifty miles and falling about 200 miles away from the launching point. Its top speed was about 4,000 miles an hour, and the whole flight took no more than three or four minutes.

At the end of August it seemed that our armies might expel the enemy from all territory within the 200-mile range of the rocket from London, but he managed to hold Walcheren and The Hague. On September 8, a week after the main V-1 bombardment ceased, the Germans launched their first two rockets against London. The first V-2 fell at Chiswick at seventeen minutes to seven in the evening, the other at Epping sixteen seconds later. About 1,300 were fired against England in the seven months before our armies could liberate The Hague, whence most rockets were launched. Many fell short, but about 500 hit London. The total casualties caused by the V-2 in England were 2,724 killed and 6,476 seriously injured. On the average each rocket caused about twice as many casualties as a flying bomb. Although the war heads were of much the same size, the strident engine of the flying bomb warned people to take cover. The rocket approached in silence.

Many countermeasures were tried, and still more were explored. The raid on Peenemünde over a year before did more than everything else to alleviate the threat. The V-2 attack would otherwise have started at least as early as the V-1 attack, and it would have been from a shorter range, and therefore more accurate in June than it was in September and after. The United States Air Force continued to bomb Peenemünde in July and August, and both they and Bomber Command attacked factories making rocket components. We owe it to our armies that they had pushed the rocket back to the limit of its range before the Germans were at last ready to open fire. Our fighters and tactical bombers continually worried the launching points near The Hague. We made ready to jam the radio control of the rockets, should the Germans use it, and we even considered attempting to burst the rockets in the air by gunfire as they fell.

Our efforts confined the attack to four or five hundred rockets a month, shared between London and the Continent, compared with an intended rate of 900. Thus, although we could do little against the rocket once it was launched, we postponed and substantially reduced the weight of the onslaught. About 200 rockets a month were aimed against London, most of the rest against Antwerp, and a few against other Continental targets. The enemy made no mention of his new missiles until November 8, and I did not feel the need for a public statement until November 10. I was then able to assure the House that the scale and effects of the attack had not hitherto been serious. This fortunately continued to be true throughout the remaining months of the war.

Despite the great technical achievements, Speer, the highly competent German Minister of Munitions, deplored the effort that had gone into making rockets. He asserted that each one took as long to produce as six or seven fighters, which would have been far more useful, and that twenty flying bombs could have been made for the cost of one rocket. This postwar information confirms the views Lord Cherwell had so often expressed before the event.

It was fortunate that the Germans spent so much effort on rockets instead of on bombers. Even our Mosquitoes, each one of which was probably no dearer than a rocket, dropped on the average 125 tons of bombs per aircraft within one mile of the target during their life, whereas the rocket dropped one ton only, and that with an average error of fifteen miles.

WHILE I have here recorded the story of Hitler's "Retaliation" campaign against England, we must not forget that Belgium suffered with equal bitterness when the Germans attempted to use the same vindictive weapons against her liberated cities. We did not of course allow the German attack to go unparried. Our bombing of German production centres, and other targets, happily reduced the scale of effort against Belgium as much as against ourselves; but it was not easy to re-deploy fighter and gun defences, with all their elaborate control, in the newly won territories. German records show that by the end of the war Antwerp had been the target for 8,696 flying bombs and 1,610 rockets. Of all these 5,960 fell within eight miles of the city centre, and between them they killed 3,470 Belgian citizens and 682 Allied Servicemen. A further 3,141 flying bombs were aimed against Liége, and 151 rockets against Brussels. The people of Belgium bore this senseless bombardment in a spirit equal to our own.

Such is the tale of the new weapons on which Hitler pinned his stubborn hopes for many months, and of their defeat by the foresight of the British Administration, the skill of the Services, and the fortitude of the people who, by their conduct for the second time in this war, gave "Greater London" a prouder meaning.

In the deepening dusk, three Stirling bombers of the R.A.F. fly over English farms on their way to drop fire and destruction on Germany

THE AVENGERS

Nightly Rain
of British Bombs

"The Fighters are our salvation, but the Bombers alone provide the means of victory," said Churchill in September 1940. It took 18 months for the R.A.F. to catch up with the Luftwaffe and destroy an area roughly equal to what the Germans had destroyed in England—780 acres. Then began a campaign of systematic destruction. By 1944 the Germans could no longer look forward to a bomb-free night.

The R.A.F. developed night bombing because it had lost too many bombers by day. Except in bright moonlight, this meant it was impossible to aim at a particular target. The crews simply looked for the outlines of a city and assumed that anything they hit within city limits would at least interrupt some war production and shake some civilian morale. In fair weather and foul, the bombers kept coming. Flares, tracers, searchlights, crashing planes and the thick flames of burning cities—all lit up the German sky in a ghastly carnival nights without end. When day came, the American bombers took over (*pages 420-421*).

Converging searchlights pinpoint a British bomber as an antiaircraft crew prepares for the kill. Paintings on these pages are by German artists who had survived the mass raids on Hamburg and Berlin.

Electronic computer is operated by German crew to help plot the size and direction of approaching bomber fleets. Antiaircraft defense and repair work tied down over a million and a half Germans.

A dome of fire (*opposite*), caused by an exploding bomb, appears over Berlin. Such concentrations of flame sometimes set off a "fire storm," igniting every bit of combustible matter within a mile.

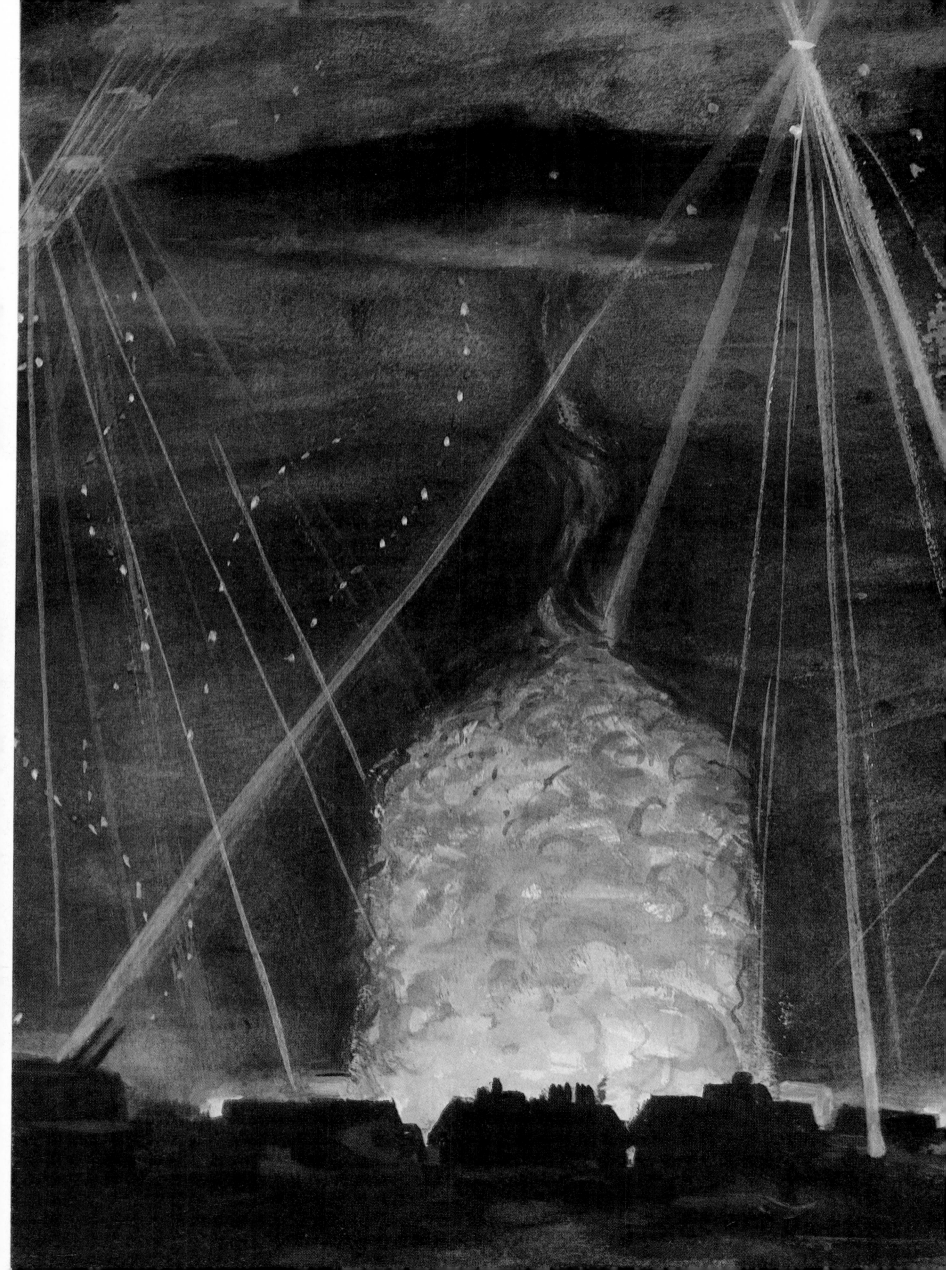

Daylight Punch from U.S. Bombers

On the evening of August 17, 1942, Air Force generals and the Anglo-American press were out in scores along with the ground crews to witness the landing painted below by Peter Hurd. Twelve American B-17s—the first to make a raid on Hitler's Europe—were coming back from a strike at the Rouen railroad yard. They had done some damage—much less than they thought—but the big news was that

all twelve came back. They had proved that daylight bombing with fighter escort was feasible. Coupled with the R.A.F.'s nighttime attacks, this meant that the bombing of Germany could proceed unremittingly around the clock.

As U.S. war production swelled, so did the size of the bomber fleets—to 1,500 and more—which alternated with the British raiders in hitting every corner of the enemy empire. American theory called for pinpointing targets vital to the German war machine. In practice the bombers could not be so precise. To the Germans it made little difference. The factories the Americans missed might be engulfed in the conflagrations set off by British "area" raids. Or the houses the British left standing would tumble down under the misses of American "precision" attacks.

The Daily Drama at the Bases

England's already overcrowded isle seemed to shrink still more as bulldozers levelled off miles of farmland for the runways, the bomb depots and barracks of the U.S. Eighth Air Force, the biggest of the overseas air commands. Each base was virtually a self-contained American community with as many as 1,000 men to fly the big bombers and as many more to arm and fuel and repair them.

Every day when the weather was not hopeless was a day of battle. The big B-17s and B-24s took off at three-minute intervals and gathered in huge formations at rendezvous points off the coast, where they picked up fighter escorts. As they passed the coasts of Europe, black puffs of anti-aircraft fire began appearing among the formations. On the bombers went, sometimes to the furthest corners of Germany, and in that case it might take them eight hours to return. When they got back, the fliers were greeted by the ground crews with boisterous receptions and their planes were decorated anew with painted swastikas, one for each Luftwaffe fighter the bomber gunners had shot down (the numbers generally were wildly exaggerated).

Many did not come back. In the long hours through the murderous "Flak Alleys" and amid the swarms of German fighters, the bombers often suffered losses greater than the five percent considered the maximum they could bear. Altogether, 9,949 American bombers went down over German-held territory, and nearly 70,000 Americans died in them.

Dejected crew of ground mechanics, after waiting three hours in the hope their bomber might return from its mission, walk off in resignation, carrying with them their replacement parts and tool boxes.

Flying mascots, a dog and a monkey, ham it up with the crew of a B-17 named Honey Chile. Several animals with improvised oxygen masks went on raids, although the Air Force frowned on the practice.

Wounded flier (*below*), hurriedly treated beneath his returned plane, is given plasma at an English base. He had lost much blood since he was wounded in a bombing mission over Bremen, 375 miles away.

Exuberant reunion of flight and ground crews marks the end of a successful raid. In the background, a flier indicates where a new bomb will be added to the record of the plane's successful missions.

Ceremonial dunking in a water-filled trailer is given a pilot who has beaten the law of averages and safely completed his twenty-sixth mission. Now he can finish his Air Force service on the ground.

High above Germany, a flight of B-17s—here painted by Floyd Davis—drones above the clouds amid vicious bursts of German flak on the way to Hamburg. The stepped formation gave the maximum sweep of bomber guns against German fighters, and the sheer size of sky-filling raids like this swamped the German defenses. Hamburg was pulverized by four days of combined day and night attacks in midsummer of 1943. This was the deadliest stroke of the whole strategic-bombing campaign. It killed over 60,000 civilians, destroyed nearly two-thirds of the city's buildings, and knocked out the ship-building and other war industries of Germany's second city for almost five months.

The Brand the Bombers Left

When the Eighth Air Force took its ground crews on an aerial tour of Europe after the German surrender, it offered them a view of the most colossal devastation ever performed by man. The five billion pounds of high explosive dropped by the British and American heavy bombers had wrecked one out of every five buildings in Germany and killed more than 300,000 civilians. Appallingly impressive as these results were, they fell short of the aims of the strategic bombing advocates who had confidently expected to knock Germany out of the war by their own efforts. Like the Luftwaffe in 1940, the Allied air forces underestimated both the resiliency of bombed industry and the toughness of bombed civilians. Only in the last months of the fighting did strategic bombing succeed in delivering mortal blows to the German war machine—and by that time the war had been won on the ground.

Black smoke at Ploesti, almost 500 miles inside enemy territory, marks the bold strike in August 1943 by unescorted B-24s which tried—with limited success—to cut Hitler's Romanian oil supply.

Total ruin at Wesel (*opposite*) leaves only a faint ribbon of railroad track (*foreground*) and a few stone walls to mark the site of a thriving town and key staging point for the German Army on the Rhine.

D-Day armada heads for Normandy under a canopy of barrage balloons. Composed of more than 4,000 U.S., British, Canadian, French, Dutch and Norwegian ships, it was the largest fleet ever assembled in the history of war.

18

THE LIBERATION OF FRANCE

Preparations for 'Overlord'

THOUGHT arising from factual experience may be a bridle or a spur. The reader will be aware that while I was always willing to join with the United States in a direct assault across the Channel on the German sea front in France, I was not convinced that this was the only way of winning the war, and I knew that it would be a very heavy and hazardous adventure. The fearful price we had had to pay in human life and blood for the great offensives of the First World War was graven in my mind. Memories of the Somme and Passchendaele and many lesser frontal attacks upon the Germans were not to be blotted out by time or reflection. It still seemed to me, after a quarter of a century, that fortifications of concrete and steel armed with modern firepower, and fully manned by trained, resolute men, could only be overcome by surprise in time or place by turning their flanks, or by some new and mechanical device like the tank. Superiority of bombardment, terrific as it may be, was no final answer. The defenders could easily have ready other lines behind their first, and the intervening ground which the artillery could conquer would become impassable crater-fields. These were the fruits of knowledge which the French and British had bought so dearly from 1915 to 1917.

Since then new factors had appeared, but they did not all tell the same way. The firepower of the defence had

vastly increased. The development of mine fields both on land and in the sea was enormous. On the other hand, we, the attackers, held air supremacy, and could land large numbers of paratroops behind the enemy's front, and above all block and paralyse the communications by which he could bring reinforcements for a counterattack.

Throughout the summer months of 1943 General Morgan and his Allied Inter-Service Staff had laboured at the plan. In a previous chapter I have described how it was presented to me during my voyage to Quebec for the "Quadrant" Conference with Mr. Roosevelt. There the scheme was generally approved, but there was one feature of it which requires comment. The size and scope of the first assault on the Normandy beaches was necessarily and inevitably limited by the numbers of landing craft available. General Morgan's instructions were to plan an assault by three divisions, with two divisions as an immediate follow-up. He accordingly proposed to land the three divisions on the coast between Caen and Carentan. He would have liked to land part of the force north of Carentan, nearer to Cherbourg, but he thought it unwise to divide so small a force. The estuary of the river Vire at Carentan was marshy and it would have been difficult for the two wings of the attack to keep in touch. No doubt he was right. I would certainly have preferred a stronger attack on a broader front, but at that time, ten months before the event, we could not be sure of having enough landing craft.

It was the absence of important harbours in all this stretch of coast which had impelled Mountbatten's staff to propose the synthetic harbours. The decisions at Quebec confirmed the need and clarified the issues. I kept in close touch with the development of this project, which was pressed forward by a committee of experts and Service representatives, summoned by Brigadier Bruce White of the War Office, himself an eminent civil engineer. It was a tremendous undertaking, and high credit is due to many, not least to Major-General Sir Harold Wernher, whose task it was to co-ordinate the many interests concerned. Here too should be mentioned "Pluto," the submarine pipelines which carried petrol from the Isle of Wight to Normandy and later from Dungeness to Calais. This idea and many others owed much to Mountbatten's staff. Space forbids description of the many contrivances devised to overcome the formidable obstacles and minefields guarding the beaches. Some were fitted to our tanks to protect their crews; others served the landing craft. All these matters aroused my personal interest, and, when it seemed necessary, my intervention. General Morgan and his staff were well content with the approval given at the Quebec Conference to their proposals. The troops could now begin their training and their special equipment could be made. For this Morgan had been given powers greater than a Staff officer usually wields.

The discussions which resulted in the appointment of General Eisenhower to the Supreme Command of the Allied Forces and of General Montgomery to command the expeditionary army have been related. Eisenhower's Deputy was Air Chief Marshal Tedder. Air Marshal Leigh-Mallory was appointed to the Air and Admiral Ramsay to the Naval Command. General Eisenhower brought with him General Bedell Smith as his Chief of Staff, to whom General Morgan was appointed Deputy.

Eisenhower and Montgomery disagreed with one important feature of the plan. They wanted an assault in greater strength and on a wider front, so as to gain quickly a good-sized bridgehead in which to build up their forces for the break-out. Also it was important to capture the Cherbourg docks earlier than had been planned. They wanted a first assault by five divisions instead of three. Of course this was perfectly right. General Morgan himself had advocated an extension of the initial landing, but had not been given enough resources. But where were the extra landing craft to come from? Southeast Asia had already been stripped.

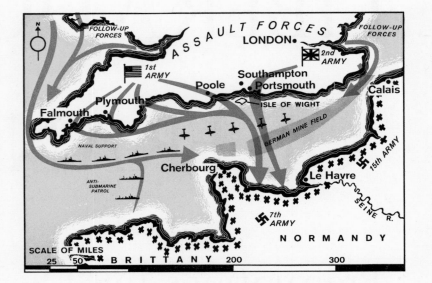

Invasion strategy for Normandy called for first wave of two Allied armies (*red*) to sail from England's south coast and cross Channel through gaps swept in German mine field. Meanwhile, naval and air support would soften up German defenses and keep off U-boats.

There were sufficient in the Mediterranean to carry two divisions, but these were needed for "Anvil," the seaborne assault on Southern France which was to take place at the same time as "Overlord" and draw German troops away from the battlefields in the North. If "Anvil" were to be reduced it would be too weak to be helpful. It was not until March that General Eisenhower, in conference with the British Chiefs of Staff, made his final decision. The American Chiefs of Staff had agreed that he should speak for them. Having recently come from the Mediterranean, he knew all about "Anvil," and now as Supreme Commander of "Overlord" he could best judge the needs of both. It was agreed to take the ships of one division from "Anvil" and to employ them for "Overlord." The ships for a second division could be found by putting off Operation "Overlord" until the period of the June moon. The output of all our new landing craft in that month would fill the gap. As for the additional troops needed, Britain and the United States would each contribute one division to bring the total up to five, and the United States also agreed to provide naval support for their extra division. Thus the naval forces allocated to the operation were roughly 80 per cent British and 20 per cent American. Planning now went ahead on this revised and greatly improved foundation. Once the size of the expedition had been determined it was possible to go ahead with intensive training. Not the least of our difficulties was to find enough room. A broad partition was arranged between British and American forces, whereby the British occupied the southeastern and the Americans the southwestern parts of England. The inhabitants of coastal areas accepted all the inconveniences in good part. One British division with its naval counterpart did all its earlier training in the Moray Firth area in Scotland. The winter storms prepared them for the rough-and-tumble of D-Day.

The theory and practice of amphibious operations had long been established by the Combined Operations Staff, under Admiral Mountbatten, who had been succeeded by General Laycock. It had now to be taught to all concerned, in addition to the thorough general training needed for modern warfare. This of course had long been going on in Britain and America in exercises great and small with live ammunition. Many officers and men entered into battle for the first time, but all bore themselves like seasoned troops.

Lessons from previous large-scale exercises, and of course from our hard experience at Dieppe, were applied in final rehearsals by all three Services, which culminated in early May. All this activity did not pass unnoticed by the enemy.

We did not object, and special pains were taken that they should be remarked by watchers in the Pas-de-Calais, where we wanted the Germans to believe we were coming.

Our plans had to be altered and kept up to date as fresh information came in about the enemy. We knew the general layout of his troops and his principal defences, the gun positions, the strong points and entrenchments along the coast, but after Rommel took command in late January great additions and refinements began to appear. In particular we had to discover any new types of obstacle that might be installed, and contrive the antidote.

Constant air reconnaissance kept us informed of what was going on across the Channel. And of course there were other ways of finding out. Many trips were made by parties in small craft to resolve some doubtful point, to take soundings inshore, to examine new obstacles, or to test the slope and nature of a beach. All this had to be done in darkness, with silent approach, stealthy reconnaissance, and timely withdrawal.

An intricate decision was the choice of D-Day and H-Hour, the moment at which the leading assault craft should hit the beach. From this many other timings had to be worked backwards. It was agreed to approach the enemy coast by moonlight, because this would help both our ships and our airborne troops. A short period of daylight before H-Hour was also needed to give order to the deployment of the small craft and accuracy to the covering bombardment. But if the interval between first light and H-Hour was too long the enemy would have more time to recover from their surprise and fire on our troops in the act of landing.

Then there were the tides. If we landed at high tide the underwater obstacles would obstruct the approach; if at low tide the troops would have far to go across the exposed beaches. Many other factors had to be considered, and it was finally decided to land about three hours before high water. But this was not all. The tides varied by forty minutes between the eastern and western beaches, and there was a submerged reef in one of the British sectors. Each sector had to have a different H-Hour, which varied from one place to another by as much as eighty-five minutes.

Only on three days in each lunar month were all the desired conditions fulfilled. The first three-day period after May 31, General Eisenhower's target date, was June 5, 6, and 7. Thus was June 5 chosen. If the weather were not propitious on any of those three days the whole operation would have to be postponed at least a fortnight—indeed, a whole month if we waited for the moon.

†   †   †

By April our plans were taking final shape. From the embarkation ports, stretching from Felixstowe on the east to the Bristol Channel on the west, shipping would be brought coastwise in convoy to a rendezvous near the Isle of Wight. From here the vast armada would sail to Normandy. Twenty-nine flotillas of mine sweepers were assembled, amounting to about 350 craft, who would sweep ten separate channels through the enemy mine barrier. Because of the great congestion in our southern ports and to help our deception plans, the heavy naval bombarding forces would assemble in the Clyde and at Belfast. Of course we had not only to plan for what we were really going to do. The enemy were bound to know that a great invasion was being prepared; we had to conceal the place and time of attack and make him think we were landing somewhere else and at a different moment. This alone involved an immense amount of thought and action. Coastal areas were banned to visitors; censorship was tightened; letters after a certain date were held back from delivery; foreign embassies were forbidden to send cipher telegrams, and even their diplomatic bags were delayed.

Our major deception was to pretend that we were coming across the Strait of Dover. It would not be proper even now to describe all the methods employed to mislead the enemy, but the obvious ones of simulated concentrations of troops in Kent and Sussex, of fleets of dummy ships collected in the Cinque Ports, of landing exercises on the nearby beaches, of increased wireless activity, were all used. More reconnaissances were made at or over the places we were *not* going to than at the places we were. The final result was admirable. The German High Command firmly believed the evidence we put at their disposal. Field-Marshal Karl von Rundstedt, the Commander-in-Chief on the Western Front, was convinced that the Pas-de-Calais was our objective.

THE concentration of the assaulting forces—176,000 men, 20,000 vehicles, and many thousand tons of stores, all to be shipped in the first two days—was in itself an enormous task. It was handled principally by the War Office and the railway authorities, and with great success. From their normal stations all over Britain the troops were brought to the southern counties, into areas stretching from Ipswich round to Cornwall and the Bristol Channel. The three airborne divisions which were to drop on Normandy before the sea assault were assembled close to the airfields whence they would set out. From their concentration areas in rear troops were brought forward for embarkation in assigned priority to camps in marshalling areas near the coast. At the marshalling camps they were divided up into detachments corresponding to the ship- or boat-loads in which they would be embarked. Here every man received his orders. Once briefed, none were permitted to leave camp. The camps themselves were situated near to the embarkation points. These were ports or "hards"—*i.e.*, stretches of beach concreted to allow of easy embarkation on smaller craft. Here they were to be met by the naval ships.

It seemed most improbable that all this movement by sea and land would escape the attentions of the enemy. There were many tempting targets for their Air, and full precautions were taken. Nearly seven thousand guns and rockets and over a thousand balloons protected the great masses of men and vehicles. But there was no sign of the Luftwaffe. How different things were four years before! The Home Guard, who had so patiently waited for a worthwhile job all those years, now found it. Not only were they manning sections of antiaircraft and coast defences, but they also took over many routine and security duties, thus releasing other soldiers for battle.

All Southern England thus became a vast military camp, filled with men trained, instructed, and eager to come to grips with the Germans across the water.

On The Eve

EVENTS now began to move swiftly and smoothly to the climax. On May 15 His Majesty visited each of the assault forces at their ports of assembly. On May 28 subordinate commanders were informed that D-Day would be June 5. From this moment all personnel committed to the assault were "sealed" in their ships or at their camps and assembly points ashore. All mail was impounded and private messages of all kinds forbidden except in case of personal emergency. On June 1 Admiral Ramsay assumed control of operations in the Channel, the functions of the naval Commanders-in-Chief in the home ports being subordinated to his requirements.

I thought it would not be wrong for me to watch the preliminary bombardment in this historic battle from one of our cruiser squadrons, and I asked Admiral Ramsay to make a plan. He arranged for me to embark in H.M.S. *Belfast*, in the late afternoon of the day before D-Day. She was one of the bombarding ships attached to the centre British force, and I would spend the night in her and watch the dawn attack. I was then to make a short tour of the beaches, with due regard to the unswept mine areas, and come back in a destroyer.

Admiral Ramsay felt it his duty however to tell the Supreme Commander of what was in the air. Eisenhower protested against my running such risks. As Supreme Commander he could not bear the responsibility. I sent him word, as he has described, that while we accepted him as Supreme Commander of the British forces involved, which in the case of the Navy were four to one compared with those of the United States, we did not in any way admit his right to regulate the complements of the British ships in the Royal Navy. He accepted this undoubted fact, but dwelt on the addition this would impose upon his anxieties. This appeared to be out of proportion both to the scale of events and to our relations. I too had responsibilities, and felt I must be my own judge of my movements. The matter was settled accordingly.

However, a complication occurred which I have His late Majesty's permission to recount. When I attended my weekly luncheon with the King on Tuesday, May 30, His Majesty asked me where I intended to be on D-Day. I replied that I proposed to witness the bombardment from one of the cruiser squadrons. His Majesty immediately said he would like to come too. He had not been under fire except in air raids since the Battle of Jutland, and eagerly welcomed the prospect of renewing the experiences of his youth. I thought about this carefully, and was not unwilling to submit the matter to the Cabinet. It was agreed to discuss the matter with Admiral Ramsay first.

Meanwhile the King came to the conclusion that neither he nor I ought to go. He was greatly disappointed, and wrote me the following letter:

BUCKINGHAM PALACE
May 31, 1944

MY DEAR WINSTON,

I have been thinking a great deal of our conversation yesterday, and I have come to the conclusion that it would not be right for either you or I to be where we planned to be on D-Day. I don't think I need emphasise what it would mean to me personally, and to the whole Allied cause, if at this juncture a chance bomb, torpedo, or even a mine, should remove you from the scene; equally a change of Sovereign at this moment would be a serious matter for the country and Empire. We should both, I know, love to be there, but in all seriousness I would ask you to reconsider your plan. Our presence, I feel, would be an embarrassment to those responsible for fighting the ship or ships in which we were, despite anything we might say to them.

So, as I said, I have very reluctantly come to the conclusion that the right thing to do is what normally falls to those at the top on such occasions, namely, to remain at home and wait. I hope very much that you will see it in this light too. The anxiety of these coming days would be very greatly increased for me if I thought that, in addition to everything else, there was a risk, however remote, of my losing your help and guidance.

Believe me, Yours very sincerely,
GEORGE R.I.

At 3:15 p.m. on June 1 the King, with Sir Alan Lascelles in attendance, came to the Map Room at the Annexe, where I and Admiral Ramsay awaited him. The Admiral, who did not then know that there was any idea of the King coming, explained what the *Belfast* would do on the morning of D-Day. It was clear from what he said that those on board the ship would run considerable risks, and also would see very little of the battle. The Admiral was then asked to withdraw for a few minutes, during which it was decided to ask his opinion on the advisability of His Majesty also going to sea in the *Belfast*. The Admiral immediately made it clear that he was not in favour of this. The King said that if it was not right for him to go neither was it right for me. I replied I was going as Minister of Defence in the exercise of my duty. Sir Alan Lascelles, who the King remarked was "wearing a very long face," said that "His Majesty's anxieties would be increased if he heard his Prime Minister was at the bottom of the English Channel." I replied that that was all arranged for, and that moreover I considered the risk negligible. The King then returned to Buckingham Palace.

On the morning of Friday, June 2, I set out in my train for our siding by Eisenhower's headquarters near Portsmouth, with Field-Marshal Smuts, Mr. Ernest Bevin, General Ismay, and my personal staff. Just before we started a further letter arrived.

BUCKINGHAM PALACE
June 2, 1944

MY DEAR WINSTON,

I want to make one more appeal to you not to go to sea on D-Day. Please consider my own position. I am a younger man than you, I am a sailor, and as King I am the head of all these Services. There is nothing I would like better than to go to sea, but I have agreed to stay at home; is it fair that you should then do exactly what I should have liked to do myself? You said yesterday afternoon that it would be a fine thing for the King to lead his troops into battle, as in old days; if the King cannot do this, it does not seem to me right that his Prime Minister should take his place.

Then there is your own position. You will see very little, you will run a considerable risk, you will be inaccessible at a critical time, when vital decisions might have to be taken, and however unobtrusive you may be your mere presence on board is bound to be a very heavy additional responsibility to the Admiral and Captain. As I said in my previous letter, your being there would add immeasurably to my anxieties, and your going without consulting your colleagues in the Cabinet would put them in a very difficult position, which they would justifiably resent.

I ask you most earnestly to consider the whole question again, and not let your personal wishes, which I very well understand, lead you to depart from your own high standard of duty to the State.

Believe me, Your very sincere friend,
George R.I.

Meanwhile my train lay just outside Southampton, and we were soon connected by telephone with Eisenhower's headquarters. That afternoon we paid him a visit. His tents and caravans were very well concealed in a wood near by. His Majesty was concerned at not having had a reply from me to his letter. At 11:30 p.m., in response to inquiries, I spoke to Lascelles at Windsor Castle on the scrambler telephone, and said that I had cancelled my arrangements in deference to His Majesty's desire. I wrote the following letter in the small hours of the morning and sent it at once by dispatch-rider to Windsor.

June 3, 1944

Sir,

I must excuse myself for not having answered Your Majesty's letter earlier. It caught me just as I was leaving by the train, and I have been in constant movement ever since. I had a dispatch-rider standing by in order to take it to you to-night.

Sir, I cannot really feel that the first paragraph of your letter takes sufficient account of the fact that there is absolutely no comparison in the British Constitution between a Sovereign and a subject. If Your Majesty had gone, as you desire, on board one of your ships in this bombarding action it would have required the Cabinet approval beforehand, and I am very much inclined to think, as I told you, that the Cabinet would have advised most strongly against Your Majesty going.

On the other hand, as Prime Minister and Minister of Defence I ought to be allowed to go where I consider it necessary to the discharge of my duty, and I do not admit that the Cabinet have any right to put restrictions on my freedom of movement. I rely on my own judgment, invoked in many serious matters, as to what are the proper limits of risk which a person who discharges my duties is entitled to run. I must most earnestly ask Your Majesty that no principle shall be laid down which inhibits my freedom of movement when I judge it necessary to acquaint myself with conditions in the various theatres of war. Since Your Majesty does me the honour to be so much concerned about my personal safety on this occasion, I must defer to Your Majesty's wishes, and indeed commands. It is a great comfort to me to know that they arise from Your Majesty's desire to continue me in your service. Though I regret that I cannot go, I am deeply grateful to Your Majesty for the motives which have guided Your Majesty in respect of

Your Majesty's humble and devoted servant and subject,
Winston S. Churchill

I may add that the cruiser concerned was, as I had estimated, not exposed to any undue danger. In fact, it did not sustain a single casualty. I should not have referred to this matter if it had not been publicised in a friendly but unwittingly inaccurate form by General Eisenhower.

I MAY here set down the view I have formed over many years on this sort of thing. A man who has to play an effective part in taking, with the highest responsibility, grave and terrible decisions of war may need the refreshment of adventure. He may need also the comfort that when sending so many others to their death he may share in a small way their risks. His field of personal interest, and consequently his forces of action, are stimulated by direct contact with the event. As a result of what I saw and learned in the First World War, I was convinced that generals and other high commanders should try from time to time to see the conditions and aspect of the battle scene themselves. I had seen many grievous errors made through the silly theory that valuable lives should not be endangered. No one was more careful of his personal safety than I was, but I thought my view and theme of the war were sufficiently important and authoritative to entitle me to full freedom of judgment as to how I discharged my task in such a personal matter.

The weather now began to cause anxiety. A fine spell was giving way to unsettled conditions, and from June 1 onwards a commanders' meeting was held twice daily to study the weather reports. At their first meeting poor conditions were predicted for D-Day, with low clouds. This was of prime importance to the Air Forces, affecting both the bombing and the airborne landings. The next evening the first warships sailed from the Clyde, as well as two midget submarines from Portsmouth, whose duty was to mark the assault areas. June 3 brought little encouragement. A rising westerly wind was whipping up a moderate sea; there was heavy cloud and a lowering cloud base. Predictions for June 5 were gloomy.

That afternoon I drove down to Portsmouth harbour with Mr. Ernest Bevin and Field-Marshal Smuts and saw a

---

2 Apr 44

Prime Minister to General Ismay,
for Chiefs of Staff and Vice-Chiefs of Staff

By all means dispose of the antiaircraft defences in the United Kingdom as may be necessary to sustain the "Overlord" ports. You are answerable that reasonable, though reduced, security is provided elsewhere. It is quite understood that the British public will take their share of anything that is going.

---

large number of troops embarking for Normandy. We visited the headquarters ship of the 50th British Division, and then cruised down The Solent in a launch, boarding one ship after another.

On the way back we stopped at General Eisenhower's camp and wished him luck. We got back to the train in time for a very late dinner. While it was in progress Ismay was called to the telephone by Bedell Smith, who told him that the weather was getting worse and that the operation would probably have to be postponed for twenty-four hours. General Eisenhower would wait until the early hours of June 4 before making a definite decision. Meanwhile units of the great armada would continue to put to sea according to programme.

Ismay came back and reported the bleak news. Those who had seen the array in The Solent felt that the vast movement was now as impossible to stop as an avalanche. We were haunted by the knowledge that if the bad weather continued and the postponement had to be prolonged beyond June 7 we could not again get the necessary combination of moon and tide for at least another fortnight. Meanwhile the troops had all been briefed. They clearly could not be kept on board these tiny ships indefinitely. But how was a leakage to be prevented?

We went to bed at about half-past one. Ismay told me that he would wait up to hear the result of the morning conference. As there was nothing I could do about it, I said that I was not to be woken to hear the result. At 4:15 a.m. Eisenhower again met his commanders, and heard from the weather experts the ominous report, sky overcast, cloud ceiling low, strong southwesterly wind, with rain and moderate sea. The forecast for the 5th was even worse. Reluctantly he ordered a postponement of the attack for twenty-four hours, and the whole vast array was put into reverse in accordance with a carefully prepared plan. All convoys at sea turned about and small craft sought shelter in convenient anchorages. Only one large convoy, comprising a hundred and thirty-eight small vessels, failed to receive the message, but this too was overtaken and turned round without arousing the suspicions of the enemy. It was a hard day for the thousands of men cooped up in landing craft all round the coast. The Americans who came from the West Country ports had the greatest distance to go and suffered most.

At about five o'clock that morning Bedell Smith again telephoned Ismay confirming the postponement, and Ismay went to bed. Half an hour later I woke up and sent for him. He told me the news. He says I made no comment.

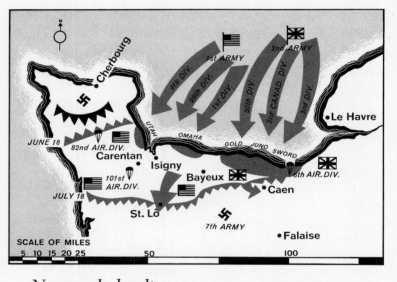

Normandy landings by three Allied paratroop and six seaborne divisions (*red arrows*) secured red areas on beach in first 24 hours. Allies pushed inland over next six weeks to establish lines (*red*) across peninsula and isolate Germans (*black*) in Cherbourg.

The hours dragged slowly by until, at 9:15 p.m. on the evening of June 4, another fateful conference opened at Eisenhower's battle headquarters. Conditions were bad, typical of December rather than June, but the weather experts gave some promise of a temporary improvement on the morning of the 6th. After this they predicted a return of rough weather for an indefinite period. Faced with the desperate alternatives of accepting the immediate risks or of postponing the attack for at least a fortnight, General Eisenhower, with the advice of his commanders, boldly, and as it proved wisely, chose to go ahead with the operation, subject to final confirmation early on the following morning. At 4 a.m. on June 5 the die was irrevocably cast: the invasion would be launched on June 6.

In retrospect this decision rightly evokes admiration. It was amply justified by events, and was largely responsible for gaining us the precious advantage of surprise. We now know that the German meteorologic officers informed their High Command that invasion on the 5th or 6th of June would not be possible owing to the stormy weather, which might last several days. The fact that such a complex series of movements could be accomplished without detection by a wary and determined enemy is a remarkable tribute to the work of the Allied Air Forces and the excellence of our deception plans.

All day on June 5 the convoys bearing the spearhead of the invasion converged on the rendezvous south of the Isle of Wight. Thence, in an endless stream, led by the minesweepers on a wide front and protected on all sides by the might of the Allied Navies and Air Forces, the greatest armada that ever left our shores set out for the coast of France. The rough conditions at sea were a severe trial to troops on the eve of battle, particularly in the terrible discomfort of the smaller craft. Yet, in spite of all, the vast movement was carried through with almost the precision of a parade, and, although not wholly without loss, such casualties and delays as did occur, mostly to small craft in tow, had no appreciable effect on events.

Round all our coasts the network of defence was keyed to the highest pitch. The Home Fleet was alert against any move by German surface ships, while air patrols watched the enemy coast from Norway to the Channel. Far out at sea, in the Western Approaches and the Bay of Biscay, aircraft of Coastal Command, in great strength, supported by flotillas of destroyers, kept watch for enemy reactions. Our intelligence told us that over fifty U-boats were concentrated in the French Biscay ports, ready to intervene when the moment came. The hour was now striking.

D-Day, June 6, 1944

OUR long months of preparation and planning for the greatest amphibious operation in history ended on D-Day, June 6, 1944. During the preceding night great armadas of convoys and their escorts sailed, unknown to the enemy, along the swept channels from the Isle of Wight to the Normandy coast. Heavy bombers of the Royal Air Force attacked enemy coast-defence guns in their concrete emplacements, dropping 5,200 tons of bombs. When dawn broke the United States Air Force came on the scene to deal with other shore defences, followed by medium and fighter-bombers. In the twenty-four hours of June 6 the Allies flew over 14,600 sorties. So great was our superiority in the air that all the enemy could put up during daylight over the invasion beaches was a mere hundred sorties. From midnight three airborne divisions were alighting, the British 6th Airborne Division northeast of Caen to seize bridgeheads over the river between the town and the sea, and two American airborne divisions north of Carentan to assist the sea-borne assault on the beaches and to check the movement of enemy reserves into the Cotentin peninsula. Although in places the airborne divisions were more widely scattered than had been intended, the object was in every case achieved.

As dawn came and the ships, great and small, began to file into their prearranged positions for the assault the scene might almost have been a review. Immediate opposition was limited to an attack by torpedo boats, which sank a Norwegian destroyer. Even when the naval bombardment began the reply from the coastal batteries was desultory and ineffective. There was no doubt that we had achieved a tactical surprise. Landing and support craft with infantry, with tanks, with self-propelled artillery, and a great variety of weapons, and engineer demolition teams to deal with the beach obstacles, all formed up into groups and moved towards the beaches. Among them were the DD ("swimming") tanks, which made their first large-scale appearance in battle. It was still very rough from the bad weather of the day before, and a good many of the "swimming" tanks foundered on the way.

Destroyers and gun and rocket batteries mounted on landing craft pounded the beaches, while farther to seaward battleships and cruisers kept down the fire of the defending batteries. Opposition was slight until the first landing craft were a mile from the shore, but then mortar and machine-gun fire grew. Surf and partly submerged obstacles and mines made the landings hazardous, and many craft were wrecked after setting down their troops, but the advance went on.

As soon as the infantry got ashore they dashed forward towards their objectives, and in every case except one made good progress. On "Omaha" beach, northwest of Bayeux, the V American Corps ran into severe resistance. By an unlucky chance this sector had recently been taken over by a German division in full strength and on the alert. Our Allies had a very stiff fight all day to make any lodgment at all, and it was not until the 7th that, after losing several thousand men, they were able to force their way inland.

Although we did not gain all we sought, and in particular Caen remained firmly in enemy hands, the progress made on the first two days of the assault was judged very satisfactory.

From the Biscay ports a stream of U-boats, facing all risks and moving on the surface at high speed, sought to break up the invasion. In the first crucial four days six were sunk by air attack and a similar number damaged. They were not able to make any impression on the invasion convoys, which continued to move to their objectives with trifling loss. Thereafter they were more cautious, but no more successful.

At noon on June 6 I asked the House of Commons to "take formal cognisance of the liberation of Rome by the Allied Armies under the command of General Alexander," the news of which had been released the night before. There was intense excitement about the landings in France, which everyone knew were in progress at the moment. Nevertheless I devoted ten minutes to the campaign in Italy and in paying my tribute to the Allied Armies there. After thus keeping them on tenterhooks for a little I gave them an account of what had happened.

BY the afternoon I felt justified in reporting to Stalin: "Everything has started well. The mines, obstacles, and land batteries have been largely overcome. The air landings were very successful, and on a large scale. Infantry landings are proceeding rapidly, and many tanks and self-propelled guns are ashore."

His answer was prompt, and contained welcome news of the highest importance. "I have received," he cabled, "your communication about the success of the beginning of the 'Overlord' operations. It gives joy to us all and hope of further successes. The summer offensive of the Soviet forces, organised in accordance with the agreement at the Tehran Conference, will begin towards the middle of June on one of the important sectors of the front. . . . At the end of June and during July offensive operations will become a general offensive of the Soviet forces."

I was actually sending him a fuller account of our progress when this telegram arrived. "I am well satisfied," I answered, "with the situation up to noon today [June 7]. Only at one American beach has there been serious difficulty, and that has now been cleared up. 20,000 airborne troops are safely landed behind the flanks of the enemy's lines, and have made contact in each case with the American and British sea-borne forces. We got across with small losses. We had expected to lose about 10,000 men. . . ."

Stalin telegraphed again a few days later:

"As is evident, the landing, conceived on a grandiose scale, has succeeded completely. My colleagues and I cannot but admit that the history of warfare knows no other like undertaking from the point of view of its scale, its vast conception, and its masterly execution. As is well known, Napoleon in his time failed ignominiously in his plan to force the Channel. The hysterical Hitler, who boasted for two years that he would effect a forcing of the Channel, was unable to make up his mind even to hint at attempting to carry out his threat. Only our Allies have succeeded in realising with honour the grandiose plan of the forcing of the Channel. History will record this deed as an achievement of the highest order.''

The word ''grandiose'' is the translation from the Russian text which was given me. I think ''majestic'' was probably what Stalin meant. At any rate, harmony was complete.

LET us survey the enemy's dispositions and plans as we now know them. Rundstedt, with sixty divisions, commanded the whole Atlantic Wall, from the Low Countries to the Bay of Biscay, and from Marseilles along the Riviera shore. Under him Rommel held the coast from Holland to the Loire. His Fifteenth Army with nineteen divisions held the sector about Calais and Boulogne, and his Seventh Army had nine infantry and one Panzer division at hand in Normandy. The ten Panzer divisions on the whole Western Front were spreadeagled from Belgium to Bordeaux. How strange that the Germans, now on the defensive, made the same mistake as the French in 1940 and dispersed their most powerful weapon of counterattack!

When Rommel took up his command in late January he had been displeased with the defences he found, and his energy improved them greatly. Along the coast there was a line of concrete works with all-round defence, many mines and difficult obstacles of various patterns, especially below high-water mark. Fixed guns pointed seaward, and field artillery covered the beaches. While there was no complete second line of defence, villages in rear were strongly fortified. Rommel was not content with the progress made, and had more time been left him our task would have been harder. Our opening bombardment by sea and air did not destroy many of the concrete works, but by stunning their defenders reduced their fire and also upset their radar.

The German warning system had been completely paralysed. From Calais to Guernsey the Germans had no fewer than one hundred and twenty major pieces of radar equipment for finding our convoys and directing the fire of their shore batteries. These were grouped in forty-seven stations. We discovered them all, and attacked them so successfully with rocket-firing aircraft that on the night before D-Day not one in six was working. The serviceable ones were deceived by the device of tin-foil strips known as ''Window,'' which simulated a convoy heading east of Fécamp, and they thus failed to detect the real landings. Nor was this the only menace which was overcome. Encouraged by their success two years before in concealing the passage up the Channel of the *Scharnhorst* and *Gneisenau*, the enemy had built many more jamming stations for thwarting both the ships which directed our night fighters and the radar beams upon which many of our forces depended for an accurate landfall. But they too were discovered. All were obliterated, and our radio and radar aids were secure.

It is indeed remarkable that the vast, long-planned assault fell on the enemy as a surprise both in time and place. The German High Command was told that the weather would be too rough that day for amphibious operations, and had received no recent air reports of the assembly of our thousands of ships along the English shore. Early on June 5 Rommel left his headquarters to visit Hitler at Berchtesgaden, and was in Germany when the blow fell.

There had been much argument about which front the Allies would attack. Rundstedt had consistently believed that our main blow would be launched across the Strait of Dover, as that was the shortest sea route and gave the best access to the heart of Germany. Rommel for long agreed with him. Hitler and his staff however appear to have had reports indicating that Normandy would be the principal battleground. Even after we had landed uncertainties continued. Hitler lost a whole critical day in making up his mind to release the two nearest Panzer divisions to reinforce the front. The German Intelligence Service grossly overestimated the number of divisions and the amount of suitable shipping available in England. On their showing there were ample resources for a second big landing, so Normandy might be only a preliminary and subsidiary one. On June 19 Rommel reported to von Rundstedt, ''. . . a large-scale landing is to be expected on the Channel front on both sides of Cap Gris Nez or between the Somme and Le Havre,'' and he repeated the warning a week later. Thus it was not until the third week in July, six weeks after D-Day, that reserves from the Fifteenth Army were sent south from the Pas-de-Calais to join the battle.

ON June 10 Montgomery was sufficiently established ashore to receive a visit. I therefore set off in my train to Portsmouth, with Smuts, Brooke, General Marshall, and Admiral King. All three American Chiefs of Staff had flown to the United Kingdom on June 8 in case any vital military decision had to be taken at short notice. A British and an American destroyer awaited us. Smuts, Brooke, and I embarked in the former and General Marshall and Admiral King, with their staffs, in the latter, and we crossed the Channel without incident to our respective fronts. Montgomery, smiling and confident, met me at the beach as we scrambled out of our landing craft. His army had already penetrated seven or eight miles inland. There was very little firing or activity. The weather was brilliant. We drove through our limited but fertile domain in Normandy. It was pleasant to see the prosperity of the countryside. The fields were full of lovely red and white cows basking or parading in the sunshine. The inhabitants seemed quite buoyant and well nourished and waved enthusiastically. Montgomery's headquarters, about five miles inland, were in a château with lawns and lakes around it. We lunched in a tent looking towards the enemy. The General was in the highest spirits. I asked him how far away was the actual front. He said about three miles. I asked him if he had a continuous line. He said, ''No.'' ''What is there then to prevent an incursion of German armour breaking up our luncheon?'' He said he did not think they would come. The staff told me the château had been heavily bombed the night before, and certainly there were a good many craters around it. I told him he was taking too much risk if he made a habit of such proceedings. Anything can be done once or for a short time, but custom, repetition, prolongation, is always to be avoided when possible in war. He did in fact move two days later, though not till he and his staff had had another dose.

The weather continued fine, and apart from occasional air alarms and antiaircraft fire there seemed to be no fighting. We made a considerable inspection of our limited bridgehead. I was particularly interested to see the local ports of Port en Bessin, Courseulles, and Quistreham. We had not counted much on these little harbours in any of the plans we had made for the great descent. They proved a most valuable acquisition, and soon were discharging about two thousand tons a day. I dwelt on these agreeable facts as we drove or walked round our interesting but severely restricted conquest.

Smuts, Brooke, and I went home in the destroyer *Kelvin*. Admiral Vian, who now commanded all the flotillas and light craft protecting the Arromanches harbour, was on board. He proposed that we should go and watch the bombardment of the German position by the battleships and cruisers protecting the British left flank. Accordingly we passed between the two battleships, which were firing at twenty thousand yards, and through the cruiser squadron, firing at about fourteen thousand yards, and soon we were within seven or eight thousand yards of the shore, which was thickly wooded. The bombardment was leisurely and continuous, but there was no reply from the enemy. As we were about to turn I said to Vian, "Since we are so near, why shouldn't we have a plug at them ourselves before we go home?" He said, "Certainly," and in a minute or two all our guns fired on the silent coast. We were of course well within the range of their artillery, and the moment we had fired Vian made the destroyer turn about and depart at the highest speed. This is the only time I have ever been on board a naval vessel when she fired "in anger" —if it can be so called. I admired the Admiral's sporting spirit. Smuts too was delighted. I slept soundly on the four-hour voyage to Portsmouth. Altogether it had been a most interesting and enjoyable day.

Soon afterwards I wrote to the President about various questions, including de Gaulle's visit to France, which I had arranged without consulting Roosevelt beforehand:

"I had a jolly day on Monday on the beaches and inland. There is a great mass of shipping extended more than fifty miles along the coast. It is being increasingly protected against weather by the artificial harbours. The power of our air and of our anti-U-boat forces seems to ensure it a very great measure of protection. After doing much laborious duty we went and had a plug at the Hun from our destroyer, but although the range was six thousand yards he did not honour us with a reply. Marshall and King came back in my train. They were greatly reassured by all they saw on the American side, and Marshall wrote out a charming telegram to Mountbatten, saying how many of these new craft had been produced under his organisation and what a help they had been. You used the word 'stupendous' in one of your early telegrams to me. I must admit that what I saw could only be described by that word, and I think your officers would agree as well. . . . How I wish you were here!"

Normandy to Paris

THE enemy fought stubbornly and were not easily overcome. In the American sector the marshes near Carentan and at the mouth of the river Vire hampered our movements, and everywhere the country was suited to infantry defence. The *bocage* which covers much of Normandy consists of a multitude of small fields divided by banks, with ditches and very high hedges. Artillery support for an attack is thus hindered by lack of good observation and it was extremely difficult to use tanks. It was infantry fighting all the way, with every little field a potential strong point. Nevertheless good progress was made, except for the failure to capture Caen.

This small but famous town was to be the scene of bitter struggles over many days. To us it was important, because, apart from the fact that there was good ground to the east for constructing airstrips, it was the hinge on which our whole plan turned. Montgomery's intention was to make a great left wheel by the American forces, with Caen as their left-hand pivot. It was equally important for the Germans. If their lines were pierced there the whole of their Seventh Army would be forced southeastward toward the Loire, opening a gap between it and the Fifteenth Army in the north. The way to Paris would then be open. Thus in the following weeks Caen became the scene of ceaseless attacks and the most stubborn defence, drawing towards it a great part of the German divisions, and especially their armour. This was a help as well as a hindrance.

The Germans, though the reserve divisions of their Fifteenth Army were still held intact north of the Seine, had of course been reinforced from elsewhere, and by June 12 twelve divisions were in action, four of them Panzers. This was less than we had expected. The tremendous air offensive had hampered all the enemy's communications. Not only were the enemy unable to reinforce quickly, but their divisions arrived piecemeal, short of equipment, and fatigued by long night marches, and they were thrown into the line as they came. The German command had no chance to form a striking force behind the battle for a powerful, well-concerted counteroffensive.

By June 11 the Allies had formed a continuous front inland, and our fighters were operating from half a dozen forward airstrips. The next task was to secure a lodgment area big enough to hold sufficient forces for the decisive break-out. The Americans thrust westward across the Cherbourg peninsula towards Barneville, on the western coast, which they reached on June 17. Simultaneously they advanced northwards, and after sharp fighting stood before the outer defences of Cherbourg on the 22nd. The enemy resisted stoutly till the 26th in order to carry out demolitions. These were so thorough that heavy loads could not be brought in through the port till the end of August.

Beyond the battlefield other events influenced the future. On June 17, at Margival, near Soissons, Hitler held a conference with Rundstedt and Rommel. His two generals pressed on him strongly the folly of bleeding the German Army to death in Normandy. They urged that before it was destroyed the Seventh Army should make an orderly withdrawal towards the Seine, where, together with the Fifteenth Army, it could fight a defensive but mobile battle with at least some hope of success. But Hitler would not agree. Here, as in Russia and Italy, he demanded that no ground should be given up and all should fight where they stood. The generals were of course right. Hitler's method of fighting to the death at once on all fronts lacked the important element of selection.

In the battle area along the coast our consolidation was making headway. In the first six days 326,000 men, 54,000 vehicles, and 104,000 tons of stores were landed. In spite of serious losses among landing craft an immense supply organisation was rapidly taking shape. By June 19 the two "Mulberry" harbours, one of Arromanches, the other ten miles farther west, in the American sector, were making good progress. But then a four-day gale began. The harbour in the American sector was ruined, and its serviceable parts were used to repair Arromanches. This gale, the like of which had not been known in June for forty years, was a severe misfortune. We were already behind our programme of unloading. The break-out was equally delayed, and on June 23 we stood only on the line we had prescribed for the 11th. Nevertheless, by the middle of July thirty Allied divisions were ashore. Half were American and half British and Canadian. Against these the Germans had gathered twenty-seven divisions. But they had suffered 160,000 casualties, and General Eisenhower estimated their fighting value as no higher than sixteen divisions.

An important event then occurred. On July 17 Rommel was severely wounded. His car was attacked by our low-flying fighters, and he was carried to hospital in what was thought a dying condition. He made a wonderful recovery, in time to meet his death later on at Hitler's orders.

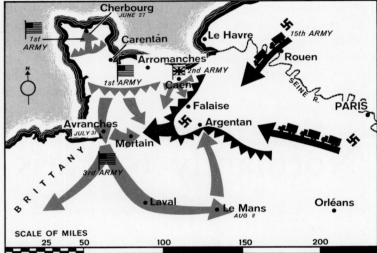

Breakout from Normandy by Allies (*red*) was made by U.S. Third Army under Patton as First Army took Cherbourg. Sweeping south, Patton sent force into Brittany, liberated Le Mans, then wheeled north to cripple German attack (*black*) near Falaise.

Montgomery's general offensive, planned for July 18, now approached. The British Army attacked with three corps, with the aim of enlarging their bridgeheads and carrying them well beyond the river Orne. The operation was preceded by an immense bombardment by the Allied Air. The German Air Force was totally prevented from interfering. Good progress was made to the east of Caen, until clouded skies began to hamper our planes and led to a week's delay in launching the break-out from the American sector. I thought this was an opportunity to visit Cherbourg and to spend a few days in the "Mulberry" harbour. On the 20th I flew direct in an American Army Dakota to their landing ground on the Cherbourg peninsula, and was taken all round the harbour by the United States commander. Here I saw for the first time a flying bomb launching point. It was a very elaborate affair. I was shocked at the damage the Germans had done to the town,

and shared the staff disappointment at the inevitable delay in getting the port to work. The basins of the harbour were thickly sown with contact mines. A handful of devoted British divers were at work day and night disconnecting these at their mortal peril. Warm tributes were paid to them by their American comrades.

After a long and dangerous drive to the United States beachhead known as Utah Beach I went aboard a British motor torpedo-boat, and thence had a rough passage to Arromanches. As one gets older seasickness retreats. I did not succumb, but slept soundly till we were in the calm waters of our synthetic lagoon. I went aboard the cruiser *Enterprise*, where I remained for three days, making myself thoroughly acquainted with the whole working of the harbour, on which all the armies now almost entirely depended, and at the same time transacting my London business. The nights were very noisy, there being repeated raids by single aircraft, and still more numerous alarms. By day I studied the whole process of the landing of supplies and troops, both at the piers, in which I had so long been interested, and on the beaches. On one occasion six tank landing craft came to the beach in line. As soon as their prows grounded, their drawbridges fell forward and out came the tanks, three or four from each, and splashed ashore. In less than eight minutes by my stop watch the tanks stood in column of route on the highroad ready to move into action. This was an impressive performance, and typical of the rate of discharge which had now been achieved. I was fascinated to see the DUKWs swimming through the harbour, waddling ashore, and then hurrying up the hill to the great dump where the lorries were waiting to take their supplies to the various units. Upon the wonderful efficiency of this system, now yielding results far greater than we had ever planned, depended the hopes of a speedy and victorious action.

On my last day at Arromanches I visited Montgomery's headquarters, a few miles inland. The Commander-in-Chief was in the best of spirits on the eve of his largest operation, which he explained to me in all detail. He took me into the ruins of Caen and across the river, and we also visited other parts of the British front. Then he placed at my disposal his captured Storch aeroplane, and the Air Commander himself piloted me all over the British positions. This aircraft could land at a pinch almost anywhere, and consequently one could fly at a few hundred feet from the ground, gaining a far better view and knowledge of the scene than by any other method. I also visited several of the air stations, and said a few words to gatherings of officers and men. Finally I went to the field hospital, where, though it was a quiet day, a trickle of casualties was coming in. One poor man was to have a serious operation, and was actually on the table about to take the anaesthetic. I was slipping away when he said he wanted me. He smiled wanly and kissed my hand. I was deeply moved, and very glad to learn later that the operation had been entirely successful.

†   †   †

At this time the orders which had held the German Fifteenth Army behind the Seine were cancelled, and several fresh divisions were sent to reinforce the hard-pressed Seventh. Their transference, by rail, road or across the Seine by the ferries which had replaced the broken bridges, was greatly delayed and injured by our air forces. The long-withheld aid reached the field too late to turn the scale.

The hour of the great American break-out under General Omar Bradley came at last. On July 25 their VII Corps struck southward from St. Lô, and on the next day the VIII Corps joined the battle. The United States Air Force bombardment had been devastating, and the infantry assault prospered. Then the armour leaped through and swept on to the key point of Coutances. The German escape route down that coast of Normandy was cut, and the whole German defence west of the Vire was in jeopardy and chaos. The roads were jammed with retreating troops, and the Allied bombers and fighter-bombers exacted a destructive toll of men and vehicles.

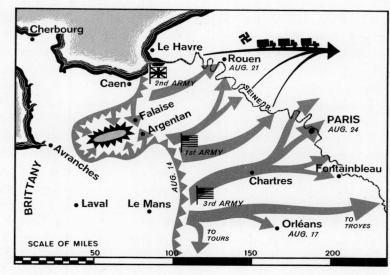

Advance to Seine by Allies (*red*) liberated Paris and Rouen, threatened eastern France and forced Germans (*black*) in northern France to flee for Germany. Remnants of the abortive enemy counterattack near Falaise (*left*) were encircled and had to surrender.

On August 7 I went again to Montgomery's headquarters by air, and after he had given me a vivid account with his maps an American colonel arrived to take me to General Bradley. The route had been carefully planned to show me the frightful devastation of the towns and villages through which the United States troops had fought their way. All the buildings were pulverised by air bombing. We reached Bradley's headquarters about four o'clock. The General welcomed me cordially, but I could feel there was great tension, as the battle was at its height and every few minutes messages arrived. I therefore cut my visit short and motored back to my aeroplane, which awaited me. I was about to go on board when, to my surprise, Eisenhower arrived. He had flown from London to his advanced headquarters, and, hearing of my movements, intercepted me. He had not yet taken over the actual command of the army in the field from Montgomery; but he supervised everything with a vigilant eye, and no one knew better than he how to stand close to a tremendous event without impairing the authority he had delegated to others.

The Third United States Army, under General Patton, had now been formed and was in action. He detached two armoured and three infantry divisions for the westward and southerly drive to clear the Brittany peninsula. The cut-off enemy at once retreated towards their fortified ports. The French Resistance Movement, which here numbered 30,000 men, played a notable part, and the peninsula was quickly overrun. By the end of the first week in August the Germans, amounting to 45,000 garrison troops and remnants of four divisions, had been pressed into their defensive perimeters at St. Malo, Brest, Lorient, and St. Nazaire. Here they could be penned and left to wither, thus saving the unnecessary losses which immediate assaults would have required. Brest, however, which held a large garrison, under an active commander, was dangerous, and had to be eliminated. It surrendered on September 19 to violent attacks by three U.S. divisions. While Britanny was being cleared or cooped the rest of Patton's Third Army drove eastward in the "long hook" which was to carry them to the gap between the Loire and Paris and then down the Seine towards Rouen. The town of Laval was entered on August 6, and Le Mans on August 9. Few Germans were found in all this wide region; the main difficulty was supplying the advancing Americans over long and ever-lengthening distances. Except for a limited airlift, everything had still to come from the beaches of the original landing and pass down the western side of Normandy through Avranches to reach the front. Avranches therefore became the bottleneck, and offered a tempting opportunity for a German attack striking westward from the neighbourhood of Falaise. The idea caught Hitler's fancy, and he gave orders for the maximum possible force to attack Mortain, burst its way through the Avranches, and thus cut Patton's communications. The German commanders were unanimous in condemning the project. Realising that the battle for Normandy was already lost, they wished to use four divisions which had just arrived from the Fifteenth Army in the north to carry out an orderly retreat to the Seine. They thought that to throw any fresh troops westward was merely to "stick out their necks," with the certain prospect of having them severed. Hitler insisted on having his way, and on August 7 five Panzer and two infantry divisions delivered a vehement attack on Mortain from the east.

The blow fell on a single U.S. division, but it held firm and three others came to its aid. After five days of severe fighting and concentrated bombing from the air the audacious onslaught was thrown back in confusion, and, as the

439

enemy generals had predicted, the whole salient from Falaise to Mortain, full of German troops, was at the mercy of converging attacks from three sides. The Allied air forces swept on to the crowded Germans within the long and narrow pocket, and with the artillery inflicted fearful slaughter. The Germans held stubbornly on to the jaws of the gap at Falaise and Argentan, and, giving priority to their armour, tried to extricate all that they could. But on August 17 command and control broke down and the scene became a shambles. The jaws closed on August 20, and although by then a considerable part of the enemy had been able to scramble eastward no fewer than eight German divisions were annihilated. What had been the Falaise pocket was their grave.

† † †

The Third United States Army, besides clearing the Brittany peninsula and contributing with their "short hook" to the culminating victory at Falaise, thrust three corps eastward and northeastward from Le Mans. On August 17 they reached Orléans, Chartres, and Dreux. Thence they drove northwestward down the left bank of the river to meet the British advancing on Rouen. Our Second Army had experienced some delay. They had to reorganise after the Falaise battle, and the enemy found means to improvise rear-guard positions. However, the pursuit was pressed hotly, and all the Germans south of the Seine were soon seeking desperately to retreat across it, under destructive air attacks. None of the bridges destroyed by previous air bombardments had been repaired, but there were a few pontoon bridges and a fairly adequate ferry service. Very few vehicles could be saved. South of Rouen immense quantities of transport were abandoned. Such troops as escaped were in no condition to resist on the farther bank of the river.

Eisenhower, who had taken up supreme command, was determined to avoid a battle for Paris. Stalingrad and Warsaw had proved the horrors of frontal assaults and patriotic risings, and he therefore resolved to encircle the capital and force the garrison to surrender or flee. By August 20 the time for action had come. Patton had crossed the Seine near Mantes, and his right flank had reached Fontainebleau. The French Underground had revolted. The police were on strike. The Prefecture was in Patriot hands. An officer of the Resistance reached Patton's headquarters with vital reports, and on the morning of Wednesday, August 23, these were delivered to Eisenhower at Le Mans.

Attached to Patton was the French 2nd Armoured Division, under General Leclerc, which had landed in Normandy on August 1, and played an honourable part in the advance. That evening the news of street-fighting in the capital decided Eisenhower to act, and Leclerc was told to march. Leclerc wrote to de Gaulle: "I have had the impression of living . . . the situation of 1940 in reverse. . . ." On August 24 the first detachments moved on the city from Rambouillet, where they had arrived from Normandy the day before. The main thrust, led by Colonel Billotte, son of the commander of the First French Army Group, who was killed in May 1940, moved up from Orléans. That night a vanguard of tanks reached the Porte d'Orléans, and at 9:22 precisely entered the square in front of the Hotel de Ville. Early next morning Billotte's armoured columns held both banks of the Seine opposite the Cité. By the afternoon the headquarters of the German commander, General von Cholitz, in the Hotel Meurice, had been surrounded, and Cholitz surrendered to a French lieutenant, who brought him to Billotte. Leclerc had meanwhile arrived and established himself at the Gare Montparnasse, moving down in the afternoon to the Prefecture of Police. About four o'clock von Cholitz was taken before him. This was the end of the road from Dunquerque to Lake Chad and home again. In a low voice Leclerc spoke his thoughts aloud: "Maintenant, ça y est," and then in German he introduced himself to the vanquished. After a brief and brusque discussion the capitulation of the garrison was signed, and one by one their remaining strong points were occupied by the Resistance and the regular troops.

The city was given over to a rapturous demonstration. German prisoners were spat upon, collaborators dragged through the streets, and the liberating troops feted. On this scene of long-delayed triumph there arrived General de Gaulle. At 5 p.m. he reached the Rue St. Dominique, and set up his headquarters in the Ministry of War. Two hours later at the Hotel de Ville he appeared for the first time as the leader of Free France before the jubilant population in company with the main figures of the Resistance and Generals Leclerc and Juin. There was a spontaneous burst of wild enthusiasm. Next afternoon, on August 26, de Gaulle made his formal entry on foot down the Champs Élysées to the Place de la Concorde, and then in a file of cars to Notre Dame. There was some firing from inside and outside the cathedral by hidden collaborators. The crowd scattered, but after a short moment of panic the solemn dedication of the liberation of Paris proceeded to its end.

† † †

By August 30 our troops were crossing the Seine at many points. Enemy losses had been tremendous: 400,000 men, half of them prisoners, 1,300 tanks, 20,000 vehicles, 1,500 field guns. The German Seventh Army, and all divisions that had been sent to reinforce it, were torn to shreds. The Allied break-out from the beachhead had been delayed by bad weather and Hitler's mistaken resolve. But once that battle was over everything went with a run, and the Seine was reached six days ahead of the planned time. There has been criticism of slowness on the British front in Normandy, and the splendid American advances of the later stages seemed to indicate greater success on their part than on ours. It is therefore necessary to emphasise again that the whole plan of campaign was to pivot on the British front and draw the enemy's reserves in that direction in order to help the American turning movement. The object of the Second British Army was described in its original plan as "to protect the flank of the U.S. armies while the latter captured Cherbourg, Angers, Nantes, and the Brittany ports." By determination and hard fighting this was achieved. General Eisenhower, who fully comprehended the work of his British comrades, wrote in his official report: "Without the great sacrifices made by the Anglo-Canadian armies in the brutal, slugging battles for Caen and Falaise the spectacular advances made elsewhere by the Allied forces could never have come about."

Paying a last-minute call, General Eisenhower visits with American paratroopers, their faces blackened for nighttime combat in Normandy

THE INVADERS

The Great Assault Gets under Way

At the beginning of the single day when a single man's wrong decisions could lose the war, the man who had the decisions to make went to visit his airborne spearhead (*page 441*). His air commander had told him that, flying at low altitude in moonlight, 80 percent of these men would fall to German antiaircraft fire in a "futile slaughter." Watching them take off, said an aide, was Eisenhower's toughest moment in the whole operation.

An hour and a half later, the first paratroopers were down in Normandy and fighting. From the airports of southern England (*below*), planes were flying the first of 14,600 D-Day sorties. From English harbors (*right*), the immense convoys were under way. At dawn the naval bombardment began, and by 0630 the landing craft were running up the beaches as ordered by the Combined Chiefs of Staff: "You will enter the continent of Europe and . . . undertake operations aimed at the heart of Germany."

By noon, Churchill was reporting to the Commons: "Everything is proceeding according to plan. And what a plan! This vast operation is undoubtedly the most complicated and difficult that has ever taken place."

To the men ashore, the complications and difficulties loomed larger than the plan, and the battle was a chaotic succession of gambles taken, blunders retrieved, local defeats and triumphs. The biggest gamble of all—that the "comparatively small area of high pressure" noted by the Allied weathermen over Greenland would calm down the seas—was successful: the Germans, thinking the waves too rough, had not even sent out patrol boats the night before. Allied Intelligence underestimated the defenses of Omaha Beach with bloody consequences, but German Intelligence underestimated the whole invasion force. The U.S. 4th Division landed on the wrong beach, but it proved to be better than the right one. A German tank column which had driven to the coast saw parachutes falling in its rear (they were only carrying supplies) and turned tail, throwing away the last opportunity to disrupt the landings.

Thus on the whole the chances of war decisively favored the Allied armies. By midnight there were 150,000 men ashore. They were miles behind the plan, but the walls of Hitler's "Fortress Europe" were irreparably cracked.

Ground-support planes (*left*), painted with zebra stripes for easy identification, have guns cleaned in England between strikes. They kept the Germans from reinforcing the beaches all through D-Day.

Embarkation fleet crowds a harbor in Southern England as every conceivable kind of transport, landing craft and cargo ship takes on its charge of supplies and men and lines up ready to sail for France. In the center foreground of this painting by Richard Eurich, an LST is standing on the beach with red jaws wide open to receive a line of tanks and ambulances moving on board under a camouflage netting.

The smoke of battle lies ahead

as the U.S. 1st Division wades ashore...

. . . On to the hell of Omaha Beach

In this extraordinary picture taken by LIFE Photographer Robert Capa from the shore of Omaha Beach when it was quivering with the impact of a thousand guns, an American infantryman wades chest-deep through the water after getting successfully past a jungle of underwater obstacles (*background*). Ahead of him lie pillboxes, boobytraps, dugouts and enfiladed batteries—enough to kill or wound 8,600 men that first day.

German prisoners come over a hilltop on Utah Beach with their hands up. Many of the enemy troops in Normandy were Russian prisoners enrolled in the Wehrmacht and not at all anxious to fight.

Fallen American (*below*) lies dead on Omaha Beach while survivors group for a new assault. He was in one of the demolition teams that blasted paths through the beach obstacles under murderous fire.

Buildup on the beach reaches impressive proportions with the help of breakwater (*background*) formed by ships towed from England and sunk—a plan first suggested by Churchill in 1917. This striking panorama, taken a few days after the landings, shows a convoy coming in from across the Channel, LCT's and LST's unloading supplies, trucks on their way inland, and men bivouacked for their first night in France.

449

Somber column of men in the U.S. 1st Division marches up the shell-pocked, wreckage-littered Omaha Beach. When Aaron Bohrod painted this scene about a week after D-Day, troops were still landing on the invasion beaches within earshot of the battle. They had barely time to line up before they were led off inland to fight through the fields and hedgerows on the beachhead's expanding perimeter a few miles away.

Point-blank fire from an American antitank gun blasts a German strong point on the Cherbourg front while infantrymen take cover behind a wall. Hitler had ordered his men not to retreat a foot, and fighting on ideal defensive terrain like this they made the Allies pay for every foot they gained—73,000 American and 49,000 British and Canadian casualties between D-Day and the break-out.

The Slow Struggle
for Normandy

In the three weeks after D-Day, the beachhead thickened out a little and on its right flank absorbed the Cherbourg peninsula with its great, but wrecked, port. In the next month the lines of battle on the map moved hardly more than they had done during the massacres in Flanders in the First World War. On D+50 the Allied lines were approximately those that had been planned for D+5. Yet these fifty days had broken the power of the German Army to resist.

It was a highly mobile battle in its constricted space, thrust following counterthrust across a patchwork of apple orchards and pastures where every field, surrounded by earthen banks and thick hedges, was a fortress. Both sides were trying by continuous local attacks to keep each other off balance and unable to concentrate for a decisive blow. Using to the full their supremacy on the sea and in the air, the Allies succeeded. But it was the footsoldier who won this long and fearful battle, flushing the German out of hedge and dugout and fortified farmhouse, wearing him down till his thin lines could no longer hold back the tremendous power straining to break out of the beachhead.

On the double (right) a pair of footsoldiers dash across a road strewn with the debris of battle in the Periers sector. Here the Allied advance cut off the defenders of the Cherbourg peninsula.

The breakthrough at St. Lô, which opened the way to Paris, is spearheaded by American Sherman tanks with their infantry escort. This painting by Ogden Pleissner shows them plunging through

the sea of rubble around the mutilated cathedral, exploiting the gap
that had been blasted in the German defense lines by an aerial attack by
2,500 bombers which practically annihilated a whole Panzer division.

A tank explodes on a German mine at Coutances during the breakthrough battle. At the left is an overturned jeep, its soldier passengers lying dead among the flowers French civilians had thrown to them.

A town revives (*below*) as civilians drift back after the battle. U.S. engineers are still hunting for German mines, and German road signs still hang at the foot of a monument to the dead of another war.

A roadside cross, outside the village of Pont-l'Abbé in Brittany, is pressed into service as an emergency telephone pole, while on the steps below an American military policeman waves on a Sherman tank. The tank is part of one of the flying columns in General George Patton's Third Army, which rolled up the left flank of the German line and went rampaging at a real blitzkrieg clip right across France.

Terror and Joy on the Road to Paris

In the six glorious weeks that followed the American breakthrough at St. Lô, the people of France saw great motorized armies sweep over the land in pursuit of a demoralized foe, just as they had in the six weeks following the breakthrough at the Meuse in 1940. But this time it was their enslavers who were on the run, and revenge was sweet. Well organized though inadequately armed, the French Forces of the Interior came out of hiding to help the Allied invaders by continual acts of sabotage (in some months they wrecked more locomotives than the Allied air forces), by spying on the enemy and by attacking his stragglers and isolated garrisons. Many privations and disappointments still lay ahead, but the French turned out by millions on those fine summer days to vent their hatred on the traitors among them and to shout their delirious joy as the liberating armies rolled down every road to Paris and beyond.

A collaborationist cowers on a sidewalk before a group of lightly armed patriots in Rennes who, on the day of their liberation, take the administration of justice for traitors into their own hands.

Parisians rejoice (*opposite*) around the Arc de Triomphe, illuminated and hung with the flags of France and her Allies, the night after the German garrison surrendered to a French armored division.

A harrowed Marine stares with bloodshot eyes as he awaits word to fight once again on the limestone crags of Peleliu, where a suicidal Japanese garrison set up a bloody roadblock to the American advance on the Philippines.

19

CLIMAX
IN THE PACIFIC

Japan in Retreat

OCEAN war against Japan now reached its climax. From the Bay of Bengal to the Central Pacific, Allied maritime power was in the ascendant. The organisation and production of the United States were in full stride, and had attained astonishing proportions. A single example may suffice to illustrate the size and success of the American effort. In the autumn of 1942 only three American aircraft carriers were afloat; a year later there were fifty; by the end of the war there were more than a hundred. This achievement had been matched by an increase in the production of aircraft which was no less remarkable. The advance of these great forces was animated by an aggressive strategy and an elaborate, novel, and effective tactic. The task which confronted them was formidable.

A chain of island groups, nearly 2,000 miles in length, stretches southward across the Pacific from Japan to the Marianas and the Carolines. Many of these islands had been fortified by the enemy and equipped with good airfields, and near the southernmost end of the chain was the Japanese naval base of Truk. Behind this shield of archipelagos lay Formosa, the Philippines, and China, and in its shelter ran the supply routes for the more advanced enemy positions. It was thus impossible to invade or bomb Japan itself. The chain must first be broken and penetrated. It would take too long to conquer and subdue every fortified island, and the Americans had accordingly advanced leapfrog fashion. They seized only the more important islands and bypassed the rest; but their maritime strength was now so great and was growing so fast that they were able to establish their own lines of communication and break the enemy's, leaving the defenders of the bypassed islands immobile and powerless. Their method of assault was equally successful. First came softening attacks by planes from the aircraft carriers, then heavy and sometimes prolonged bombardment from the sea, and finally amphibious landings and the struggle ashore. When an island had been won and garrisoned, land-based planes moved in and beat off counterattacks. At the same time they helped in the next onward surge. The fleets worked in echelons. While one group waged battle another prepared for a new leap. This needed very large resources, not only for the fighting, but also for developing bases along the line of advance. The Americans took it all in their stride.

By the latter half of 1943 the Japanese had lost the eastern end of New Guinea. Before he could attack the Philippines, General MacArthur had first to reoccupy all its northern shore. Part of the 41st U.S. Division worked their way towards Salamaua, and at the end of June other troops landed near it from the sea. They were joined by the 3rd Australian Division from Wau, and began their attack on Salamaua. It was purposely deliberate, so as to draw reinforcements from Lae, the next major objective. The attack on Lae began on September 4, 1943, when the 9th Australian Division, of Alamein fame, landed on the coast ten miles east of the town. Next day American parachutists dropped on Nadzab, in the Markham valley, and, with the help of Australian pioneers, rapidly made an airfield. The 7th Australian Division flew in, and immediately advanced. Attacked from two sides, Lae was taken on September 16. Salamaua had fallen a few days before, and Finschhafen fell on October 2. All were fiercely defended. The Markham valley, running northwest from Lae, had many potential airfields, and the 7th Australian Division, swift to exploit success, occupied its length in a series of airborne assaults. All the operations were well conceived and skilfully executed, and the co-operation of all three Services was brought to a high pitch.

The Australian capture of Finschhafen was followed by fierce Japanese counterattacks, and there was much fighting during the last fortnight of October. Then by the middle of November, the 5th Australian Division was moving forward through the mountains of the Huon Peninsula, overcoming a series of strongly held positions, while the 9th Australian Division was clearing the heights overlooking the Markham valley. Part of the 32nd U.S. Division made a landing at Saidor in the early days of January 1944, where they were joined on February 11 by the 5th Australian Division. It had taken five months to clear the Huon Peninsula. Out of the 12,000 Japanese troops who had been engaged there not more than 4,200 survived.

In April General MacArthur made an amphibious leap of 400 miles. He bypassed 50,000 Japanese around Wewak, and landed an American division at Aitape and two more near Hollandia. The Japanese Air Force had been thoroughly pounded, and 380 machines were found destroyed. Allied superiority by sea and air was henceforward so decisive that MacArthur could select whatever objectives suited him best and leave behind him large pockets of Japanese to be dealt with later. His final bound was to Biak Island, where the 41st U.S. Division had a fierce struggle against an enemy garrison nearly 10,000 strong. A convoy of a dozen Japanese warships was destroyed or crippled by air attack as they tried to bring reinforcements, and the

island was effectively in American possession before the end of June 1944. This marked the end of the two-year struggle in New Guinea, where the stubborn resistance of the enemy, the physical difficulties of the country, the ravages of disease, and the absence of communications made the campaign as arduous as any in history.

Farther east, at the beginning of July 1943, and simultaneously with General MacArthur's attack on Salamaua, Admiral Halsey had struck in New Georgia. After several weeks of severe fighting both this and the adjacent islands were won. Air fighting again dominated the scene, and the ascendancy of the American airmen soon proved decisive. Japanese losses in the air now exceeded those of the Americans by four or five to one.

In July and August a series of naval actions gave the Americans command of the sea. By September the backbone of Japanese resistance had been broken, and although much severe fighting continued both at Bougainville and in other islands the campaign in the Solomons was ended by December 1943. Such positions as remained in the enemy's hands had been neutralised and could now be safely bypassed and left to wilt.

Rabaul itself, in New Britain, became the next centre of attack. During November and December it was heavily and repeatedly struck by Allied air forces, and in the last days of 1943 General MacArthur's amphibious forces successfully landed on the western extremity of New Britain at Cape Gloucester. It was now decided to bypass Rabaul. An alternative base was therefore needed to sustain the advance to the Philippines, and this was within MacArthur's grasp at Manus Island, a part of the Admiralty group. In February 1944 the first stage of this envelopment was accomplished by the seizure of Green Islands, 120 miles east of Rabaul. This was followed by the brilliant capture of the whole Admiralty group, to the westward. In March Emirau Island, immediately to the north, was taken by Admiral Halsey, and the isolation of Rabaul was complete. The air and sea surrounding these islands thus passed entirely under American control.

Meanwhile the main American maritime forces, under Admiral Nimitz, began to concentrate for his drive through the island groups near the equator, which were the outposts defending the Japanese fleet base at Truk, in the Carolines. The most easterly of these groups, the Gilberts,

Paths to Philippines were cleared by the Allies in three amphibious drives (*blue*) through Japan's outer and inner defense lines. Sweeps across Pacific (*right*) and up Solomons (*middle*) were made by Navy and Marines, push up from New Guinea by Army (*left*).

seized from the British in 1941, was chosen for the first attack. In October 1943 Admiral Spruance, who had gained fame at Midway, was appointed to command the Central Pacific force. In November, while Halsey was attacking Bougainville, Spruance struck at Tarawa, in the Gilberts. The island was strongly fortified, and was held by about 3,500 Japanese troops. The landing by the 2nd Marine Division was bitterly contested, in spite of heavy preliminary air attacks. After four fierce days, in which casualties were severe, the island was captured.

With Tarawa eliminated the way was clear for attack on the Marshall group, to the north and west of the Gilberts. In February 1944 they were the object of amphibious operations on the greatest scale yet attempted in the Pacific, and by the end of the month the Americans were victorious. Without pause Admiral Spruance began the next phase of his advance, namely the softening by air attack of Japanese defences in the Carolines and Marianas. The flexibility of sea-borne attack in an ocean area is the most remarkable feature of these operations. While we in Europe were making our final preparations for "Overlord" with immense concentration of force in the narrow waters of the Channel, Spruance's carriers were ranging over huge areas, striking at islands in the Marianas, the Palau group, and the Carolines, deep within the Japanese defensive perimeter, and at the same time helping General MacArthur in his attack on Hollandia. On the eve of "Overlord" Japan's strength was everywhere on the wane; her defence system in the Central Pacific had been breached at many points and was ripe for disruption.

Summing up these remarkable and intricate operations in the Southwest Pacific, General Marshall could report that in a little over twelve months the United States and her Allies had "pushed 1,300 miles closer to the heart of the Japanese Empire, cutting off more than 135,000 enemy troops beyond hope of rescue."

The Second Quebec Conference

ON Tuesday, September 5, 1944, we sailed once again from the Clyde in the *Queen Mary*. All the Chiefs of Staff came with me, and met daily, and sometimes twice a day, during our six days' voyage. I wanted, before meeting our American friends, to harmonise and grip the many plans and projects which were now before us. In Europe, "Overlord" was not only launched, but triumphant. How, when, and where could we strike at Japan, and assure for Britain an honourable share in the final victory there? We had lost as much, if not more, than the United States. Over 160,000 British prisoners and civilian internees were in Japanese hands. Singapore must be redeemed and Malaya freed. For nearly three years we had persisted in the strategy of "Germany First." The time had now come for the liberation of Asia, and I was determined that we should play our full and equal part in it.

Our main contribution must obviously be on the sea and in the air. Most of our Fleet was now free to move eastward, and I resolved that our first demand on our American Allies should be for its full participation in the main assault on Japan. The Royal Air Force should follow as soon as possible after Germany was defeated. But I was by no means certain that Germany would be defeated in 1944. It was true that we had had nearly seven weeks of unbroken military success. Paris was liberated and large areas of France had been cleared of the enemy. Our advance in Italy continued. The Soviet offensive, though temporarily halted, might at any moment surge forward again. Greece would soon be free. Hitler's "secret weapons" were almost mastered, and there was no evidence that he had learned how to make the atomic bomb. All these and many other factors induced a belief in our military circle that the Nazis would soon collapse. But I was not convinced.

Another matter lay heavy on my mind. I was very anxious to forestall the Russians in certain areas of Central Europe. The Hungarians, for instance, had expressed their intention of resisting the Soviet advance, but would surrender to a British force if it could arrive in time. If the Germans either evacuated Italy or retired to the Alps I much desired that Alexander should be enabled to make his amphibious thrust across the Adriatic, seize and occupy the Istrian Peninsula, and try to reach Vienna before the Russians. It seemed much too early to start sending his troops to Southeast Asia. The C.I.G.S. agreed that there should be no question of withdrawing any of Alexander's troops until Kesselring had been driven across the Piave. Our front would then be considerably less than half its present width. For the time being only the first of the Indian divisions needed for Burma would be taken from Alexander. I was discontented even at this prospect.

As for landing in the Istrian Peninsula, I was told that we should either have to borrow American landing craft which were due to leave for the Pacific or weaken the campaign in France. The rest of our craft were needed for taking Rangoon. This must be done before the May monsoon, and if we used these vessels in the Adriatic they would not get there in time.

As a result of our lengthy talks on the voyage we reached agreement about what we should say to our great Ally.

We landed at Halifax on September 10, and reached Quebec the following morning. The President and Mrs. Roosevelt, who were our guests, had arrived just before us, and the President waited at the station to greet me. Once again the Citadel was our home, while the staffs again monopolised the Château Frontenac. But this time, alas, there was no Harry Hopkins. He had sent me a telegram just before I left England: "Although I am now feeling much better, I still must take things easy, and I therefore feel that I should not run the risk of a setback in health by attempting to fight the Battle of Quebec on the Plains of Abraham, where better men than I have been killed." I was not then aware of the change in the character of his relationship with the President, but I was sure that he would be sorely missed.

Mr. Roosevelt asked me to open the discussion. I thereupon made a general survey of the war which I had prepared on the voyage. Since our meeting in Cairo the affairs of the United Nations had taken a revolutionary turn for the better. Everything we had touched had turned to gold, and during the last seven weeks there had been an unbroken run of military success. In Italy General Alexander had resumed the offensive at the end of August. I explained that I had been anxious lest he might be short of certain essentials for the vigorous prosecution of his campaign, but I now understood that the Combined Chiefs of Staff had agreed to withdraw nothing from his army until either Kesselring's troops had been destroyed or were on the run out of Italy.

General Marshall confirmed this undertaking, and I accordingly emphasised that in that case we should have to look for fresh woods and pastures new. It would never do for our armies to remain idle. I said I had always been attracted by a right-handed movement to give Germany a stab in the Adriatic armpit. Our objective should be Vienna. If German resistance collapsed we should of course be able to reach the city more quickly and more easily. If not I had given considerable thought to aiding this movement by capturing Istria and occupying Trieste and Fiume. I had been relieved to learn that the United States Chiefs of Staff were willing to leave in the Mediterranean certain landing craft now engaged in the attack on the south of France to provide an amphibious lift for such an operation, if this was found desirable and necessary. Another reason for this right-handed movement was the rapid encroachment of the Russians into the Balkan Peninsula and the dangerous spread of Soviet influence there.

I THEN turned to the Far East. Certain troublemakers had said that we would take no share in the war against Japan once Germany had been defeated. Far from shirking this task, the British Empire was eager to play the greatest possible part in it. We had every reason for doing so. Japan was as much the bitter enemy of the British Empire as of the United States. British territory had been captured in battle and grievous losses had been suffered. The offer I now made was for the British main fleet to take part in the major operations against Japan under United States Supreme Command. The President intervened to say that the British Fleet was no sooner offered than accepted. In this, though the fact was not mentioned, he overruled Admiral King's opinion.

I continued that placing a British fleet in the Central Pacific would not prevent us sending a detachment to General MacArthur in the Southwest Pacific if this was desired. We had of course no intention of interfering in any way with his command. As a further contribution to the defeat of the enemy, the Royal Air Force would like to take part in the heavy bombardment of Japan. A bomber force of no mean size could be made available, and would feel honoured to share with their American colleagues the dangers of striking at the heart of the enemy.

The President thanked me for this review, and said it was a matter of profound satisfaction that at each succeeding Conference between the Americans and the British there had been ever-increasing solidarity of outlook and identity of basic thought. Added to this there had always been an atmosphere of cordiality and friendship. Our fortunes had prospered, but it was still not quite possible to

forecast when the war with Germany would end. It was clear that the Germans were withdrawing from the Balkans, and it seemed likely that in Italy they would retire to the Alps. The Russians were on the edge of Hungary. The Germans had shown themselves good at staging withdrawals, and had been able to save many men, although they had lost much matériel. If Alexander's battle went well we should reach the Piave reasonably soon. All forces in Italy should be engaged to the maximum intensity. In the West it seemed probable that the Germans would retire behind the Rhine. Its right bank would be the western rampart of their defence and would present a formidable obstacle. We should have to attack them either from the east or from the west, and our plans must therefore be flexible. The Germans could not yet be counted out. One more big battle would have to be fought, and our operations against Japan would to some extent depend on what happened in Europe.

AS for Burma, the President agreed we should not remain there any longer than was necessary to clean up the Japanese in that theatre. The American plan was to regain the Philippines and to dominate the mainland of Japan from there or Formosa, and from bridgeheads which would be seized in China. If forces could be established on the mainland of China, China could be saved. American experience had been that the "end run" method paid a handsome dividend. Rabaul was an example of this bypassing technique which had brought considerable success at small cost of life. Would it not be possible, he asked, to bypass Singapore by seizing an area to the north or east of it, such as Bangkok? He said that he had not hitherto been greatly attracted to the Sumatra plan, but now the operation had acquired greater merit.

I said that all these projects were being examined and would be put in order. No decision could be reached until after we had taken Rangoon. It should not be overlooked that Stalin had volunteered a solemn undertaking at Tehran that Russia would enter the war against Japan the day that Hitler was beaten. There was no reason to doubt that Stalin would be as good as his word. The Russians undoubtedly had great ambitions in the East. If Hitler was beaten by, say, January, and Japan was confronted with the three most powerful nations in the world, she would undoubtedly think twice about continuing the fight.

I then cast back to make sure where we stood, and asked for a definite undertaking about employing the British Fleet in the main operations against Japan. "I should like," said the President, "to see the British Fleet wherever and whenever possible." Admiral King said that a paper had been prepared for the Combined Chiefs of Staff, and the question was being actively studied. "The offer of the British Fleet has been made," I repeated. "Is it accepted?" "Yes," said Mr. Roosevelt.

"Will you also let the British Air Force take part in the main operations?" Here it was much more difficult to get a direct answer. Marshall said that General Arnold and he were trying to see how to use the greatest number of aircraft they could. "Not so long ago," he explained, "we were crying out for planes. Now we have a glut. If you are going to be heavily engaged in Southeast Asia and Malaya won't you need most of your Air Force? Or is Portal's plan to bomb Japan something quite separate?" "Quite separate," answered Portal. "If our Lancaster bombers are refuelled in the air they can go nearly as far as your B-29s."

I said that for the sake of good relations, on which so much depended in the future, it was of vital importance that the British should be given their fair share in the main operations against Japan. The United States had given us the most handsome assistance in the fight against Germany. It was only to be expected that the British Empire in return should wish to give the United States all the help in their power towards defeating Japan.

During the days which followed I had a number of conversations with the President and his advisers, and we held our last meeting at midday on Saturday, September 16. The Combined Chiefs of Staff had now completed their final report to the President and myself, and at Mr. Roosevelt's request Admiral Leahy read it out to us paragraph by paragraph. The principal passages were as follows:

"The Supreme Commander's broad intention is to press on with all speed to destroy the German armed forces and occupy the heart of Germany. He considers his best opportunity of defeating the enemy in the West lies in striking at the Ruhr and Saar, since he is convinced that the enemy will concentrate the remainder of his available forces in the defence of these essential areas. . . .

"We have approved General Eisenhower's proposals and drawn his attention (a) to the advantages of the northern line of approach into Germany, as opposed to the southern, and (b) to the necessity for the opening up of the north-west ports, particularly Antwerp and Rotterdam, before bad weather sets in."

I had no quarrel with these broad intentions, but the reader will remember the doubts which I had voiced to the British Chiefs of Staff during our voyage across the Atlantic about the imminence of Germany's defeat. I had also written a paper in this sense. Rundstedt's counter-stroke was still to come, and the crossing of the Rhine was not to be achieved for more than another six months.

The military recommendations about Italy included the following: ". . . no major units should be withdrawn from Italy until the outcome of General Alexander's present offensive is known." Here I had to beware of bargains. No major units to be withdrawn until we knew the result of Alexander's offensive; so far, so good. But how far was the offensive to be pushed? If he was only to be allowed to go to the Rimini line, for instance, then the proposal was quite unacceptable. I accordingly said I presumed he would be allowed to invade and dominate the valley of the Po, and I was much relieved when Marshall and Leahy agreed that this was what they meant.

I then thanked Admiral King for promising to lend us his landing craft for an attack on the Istrian Peninsula. He stressed that they would also be wanted for the assault on Rangoon, and we must therefore make up our minds about invading Istria by October 15. The rest of the report was approved with little or no discussion. The planning date for the end of the war against Japan was set for the time being at eighteen months after the defeat of Germany.

On Sunday, September 17, I left Quebec by train with my wife and daughter Mary to pay a farewell visit to the President at Hyde Park. I lunched there on September 19. Harry Hopkins was present. He was obviously invited to please me. He explained to me his altered position. He had declined in the favour of the President. There was a curious incident at luncheon, when he arrived a few minutes late and the President did not even greet him. It was remarkable how definitely my contacts with the President improved and our affairs moved quicker as Hopkins appeared to regain his influence. In two days it seemed to be like old times. He said to me, "You must know I am not what I was." He had tried too much at once. Even his fullness of spirit broke under his variegated activities.

After dinner I left for New York, and boarded the *Queen Mary* the following morning. The voyage home was without incident. We arrived in the Clyde on September 25, and left immediately by train for London.

Burma and Beyond

THE curtain must now rise on a widely different scene in Southeast Asia. For more than eighteen months the Japanese had now been masters of a vast defensive arc covering their early conquests. This stretched from the jungle-covered hills and mountains of Northern and Western Burma, where our British and Indian troops were at close grips with them, across the sea to the Andamans and the great Dutch dependencies of Sumatra and Java, and thence in an easterly bend along the string of lesser islands to New Guinea.

The Americans had established a bomber force in China which was doing good work against the enemy's sea communications between the mainland and the Philippines. They wanted to extend this effort by basing long-range aircraft in China to attack Japan itself. The Burma Road was cut, and they were carrying all supplies for them and the Chinese armies by air over the southern spurs of the Himalayas, which they called "the Hump." This was a stupendous task. The American wish to succour China, not only by an ever-increasing airlift but also by land, led to heavy demands both upon Britain and the Indian Empire. They pressed as a matter of the highest urgency and importance the making of a new motor road from the existing roadhead at Ledo through 500 miles of jungles and mountains into Chinese territory. Only one metre-gauge, single-line railway ran through Assam to Ledo. It was already in constant use for many other needs, including the supply of the troops who held the frontier positions, but in order to build the road to China the Americans wanted us to reconquer Northern Burma first and quickly.

Certainly we favoured keeping China in the war and operating air forces from her territory, but a sense of proportion and the study of alternatives were needed. I disliked intensely the prospect of a large-scale campaign in Northern Burma. One could not choose a worse place for fighting the Japanese. Making a road from Ledo to

China was also an immense, laborious task, unlikely to be finished until the need for it had passed. Even if it were done in time to replenish the Chinese armies while they were still engaged it would make little difference to their fighting capacity. The need to strengthen the American air bases in China would also, in our view, diminish as Allied advances in the Pacific and from Australia gained us airfields closer to Japan. On both counts therefore we argued that the enormous expenditure of manpower and matériel would not be worth while. But we never succeeded in deflecting the Americans from their purpose. Their national psychology is such that the bigger the Idea the more wholeheartedly and obstinately do they throw themselves into making it a success. It is an admirable characteristic provided the Idea is good.

WE of course wanted to recapture Burma, but we did not want to have to do it by land advances from slender communications and across the most forbidding fighting country imaginable. The south of Burma, with its port of Rangoon, was far more valuable than the north. But all of it was remote from Japan. I myself wished, on the contrary, to contain the Japanese in Burma, and to break into or through the great arc of islands forming the outer fringe of the Netherlands Indies. Our whole British Indian Imperial front would thus advance across the Bay of Bengal into close contact with the enemy, by using amphibious power at every stage. This divergence of opinion, albeit honestly held and frankly discussed, and with decisions loyally executed, continued. It is against this permanent background of geography, limited resources, and clash of policies that the story of the campaign should be read.

It had opened in December 1943, when General Stilwell, with two Chinese divisions which he had organised and trained in India, crossed the watershed from Ledo into the jungles below the main mountain ranges. He was opposed by the renowned Japanese 18th Division, but forged ahead steadily, and by early January had penetrated forty miles, while the road makers toiled behind him. In the south a British Corps began to advance down the Arakan coast of the Bay of Bengal, and at the same time, with the aid of newly arrived Spitfires, we gained a degree of air superiority which was shortly to prove invaluable.

In February our advance was suddenly halted. The Japanese also had a plan. Since November they had increased their strength in Burma from five divisions to eight, and they now proposed to invade Eastern India and raise the flag of rebellion against the British. Their first stroke was an offensive in the Arakan towards the port of Chittagong, which would draw off our reserves and also our attention. Holding our 5th Division frontally on the coast, they passed the better part of a division through the jungle and round the flank of the 7th Division, which was farther inland. Within a few days it was surrounded and the enemy threatened to cut the coastal road behind the 5th Division. They fully expected both divisions to withdraw, but they had reckoned without one factor, supply by air. The 7th Division grouped themselves into perimeters, stood their ground, and fought it out. For a fortnight food, water, and ammunition were delivered to them, like manna, from above. The enemy had no such facilities; they had taken with them only ten days' supply, and the obstinacy of the 7th Division prevented more reaching them. Unable to overwhelm our forward troops, pressed from the north by a division we brought from reserve, they broke up into small parties to fight their way back through the jungle, leaving 5,000 dead behind. This terminated the legend of Japanese invincibility in the jungle.

More, however, was to come. In this same February of 1944 there were sure signs that our central front at Imphal would also be attacked. We ourselves were preparing to advance to the Chindwin river, and the now famous Chindits, the familiar name for Wingate's Long-Range Penetration Force, were poised for a daring stroke against the enemy supply lines and communications, notably those of the Japanese Division with whom Stilwell was at close grips.

Although it was clear that the Japanese would get their blow in first it was decided that Wingate's brigades should carry on with their task. One of his brigades had already started on February 5. They marched across 450 miles of mountain and jungle and were supplied solely from the air. On March 5, sustained by an American "Air Commando" of 250 machines, the fly-in of two more Brigades of British and Gurkha troops began. After assembly at their rallying point they set out and cut the railway north of Indaw. Wingate did not live long to enjoy this first success or to reap its fruits. On March 24, to my great distress, he was killed in the air. With him a bright flame was extinguished.

The main enemy blow fell, as we expected, on our central front. On March 8 three Japanese divisions attacked. General Scoones withdrew his IV Corps, also of three divisions, to the Imphal plateau, so as to fight concentrated on ground of his own choosing. The Japanese repeated the tactics they had used with misfortune in the Arakan. They counted on capturing our stores at Imphal to feed themselves. They intended to cut both the road to Dimapur and also the railway there, and thus sever the supply route maintaining Stilwell's force and the United States airlift to China. Important issues were at stake.

THE key lay again in transport aircraft. Mountbatten had considerable resources but they were not nearly enough. He sought to retain twenty United States aircraft already borrowed from "the Hump" traffic, and asked for seventy more. This was a hard requirement to make or to procure. In the anxious weeks that followed I gave him my strongest support. We halted our operations on the Arakan coast, withdrew the victorious Indian divisions, and flew them to his aid. The 5th went to Imphal, where the enemy were now pressing hard on the fringes of the plain from three sides; the 7th to Dimapur. Thither by rail also came the headquarters of General Stopford's XXXII Corps, together with a British division and another two brigades. The road through the mountains was now cut, and these new forces began to fight their way upwards.

Between them and Imphal lay the roadside township of Kohima, which commanded the pass to the Assam valley, and here, on April 4, the Japanese launched yet another furious onslaught. They used a whole division. Our garrison consisted of a battalion of the Royal West Kent, a

Nepalese battalion, and a battalion of the Assam Rifles, with every man, and even convalescents from the hospital, who could bear arms. They were slowly forced back into a diminishing area, and finally on to a single hill. They had no supplies except what was dropped on them by parachutes. Attacked on every side, they held on steadfastly, supported by bombing and cannon fire from the air, until General Stopford relieved them on the 20th. Four thousand Japanese were killed. The valiant defence of Kohima against enormous odds was a fine episode.

The climax came in May 1944. Sixty thousand British and Indian soldiers, with all their modern equipment, were confined in a circle on the Imphal plain. I could feel the stress amid all other business. All depended on the transport planes. On the principle "Nothing matters but the battle" I used my authority. On the 4th I telegraphed to Admiral Mountbatten: "Let nothing go from the battle that you need for victory. I will not accept denial of this from any quarter, and will back you to the full."

Most of his needs were met in the end, but for more than another month the situation was at full strain. Our Air was dominant, but the monsoon was hindering the air supply, on which our success depended. All four divisions of the IV Corps were slowly pushing outwards against their encirclement. All along the Kohima road the relieving force and the besieged were fighting their way towards each other. It was a race against time. We marked their progress with tense feelings. On June 22 I cabled to Mountbatten: "Chiefs of Staff have expressed anxiety about the situation in Imphal, particularly in respect of reserves of supplies and ammunition. You are absolutely entitled to ask for all aircraft necessary to maintain the situation, whether they come from 'the Hump' or any other source. 'The Hump' must be considered the current reserve, and should be drawn upon whenever necessary. . . . If you fail to make your demands in good time, invoking me if necessary to help from here, it will be no good complaining afterwards if it is not a success. Keep your hand close on the job, which seems to me both serious and critical. Every good wish."

The finale came while this message was on the way. I quote his report: "In the third week in June the situation was critical, and it seemed possible, after all the efforts of the previous two months, that early in July the IV Corps would finally run out of reserves. But on June 22, with a week and a half in hand, the 2nd British and 5th Indian Divisions met at a point twenty-nine miles north of Imphal and the road to the plain was open. On the same day the convoys began to roll in."

Thus ended Japan's invasion of India. Their losses had been ruinous. Over 13,000 dead were counted on the

---

8 Aug 43

PRIME MINISTER TO GENERAL ISMAY

Operations in which large numbers of men may lose their lives ought not to be described by code words which imply a boastful and overconfident sentiment or which are calculated to invest the plan with an air of despondency, such as "Woebetide." They ought not to be names of a frivolous character, such as "Bunnyhug," "Billingsgate," "Aperitif," and "Ballyhoo."

2. After all, the world is wide, and intelligent thought will readily supply names which do not suggest the character of the operation or disparage it in any way and do not enable some widow or mother to say that her son was killed in an operation called "Bunnyhug," or "Ballyhoo."

---

battlefields, and, allowing for those who died of wounds, disease, or hunger, the total amounted on a Japanese estimate to 65,000 men.

The monsoon, now at its height, had in previous years brought active operations to a standstill, and the enemy doubtless counted on a pause during which they could extricate and rebuild their shattered forces. They were given no such respite. The British Indian Fourteenth Army, under the able and forceful leadership of General Slim, took the offensive. All along the mountain tracks they found evidence of disaster—quantities of abandoned guns, transport, and equipment; thousands dead or dying. Progress, measured in miles a day, was very slow. But our men were fighting in tropical rainfall, soaked to the skin by day and night. The so-called roads were mostly fair-weather dust tracks, now churned into deep mud, through which guns and vehicles had often to be manhandled. It was not the slowness of advance but the fact that any advance was made at all that should cause surprise.

The Chindits had meanwhile been reinforced, and five of their brigades were now working their way northward up the railway from Indaw, preventing passage of reinforcements and destroying dumps as they went. Despite the havoc they caused, the Japanese withdrew nothing from the Imphal front and only one battalion from Stilwell's. They brought their 53rd Division from Thailand and tried, at the cost of over 5,400 killed, but without success, to quell the nuisance. Stilwell continued his steady progress and captured Myitkyina on August 3, thus providing a staging post for the American airlift to China. The "Hump" traffic had no longer to make the direct and often dangerous flight from Northern Assam over the great mountains to Kunming. Work proceeded on the long road from Northern Assam, destined later to link up with the former road from Burma to China, and the strain on rearward communications was relieved by a new 750-mile oil pipeline laid from Calcutta, a greater span than the famous desert pipeline from Iraq to Haifa.

At this juncture I was in conference with the President at Quebec, and in spite of these successes I continued to urge that it was most undesirable that the fighting in the jungles should go on indefinitely. I desired an amphibious stroke across the Bay of Bengal on Rangoon, at the base of the Burmese land mass. If the Fourteenth Army then swept down from Central Burma we might clear the way for an assault on Sumatra. But all these projects called for men and matériel, and there was not enough in Southeast Asia. The only place they could come from was Europe. Landing craft would have to be taken either from the Mediterranean or from "Overlord," and the troops from Italy and elsewhere, and they would have to leave soon. It was now September. Rangoon lies forty miles up a winding estuary, complicated with backwaters and mud banks. The monsoon starts in early May, and we should therefore have to attack by April 1945 at the latest. Was it yet safe to start weakening our effort in Europe? We carried the Americans with us on the Rangoon plan, but the sanguine hopes, which I had not shared, that Germany would collapse before the end of the year faded. It became obvious that German resistance would continue into and beyond the winter, and Mountbatten was accordingly instructed, not for the first time, that he must do what he could with what he had got.

And so the Fourteenth Army forged slowly ahead in the largest land engagement with Japan which had so far been attained. The good hygiene discipline now practised by all our units, the use of the new drug mepacrine, and constant spraying with D.D.T. insecticide, kept the sick rate admirably low. The Japanese were not versed in these precautions and died in hundreds. The Fourteenth Army joined hands with the Chinese and the Americans from the north, who now included a British division, and by early December, with two bridgeheads across the Chindwin, was poised for the main advance into the central plain of Burma.

In defiance of chronology, we may here pursue the story to its victorious conclusion. Formidable administrative problems now intervened. Far away in Southeast China, the Japanese had begun an advance on Chungking, the Generalissimo's capital, and Kunming, the delivery point of the American supply airlift. The Americans took a serious view of this situation. Their forward Air Force bases were being overrun. Chiang Kai-shek's troops gave little promise, and General Wedemeyer now appealed for two of the Chinese divisions in North Burma, and also for more American air squadrons, in particular for three transport squadrons. These were hard tidings, but we had no choice but to accept. The loss of two good Chinese divisions was not so grave an inconvenience as parting with the transport squadrons. The Fourteenth Army was 400 miles beyond its railhead and General Slim relied on air supply to help the tenuous road link. The squadrons had to go, and although later replaced, mostly from British sources, their absence inflicted severe delay on the campaign. In spite of all this the Fourteenth Army broke out of the hills into the plain northwest of Mandalay, and by the end of January 1945, General Sultan, who had succeeded Stilwell, reopened the land route to China.

Hard strategic decisions faced Admiral Mountbatten when the decisive battle across the Irrawaddy began in the following month. His instructions were to liberate Burma,

for which purpose he was not to expect greater resources than he already had, and then to occupy Malaya and open the Malacca Strait. Weather was dominant. The first task was to occupy the central plain of Burma and capture Rangoon before the monsoon, and the monsoon was due in early May. He could either concentrate the whole Fourteenth Army on a decisive battle in the Mandalay plain and make a swift advance to the south, or use some of his troops for an amphibious operation against Rangoon. In either case, much depended on air supply, in which United States aircraft played a big part. Aid to China still dominated American policy, and more planes might be withdrawn and his plans ruined. In face of these dangers, soon to become acute, Mountbatten now decided on a single, fully supported operation against the main enemy body west of Mandalay, and a subsequent advance on Rangoon, which, he was advised, could be reached by April 15.

Henceforward events moved swiftly. One of his divisions had already seized bridgeheads across the Irrawaddy about forty miles north of Mandalay, and throughout February they beat off a series of fierce counterattacks. On February 12 the 20th Division crossed the river lower down and to the west of Mandalay. For a fortnight they had a hard fight to hold their gains, but by then they were joined by the 2nd British Division. This convinced the Japanese High Command that a decisive battle was imminent, and they sent heavy reinforcements. They did not believe that a serious flank attack was also possible, and even dispatched to Thailand a division they could ill spare. This however was precisely the stroke which General Slim had prepared.

On February 13 the 7th Division crossed the Irrawaddy south of Pakokku and formed a bridgehead. The enemy thought this was a mere diversion, but he was soon to be better informed. On the 21st two motorised brigades of the 17th Division and a brigade of tanks broke out from the bridgehead, and reached Meiktila on the 28th. Here was the principal administrative centre of the Japanese main front, a nodal point of their communications and the focus of several airfields. It was strongly defended, and the enemy sent two divisions posthaste to aid the garrison, but they were held at a distance until our reinforcements arrived. After a week of bitter fighting the town was in our hands, and all attempts to recapture it were repulsed. The Japanese admit losing 5,000 men and as many wounded in a battle which their Commander-in-Chief has since described as "the master stroke of Allied strategy."

Far off to the northeast General Sultan was also on the move, and by mid-March he had reached the road from

Retaking of Burma followed failures of Japanese (*black*) to invade India in 1944. British drive south (*brown*) was aided by U.S. and Chinese attacks in north and by landing at Rangoon in May.

Lashio to Mandalay. But Chiang Kai-shek now imposed a halt. He would not allow his Chinese divisions to continue. He insisted on removing them and suggested that General Slim should halt his advance when Mandalay was taken. This was precisely what Mountbatten and his Staff had feared when he made his plans a month before, and in the event the Japanese were able to take two of their three divisions from this front and march them against our Fourteenth Army.

The conjoint battles of Mandalay and Meiktila raged through March. The 19th Division broke out of its bridgeheads, fought down the east bank of the Irrawaddy and entered Mandalay on the 9th. Mandalay Hill, 780 feet above the surrounding country, was taken in two days, but the Japanese resisted strongly and the massive walls of Fort Dufferin were impenetrable to ordinary missiles. Finally a breach was made with 2,000-pound bombs, and on the 20th the enemy fled. The rest of XXXIII Corps meanwhile fought on to Meiktila. They met great opposition, as the Japanese Commander-in-Chief, in spite of the intervention of the 17th Division behind his front, showed no signs as yet of withdrawing, and the armies were well matched. But at the end of the month the enemy gave up the struggle and began to fall back down the main road to Toungoo and Rangoon, and through the mountains to the east.

The battles, however, had lasted much longer than we expected. General Sultan was halted on the Lashio road, and there was now no prospect of the Fourteenth Army reaching Rangoon by mid-April. Indeed, it was very doubtful if they could get there before the monsoon descended. Mountbatten accordingly decided to make an amphibious assault on the town after all. This would have to be much smaller than we had hoped, and even so it could not be launched before the first week in May. By then it might be too late. General Slim was nevertheless determined not only to reach Rangoon but to draw a double net down Southern Burma and trap the enemy within it. The XXXIII Corps from Meiktila accordingly drove down the Irrawaddy with overlapping thrusts and reached Prome on May 2. The IV Corps, victors at Imphal and Mandalay, advanced even more swiftly along the road and the railway to the east. An armoured column, and the mechanised brigades of the 5th and 17th Divisions, leapfrogging over each other, reached Toungoo on April 22. The next bound was to Pegu, whose capture would close the enemy's southernmost escape route from Lower Burma. Our advance troops reached it on April 29. That afternoon torrential rain fell, heralding an early monsoon. Forward airstrips were out of action; tanks and vehicles could not move off the roads. The Japanese mustered every possible man to hold the town and the bridges over the river. On May 2 the 17th Division finally broke through, and, hoping to be first in Rangoon, prepared to advance the few remaining miles.

BUT May 2 was also the D-Day of the amphibious assault. For two days beforehand Allied heavy bombers attacked the defences at Elephant Point which barred the entrance to Rangoon River. On May 1 a parachute battalion dropped on the defenders and the channel was opened for mine sweeping. Next day ships of the 26th Division, supported by 224 Group R.A.F., reached the river mouth. A Mosquito aircraft flew over Rangoon and saw no signs of the enemy. The crew landed at a nearby airfield, walked into the city, and were greeted by a number of our prisoners of war. In the belief that an amphibious attack was no longer likely, the Japanese garrison had departed some days before to hold Pegu. That afternoon the monsoon broke in all its violence, and Rangoon fell with only a few hours to spare.

The amphibious force soon reached up to Pegu and to Prome. Many thousands of Japanese were trapped, and during the next three months great numbers perished in attempts to escape eastwards. Thus ended the long struggle in Burma in which the Fourteenth Army had fought valiantly, overcome all obstacles, and achieved the seemingly impossible.

The Battle of Leyte Gulf

BY June 1944 Japan's only hope of survival lay in victory at sea. To conserve her strength for this perilous but vital hazard the main body had withdrawn from Truk and was now divided between the East Indies and her home waters; but events soon brought it to battle. At the beginning of June Admiral Spruance struck with his carriers at the Marianas, and on the 15th he landed on the fortified island of Saipan. If he captured Saipan and the adjacent islands of Tinian and Guam the enemy's defence perimeter would be broken. The threat was formidable, and the Japanese Fleet resolved to intervene. That day five of their battleships and nine carriers were sighted near the Philippines, heading east. Spruance had ample time to make his dispositions. His main purpose was to protect the landing at Saipan. This he did. He then gathered his ships, fifteen of which were carriers, and waited for the enemy to the west of the island. On June 19 Japanese carrier-borne aircraft attacked the American carrier fleet from all directions, and air fighting continued throughout the day. The Americans suffered little damage, and so shattered the Japanese air squadrons that their carriers had to withdraw.

That night Spruance searched in vain for the vanished enemy. Late in the afternoon of the 20th he found them about 250 miles away. Attacking just before sunset, the American airmen sank one carrier and damaged four others, besides a battleship and a heavy cruiser. The previous day American submarines had sunk two other large carriers. No further attack was possible, and remnants of the enemy fleet managed to escape, but its departure sealed the fate of Saipan. Though the garrison fought hard the landings continued, the buildup progressed, and by July 9 all organised resistance came to an end. The neighbouring islands of Guam and Tinian were overcome, and by the first days of August the American grip on the Marianas was complete.

The fall of Saipan was a great shock to the Japanese High Command, and led indirectly to the dismissal of

General Tojo's Government. The enemy's concern was indeed well founded. The fortress was little more than 1,300 miles from Tokyo. They had believed it was impregnable; now it was gone. Their southern defence regions were cut off and the American heavy bombers had gained a first-class base for attacking the very homeland of Japan. For a long time United States submarines had been sinking Japanese merchantmen along the China coast, and now the way was open for other warships to join in the onslaught. Japan's oil and raw materials would be cut off if the Americans advanced any farther. The Japanese Fleet was still powerful, but unbalanced, and so weak in destroyers, carriers, and aircrews that it could no longer fight effectively without land-based planes. Fuel was scarce, and not only hampered training but made it impossible to concentrate the ships in one place, so that in the late summer most of the heavy vessels and cruisers lay near Singapore and the oil supplies of the Netherlands Indies, while the few surviving carriers remained in Japan's home waters, where their new air groups were finishing their training.

The plight of the Japanese Army was little better. Though remaining strong in numbers, it sprawled over China and Southeast Asia or languished in remote islands beyond reach of support. The more sober-minded of the enemy leaders began to look for some way of ending the war; but their military machine was far too strong for them. The High Command brought reinforcements from Manchuria and ordered a fight to the finish both in Formosa and the Philippines. Here and in the homeland the troops would die where they stood. The Japanese Admiralty were no less resolute. If they lost the impending battle for the islands the oil from the East Indies would be cut off. There was no purpose, they argued, in preserving ships without fuel. Steeled for sacrifice but hopeful of victory, they decided in August to send the entire Fleet into battle.

On September 15 the Americans made another advance. General MacArthur seized Morotai Island, midway between the western tip of New Guinea and the Philippines, and Admiral Halsey, who had now assumed command of the United States naval forces, captured an advanced base for his fleet in the Palau group. These simultaneous moves were of high importance. At the same time Halsey continually probed the defences of the enemy with his whole

force. Thus he hoped to provoke a general action at sea which would enable him to destroy the Japanese Fleet, particularly its surviving carriers. The next leap would be at the Philippines themselves, and there now occurred a dramatic change in the American plan.

Till then our Allies had purposed to invade the southernmost portion of the Philippines, the island of Mindanao, and planes from Halsey's carriers had already attacked the Japanese airfields both there and in the large northern island of Luzon. They destroyed large numbers of enemy aircraft, and discovered in the clash of combat that the Japanese garrison at Leyte was unexpectedly weak. This small but now famous island, lying between the two larger but strategically less important land masses of Mindanao and Luzon, became the obvious point for the American descent. On September 13, while the Allies were still in conference at Quebec, Admiral Nimitz, at Halsey's suggestion, urged its immediate invasion. General MacArthur agreed, and so within two days the American Chiefs of Staff resolved to attack on the 20th of October, two months earlier than had been planned. Such was the genesis of the Battle of Leyte Gulf.

On October 10 the Americans opened their new campaign with raids on airfields between Japan and the Philippines. Devastating and repeated attacks on Formosa provoked the most violent resistance, and from the 12th to the 16th there was a heavy and sustained air battle between shipborne and land-based aircraft. The Americans inflicted grievous losses both in the air and on the ground, but suffered little themselves, and their carrier fleet withstood powerful land-based air attack. The result was decisive. The enemy's Air Force was broken before the battle for Leyte was joined. Many Japanese naval aircraft destined for the fleet carriers were improvidently sent to Formosa as reinforcements and there destroyed. Thus in the supreme naval battle which now impended the Japanese carriers were manned and fought by little more than a hundred partially trained pilots.

To comprehend the engagements which followed, a study of the accompanying maps is necessary. The two large islands of the Philippines, Luzon in the north and Mindanao in the south, are separated by a group of smaller islands, of which Leyte is the key and centre. This central group is pierced by two navigable straits, both of them destined to dominate this famous battle. The northerly strait is

Battle for Leyte began as U.S. invasion fleets (*blue*) were menaced by three Japanese fleets (*black*). When bombed, center enemy force pretended to flee. This prompted U.S. Third Fleet to go for decoy force in north, leaving San Bernardino Strait unguarded.

San Bernardino, and about 200 miles to the south of it, leading directly to Leyte, is the strait of Surigao. The Americans, as we have seen, intended to seize Leyte, and the Japanese were inflexibly resolved to stop them and to destroy their fleet.

The plan was simple and desperate. Four divisions under General MacArthur would land on Leyte, protected by the guns and planes of the American fleet—so much they knew or guessed. Draw off this fleet, entice it far to the north, and engage it in a secondary battle—such was the first step. But this would be only a preliminary. As soon as the main fleet was lured away two strong columns of warships would sail through the straits, one through San Bernardino and the other through Surigao, and converge on the landings. All eyes would be on the shores of Leyte, all guns trained on the beaches, and the heavy ships and the big aircraft carriers which alone could withstand the assault would be chasing the decoy force in the far north. The plan very nearly succeeded.

On October 17 the Japanese Commander-in-Chief ordered his fleet to sail. The decoy force, under Admiral Ozawa, the Supreme Commander, sailing direct from Japan, steered for Luzon. It was a composite force, including battleships, carriers, cruisers, and destroyers. Ozawa's task was to appear on the eastern coast of Luzon, engage the American fleet, and draw it away from the landings in Leyte Gulf. The carriers were short of both planes and pilots, but no matter. They were only bait, and bait is made to be eaten. Meanwhile the main Japanese striking forces made for the straits. The larger, or what may be termed the Centre Force, coming from Singapore, and consisting of five battleships, twelve cruisers, and fifteen destroyers, under Admiral Kurita, headed for San Bernardino to curl round Samar Island to Leyte; the smaller, or Southern Force, in two independent groups, comprising in all two battleships, four cruisers, and eight destroyers, sailed through Surigao.

On October 20 the Americans landed on Leyte. At first all went well. Resistance on shore was weak, a bridgehead was quickly formed, and General MacArthur's troops began their advance. They were supported by Admiral Kinkaid's Seventh United States Fleet, which was under MacArthur's command, and whose older battleships and small aircraft carriers were well suited to amphibious

operations. Further away to the northward lay Admiral Halsey's main fleet, shielding them from an attack by sea.

The crisis however was still to come. On October 23 American submarines sighted the Japanese Centre Force (Admiral Kurita) off the coast of Borneo and sank two of his heavy cruisers, one of which was Kurita's flagship, and damaged a third. Next day, October the 24th, planes from Admiral Halsey's carriers joined in the attack. The giant battleship *Musashi*, mounting nine eighteen-inch guns, was sunk, other vessels were damaged, and Kurita turned back. The reports of the American airmen were optimistic and perhaps misleading, and Halsey concluded, not without reason, that the battle was won, or at any rate this part of it. He knew that the second or Southern enemy force was approaching the Surigao Strait, but he judged, and events were to prove him right, that it could be repelled by Kinkaid's Seventh Fleet. But one thing disturbed him. During the day he had been attacked by Japanese naval planes. Many of them were shot down, but the carrier *Princeton* was damaged and had later to be abandoned. The planes, he reasoned, probably came from carriers, for it was most unlikely that the enemy had sailed without them. Yet none had so far been found. The main Japanese fleet, under Admiral Kurita, had been located, and was apparently in retreat, but Kurita had no carriers, neither were there any in the Southern Force. Surely there must be a carrier force, and it was imperative to find it. He accordingly ordered a search to the north,

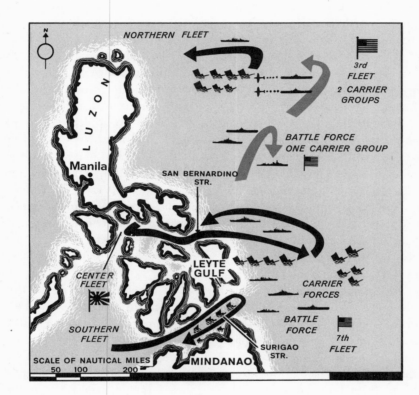

Crisis in Leyte Gulf arose when the Japanese center fleet turned back to maul U.S. force of escort carriers lying off beachhead. Although bulk of U.S. forces were away in north and south disposing of other threats, Japanese center fleet then unaccountably withdrew.

and late in the afternoon of October 24 his flyers came upon Admiral Ozawa's decoy force, far to the northeast of Luzon and steering south. Four carriers, two battleships equipped with flying decks, three cruisers, and ten destroyers! Here, he concluded, was the source of trouble and the real target. If he could now destroy these carriers, he and his Chief of Staff, Admiral Carney, rightly considered that the power of the Japanese fleet to intervene in future operations would be broken irretrievably. This was a dominating factor in his mind, and would be of particular advantage when MacArthur came later to attack Luzon. Halsey could not know how frail was their power, nor that most of the attacks he had endured came not from carriers at all but from airfields in Luzon itself. Kurita's Centre Force was in retreat. Kinkaid could cope with the Southern Force and protect the landings at Leyte, the way was clear for a final blow, and Halsey ordered his whole fleet to steam northward and destroy Admiral Ozawa next day. Thus he fell into the trap. That same afternoon Kurita again turned east, and sailed once more for the San Bernardino Strait. This time there was nothing to stop him.

Meanwhile the Southern Japanese Force was nearing Surigao Strait, and that night they entered it in two groups. A fierce battle followed, in which all types of vessel, from battleships to light coastal craft, were closely engaged. The first group was annihilated by Kinkaid's fleet, which was concentrated at the northern exit; the second group tried to break through in the darkness and confusion, but was driven back. All seemed to be going well, but the Americans had still to reckon with Admiral Kurita.

WHILE Kinkaid was fighting in the Surigao Strait and Halsey was steaming in hard pursuit of the decoy force far to the northward, Kurita had passed unchallenged in the darkness through the strait of San Bernardino, and in the early morning of October 25 he fell upon a group of escort carriers who were supporting General MacArthur's landings. Taken by surprise and too slow-moving to escape, they could not at once rearm their planes to repel the onslaught from the sea. For about two and a half hours the small American ships fought a valiant retreat under cover of smoke. Two of their carriers, three destroyers, and over a hundred planes were lost, one of the carriers by suicide bomber attack; but they succeeded in sinking three enemy cruisers and damaging others. Help was far away. Kinkaid's heavy ships were now well south of Leyte, having routed the Southern Force, and were short of ammunition and fuel. Halsey, with ten carriers and all his fast battleships, was even yet more distant, and although another of his carrier groups had been detached to refuel and was now recalled it could not arrive for some hours. Victory seemed to be in Kurita's hands. There was nothing to stop him steaming into Leyte Gulf and destroying MacArthur's amphibious fleet.

But once again Kurita turned back. His reasons are obscure. Many of his ships had been bombed and scattered by Kinkaid's light escort carriers, and he now knew that the Southern Force had met with disaster. He had no information about the fortunes of the decoys in the north and he was uncertain of the whereabouts of the American fleets. Intercepted signals made him think that Kinkaid and Halsey were converging on him in overwhelming strength and that MacArthur's transports had already managed to escape. Alone and unsupported, he now abandoned the desperate venture for which so much had been sacrificed and which was about to gain its prize, and, without attempting to enter Leyte Gulf, he turned about and steered once more for the San Bernardino Strait. He hoped to fight a last battle on the way with Halsey's fleet, but even this was denied him.

In response to Kinkaid's repeated calls for support Halsey had indeed at last turned back with his battleships, leaving two carrier groups to continue the pursuit to the north. During the day these destroyed all four of Ozawa's carriers. But Halsey himself got back to San Bernardino too late. The fleets did not meet. Kurita escaped. Next day Halsey's and MacArthur's planes pursued the Japanese

admiral and sank another cruiser and two more destroyers. This was the end of the battle. It may well be that Kurita's mind had become confused by the pressure of events. He had been under constant attack for three days, he had suffered heavy losses, and his flagship had been sunk soon after starting from Borneo. Those who have endured a similar ordeal may judge him.

The Battle of Leyte Gulf was decisive. At a cost to themselves of three carriers, three destroyers, and a submarine the Americans had conquered the Japanese Fleet. The struggle had lasted from October 22 to October 27. Three battleships, four carriers, and twenty other enemy warships had been sunk, and the suicide bomber was henceforward the only effective naval weapon left to the foe. As an instrument of despair it was still deadly, but it carried no hope of victory.

Long should this victory be treasured in American history. Apart from valour, skill, and daring, it shed a light on the future more vivid and far-reaching than any we had seen. It shows a battle fought less with guns than by predominance in the air. I have told the tale fully because at the time it was almost unknown to the harassed European world. Perhaps the most important single conclusion to be derived from study of these great events is the vital need for unity of command in conjoint operations of this kind in place of the concept of control by co-operation such as existed between MacArthur and Halsey at this time. The Americans learnt this lesson, and in the final operations planned against the homeland of Japan they intended that supreme command should be exercised by either Admiral Nimitz or General MacArthur, as might be advisable at any given moment.

IN the following weeks the fight for the Philippines spread and grew. By the end of November nearly a quarter of a million Americans had landed in Leyte, and by mid-December Japanese resistance was broken. MacArthur pressed on with his main advance, and soon landed without opposition on Mindoro Island, little more than a hundred miles from Manila itself. On January 9, 1945, a new phase opened with the landing of four divisions in Lingayen Gulf, north of Manila, which had been the scene of the major Japanese invasion three years before. Elaborate deception measures kept the enemy in doubt as to where the blow would fall. It came as a surprise and was only lightly opposed. As the Americans thrust towards Manila resistance stiffened, but they made two more landings on the west coast and surrounded the city. A desperate defence held out until early March, when the last survivors were killed. Sixteen thousand Japanese dead were counted in the ruins.

Attacks by suicide aircraft were now inflicting considerable losses, sixteen ships being hit in a single day. The cruiser *Australia*, unlucky once before, was hit five times in four days, but stayed in action. This desperate expedient however caused no check to the fleets. In mid-January Admiral Halsey's carriers broke unmolested into the South China Sea, ranging widely along the coast and attacking airfields and shipping as far west as Saigon. At Hong Kong on January 16 widespread damage was inflicted, and great oil fires were started at Canton.

In the first wary move from beach to jungle fringe on the island of Rendova in the Solomons, a soldier sets up the tripod for his machine gun

STEPS TO TOKYO

The Swampy Road
up the Solomons

In the foul water and rotting leaves of Bougainville, painted below by Kerr Eby, Marines slogging knee-deep through the island jungle in November of 1943 could see the progress of the Southwest Pacific war only as an agonizing crawl. In terrain where the enemy might be invisibly posed 15 feet away, advances were slow and stumbling, and the reward for success was only a chance to take a crack at still

another sodden, malarial and undesirable island. But the truth was that these soldiers were taking a strategic giant step. The first American counteroffensives on Guadalcanal and New Guinea had revealed that the Japanese would fight for their outposts until the last man had been blasted out or burned alive. Now, with increasing Allied command of the sea and air, it had become possible to go around the principal Japanese strongholds and to "hit them where they ain't" by landing on unoccupied or lightly held coastlines, setting up bases for further advances and letting the bypassed garrisons starve and rot where they were. Bougainville was 400 miles up the ladder of the Solomon Islands from the first landing at Guadalcanal. Tokyo was still 3,000 miles to go, but the Americans were on their way.

A hail of fire meets U.S. soldiers paddling to shore near Arawe. Forming a diversionary attack intended to draw the Japanese away from the main landings, the soldiers expected to land on an undefended beach.

But Japanese machine guns were in position, and the boats made easy targets in the moonlight. Both paintings here are by David Fredenthal, who was in one of the three boats that missed being sunk that night.

A Night Landing on New Britain

As they island-hopped toward Tokyo, the Allies closed in on Rabaul, the once-sleepy trading port on New Britain which the Japanese had built into their mightiest base in the Southwest Pacific. Rabaul was the heart of Japan's outermost line of defenses and prevented an approach to her vital conquests in the East Indies and the Philippines.

To avoid a direct attack on this bristling fortress the Allies grabbed a number of islands and jungle beachheads in a wide circle around it. At Arawe, 300 impenetrable jungle miles from Rabaul, they crushed the small Japanese garrison after bitter engagements like the one shown here. On the captured outposts, airfields were built from which Rabaul was kept under constant attack. There, 100,000 Japanese garrison troops found themselves with nothing to do between air raids but watch their equipment rust and their food stocks dwindle, all the rest of the war.

Naked survivors (*right*), who had torn off their clothes to swim easily, cling to a boat overloaded with wounded as a sub-chaser comes to the rescue. All but 16 of the men in this action were eventually saved.

Rain of Fire
on Coral Islands

While the slow advance up the Solomons across the Southwest Pacific ground on through 1943, a straighter, harder blow at Japan was launched in the vast spaces of the Central Pacific. There, the Japanese had built a web of fortresses out of every coral atoll where ships could anchor or planes could land. Through them the U.S. Navy was now ready to move in force.

First goal was Tarawa. There the 2nd Marine Division got into landing boats on November 20 and soon found that two mistakes had been made. The naval bombardment which was supposed to obliterate the island's defenses had had little effect on the concrete and log bunkers which overlooked the beaches. And the planners had failed to foresee that the neap tide would lower the water over the fringing reef so far that the assault boats stuck and some of the men had to wade as much as 700 yards to shore under direct fire. The Marines did not turn back and—though they had 3,030 killed and wounded—they conquered Tarawa in eight days. Every man but 146 of the more than 4,500 in the Japanese garrison was killed.

The hard lesson of Tarawa was quickly learned. More devastating bombardments, more careful preparation and improved amphibious equipment brought the Americans in two prodigious leaps across the Pacific, 540 miles to Kwajalein and 360 more to Eniwetok, with only minor losses.

Burned alive (*left*), a Japanese on Eniwetok is enveloped with blazing oil from a flame-thrower capable of shooting a stream of fire 125 feet, the most effective weapon for getting at the deep Japanese defenses.

Braving cross fire from the maze of Japanese strong points on Tarawa, U.S. Marines storm the sand-banked slopes of a bombproof shelter used for defense by the Japanese. Their roofs, six feet thick, could take anything but the heaviest shells. But, impressive as these constructions were, they were less deadly to the Marines than the hundreds of camouflaged pillboxes and gun emplacements covering the beaches.

479

Cleaning out a cave on Saipan, U.S. Marines perched on a seaside cliff lower a charge of explosives and swing it into the cave opening in the sheer rock wall to blow up any enemy troops who may be still holed up inside. On the ledge is a dead Japanese sniper who, only minutes earlier, had been shooting down at soldiers and civilians at the ocean's edge below and was picked off himself by a Marine sharpshooter.

Clean-up in the Saipan Caves

In the same month that the great Allied invasion fleet was crossing the English Channel to deliver the decisive blow against Germany, another force no less imposing was sailing the Central Pacific over distances far greater to crack the defensive perimeter around Japan. From bases thousands of miles to the east and south, 535 naval ships with 127,000 men on board were converging on Saipan.

When the Marines landed on June 15, they found a big, mountainous island, very different from the flat coral islands of Tarawa but just as fanatically defended. Beaten at the beaches, the defenders burrowed into the hillsides and finally were killed there. Even the Japanese civilians on Saipan were so afraid of surrendering that hundreds of them jumped into the sea or blew themselves up.

The loss of Saipan—together with three big Japanese aircraft carriers and 476 planes—was recognized in Tokyo as a major disaster. "Hell is on us," said the Emperor's naval adviser. General Tojo was dismissed as prime minister. Japan's rulers knew by now that they were beaten, but they did not yet know how to go about giving up.

Terrified civilians, hiding in a hole in the ground (*top*) and expecting the worst from American soldiers, decide that they can trust them after all and come crawling out (*bottom*), with their children.

Abandoned infant is tenderly lifted up by the American soldier who found it lying wedged head down in the earth. Naked and diseased, the baby was sent straight on to a front-line hospital for care.

481

Forgotten Front in Burma and China

While the Americans steadily advanced through Japan's strongholds in the Pacific, the front in China stagnated. There the Chinese—who had been fighting Japan since 1937—were battered and weary, and the fall of Burma in 1942 had cut them off from overland contact with the Allies who alone could supply them with modern arms.

All through the war, the Allies squabbled over how much aid they could afford to send to China, and when it came to allocating matériel, the China-Burma-India theater was always at the bottom of the priority list. But troops worked heroically to maintain contact with the Chinese. To send them a minimum of supplies, American pilots flew regularly over the menacing "Hump" of 20,000-foot-high Himalaya ranges. The Chinese built airfields from which American B-29s made harassing raids on Japan. Americans and Chinese hacked out a spectacular new supply road over mountain and jungle. Chinese troops trained by General Joseph ("Vinegar Joe") Stilwell reconquered northern Burma, while guerrilla outfits led by British General Orde Wingate and U.S. General Frank Merrill harried the Japanese rear. Eventually, in a long and arduous campaign, the British-Indian Fourteenth Army cleared the enemy out of Burma, but not before 20,000 Allied prisoners of the Japanese had died wretchedly at forced labor on a "railroad of death" to supply troops in the jungle.

All this effort and suffering bore little strategic fruit. It had been undertaken in the belief that the war would be decided, in the end, on the Chinese mainland. Instead the death blow was delivered in the Pacific, and Japan was to give up all her conquests inside China without a battle.

Back to Mandalay (above) come British soldiers pushing past a pagoda in the brilliant six-month campaign during which the British-Indian Fourteenth Army annihilated three Japanese armies in Burma.

Chinese coolies (*below*), yoked by the scores to a road roller, level a landing field in south China for use by giant American B-29 bombers in attacks on cities in Japan and on shipping off the China coast.

The Burma road, reopened in 1945, snakes upward through the Himalayas. Over it—despite perpetual danger from floods, landslides and encroaching jungle—some 30,000 tons of supplies passed monthly.

The Fearful Fight for Peleliu

In the Tom Lea painting below, the young Marine wearing the smears of jungle camouflage and gripping the side of a landing barge was headed for Peleliu, last steppingstone on the way back across the Pacific to the Philippines. This tiny island was considered a fairly easy prize to snatch, and the admiral commanding the pre-invasion bombardment, which blew most of the jungle growth off its hills, boasted

after three days, "We have run out of targets." But the Marines who hit the beaches on September 15, 1944 discovered that thousands of Japanese were safely hidden in a series of interlocking caves deep in the limestone of the Umurbrogol Ridge, which was soon nicknamed "Bloody Nose Ridge." Safe from bomb or shell, enemy soldiers could pop open camouflaged steel doors in the hillside, let go a salvo at the Marines and then disappear again. Their cave entrances commanded the airfield which was the sole strategic object of value at Peleliu, so the Marines had no choice but to clear the caves. It took them ten weeks to do it. For months after that, 30 or so Japanese subsisted in the blackness deep under Bloody Nose and killed any foolhardy Americans who went poking around for souvenirs.

Death and Prayer on the Battlefield

Hit as he landed, a Marine is portrayed by Tom Lea, who saw him come ashore in the first wave at Peleliu, where Japanese gun fire ripped one arm and half his face into red pulp. "His eyes searched for a fight," wrote Lea. "Then something exploded. He scrambled up from the ground as if embarrassed at falling. He looked at his left arm, stumbled back to the beach. He never saw a Jap, never fired a shot."

Last rites for the dead are shown by Lea at a sick bay close to the front line where one of the 1,200 Marines who were killed at Peleliu lies on a stretcher. "The padre," wrote Lea, "towered over the crouching figures like a plaster saint with canteens and a Bible. Amid the frenzy, the wreckage and snipers' bullets, he looked very lonely, very close to God as he intoned his prayers over the shattered men."

The Liberation of the Philippines

In October 1944, two great arms of the American offensive came together when General MacArthur led his avenging armies ashore at Leyte in the Philippines. The Japanese now had their backs to the wall and threw in everything they had. Their navy came out to fight because, as the Japanese naval commander in chief said, "there would be no sense in saving the fleet at the expense of the Philippines." In the end, the Japanese lost both. Japanese ground forces made their usual stubborn fight, but they too were annihilated. In just about eight months, more than 340,000 men of the Japanese Fourteenth and Thirty-fifth Armies were reduced to a few hundred demoralized individuals dying of malnutrition in the jungle.

The reconquest of the Philippines was also a war of liberation, in which the native population gave the U.S. enthusiastic help. For two and a half years, guerrilla fighters had been operating in the islands, and now they came out to aid the invaders by spying, signalling (*right*), and fighting side by side with the Americans to clear their country of the nightmare of years of brutal occupation.

Assault on Corregidor by air and sea overwhelms the defenses of the island fortress on February 16, 1945, two years and nine months after the American flag there was hauled down by the Japanese.

Signal on Luzon (*opposite*)—indicating that the Japanese have already fled from the beaches—is waved by Filipino guerrilla wading into the surf while a pre-invasion bombardment from the U.S. fleet is raging.

Shock of Freedom
in Prison Camps

As the U.S. Army fought its way toward Manila, General MacArthur sent special detachments ahead to break into the compounds where American soldiers and civilians rounded up in the dark days of defeat had been imprisoned for three years. Disease and beatings had killed thousands of them off, and the news of Japanese defeats was making the guards even more savage. But the rescue teams now got them all out safe, without the loss of a prisoner's life.

The men behind the barbed wire were skeleton-thin and listless from the slow seepage of will brought on by undernourishment. In Bilibid prison in Manila, prisoners had been living since 1942 on a diet of wormy corn, rice and soybeans. At Cabanatuan, 486 worn-out survivors of the Bataan Death March simply looked up incuriously as U.S. Rangers, who had cut 60 miles inside the enemy lines, burst the walls of the stockade and massacred the guards. Many of the debilitated prisoners had to be carried out on the Rangers' backs, but soon they were wriggling off, insistent on shambling their own way to freedom (*below*).

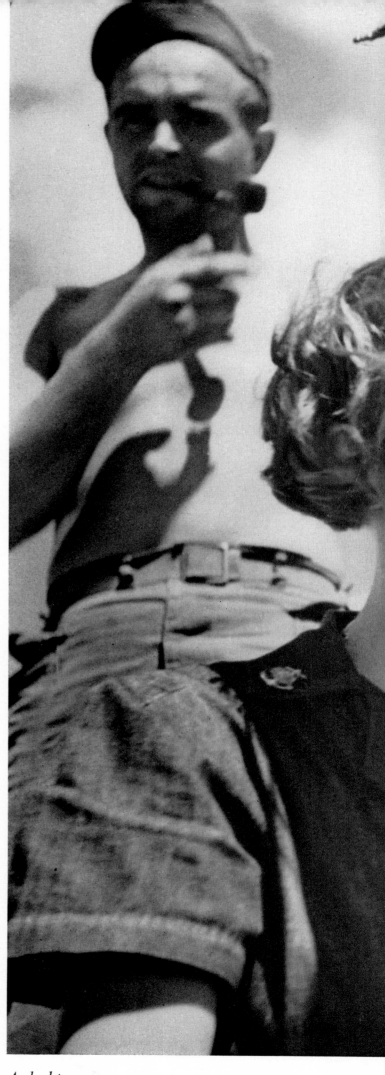

A shaking step out of captivity (*left*) is taken by two survivors of Bataan, still dazed with excitement and the weariness of three years' waiting, as they pass the gate of Cabanatuan prison camp north of Manila.

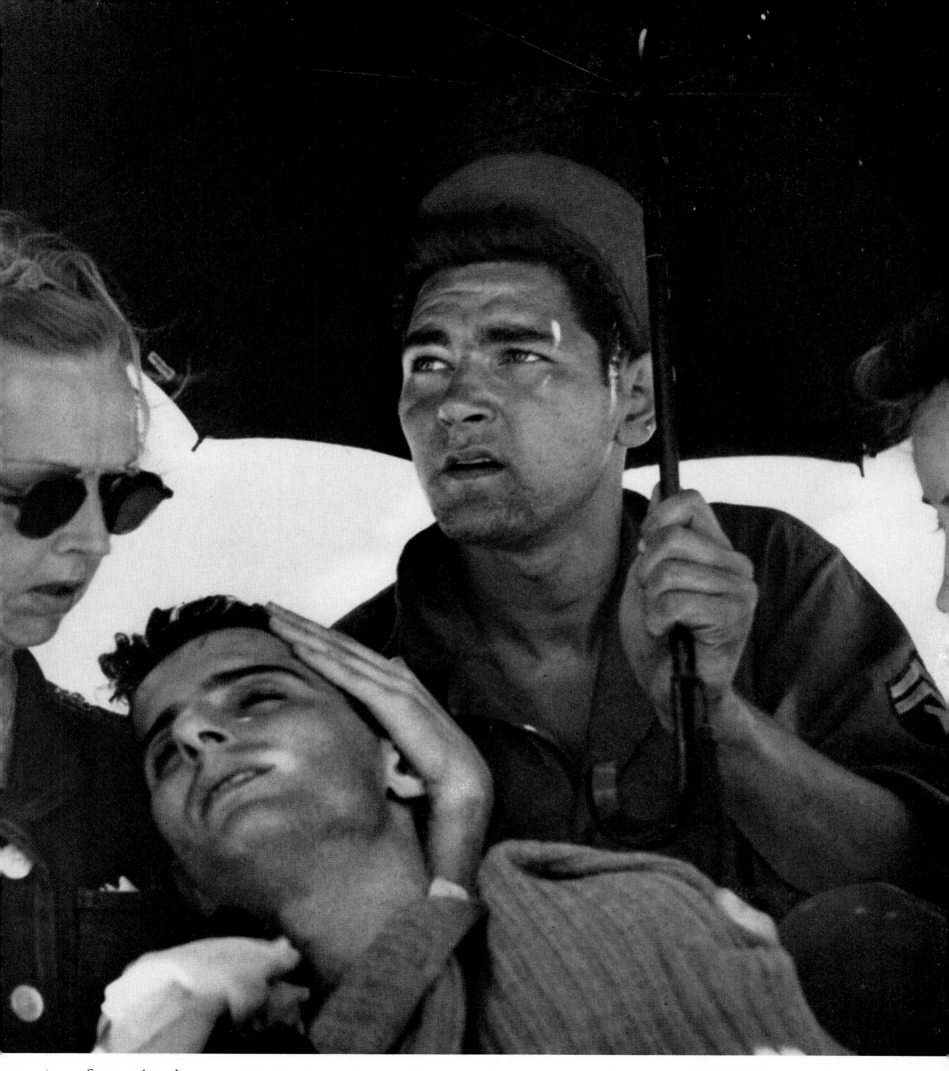

A comforting hand holds the head of a freed internee who has fainted from heat and exhaustion while walking from the Los Baños prison camp. The woman is a Navy nurse who, like him, was captured in the first Philippine campaign of 1942. Holding an umbrella to shield the prostrated man is a soldier (*right*) on the crew of the amphibious vehicle taking the prisoners to the ship that will bring them back to America.

491

The martyrdom of Warsaw is symbolized in this image of grief and death by Zygmunt Menkes, an American artist born in Poland. All his family were slaughtered by the Nazis during the German occupation of his homeland.

20

ONSLAUGHT FROM THE EAST

Italy and the Riviera Landing

LIBERATING Normandy was a supreme event in the European campaign of 1944, but it was only one of several concentric strokes upon Nazi Germany. In the east the Russians were flooding into Poland and the Balkans, and in the south Alexander's armies in Italy were pressing towards the river Po. Decisions had now to be taken about our next move in the Mediterranean, and it must be recorded with regret that these occasioned the first important divergence on high strategy between ourselves and our American friends.

The design for final victory in Europe had been outlined in prolonged discussion at the Tehran Conference in November 1943. Its decisions still governed our plans, and it would be well to recall them. First and foremost we had promised to carry out "Overlord." Here was the dominating task, and no one disputed that here lay our prime duty. But we still wielded powerful forces in the Mediterranean, and the question had remained, what should they do? We had resolved that they should capture Rome, whose nearby airfields were needed for bombing Southern Germany, and then advance up the peninsula as far as the Pisa-Rimini line. There they would hold as many enemy divisions as possible.

This however was not all. A third operation was also agreed upon, namely, an amphibious landing in the south of France, and it was on this project that controversy was about to descend. It was originally conceived as a feint or threat to keep German troops on the Riviera and stop them joining the battles in Normandy, but the Americans had pressed for a real attack by ten divisions, and Stalin had supported them. I accepted the change, largely to prevent undue diversions to Burma, although I contemplated other ways of exploiting success in Italy, and the plan had been given the code name "Anvil."

But there were several reservations. Many of the forces would have to come from Italy, and they had first to accomplish the arduous and important task of seizing Rome and the airfields. Until this was done little could be spared or taken from Alexander. Rome must fall before "Anvil" could start. And it must also start about the same time as "Overlord." The troops would have a long way to go before they could reach Eisenhower's armies in Normandy, and unless they landed in good time they would be too late to help and the battle of the beaches would be over. All turned on the capture of Rome. At Tehran we had confidently expected to reach it early in the spring, but this had proved impossible. The descent at Anzio to accelerate its capture had drawn eight or ten German divisions away from the vital theatre, or more than was expected to be attracted to the Riviera by "Anvil." This in effect

493

superseded it by achieving its object. Nevertheless the Riviera project went forward as if nothing had happened.

Apart from ''Anvil'' hanging somewhat vaguely in the future, some of the finest divisions of the armies of Italy had rightly been assigned to the main operation of ''Overlord'' and had sailed for England before the end of 1943. Alexander had thus been weakened and Kesselring had been strengthened. The Germans had sent reinforcements to Italy, had parried the Anzio swoop, and had stopped us entering Rome until just before D-Day. The hard fighting had of course engulfed important enemy reserves which might otherwise have gone to France, and it certainly helped ''Overlord'' in its critical early stages, but none the less our advance in the Mediterranean had been gravely upset. Landing craft were another obstacle. Many of them had been sent to ''Overlord.'' ''Anvil'' could not be mounted until they came back, and this in its turn depended on events in Normandy.

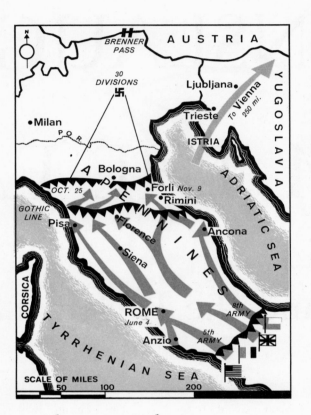

These facts had been long foreseen, and as far back as March 21 General Maitland Wilson, the Supreme Commander in the Mediterranean, reported that ''Anvil'' could not be launched before the end of July. Later he put it at mid-August, and declared that the best way to help ''Overlord'' was to abandon any attack on the Riviera and concentrate on Italy. Both he and Alexander thought their best contribution to the common end would be to press forward with all their resources into the Po valley. Thereafter, with the help of an amphibious operation against the Istrian peninsula, at the head of the Adriatic, which is dominated by and runs south from Trieste, there would be attractive prospects of advancing through the Ljubljana Gap into Austria and Hungary and striking at the heart of Germany from another direction.

When Rome fell on June 4 the problem had to be reviewed. Should we go on with ''Anvil'' or should we make a new plan? General Eisenhower naturally wanted to strengthen his attack in Northwest Europe by all available means. Strategic possibilities in Northern Italy did not attract him, but he consented to return the landing craft as soon as possible if this would lead to a speedy ''Anvil.'' The American Chiefs of Staff agreed with Eisenhower, holding rigidly to the maxim of concentration at the decisive point, which in their eyes meant only Northwest Europe. They were supported by the President, who was mindful of the agreements made with Stalin many months before at Tehran. Yet all was changed by the delay in Italy. Mr. Roosevelt admitted that an advance through the Ljubljana Gap might contain German troops, but it would

Advances in Italy to Gothic Line in the north took Allies (*blue*) seven months in 1944. Churchill would have liked to divert this energy to drive (*light blue*) over Adriatic to Yugoslavia.

not draw any divisions from France. This direct conflict of opinions, honestly held and warmly argued by either side, could only be settled, if at all, between the President and myself, and an interchange of telegrams now took place.

''The deadlock,'' I telegraphed on June 28, ''between our Chiefs of Staff raises most serious issues. Our first wish is to help General Eisenhower in the most speedy and effective manner. But we do not think this necessarily involves the complete ruin of all our great affairs in the Mediterranean, and we take it hard that this should be demanded of us. . . . I most earnestly beg you to examine this matter in detail for yourself. . . . Please remember how you spoke to me at Tehran about Istria, and how I introduced it at the full Conference. This has sunk very deeply into my mind, although it is not by any means the immediate issue we have to decide.''

But Mr. Roosevelt's reply was prompt and adverse. He was resolved to carry out what he called the ''grand strategy'' of Tehran, namely, exploiting ''Overlord'' to the full, ''victorious advances in Italy, and an early assault on Southern France.'' Political objects might be important, but military operations to achieve them must be subordinated to striking at the heart of Germany by a campaign in Europe. Stalin himself had favoured ''Anvil'' and had classified all other operations in the Mediterranean as of lesser importance, and the President declared that he could never abandon it without consulting him. The President continued: ''We can—and General Wilson confirms this is so—immediately withdraw five divisions (three of them United States and two French) from Italy for 'Anvil.' *The remaining twenty-one divisions,*'' he wrote, ''*plus numerous separate brigades, will certainly provide Alexander with adequate ground superiority.*''

But it was Mr. Roosevelt's objections to a descent on the Istrian peninsula and a thrust against Vienna through the Ljubljana Gap that revealed both the rigidity of the American military plans and his own suspicion of what he called a campaign ''in the Balkans.'' He claimed that Alexander and Smuts, who also favoured my view, ''for several natural and very human reasons,'' were inclined to disregard two vital considerations. First, the operation infringed ''the grand strategy.'' Secondly, it would take too long and we could probably not deploy more than six divisions. ''I cannot agree,'' he wrote, ''to the employment of United States troops against Istria *and into the Balkans*, nor can I see the French agreeing to such use of French troops. . . . For purely political considerations over here, I should never survive even a slight setback in

'Overlord' *if it were known that fairly large forces had been diverted to the Balkans.''* No one involved in these discussions had ever thought of moving armies into the Balkans; but Istria and Trieste were strategic and political positions, which, as he saw very clearly, might exercise profound and widespread reactions, especially after the Russian advances. I was sure that if we could have met, as I so frequently proposed, we should have reached a happy agreement. For the time being, however, I resigned myself, and on July 2 General Wilson was ordered to attack the south of France on August 15. Preparations began at once, but the reader should note that "Anvil" was renamed "Dragoon." This was done in case the enemy had learnt the meaning of the original code word. By early August however a marked change had come over the battlefield in Normandy and great developments impended, and on the 7th I visited Eisenhower at his headquarters near Portsmouth and unfolded to him my last hope of stopping an assault on the south of France. After an agreeable luncheon we had a long and serious conversation. Eisenhower had with him Bedell Smith and Admiral Ramsay. I had brought the First Sea Lord, as the movement of shipping was the key.

Briefly, what I proposed was to continue loading the "Dragoon" expedition, but when the troops were in the ships to send them through the Strait of Gibraltar and enter France at Bordeaux. The matter had been long considered by the British Chiefs of Staff, and the operation was deemed to be feasible. I showed Eisenhower a telegram I had sent to the President, whose reply I had not yet received, and did my best to convince him. The First Sea Lord strongly supported me. Admiral Ramsay argued against any change of plan. Bedell Smith, on the contrary, declared himself strongly in favour of this sudden deflection of the attack, which would have all the surprise that sea power can bestow. Eisenhower in no way resented the views of his Chief of Staff. He always encouraged free expression of opinion in council at the summit, though of course whatever was settled would receive every loyalty in execution.

However, I was quite unable to move him, and next day I received the President's reply. "It is my considered opinion," he cabled, "that 'Dragoon' should be launched as planned at the earliest practicable date, and I have full confidence that it will be successful and of great assistance to Eisenhower in driving the Huns from France."

There was no more to be done about it. It is worth noting that we had now passed the day in July when for the first time in the war the movement of the great American

Landings on Riviera by the Allies (*blue*) were supported from Corsica. They took Toulon and Marseille, then pushed up the Rhône to Sombernon and met forces from Normandy.

armies into Europe and their growth in the Far East made their numbers in action greater than our own. Influence on Allied operations is usually increased by large reinforcements. It must also be remembered that had the British views on this strategic issue been accepted the tactical preparations might well have caused some delay, which again would have reacted on the general argument.

I now decided to go myself to Italy, where many questions could be more easily settled on the spot than by correspondence. It would be a great advantage to see the commanders and the troops from whom so much was being demanded, after so much had been taken. General Alexander, though sorely weakened, was preparing his armies for a further offensive. I was anxious to meet Tito, who could easily come to Italy from the island of Vis, where we were protecting him. The Greek Prime Minister, M. Papandreou, and some of his colleagues could come from Cairo, and plans could then be made to help them back to Athens when the Germans departed. I reached Naples on the afternoon of August 11 and was installed in the palatial though somewhat dilapidated Villa Rivalta, with a glorious view of Vesuvius and the bay. Here General Wilson explained to me that all arrangements had been made for a conference next morning with Tito and Subašić, the new Yugoslav Prime Minister of King Peter's Government in London. They had already arrived in Naples, and would dine with us the next night.

On the morning of August 12 Marshal Tito came up to the villa. He wore a magnificent gold and blue uniform which was very tight under the collar and singularly unsuited to the blazing heat. The uniform had been given him by the Russians, and, as I was afterwards informed, the gold lace came from the United States. I joined him on the terrace of the villa, accompanied by Brigadier Maclean and an interpreter. I suggested that the Marshal might first like to see General Wilson's War Room, and we moved inside. The Marshal, who was attended by two ferocious-looking bodyguards, each carrying automatic pistols, wanted to bring them with him in case of treachery on our part. He was dissuaded from this with some difficulty, and proposed to bring them to guard him at dinner instead. I led the way into a large room, where maps of the battlefronts covered the walls, and we had a long conversation. I pointed on the map to the Istrian peninsula. He was all in favour of our attacking it, and promised to help. I explained that it would help if a small port could be opened on the Yugoslav coast so that we could send in war matériel by sea. Then and in the following days we did our best to strengthen and intensify the Yugoslav war effort and to heal the breach between him and King Peter.

On the afternoon of August 14 I flew in General Wilson's Dakota to Corsica in order to see the Riviera landing which I had tried so hard to stop, but to which I wished all success. From the British destroyer *Kimberley* we watched the long rows of boats filled with American storm troops steaming in continuously to the Gulf of St. Tropez. As far as I could see or hear not a shot was fired either at the approaching flotillas or on the beaches. The battleships stopped firing, as there seemed to be nobody there. I had at least done the civil to "Anvil-Dragoon," and I thought it was a good thing I was near the scene to show the interest I took in it.

ON the morning of August 17 I set out by motor from Naples to meet General Alexander. I was delighted to see him for the first time since his victory and entry into Rome. He drove me all along the old Cassino front, showing me how the battle had gone, and where the main struggles had occurred. Alexander brought his chief officers to dinner, and explained to me fully his difficulties and plans. The Fifteenth Group of Armies had indeed been skinned and starved. The far-reaching projects we had cherished must now be abandoned. It was still our duty to hold the Germans in the largest numbers on our front. If this purpose was to be achieved an offensive was imperative; but the well-integrated German armies were almost as strong as ours, composed of so many different contingents and races. It was proposed to attack along the whole front early on the 26th. Our right hand would be upon the Adriatic, and our immediate objective Rimini. To the westward, under Alexander's command, lay the Fifth American Army. This had been stripped and mutilated for the sake of "Anvil," but would nevertheless advance with vigour.

On August 19 I set off to visit General Mark Clark at Leghorn. We lunched in the open air by the sea. In our friendly and confidential talks I realised how painful the tearing to pieces of this fine army had been to those who controlled it. The General seemed embittered that his army had been robbed of what he thought—and I could not disagree—was a great opportunity. Still, he would drive forward to his utmost on the British left and keep the whole front blazing. It was late and I was thoroughly tired out when I got back to my château at Siena, where Alexander came again to dine.

When one writes things on paper to decide or explain large questions affecting action there is mental stress. But all this bites much deeper when you see and feel it on the spot. Here was this splendid army, equivalent to twenty-five divisions, of which a quarter were American, reduced till it was just not strong enough to produce decisive results against the immense power of the defensive. A very little more, half of what had been taken from us, and we could have broken into the valley of the Po, with all the gleaming possibilities and prizes which lay open towards Vienna. As it was, our forces, about a million strong, could play a mere secondary part in any commanding strategic conception. They could keep the enemy on their front busy at the cost and risk of a hard offensive. They could at least do their duty. Alexander maintained his soldierly cheerfulness, but

it was in a sombre mood that I went to bed. In these great matters, failing to gain one's way is no escape from the responsibility for an inferior solution.

After a brief but fruitful visit to Rome I returned by air on the 24th to Alexander's headquarters at Siena, living in the château a few miles away, and next afternoon we flew to General Leese's battle headquarters of the Eighth Army, on the Adriatic side. Here we had tents overlooking a magnificent panorama to the northward. The Adriatic, though but twenty miles away, was hidden by the mass of Monte Maggiore. General Leese told us that the barrage to cover the advance of his troops would begin at midnight. We were well placed to watch the long line of distant gun-flashes. The rapid, ceaseless thudding of the cannonade reminded me of the First World War. Artillery was certainly being used on a great scale. After an hour of this I was glad to go to bed, for Alexander had planned an early start and a long day on the front. He had also promised to take me wherever I wanted to go.

Two mornings later plenty of work arrived, both by telegram and pouch. It appeared that General Eisenhower was worried by the approach of some German divisions which had been withdrawn from Italy. I was glad that our offensive, prepared under depressing conditions, had begun. I drafted a telegram to the President explaining the position as I had learned it from the generals on the spot and from my own knowledge. I wished to convey in an uncontroversial form our sense of frustration, and at the same time to indicate my hopes and ideas for the future. If only I could revive the President's interest in this sphere we might still keep alive our design of an ultimate advance to Vienna. After explaining Alexander's plan, I ended as follows:

"I have never forgotten your talks to me at Tehran about Istria, and I am sure that the arrival of a powerful army in Trieste and Istria in four or five weeks would have an effect far outside purely military values. Tito's people will be awaiting us in Istria. What the condition of Hungary will be then I cannot imagine, but we shall at any rate be in a position to take full advantage of any great new situation."

I DID not send this message off till I reached Naples, nor did I receive the answer till after I got home. Mr. Roosevelt then replied: "I share your confidence that the Allied divisions we have in Italy are sufficient to do the task before them and that the battle commander will press the battle unrelentingly with the objective of shattering the enemy forces. . . . As to the exact employment of our forces in Italy in the future, this is a matter we can [soon] discuss. . . . With the present chaotic conditions of the Germans in Southern France, I hope that a junction of the north and south forces may be obtained at a much earlier date than was first anticipated."

Both these hopes proved vain. The army which we had landed on the Riviera at such painful cost to our operations in Italy arrived too late to help Eisenhower's first main struggle in the north, while Alexander's offensive failed, by the barest of margins, to achieve the success it deserved and we so badly needed. Italy was not to be wholly free for another eight months; the right-handed drive to Vienna was denied to us; and, except in Greece, our military power to influence the liberation of Southeastern Europe was gone.

The Russian Victories

THE Russian struggle in scale far exceeded the operations with which my account has hitherto been concerned, and formed of course the foundation upon which the British and American Armies had approached the climax of the war. The Russians had given their enemy little time to recover from their severe reverses of the early winter of 1943. In mid-January 1944 they attacked on a 120-mile front from Lake Ilmen to Leningrad and pierced the defences before the city. Farther south, by the end of February the Germans had been driven back to the shores of Lake Peipus. Leningrad was freed once and for all, and the Russians stood on the borders of the Baltic States. Further onslaughts to the west of Kiev forced the Germans back towards the old Polish frontier. The whole southern front was aflame. One great pocket of surrounded Germans was left behind at Kherson, from which few escaped. Throughout March the Russians pressed their advantage all along the line and in the air. From Gomel to the Black Sea the invaders were in full retreat, which did not end until they had been thrust across the Dniester, back into Romania and Poland. Then the spring thaw brought them a short respite. In the Crimea however operations were still possible, and in April the Russians set about destroying the Seventeenth German Army and regaining Sevastopol.

The magnitude of these victories raised issues of far-reaching importance. The Red Army now loomed over Central and Eastern Europe. What then was to happen to Poland, Hungary, Romania, Bulgaria, and above all, to Greece, for whom we had tried so hard and sacrificed so much? Would Turkey come to our side? Would Yugoslavia be engulfed in the Russian flood? Postwar Europe seemed to be taking shape and some political arrangement with the Soviets was becoming urgent.

On May 18 the Soviet Ambassador in London had called at the Foreign Office to discuss a general suggestion which Mr. Eden had made that the U.S.S.R. should temporarily regard Romanian affairs as mainly their concern under war conditions while leaving Greece to us. The Russians were prepared to accept this, but wished to know if we had consulted the United States. If so they would agree. On the 31st I accordingly sent a personal telegram to Mr. Roosevelt. But Mr. Hull was nervous of any suggestion that "might appear to savour of the creation or acceptance of the idea of spheres of influence," and Stalin, as soon as he realised the Americans had doubts, insisted on consulting them direct. In the end we were unable to reach any final agreement about dividing responsibilities in the Balkan Peninsula. Early in August the Russians dispatched from Italy by a subterfuge a mission to E.L.A.S., the military component of E.A.M., the Communist guerrillas in Northern Greece. In the light of American official reluctance and of the instance of Soviet bad faith, we abandoned our efforts to reach a major understanding until I met Stalin in Moscow two months later. By then much had happened on the Eastern Front.

In Finland, Russian troops, very different in quality and armament from those who had fought there in 1940, broke through the Mannerheim Line, reopened the railway from Leningrad to Murmansk, the terminal of our Arctic convoys, and by the end of August compelled the Finns to sue for an armistice. Their main attack on the German front began on June 23. Many towns and villages had been turned into strong positions, with all-round defence, but they were successively surrounded and disposed of, while the Red armies poured through the gaps between. At the end of July they had reached the Neman at Kaunas and Grodno. Here, after an advance of 250 miles in five weeks, they were brought to a temporary halt to replenish. The German losses had been crushing. Twenty-five divisions had ceased to exist, and an equal number were cut off in Courland. On July 17 alone, 57,000 German prisoners were marched through Moscow—who knows whither?

To the southward of these victories lay Romania. Till August was far advanced the German line from Chernovtsy to the Black Sea barred the way to the Ploesti oilfields and the Balkans. It had been weakened by withdrawal of troops to sustain the sagging line farther north, and under violent attacks, beginning on August 22, it rapidly disintegrated. Aided by landings on the coast, the Russians made short work of the enemy. Sixteen German divisions were lost. On August 23 a *coup d'état* in Bucharest, organised by the young King Michael and his close advisers, led to a complete reversal of the whole military position. The Romanian armies followed their King to a man. Within three days before the arrival of the Soviet troops the German forces had been disarmed or had retired over the northern frontiers. By September 1 Bucharest had been evacuated by the Germans. The Romanian armies disintegrated and the country was overrun. The Romanian Government capitulated.

Bulgaria, after a last-minute attempt to declare war on Germany, was overwhelmed. Wheeling to the west, the Russian armies drove up the Danube valley and through the Transylvanian Alps to the Hungarian border, while their left flank, south of the Danube, lined up on the frontier of Yugoslavia. Here they prepared for the great westerly drive which in due time was to carry them to Vienna.

IN Poland there was a tragedy which requires a more detailed account. By late July the Russian armies stood before the river Vistula, and all reports indicated that in the very near future Poland would be in Russian hands. The leaders of the Polish Underground Army, which owed allegiance to the London Government, had now to decide when to raise a general insurrection against the Germans. In order to speed the liberation of their country and prevent them fighting a series of bitter defensive actions on Polish territory, and particularly in Warsaw itself, the Polish commander, General Bor-Komorowski, and his civilian adviser were authorised by the Polish Government in London to proclaim a general insurrection whenever deemed fit. The moment indeed seemed opportune. On July 20 came the news of the German generals' attempt to assassinate Hitler, followed swiftly by the Allied break-out from the Normandy beachhead. About July 22 the Poles intercepted wireless messages from the German Fourth Panzer Army ordering a general withdrawal to the west of the Vistula. The Russians crossed the river on the same day, and their patrols pushed forward in the direction of Warsaw. A general collapse seemed imminent.

General Bor therefore decided to stage a major rising and liberate the city. He had about 40,000 men, with reserves of food and ammunition for seven to ten days' fighting. The sound of Russian guns across the Vistula could now be heard. The Soviet Air Force began bombing the Germans in Warsaw from recently captured airfields near the capital, of which the closest was only twenty minutes' flight away. At the same time a Communist Committee of National Liberation had been formed in Eastern Poland, and the Russians announced that liberated territory would be placed under their control. Soviet broadcasting stations had for a considerable time been urging the Polish population to drop all caution and start a general revolt against the Germans.

On July 29, three days before the rising began, the Moscow radio station broadcast an appeal from the Polish Communists to the people of Warsaw, which said that the guns of liberation were now within hearing, and calling upon them as in 1939 to join battle with the Germans, this time for decisive action: "For Warsaw, which did not yield but fought on, the hour of action has already arrived." After pointing out that the German plan to set up defence points would result in the gradual destruction of the city, the broadcast ended by reminding the inhabitants that "all is lost that is not saved by active effort," and that "by direct active struggle in the streets, houses, etc. of Warsaw the moment of final liberation will be hastened and the lives of our brethren saved."

On the evening of July 31 the Underground command in Warsaw got news that Soviet tanks had broken into the German defences east of the city. The German military wireless announced, "To-day the Russians started a general attack on Warsaw from the southeast." Russian troops were now at points less than ten miles away. In the capital itself the Polish Underground command ordered a general insurrection at 5 p.m. on the following day. General Bor has himself described what happened: "At exactly five o'clock thousands of windows flashed as they were flung open. From all sides a hail of bullets struck passing Germans, riddling their buildings and their marching formations. In the twinkling of an eye the remaining civilians disappeared from the streets. From the entrances of houses our men streamed out and rushed to the attack. In fifteen

Liberation of Russia was completed by September 1944 after hydra-headed Soviet offensive (*blue*). Germans (*black*) were stranded in the Crimea and in pockets southwest of Kiev.

minutes an entire city of a million inhabitants was engulfed in the fight. Every kind of traffic ceased. As a big communications centre where roads from north, south, east, and west converged, in the immediate rear of the German front, Warsaw ceased to exist. The battle for the city was on." The news reached London next day, and we anxiously waited for more. The Soviet radio was silent and Russian air activity ceased. On August 4 the Germans started to attack from strongpoints which they held throughout the city and suburbs. The Polish Government in London told us of the agonising urgency of sending in supplies by air. The insurgents were now opposed by five hastily concentrated German divisions. The Hermann Goering Division had also been brought from Italy, and two more S.S. divisions arrived soon afterwards. I accordingly telegraphed to Stalin: "At urgent request of Polish Underground Army we are dropping, subject to weather, about sixty tons of equipment and ammunition into the southwest quarter of Warsaw, where it is said a Polish revolt against the Germans is in fierce struggle. They also say that they appeal for Russian aid, which seems to be very near. They are being attacked by one and a half German divisions. This may be of help to your operation."

Stalin's reply was prompt and grim. "I have received your message about Warsaw. I think that the information which has been communicated to you by the Poles is greatly exaggerated and does not inspire confidence. One could reach that conclusion even from the fact that the Polish emigrants have already claimed for themselves that they all but captured Vilna with a few stray units of the Home Army, and even announced that on the radio. But that of course does not in any way correspond with the facts. The Home Army of the Poles consists of a few detachments, which they incorrectly call divisions. They have neither artillery nor aircraft nor tanks. I cannot imagine how such detachments can capture Warsaw, for the defence of which the Germans have produced four tank divisions, among them the Hermann Goering Division."

Meanwhile the battle went on street by street against the German "Tiger" tanks, and by August 9 the Germans had driven a wedge right across the city through to the Vistula, breaking up the Polish-held districts into isolated sectors. The gallant attempts of the R.A.F., with Polish, British, and Dominion crews, to fly to Warsaw from Italian bases were both forlorn and inadequate. Two planes appeared on the night of August 4, and three four nights later.

The Polish Prime Minister, Mikolajczyk, had been in Moscow since July 30 trying to establish some kind of terms with the Soviet Government, which had recognised the Polish Communist Committee of National Liberation, the Lublin Committee, as we called it, as the future administrators of the country. These negotiations were carried on throughout the early days of the Warsaw rising. Messages from General Bor were reaching Mikolajczyk daily, begging for ammunition and antitank weapons and for help from the Red Army. Meanwhile the Russians pressed for agreement upon the postwar frontiers of Poland and the setting up of a joint Government. A last fruitless talk took place with Stalin on August 9.

ON the night of August 16 Vyshinsky asked the United States Ambassador in Moscow to call, and, explaining that he wished to avoid the possibility of any misunderstanding, read out the following astonishing statement: "The Soviet Government cannot of course object to English or American aircraft dropping arms in the region of Warsaw, since this is an American and British affair. But they decidedly object to American or British aircraft, after dropping arms in the region of Warsaw, landing on Soviet territory, since the Soviet Government do not wish to associate themselves either directly or indirectly with the adventure in Warsaw."

Four days later Roosevelt and I sent Stalin a joint appeal, which the President had drafted: "We are thinking of world opinion if the anti-Nazis in Warsaw are in effect abandoned. We believe that all three of us should do the utmost to save as many of the patriots there as possible. We hope that you will drop immediate supplies and munitions to the patriot Poles in Warsaw, or will you agree to help our planes in doing it very quickly? We hope you will approve. The time element is of extreme importance."

This was the reply we got: "I have received the message from you and Mr. Roosevelt about Warsaw. I wish to express my opinions. Sooner or later the truth about the group of criminals who have embarked on the Warsaw adventure in order to seize power will become known to everybody. These people have exploited the good faith of the inhabitants of Warsaw, throwing many almost unarmed people against the German guns, tanks and aircraft. A situation has arisen in which each new day serves, not the Poles for the liberation of Warsaw but the Hitlerites who are inhumanly shooting down the inhabitants of Warsaw.

"From the military point of view, the situation which has arisen, by increasingly directing the attention of the Germans to Warsaw, is just as unprofitable for the Red Army as for the Poles. Meanwhile the Soviet troops, which have recently encountered new and notable efforts by the Germans to go over to the counterattack, are doing everything possible to smash these counterattacks of the Hitlerites and to go over to a new wide-scale attack in the region of Warsaw. There can be no doubt that the Red Army is not sparing its efforts to break the Germans round Warsaw and to free Warsaw for the Poles. That will be the best and most effective help for the Poles who are anti-Nazis."

Meanwhile the agony of Warsaw reached its height. "The German tank forces during last night [August 11]," cabled an eyewitness, "made determined efforts to relieve some of their strong points in the city. This is no light task however, as on the corner of every street are built huge

barricades, mostly constructed of concrete pavement slabs torn up from the streets especially for this purpose. In most cases the attempts failed, so the tank crews vented their disappointment by setting fire to several houses and shelling others from a distance. In many cases they also set fire to the dead, who litter the streets in many places. . . .

"When the Germans were bringing supplies by tanks to one of their outposts they drove before them 500 women and children to prevent the [Polish] troops from taking action against them. Many of them were killed and many wounded. The same kind of action has been reported from many other parts of the city. The dead are buried in backyards and squares. . . . The dropping of supplies has intensified the morale. Everyone wants to fight and will fight, but the uncertainty of a speedy conclusion is depressing. . . ." The battle also raged literally underground. The only means of communication between the different sectors held by the Poles lay through the sewers. The Germans threw hand grenades and gas bombs down the manholes. Battles developed in pitch-darkness between men waist-deep in excrement, fighting hand to hand at times with knives or drowning their opponents in the slime. Above ground German artillery and fighters set alight large areas of the city.

I had hoped that the Americans would support us in drastic action, but Mr. Roosevelt was adverse. On September 1, I received Mikolajczyk on his return from Moscow. I had little comfort to offer. He told me that he was prepared to propose a political settlement with the Lublin Committee, offering them fourteen seats in a combined Government. These proposals were debated under fire by the representatives of the Polish Underground in Warsaw itself. The suggestion was accepted unanimously. Most of those who took part in these decisions were tried a year later for "treason" before a Soviet court in Moscow.

When the Cabinet met on the night of September the 4th, I thought the issue so important that though I had a touch of fever I went from my bed to our underground room. We had met together on many unpleasant affairs. I do not remember any occasion when such deep anger was shown by all our members, Tory, Labour, Liberal alike. I should have liked to say, "We are sending our aeroplanes to land in your territory, after delivering supplies to Warsaw. If you do not treat them properly all convoys will be stopped from this moment by us."

BUT the reader of these pages in afteryears must realise that everyone always has to keep in mind the fortunes of millions of men fighting in a world-wide struggle, and that terrible and even humbling submissions must at times be made to the general aim. I did not therefore propose this drastic step. It might have been effective, because we were dealing with men in the Kremlin who were governed by calculation and not by emotion. They did not mean to let the spirit of Poland rise again at Warsaw. Their plans were based on the Lublin Committee. That was the only Poland they cared about. The cutting off of the convoys at this critical moment in their great advance would perhaps have bulked in their minds as much as considerations of honour, humanity, decent commonplace good faith usually count with ordinary people.

The War Cabinet in their collective capacity sent Stalin a telegram of appeal. It was the best we thought it wise to do.

"The War Cabinet wish the Soviet Government to know that public opinion in this country is deeply moved by the events in Warsaw and by the terrible sufferings of the Poles there. Whatever the rights and wrongs about the beginnings of the Warsaw rising, the people of Warsaw themselves cannot be held responsible for the decision taken. Our people cannot understand why no material help has been sent from outside to the Poles in Warsaw. The fact that such help could not be sent on account of your Government's refusal to allow United States aircraft to land on aerodromes in Russian hands is now becoming publicly known. If on top of all this the Poles in Warsaw should now be overwhelmed by the Germans, as we are told they must be within two or three days, the shock to public opinion here will be incalculable. . . .

"Out of regard for Marshal Stalin and for the Soviet peoples, with whom it is our earnest desire to work in future years, the War Cabinet have asked me to make this further appeal to the Soviet Government to give whatever help may be in their power, and above all to provide facilities for United States aircraft to land on your airfields. . . ."

On September 10, after six weeks of Polish torment, the Kremlin appeared to change their tactics. That afternoon shells from the Soviet artillery began to fall upon the eastern outskirts of Warsaw, and Soviet planes appeared again over the city. Polish Communist forces, under Soviet orders, fought their way into the fringe of the capital. From September 14 onwards the Soviet Air Force dropped supplies; but few of the parachutes opened and many of the containers were smashed and useless. The following day the Russians occupied the Praga suburb, but went no farther. They wished to have the non-Communist Poles destroyed to the full, but also to keep alive the idea that they were going to their rescue. Meanwhile, house by house, the Germans proceeded with their liquidation of Polish centres of resistance throughout the city. A fearful fate befell the population. Many were deported by the Germans. General Bor's appeals to the Soviet commander, Marshal Rokossovsky, were unanswered. Famine reigned.

My efforts to get American aid led to one isolated but large-scale operation. On September 18, 104 heavy bombers flew over the capital, dropping supplies. It was too late. On the evening of October 2 Mikolajczyk came to tell me that the Polish forces in Warsaw were about to surrender to the Germans. One of the last broadcasts from the heroic city was picked up in London:

"This is the stark truth. We were treated worse than Hitler's satellites, worse than Italy, Romania, Finland. May God, Who is just, pass judgment on the terrible injustice suffered by the Polish nation, and may He punish accordingly all those who are guilty. Your heroes are the soldiers whose only weapons against tanks, planes, and guns were their revolvers and bottles filled with petrol. Your heroes are the women who tended the wounded and carried messages under fire, who cooked in bombed and ruined cellars to feed children and adults, and who soothed and comforted the dying. Your heroes are the children who went on quietly playing among the smouldering ruins. These are the people of Warsaw.

"Immortal is the nation that can muster such universal heroism. For those who have died have conquered, and those who live on will fight on, will conquer and again bear witness that Poland lives when the Poles live."

These words are indelible. The struggle in Warsaw had lasted more than sixty days. Of the 40,000 men and women of the Polish Underground Army about 15,000 fell. Out of a population of a million, nearly 200,000 had been stricken. Suppression of the revolt cost the German Army 10,000 killed, 7,000 missing, and 9,000 wounded. The proportions attest the hand-to-hand character of the fighting.

When the Russians entered the city three months later they found little but shattered streets and the unburied dead. Such was their liberation of Poland, where they now rule. But this cannot be the end of the story.

Balkan Convulsions

THE reader must now go back to a fierce and sombre tale which the main narrative has outstripped. Since Hitler's invasion and conquest in April 1941 Yugoslavia had been the scene of fearful events. The spirited boy King took refuge in England with such of Prince Paul's ministers and other members of the Government as had defied the German assault. In the mountains there began again the fierce guerrilla with which the Serbs had resisted the Turks for centuries.

General Mihailović was its first and foremost champion, and round him rallied the surviving elite of Yugoslavia. In the vortex of world affairs their struggle was hardly noticeable. It belongs to the "unestimated sum of human pain." Mihailović suffered as a guerrilla leader from the fact that many of his followers were well-known people with relations and friends in Serbia, and property and recognisable connections elsewhere. The Germans pursued a policy of murderous blackmail. They retaliated for guerrilla activities by shooting batches of four or five hundred selected people in Belgrade. Under this pressure Mihailović drifted gradually into a posture where some of his commanders made accommodations with the German and Italian troops to be left alone in certain mountain areas in return for doing little or nothing against the enemy. Those who have triumphantly withstood such strains may brand his name, but history, more discriminating, should not erase it from the scroll of Serbian patriots. By the autumn of the year 1941 Serbian resistance to the German terror had become only a shadow. The national struggle could only be sustained by the innate valour of the common people. This however was not lacking.

A wild and furious war for existence against the Germans broke into flame among the Partisans. Among these Tito stood forth, pre-eminent and soon dominant. Tito, as he called himself, was a Soviet-trained Communist who, until Russia was invaded by Hitler, and after Yugoslavia had been assailed, had fomented political strikes along the Dalmatian coast, in accordance with the general Comintern policy. But once he united in his breast and brain his Communist doctrine with his burning ardour for his native land in her extreme torment he became a leader, with adherents who had little to lose but their lives, who were ready to die, and if to die to kill. This confronted the Germans with a problem which could not be solved by the mass executions of notables or persons of substance. They found themselves confronted by desperate men who had to be hunted down in their lairs. The Partisans under Tito wrested weapons from German hands. They grew rapidly in numbers. No reprisals, however bloody, upon hostages or villages deterred them. For them it was death or freedom. Soon they began to inflict heavy injury upon the Germans and became masters of wide regions.

I T was inevitable that the Partisan movement should also come into savage quarrels with those of their fellow countrymen who were resisting halfheartedly or making bargains for immunity with the common foe. The Partisans deliberately violated any agreements made with the enemy by the Cetniks—as the followers of General Mihailović were called. The Germans then shot Cetnik hostages, and in revenge Cetniks gave the Germans information about the Partisans. All this happened sporadically and uncontrollably in these wild mountain regions. It was a tragedy within a tragedy.

I had followed these events amid other preoccupations so far as was possible. Except for a trickle of supplies dropped from aircraft, we were not able to help. Our headquarters in the Middle East was responsible for all operations in this theatre, and maintained a system of agents and liaison officers with the followers of Mihailović.

In May 1943 we took a new departure. It was decided to send small parties of British officers and N.C.O.s to establish contact with the Yugoslav Partisans, in spite of the fact that cruel strife was proceeding between them and the Cetniks, and that Tito was waging war as a Communist not only against the German invaders but against the Serbian monarchy and Mihailović. At the end of that month Captain Deakin, an Oxford don who had helped me for five years before the war in my literary work, was dropped by parachute to set up a mission with Tito. Other British missions followed, and by June much evidence had accumulated. The Chiefs of Staff reported on June 6: "It is clear from information available to the War Office that the Cetniks are hopelessly compromised in their relations with the Axis in Hercegovina and Montenegro. During the recent fighting in the latter area it has been the well-organised Partisans rather than the Cetniks who have been holding down the Axis forces."

Having called for full information, I presided at a Chiefs of Staff conference at Downing Street on June 23. In the course of the discussion I emphasised the very great value of giving all possible support to the Yugoslav anti-Axis movement, which was containing about thirty-three Axis divisions in that area. This matter was of such importance that I directed that the small number of additional aircraft required to increase our aid must be provided, if necessary at the expense of the bombing of Germany and of the

U-boat war. Before leaving for Quebec I decided to pave the way for further action in the Balkans by appointing a senior officer to lead a larger mission to the Partisans in the field, and with authority to make direct recommendations to me about our future action towards them. Mr. Fitzroy Maclean was a member of Parliament, a man of daring character, and with Foreign Office training. This mission landed in Yugoslavia by parachute in September 1943, to find the situation revolutionised.

The news of the Italian surrender had reached Yugoslavia only with the official broadcast announcements. But, in spite of complete absence of any warning by us, Tito took quick and fruitful action. Within a few weeks six Italian divisions had been disarmed by the Partisan forces, and another two went over to fight with them against the Germans. With Italian equipment the Yugoslavs were now able to arm 80,000 more men, and to occupy for the moment most of the Adriatic coastline. There was a good chance of strengthening our general position in the Adriatic in relation to the Italian front. The Yugoslav Partisan army, totalling 200,000 men, although fighting primarily as guerrillas, was engaged in widespread action against the Germans, who continued their violent reprisals with increasing fury.

One effect of this increased activity in Yugoslavia was to exacerbate the conflict between Tito and Mihailović. Tito's growing military strength raised in an increasingly acute form the ultimate position of the Yugoslav monarchy and the exiled Government. Till the end of the war sincere and prolonged efforts were made both in London and within Yugoslavia to reach a working compromise between both sides. I had hoped that the Russians also would use their good offices in this matter, but they displayed no wish either to pool information or to discuss a plan of action. "The fighting," I telegraphed to Mr. Roosevelt, "is of the most cruel and bloody character, with merciless reprisals and executions of hostages by the Huns. . . . We hope soon to compose the Greek quarrels, but the differences between Tito's Partisans and Mihailović's Serbs are very deep-seated."

M Y gloomy forecast proved true. At the end of November Tito summoned a political congress of his movement at Jajce, in Bosnia, and not only set up a Provisional Government, "with sole authority to represent the Yugoslav nation," but also formally deprived the Royal Yugoslav Government in Cairo of all its rights. The King was forbidden to return to the country until after the liberation. The Partisans had established themselves without question as the leading elements of resistance in Yugoslavia, particularly since the Italian surrender. But it was important that no irrevocable political decisions about the future regime in Yugoslavia should be made in the atmosphere of occupation, civil war, and émigré politics.

The tragic figure of Mihailović had become the major obstacle, and by January 1944 I had been convinced by the arguments of men I knew and trusted that Mihailović was a millstone tied round the neck of the King, and he had no chance till he got rid of him. The Foreign Secretary agreed, and I wrote to Tito in this sense. But for two months longer the political wrangle over Yugoslav affairs continued in émigré circles in London. Each day lost diminished the chances of a balanced arrangement, and it was not until nearly the end of May that Mihailović was dismissed, and a moderate politician, Dr. Subašić, was asked to form a new Administration. Neither was I able to bring Tito and Subašić together until I met them in Naples in August, where I did what I could to assuage the torments both of Yugoslavia and of her southernmost neighbour, Greece, to whose affairs and fortunes we must now turn.

AFTER the withdrawal of the Allies in April 1941 Greece, like Yugoslavia, was occupied by the Axis Powers. The collapse of the Army and the retirement of the King and his Government into exile revived the bitter controversies of Greek politics. Both in the homeland and in Greek circles abroad there was hard criticism of the monarchy, which had sanctioned the dictatorship of General Metaxas, and thereby directly associated itself with the regime which had been defeated. There was much famine in the first winter, partially relieved by Red Cross shipments. The country was exhausted by the fighting and the Army was destroyed, but at the time of the surrender weapons were hidden in the mountains, and in sporadic fashion, and on a minor scale, resistance to the enemy was planned. In the towns of Central Greece starvation provided plenty of recruits.

In April 1942 the body calling itself the National Liberation Front (known by its initials in Greek as E.A.M.), which had come into being in the previous autumn, had announced the formation of the People's Liberation Army (E.L.A.S.). Small fighting groups were recruited during the following year, while in Epirus and the mountains of the northwest remnants of the Greek Army and local mountaineers gathered round the person of Colonel Napoleon Zervas. The E.A.M.–E.L.A.S. organisation was dominated by a hard core of Communist leaders. The adherents of Zervas, originally Republican in sympathy, became as time passed exclusively anti-Communist. Around these two centres Greek resistance to the Germans gathered. Neither of them had any sympathy or direct contact with the Royalist Government in London.

On the eve of Alamein we decided to attack the German supply lines leading down through Greece to the Piraeus, the port of Athens and an important base on the German route to North Africa. The first British Military Mission, under Lieut.-Colonel Myers, was accordingly dropped by parachute and made contact with the guerrillas. A viaduct on the main Athens railway line was destroyed and Greek agents made brilliant and daring sabotage against Axis shipping in the Piraeus. During the following summer the British missions were strengthened, and special efforts were made to convince the enemy that we would land in Greece on a large scale after our victory in Tunis. Anglo-Greek parties blew another railway bridge on the main Athens line, and other operations were so successful that two German divisions were moved into Greece which might have been used against us in Sicily. But this was the last direct military contribution which the Greek guerrillas and resistance fighters made to the war.

The three divergent elements, E.L.A.S., numbering 20,000 men, and predominantly under Communist control, the Zervas bands, known as E.D.E.S., totalling 5,000, and the Royalist politicians, grouped in Cairo or in London round King George II, all now thought that the Allies would probably win, and the struggle among them for political power began in earnest, to the advantage of the common foe. When the Italians capitulated in September 1943 E.L.A.S. was able to acquire most of their equipment, including the weapons of an entire division, and thus gained military supremacy. In October E.L.A.S. forces attacked E.D.E.S. (Zervas), and the British Headquarters in Cairo suspended all shipments of arms to the former.

Every effort was made by our missions to limit and end the civil war which sprawled across the ruined and occupied country, and in February 1944, British officers succeeded in establishing an uneasy truce between the two factions. But the Soviet armies were now on the borders of Romania, and as the chances of a German evacuation of the Balkans increased, and with them the possibilities of a return of the Royal Government, with British support, the E.A.M. leaders decided on a Communist coup d'état.

A Political Committee of National Liberation was set up in the mountains, and the news broadcast to the world. This was a direct challenge to the future authority of the Royal Government, and the signal for trouble and mutinies in the Greek armed forces in the Middle East and in Greek Government circles abroad. The 1st Brigade of the Greek Army in Egypt, which I was hoping could take part in the Italian campaign, mutinied against its officers. Five ships of the Royal Hellenic Navy declared for a republic, and on April 8 a Greek destroyer refused to put to sea unless a Government was formed which would include representatives of E.A.M.

I WAS at this time in charge of the Foreign Office, owing to Mr. Eden's absence. I thus had all the threads directly in my hands and with my support and personal encouragement, General Paget, who commanded the British forces in Egypt, surrounded the Brigade, which numbered 4,500 men and over fifty guns, all deployed in defensive positions against us. On the evening of the 23rd the ships were boarded by loyal Greek sailors and with about fifty casualties the mutineers were collected and sent ashore. Next day the Brigade surrendered and laid down its arms, and was evacuated to a prisoner-of-war cage, where the ringleaders were arrested. There were no Greek casualties, but one British officer, Major J. R. Copeland, was killed. The naval mutineers had surrendered unconditionally twenty-four hours earlier.

Meanwhile the King had arrived in Cairo, and on April 12 issued a proclamation that a representative Government composed largely of Greeks from within Greece would be formed. Steps were taken in secret to bring out representatives from metropolitan Greece, including M. Papandreou, the leader of the Greek Social Democratic Party, and on the 26th he took office. In May a conference of all parties, including leaders from the Greek mountains, met at a mountain resort in the Lebanon. Here it was agreed, after a fierce debate lasting three days, to set up an Administration in Cairo in which all groups would be represented under the Premiership of Papandreou, while in the mountains of Greece a united military organisation would continue to struggle against the Germans.

October in Moscow

AS the autumn drew on everything in Eastern Europe became more intense. I felt the need of another personal meeting with Stalin, whom I had not seen since Tehran, and with whom, in spite of the Warsaw tragedy, I felt new links since the successful opening of "Overlord." The Russian armies were now pressing heavily upon the Balkan scene, and Romania and Bulgaria were in their power. Belgrade was soon to fall and Hitler was fighting with desperate obstinacy to keep his grasp on Hungary. As the victory of the Grand Alliance became only a matter of time it was natural that Russian ambitions should grow. Communism raised its head behind the thundering Russian battle front. Russia was the Deliverer, and Communism the gospel she brought.

I had never felt that our relations with Romania and Bulgaria in the past called for any special sacrifices from us. But the fate of Poland and Greece struck us keenly. For Poland we had entered the war; for Greece we had made painful efforts. Both their Governments had taken refuge in London, and we considered ourselves responsible for their restoration to their own country, if that was what their peoples really wished. In the main these feelings were shared by the United States, but they were very slow in realising the upsurge of Communist influence, which slid on before, as well as followed, the onward march of the mighty armies directed from the Kremlin.

Besides these grave issues which affected the whole of Central Europe, the questions of World Organisation were also thrusting themselves upon all our minds. A lengthy conference had been held at Dumbarton Oaks, near Washington, between August and October, at which the United States, Great Britain, the U.S.S.R., and China had produced the now familiar scheme for keeping the peace of the world. The discussions had revealed many differences between the three great Allies. The Kremlin had no intention of joining an international body on which they would be outvoted by a host of small Powers, who, though they could not influence the course of the war, would certainly claim equal status in the victory. I felt sure we could only reach good decisions with Russia while we had the comradeship of a common foe as a bond. Hitler and Hitlerism were doomed; but after Hitler what?

After visiting Italy and hearing the news from the front, we alighted at Moscow on the afternoon of October 9, and were received very heartily and with full ceremonial by Molotov and many high Russian personages. This time we were lodged in Moscow itself, with every care and comfort. I had one small, perfectly appointed house and Mr. Eden another near by. We were glad to dine alone together and rest. At ten o'clock that night we held an important meeting in the Kremlin. There were only Stalin, Molotov, Eden, and I, with Major Birse and Pavlov as interpreters. It was agreed to invite the Polish Prime Minister, M. Romer, and the Foreign Minister, and M. Grabski, a grey-bearded and aged academician of much charm and quality, to Moscow at once. I telegraphed accordingly to M. Mikolajczyk that we were expecting him and his friends for discussions with the Soviet Government and ourselves, as well as with the Lublin Polish Committee.

The moment was apt for business, so I said, "Let us settle about our affairs in the Balkans. Your armies are in Romania and Bulgaria. We have interests, missions, and agents there. Don't let us get at cross-purposes in small ways. So far as Britain and Russia are concerned, how would it do for you to have ninety per cent predominance in Romania, for us to have ninety per cent of the say in Greece, and go fifty-fifty about Yugoslavia?" While this was being translated I wrote out on a half-sheet of paper:

ROMANIA	
Russia............................	90%
The others......................	10%
GREECE	
Great Britain (in accord with U.S.A.)	90%
Russia............................	10%
YUGOSLAVIA......................	50-50%
HUNGARY..........................	50-50%
BULGARIA	
Russia............................	75%
The others......................	25%

I pushed this across to Stalin, who had by then heard the translation. There was a slight pause. Then he took his blue pencil and made a large tick upon it, and passed it back to us. It was all settled in no more time than it takes to set down. Of course we had long and anxiously considered our point, and were only dealing with immediate wartime arrangements. All larger questions were reserved on both sides for what we then hoped would be a peace table when the war was won.

AFTER this there was a long silence. The pencilled paper lay in the centre of the table. At length I said, "Might it not be thought rather cynical if it seemed we had disposed of these issues, so fateful to millions of people, in such an offhand manner? Let us burn the paper." "No, you keep it," said Stalin.

"It is absolutely necessary," I reported privately to the President, "we should try to get a common mind about the Balkans, so that we may prevent civil war breaking out in several countries, when probably you and I would be in sympathy with one side and Uncle Joe with the other. I shall keep you informed of all this, and nothing will be settled except preliminary agreements between Britain and Russia, subject to further discussion and melting down with you. On this basis I am sure you will not mind our trying to have a full meeting of minds with the Russians."

To my colleagues at home I telegraphed: "The system of percentage is not intended . . . to be more than a guide, and of course in no way commits the United States, nor does it attempt to set up a rigid system of spheres of interest. It may however help the United States to see how their two principal Allies feel about these regions when the picture is presented as a whole. . . ."

The Poles from London had now arrived, and at five o'clock on the evening of October 13 we assembled at the

Soviet Government Hospitality House, known as Spirido-novka, to hear Mikolajczyk and his colleagues put their case. These talks were held as a preparation for a further meeting at which the British and American delegations would meet the Lublin Poles. I pressed Mikolajczyk hard to consider two things, namely, *de facto* acceptance of the Curzon Line, of which more hereafter, with interchange of population, and a friendly discussion with the Lublin Polish Committee so that a united Poland might be established. Changes, I said, would take place, but it would be best if unity were established now, at this closing period of the war, and I asked the Poles to consider the matter carefully that night. Mr. Eden and I would be at their disposal. It was essential for them to make contact with the Polish Committee and to accept the Curzon Line as a working arrangement, subject to discussion at the Peace Conference.

At ten o'clock on the same evening we met the so-called Polish National Committee. It was soon plain that these Lublin Poles were mere pawns of Russia. They had all learnt and had rehearsed their parts so carefully that even their masters evidently felt they were overdoing it. M. Bierut, their leader, spoke in these terms: "We are here to demand on behalf of Poland that Lvov shall belong to Russia. This is the will of the Polish people." When this had been translated from Polish into English and Russian I looked at Stalin and saw an understanding twinkle in his expressive eyes, as much as to say, "What about that for our Soviet teaching!" The lengthy contribution of another Lublin leader, Osóbka-Morawski, was equally depressing.

The whole conference lasted over six hours, but the achievement was small, and as the days passed only slight improvement was made with the festering sore of Soviet-Polish affairs. The Poles from London were willing to accept the Curzon Line "as a line of demarcation between Russia and Poland." The Russians insisted on the words "as a basis of frontier between Russia and Poland." Neither side would give way. Mikolajczyk declared that he would be repudiated by his own people, and Stalin at the end of a talk of two hours and a quarter which I had with him alone remarked that he and Molotov were the only two of those he worked with who were favourable to dealing "softly" with Mikolajczyk. I was sure there were strong pressures in the background, both party and military. Stalin was

against trying to form a united Polish Government without the frontier question being agreed. Had this been settled he would have been quite willing that Mikolajczyk should head the new Government. I myself thought that difficulties not less obstinate would arise in a discussion for a merger of the Polish Government with the Lublin Poles, whose representatives continued to make the worst possible impression on us, and who, I told Stalin, were "only an expression of the Soviet will." They had no doubt also the ambition to rule Poland, and were thus a kind of Quislings. In all the circumstances the best course was for the two Polish delegations to return whence they had come. I felt very deeply the responsibility which lay on me and the Foreign Secretary in trying to frame proposals for a Russo-Polish settlement. Even forcing the Curzon Line upon Poland would certainly excite criticism.

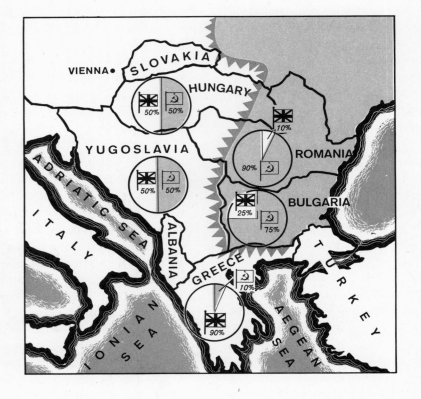

Spheres of interest in the Balkans are shown here as agreed to by Churchill and Stalin in 1944. In return for an almost free hand in Romania and Bulgaria, Russia was to share equal influence over Hungary and Yugoslavia and leave Britain the lion's portion in Greece.

We had gained considerable advantages in other directions. The resolve of the Soviet Government to attack Japan upon the overthrow of Hitler was obvious. This would have a supreme value in shortening the whole struggle. The arrangements made about the Balkans were, I was sure, the best possible, and coupled with successful military action, they should now be effective in saving Greece, and I had no doubt that our agreement to pursue a fifty-fifty joint policy in Yugoslavia was the best solution for our difficulties in view of Tito's behaviour—having lived under our protection for three or four months, he had come secretly to Moscow to confer, without telling us where he had gone—and of the arrival of Russian and Bulgarian forces under Russian command to help his eastern flank.

There is no doubt that in our narrow circle we talked with an ease, freedom, and cordiality never before attained between our two countries. Stalin made several expressions of personal regard which I feel sure were sincere. But I became even more convinced that he was by no means alone. As I said to my colleagues at home, "Behind the horseman sits black care." On the evening of October 17 we held our last meeting. The news had just arrived that Admiral Horthy had been arrested by the Germans as a precaution now that the whole German front in Hungary was disintegrating. I remarked that I hoped the Ljubljana Gap could be reached as fast as possible, and added that I did not think the war would be over before the spring.

504

Christmas at Athens

THE Greeks rival the Jews in being the most politically minded race in the world. No matter how forlorn their circumstances or how grave the peril to their country, they are always divided into many parties, with many leaders who fight among themselves with desperate vigour. It has been well said that wherever there are three Jews it will be found that there are two Prime Ministers and one leader of the Opposition. The same is true of this other famous ancient race, whose stormy and endless struggle for life stretches back to the fountain springs of human thought.

No two races have set such a mark upon the world. Both have shown a capacity for survival, in spite of unending perils and sufferings from external oppressors, matched only by their own ceaseless feuds, quarrels, and convulsions. The passage of several thousand years sees no change in their characteristics and no diminution of their trials or their vitality. They have survived in spite of all that the world could do against them, and all they could do against themselves, and each of them from angles so different have left us the inheritance of their genius and wisdom. No two cities have counted more with mankind than Athens and Jerusalem. Their messages in religion, philosophy, and art have been the main guiding lights of modern faith and culture. Centuries of foreign rule and indescribable, endless oppression leave them still living, active communities and forces in the modern world, quarrelling among themselves with an insatiable vivacity. Personally I have always been on the side of both, and believed in their invincible power to survive internal strife and the world tides threatening their extinction.

Before leaving Italy at the end of August I had asked the Chief of the Imperial General Staff to work out the details of a British expedition to Greece in case the Germans there collapsed. We gave it the code name "Manna," and by September our preparations were well advanced. M. Papandreou and his colleagues were brought to Italy and installed in a villa near Caserta. Here he set to work with the representatives of E.A.M. and their Nationalist rivals, E.D.E.S. and, aided by Mr. Harold Macmillan, as Minister Resident in the Mediterranean, and Mr. Leeper, our Ambassador to the Greek Government, a comprehensive agreement was signed on the 26th. It laid down that all guerrilla forces in the country should place themselves under the orders of the Greek Government, who in their turn put them under the British commander, General Scobie. The Greek guerrilla leaders declared that none of their men would take the law into their own hands. Any action in Athens would be taken only on General Scobie's direct orders. This document, known as the Caserta Agreement, governed our future action.

In October the liberation of Greece began. Commando units were sent into Southern Greece, and in the early hours of October 4 our troops occupied Patras. This was our first foothold since the tragic exit of 1941. On the 12th General Wilson learnt that the Germans were evacuating Athens, and next day British parachutists landed on the Mégara airfield, about eight miles west of the capital. On the 14th the rest of the paratroopers arrived and occupied the city on the heels of the German withdrawal. Our naval forces entered the Piraeus, bringing with them General Scobie and the main part of his force, and two days later the Greek Government arrived, together with our Ambassador.

The testing time for our arrangements had now come. At the Moscow conference I had obtained Russian abstention at a heavy price. We were pledged to support Papandreou's Provisional Administration, in which E.A.M. was fully represented. All parties were bound by the Caserta Agreement, and we wished to hand over authority to a stable Greek Government without loss of time. But Greece was in ruins. The Germans destroyed roads and railways as they retreated northward, and though we harassed them from the air we could do little to interfere on land. E.L.A.S. armed bands filled the gap left by the departing invaders, and their central command made little effort to enforce the solemn promises they had given. Everywhere was want and dissension. Finances were disordered and food exhausted. Our own military resources were stretched to the limit.

At the end of the month Mr. Eden visited Athens on his way home from Moscow, and received a tumultuous welcome in memory of his efforts for Greece in 1941. With him were Lord Moyne, the Minister Resident in Cairo, and Mr. Macmillan. The whole question of relief was discussed and everything humanly possible was done. Our troops willingly went on half-rations to increase the food supplies, and British sappers started to build emergency communications. By November 1 the Germans had evacuated Salonika and Flórina. Ten days later the last of their forces had crossed the northern frontier, and apart from a few isolated island garrisons, Greece was free.

BUT the Athens Government had not enough troops to control the country and compel E.L.A.S. to observe the Caserta Agreement. Disorder grew and spread. A revolt by E.A.M. was imminent, and on November 15 General Scobie was directed to make counterpreparations. Athens was to be declared a military area, and authority was given to order all E.L.A.S. troops to leave it. The 4th Indian Division was sent from Italy. So also was the Greek Brigade, which became the centre of controversy between Papandreou and his E.A.M. colleagues. It was evident that the only chance of averting civil war was to disarm the guerrillas and other forces by mutual agreement and establish a new National Army and police force under the direct control of the Government in Athens.

A draft decree for the demobilisation of the guerrillas, drawn up at M. Papandreou's request by the E.A.M. Ministers themselves, was presented to the distracted Cabinet. The regular Greek Mountain Brigade and the "Sacred Squadron" of the Air Force were to remain. E.L.A.S. were to keep a brigade of their own, and E.D.E.S. were to be given a small force. But at the last moment the E.A.M. Ministers went back on their own proposals, on which they had wasted a precious week, and demanded that the

Mountain Brigade should be disbanded. The Communist tactic was now in full swing. On December 1 the six Ministers associated with E.A.M. resigned, and a general strike in Athens was proclaimed for the following day. The rest of the Cabinet passed a decree dissolving the guerrillas, and the Communist Party headquarters moved from the capital. General Scobie, in a message to the people of Greece, stated that he stood firm behind the present constitutional Government "until the Greek State can be established with a legally armed force and free elections can be held." I issued a similar personal statement from London.

On Sunday, December 3, Communist supporters, engaging in a banned demonstration, collided with the police and civil war began. The next day General Scobie ordered E.L.A.S. to evacuate Athens and the Piraeus forthwith. Instead their troops and armed civilians tried to seize the capital by force.

AT this moment I took a more direct control of the affair. On learning that the Communists already had captured almost all the police stations in Athens, murdering the bulk of their occupants not already pledged to their attack, and were within half a mile of the Government offices, I ordered General Scobie and his 5,000 British troops, who ten days before had all been received with rapture as deliverers by the population, to intervene and fire upon the treacherous aggressors. It is no use doing things like this by halves. The mob violence by which the Communists sought to conquer the city and present themselves to the world as the Government demanded by the Greek people could only be met by firearms. There was no time for the Cabinet to be called.

Eden and I were together till about two o'clock, and were entirely agreed that we must open fire. Seeing how tired he was, I said to him, "If you like to go to bed, leave it to me." He did, and at about 3 a.m. I drafted the following telegram to General Scobie: ". . . You are responsible for maintaining order in Athens and for neutralising or destroying all E.A.M-E.L.A.S. bands approaching the city. You may make any regulations you like for the strict control of the streets or for the rounding up of any number of truculent persons. Naturally E.L.A.S. will try to put women and children in the van where shooting may occur. You must be clever about this and avoid mistakes. But do not hesitate to fire at any armed male in Athens who assails the British authority or Greek authority with which we are working. It would be well of course if your command were reinforced by the authority of some Greek Government and Papandreou is being told by Leeper to stop and help. *Do not however hesitate to act as if you were in a conquered city where a local rebellion is in progress.*

"With regard to E.L.A.S. bands approaching from the outside, you should surely be able with your armour to give some of these a lesson which will make others unlikely to try. You may count upon my support in all reasonable and sensible action taken on this basis. *We have to hold and dominate Athens. It would be a great thing for you to succeed in this without bloodshed if possible, but also with bloodshed if necessary.*"

This telegram was dispatched at 4:50 a.m. on December the 5th. I must admit that it was somewhat strident in tone. I felt it so necessary to give a strong lead to the military commander that I intentionally worded it in the sharpest terms. The fact that he had such an order in his possession would not only encourage him to decisive action but gave him the certain assurance that I should be with him in any well-conceived action he might take, whatever the consequences might be. I felt grave concern about the whole business, but I was sure that there should be no room for doubts or hedging. I had in my mind Arthur Balfour's celebrated telegram in the eighties to the British authorities in Ireland: "Don't hesitate to shoot." This was sent through the open telegraph offices. There was a furious storm about it in the House of Commons of those days, but it certainly prevented loss of life. It was one of the key steppingstones by which Balfour advanced to power and control. The setting of the scene was now entirely different. Nevertheless "Don't hesitate to shoot" hung in my mind as a prompter from those far-off days.

Now that the free world has learnt so much more than was then understood about the Communist movement in Greece and elsewhere, many readers will be astonished at the vehement attacks to which His Majesty's Government, and I in particular at its head, were subjected. The vast majority of the American Press violently condemned our action, which they declared falsified the cause for which they had gone to war. The State Department, in the charge of Mr. Stettinius, issued a markedly critical pronouncement, which they were to regret, or at least reverse, in afteryears. In England there was much perturbation. The *Times* and the *Manchester Guardian* pronounced their censures upon what they considered our reactionary policy. Stalin however adhered strictly and faithfully to our agreement of October, and during all the long weeks of fighting the Communists in the streets of Athens not one word of reproach came from *Pravda* or *Isvestia*.

IN the House of Commons there was a great stir. There was a strong current of vague opinion, and even passion, and any Government which had rested on a less solid foundation than the National Coalition might well have been shaken to pieces. But the War Cabinet stood like a rock against which all the waves and winds might beat in vain. When we recall what has happened to Poland, to Hungary, and Czechoslovakia in these later years we may be grateful to Fortune for giving us at this critical moment the calm, united strength of determined leaders of all parties. Space does not allow me to quote more than a few extracts from a speech I made on December 8:

"The charge which is made against us . . . is that we are using His Majesty's forces to disarm the friends of democracy in Greece and in other parts of Europe and to suppress those popular movements which have valorously assisted in the defeat of the enemy. . . .

"One must have some respect for democracy and not use the word too lightly. The last thing which resembles democracy is mob law, with bands of gangsters, armed with deadly weapons, forcing their way into great cities, seizing the police stations and key points of government, endeavouring to introduce a totalitarian regime with an iron hand.

"Democracy is not based on violence or terrorism, but on reason, on fair play, on freedom, on respecting the rights of other people. Democracy is no harlot to be picked up in the street by a man with a Tommy gun. I trust the people, the mass of the people, in almost any country, but I like to make sure that it is the people and not a gang of bandits who think they can overturn constituted authority.'' Only thirty members faced us in the division lobby. Nearly 300 voted confidence. Here again was a moment in which the House of Commons showed its enduring strength.

There is no doubt that the emotional expression of American opinion and the train of thought at that time being followed by the State Department affected President Roosevelt and his immediate circle. The sentiments I had expressed in the House of Commons have now become commonplace of American doctrine and policy and command the assent of the United Nations. But in those days they had an air of novelty which was startling to those who were governed by impressions of the past and did not feel the onset of the new adverse tide in human affairs.

Meanwhile British troops were fighting hard in the centre of Athens, hemmed in and outnumbered. They were engaged in house-to-house combat with an enemy of whom at least four-fifths were in plain clothes. Unlike many of the Allied newspaper correspondents in Athens, our troops had no difficulty in understanding the issues involved. M. Papandreou and his remaining Ministers had lost all authority. Previous proposals to set up a Regency under the Archbishop Damaskinos had been rejected by the King, but on December 10 Mr. Leeper revived the idea. King George was however against it.

Amid these tumults Field-Marshal Alexander and Mr. Harold Macmillan arrived in Athens. On December 12 the War Cabinet gave Alexander a free hand in all military measures. The 4th British Division, on passage from Italy to Egypt, was diverted, and their arrival during the latter half of the month in due course turned the scale, but in the meantime street fighting swayed to and fro on an enlarging scale. On the 15th Alexander warned me that it was most important to get a settlement quickly, and the best chance was through the Archbishop. ''Otherwise,'' he telegraphed, ''I fear that if rebel resistance continues at the same intensity as at present I shall have to send further large reinforcements from the Italian front to make sure of clearing the whole of Piraeus-Athens, which is fifty square miles of houses.''

A few days later I resolved to go and see for myself. It was December 24, and we had a family and children's party for Christmas Eve. We had a Christmas tree—one sent from the President—and were all looking forward to a pleasant evening, the brighter perhaps because surrounded by dark shadows. But when I had finished reading my telegrams I felt sure I ought to fly to Athens, see the situation on the spot, and especially make the acquaintance of the Archbishop, around whom so much was turning. I therefore set the telephone working and arranged for an aeroplane to be ready at Northolt that night. I also spoilt Mr. Eden's Christmas by the proposal, which he immediately accepted, that he should come too.

After having been much reproached by the family for deserting the party, I motored to meet Eden at Northolt, where the Skymaster which General Arnold had recently sent me waited, attentive and efficient. We slept soundly until about eight o'clock, when we landed at Naples to refuel. Here were several generals, and we all had breakfast together or at adjoining tables. Breakfast is not my best hour of the day, and the news we had, both from the Italian front and from Athens, was bleak. In an hour we were off again, and in perfect weather flew over the Peloponnesus and the Gulf of Corinth. Athens and the Piraeus unfolded like a map beneath us on a gigantic scale, and we gazed down upon it wondering who held what.

At about noon we landed at the Kalabáka airfield, which was guarded by about 2,000 British airmen, all well armed and active. Here were Field-Marshal Alexander, Mr. Leeper, and Mr. Macmillan. They came on board the plane, and we spent nearly three hours in hard discussion of the whole position, military and political. We were, I think, in complete agreement at the end, and about the immediate steps to be taken. I and my party were to sleep on board the *Ajax* anchored off the Piraeus, the famous light cruiser of the Plate River battle, which now seemed a long time ago. The road was reported clear, and with an escort of several armoured cars we traversed the few miles without incident. We boarded the *Ajax* before darkness fell, and I realised for the first time that it was Christmas Day. All preparations had been made by the ship's company for a jolly evening, and we certainly disturbed them as little as possible.

The sailors had a plan for a dozen of them to be dressed up in every kind of costume and disguise, as Chinese and Negroes, Red Indians, Cockneys, clowns—all to serenade the officers and warrant officers, and generally inaugurate revels suitable to the occasion. The Archbishop and his attendants arrived—an enormous tall figure in the robes and high hat of a dignitary of the Greek Church. The two parties met. The sailors thought he was part of their show of which they had not been told, and danced around him enthusiastically. The Archbishop thought this motley gang was a premeditated insult, and might well have departed to the shore but for the timely arrival of the captain, who, after some embarrassment, explained matters satisfactorily. Meanwhile I waited, wondering what had happened. But all ended happily.

He spoke to us with great bitterness against the atrocities of E.L.A.S. and the dark, sinister hand behind E.A.M.

---

26 Dec 44

PRIME MINISTER TO MRS. CHURCHILL

. . . You will have read about the plot to blow up H.Q. in the Hotel Grande-Bretagne. I do not think it was for my benefit. Still, a ton of dynamite was put in sewers by extremely skilled hands and with German mechanism between the time my arrival was known and daylight.

The conference at the Greek Foreign Office was intensely dramatic. All those haggard Greek faces round the table, and the Archbishop with his enormous hat, making him, I should think, seven feet high, whom we got to preside. The American and Russian and French Ambassadors were all very glad to be invited. . . .

Listening to him, it was quite impossible to doubt that he greatly feared the Communist, or Trotskyite as he called it, combination in Greek affairs. He told us that he had issued an encyclical condemning E.L.A.S. for taking 8,000 hostages, middle class people, many of them Egyptians, and shooting a few every day, and that he had said that he would report these matters to the Press of the world if the women were not released. Generally he impressed me with a good deal of confidence. He was a magnificent figure, and he immediately accepted the proposal of being chairman of the conference, which was to be held next day, to which E.L.A.S. had been invited to send their representatives.

ON the morning of December the 26th, "Boxing Day," I set out for the Embassy. I remember that three or four shells from the fighting which was going on a mile away on our left raised spouts of water fairly near the *Ajax* as we were about to go ashore. Here an armoured car and military escort awaited us. We rumbled along the road to the Embassy without any trouble. I again met the Archbishop, on whom we were about to stake so much. He agreed to all that was proposed. We planned the procedure at the conference to be held in the afternoon. I was already convinced that he was the outstanding figure in the Greek turmoil. Among other things, I had learned that he had been a champion wrestler before he entered the Orthodox Church.

About six o'clock that evening, the conference opened in the Greek Foreign Office. We all took our seats in a large, bleak room after darkness fell. The winter is cold in Athens. There was no heating, and a few hurricane lamps cast a dim light upon the scene. I sat on the Archbishop's right, with Mr. Eden, and Field-Marshal Alexander was on his left. Mr. MacVeagh, the American Ambassador, M. Baelen, the French Minister, and the Soviet military representative had all accepted our invitation. The three Communist leaders were late. It was not their fault. There had been prolonged bickering at the outposts. After half an hour we began our work, and I was already speaking when they entered the room. They were presentable figures in British battle dress. "It is better," I told them, "to let every effort be made to remake Greece as a factor in the victory, and to do it now. We do not intend to obstruct your deliberations. We British, and other representatives of the great united victorious Powers, will leave you Greeks to your own discussions under this most eminent and most venerable citizen, and we shall not trouble you unless you send for us again. . . . We have many other tasks to perform in this world of terrible storm. My hope is however that the conference which begins here this afternoon in Athens will restore Greece once again to her fame and power among the Allies and the peace-loving peoples of the world, will secure the Greek frontiers from any danger from the north, and will enable every Greek to make the best of himself and the best of his country before the eyes of the whole world. . . ."

Alexander added a sharp touch that Greek troops should be fighting in Italy and not against British troops in Greece. Once we had broken the ice and got the Greeks, who had done such terrible injuries to each other, to parley round the table under the presidency of the Archbishop, and the formal speeches had been made, the British members of the conference withdrew.

Bitter and animated discussions between the Greek parties occupied all the following day. At 5:30 that evening I had a final discussion with the Archbishop. As the result of his conversations with the E.L.A.S. delegates it was agreed I should ask the King of Greece to make him Regent. He would set about forming a new Government without any Communist members. We undertook to carry on the fighting in full vigour until either E.L.A.S. accepted a truce or the Athens area was clear of them. I told him that we could not undertake any military task beyond Athens and Attica, but that we would try to keep British forces in Greece until the Greek National Army was formed.

On the following morning, December 28, Mr. Eden and I left by air. I had no chance to say good-bye to M. Papandreou before leaving. He was about to resign, and was a serious loser by the whole business. I asked our Ambassador to keep in friendly touch with him.

On December 29 we arrived back in London. Mr. Eden and I sat up with the King of Greece till 4:30 in the morning, at the end of which time His Majesty agreed not to return to Greece unless summoned by a free and fair expression of the national will, and to appoint the Archbishop as Regent during the emergency. I sent his announcement at once to Mr. Leeper and the Archbishop replied to the King accepting his mandate as Regent. There was a new and living Greek Government. On January 3 General Plastiras, a vehement Republican, who was the leader of the Army revolt against King Constantine in 1922, became Premier.

Continuous fighting in Athens during December at last drove the insurgents from the capital, and by mid-January British troops controlled all Attica. The Communists could do nothing against our men in open country, and a truce was signed on January 11.

THUS ended the six weeks' struggle for Athens, and, as it ultimately proved, for Greek freedom from Communist subjugation. When three million men were fighting on either side on the Western Front and vast American forces were deployed against Japan in the Pacific the spasms of Greece may seem petty, but nevertheless they stood at the nerve centre of power, law, and freedom in the Western world. It is odd, looking back on these events, now that some years have passed, to see how completely the policy for which I and my colleagues fought so stubbornly has been justified by events. Myself, I never had any doubts about it, for I saw quite plainly that Communism would be the peril civilisation would have to face after the defeat of Nazism and Fascism. It did not fall to us to end the task in Greece. I little thought however at the end of 1944 that the State Department, supported by overwhelming American opinion, would in little more than two years not only adopt and carry on the course we had opened but would make vehement and costly exertions, even of a military character, to bring it to fruition. If Greece has escaped the fate of Czechoslovakia and survives to-day as one of the free nations, it is due not only to British action in 1944 but to the steadfast efforts of what was presently to become the united strength of the English-speaking world.

Under camouflage netting on a ship, British Commandos entertain Greek guerrillas who have come to give advice on raids against the Nazis

THE PEOPLE RISE

Guerrilla Warfare in the Aegean

A bridge blown in the night, a soldier's throat slit on a dark street, a grenade tossed into an officers' mess, mysterious accidents on military rail lines—countless episodes like these harassed the German troops who were garrisoning the occupied countries of Europe. Sometimes isolated attacks and sabotage merged to make a full-scale revolt, and entire German divisions and armies were tied down to a bloody succession of repression and reprisal.

On these pages are paintings of Greek guerrilla fighters by Bernard Perlin, an American artist who in the summer of 1944 accompanied two British raiding parties sent to reconnoiter the underground front. Silently rowed to shore on the Greek islands and mainland under cover of darkness, they slipped by the German sentries into the embattled hinterland. One raid (*below*) ran into hard luck; the other (*opposite*) wrecked a fuel dump and a Gestapo headquarters. Back in silence went the raiders. They had done little direct harm to the German war machine, but they had done their share in keeping one part of the German army occupied with worrying over where the next blow was going to fall.

Shattering explosion of a hand grenade, set off by accident, fells Commandos hiding in a Greek village. The British raiders, who had sailed from a secret base in the Aegean Sea to the mainland of Greece, made contact with the Communist-controlled E.L.A.S. guerrillas and were enthusiastically received by the local population. But the unlucky explosion left them in no shape to fight and they had to be evacuated.

Precarious shelter in a cave shields three raiders fleeing from a German patrol. Here, where the three hid for 28 hours, the artist has portrayed himself (*right foreground*) tearing up compromising papers.

Refuge for the wounded (*below*) is offered by a 13-year-old Greek girl. She hid the raiders among the other children and cats, fobbed off questioning Germans, and later guided her guests to safety.

A Heroic Failure in Warsaw

On August 1, 1944, when the German armies seemed to be in dissolution on both eastern and western fronts, the Polish underground came out in open revolt. The Nazis had erased the very name of Poland from the map and, in five years of unbridled terror, had tried to stamp out Polish national consciousness as well. Patriotism burned all the fiercer, and the people of Warsaw rose to a man with arms and a battle organization that had been secretly prepared under the grip of the Gestapo.

A mine exploding under German headquarters gave the signal for the uprising. In two days, the electric power station, the gas works and most of the center of the city were in patriot hands. The guns of the Red Army charging westward could be plainly heard in Warsaw, but soon they grew silent as the Russians elected to call off their attack on the Warsaw front and inexplicably leave the Poles to their fate. With fearful difficulty, the British and American air forces flew in some supplies, but they fell far short of the needs of the Poles, who had no reserves except for what they could capture from the Germans.

For 63 days the Poles held out against overwhelming forces under orders from Hitler to "raze Warsaw to the ground." Finally, on October 2, Warsaw succumbed. In January, when the Russians moved into the ruins, they reviled the hopeless, heroic rising as a reactionary plot.

Up from a sewer, a Pole is pulled into the open by his comrades. As the Germans cut one Polish position off from another, the only means of communication was the fetid tunnels of the sewer system.

German thugs (opposite) aim down a Warsaw street. One Nazi unit, composed of ex-convicts, committed such atrocities that their leader said to Hitler, "My Fuehrer, these men are real scoundrels."

Beaten Poles carry the white flag of surrender through the shattered city on their way to German headquarters. Altogether at least 250,000 Poles fell in the battle of Warsaw or were deported afterwards.

Triumphant Survival in Yugoslavia

Of the 17 nations overrun by Hitler, none gave him more trouble than Yugoslavia. Reduced in 1941 to a collection of puppet states and provinces handed over to foreign lands, Yugoslavia seethed with revolt and civil war, which attacks by some fifteen German, Italian and Bulgarian divisions never succeeded in subduing.

The ancient traditions, the fierce independence and love of country which imbued this people of warrior peasants were mobilized by a disciplined and dedicated band of Communists led by Josip Broz, who took the name Tito.

Some of their turbulent, enduring vitality is shown here in sketches by David Fredenthal, a LIFE artist-correspondent who lived with Tito's Partisans for two months.

More than 1,700,000 men, women and children—one-ninth of the prewar population of Yugoslavia—succumbed to German bullets and bombings, or to fratricidal massacres, or to starvation and disease. But when the Russian armies came sweeping in, the Partisans—in the only uprising in Europe that won total success—were strong enough to set themselves up as the government of their country.

Joyous villagers fiddle and dance to greet the victorious men of Tito's Partisan army as they come bearing their slogans through the countryside, after routing a part of the German army of occupation.

Stubborn peasant (opposite) goes on with his sowing as Partisan troops slog across his field, passing German tanks destroyed by Yugoslavs in one of the hundred nameless battles that devastated the land.

The Big Three, Churchill, Roosevelt and Stalin, meet with their staffs at the Livadia Palace near Yalta in February of 1945 to co-ordinate the final attacks against Germany and Japan, and to mold the shape of the postwar world.

21

DEFEAT OF GERMANY

The Liberation of Western Europe

GENERAL Eisenhower, in accordance with previous and agreed arrangements, assumed direct command of the land forces in Northern France on September 1, 1944. These comprised the British 21st Army Group, under Field-Marshal Montgomery, and the American 12th Army Group, under General Omar Bradley, whose operations Montgomery had hitherto controlled. He wielded more than thirty-seven divisions, or over half a million fighting men, and this great array was driving before it the remnants of the German armies in the West, who were harassed day and night by our dominating air forces. The enemy were still about seventeen divisions strong, but until they could re-form and were reinforced there was little fight left in most of them. General Speidel, Rommel's former Chief of Staff, has described their plight:

"An orderly retreat became impossible. The Allied motorised armies surrounded the slow and exhausted German foot divisions in separate groups and smashed them up . . . . There were no German ground forces of any importance that could be thrown in, and there was next to nothing in the air."

Eisenhower planned to thrust northeastward in the greatest possible strength and to the utmost limit of his supplies. The main effort was to be made by the British 21st Army Group, whose drive along the Channel coast would not only overrun the launching sites of the flying bomb, but also take Antwerp. Without the vast harbour of this city no advance across the lower Rhine and into the plains of Northern Germany was possible. The 12th U.S. Army Group was also to pursue the enemy, its First Army keeping abreast of the British, while the remainder, bearing eastward towards Verdun and the upper Meuse, would prepare to strike towards the Saar.

Montgomery made two counterproposals, one in late August that his Army Group and the 12th U.S. Army Group should strike north together with a solid mass of nearly forty divisions, and the second on September 4, that only one thrust should be made, either towards the Ruhr or the Saar. Whichever was chosen the forces should be given all the resources and maintenance they needed. He urged that the rest of the front should be restrained for the benefit of the major thrust, which should be placed under one commander, himself or Bradley as the case might be. He believed it would probably reach Berlin, and considered that the Ruhr was better than the Saar.

But Eisenhower held to his plan. Germany still had reserves in the homeland, and he believed that if a relatively small force were thrust far ahead across the Rhine it would play into the enemy's hands. He thought it was better for the 21st Army Group to make every effort to get a bridgehead over the Rhine, while the Twelfth advanced as far as they could against the Siegfried Line. Strategists may long debate these issues.

The discussion caused no check in the pursuit. The number of divisions that could be sustained, and the speed and range of their advance, depended, however, entirely on harbours, transport, and supplies. Relatively little ammunition was being used, but food, and above all petrol, governed every movement. Cherbourg and the "Mulberry" harbour at Arromanches were the only ports we had, and these were daily being left farther behind. The front line was still sustained from Normandy, and each day about 20,000 tons of supplies had to be carried over ever-increasing distances, together with much material for mending roads and bridges and for building airfields. The Brittany ports, when captured, would be even more remote, but the Channel ports northward from Le Havre, and Antwerp especially, if we could capture it before it was too seriously damaged, were prizes of the most vital consequence.

Antwerp was thus the immediate aim of Montgomery's Army Group, which now had its first chance to show its mobility. The 11th Armoured Division caught the commander of the Seventh German Army during his breakfast in Amiens on August 31. The frontier towns so well known to the British Expeditionary Force of 1940, and, at least by name, to their predecessors a quarter of a century before—Arras, Douai, Lille, and many others—were soon reached. Brussels, hastily evacuated by the Germans, was entered by the Guards Armoured Division on September 3, and, as everywhere in Belgium, our troops had a splendid welcome and were much helped by the well-organised Resistance. Thence the Guards turned east for Louvain, and the 11th Armoured entered Antwerp on September 4, where, to our surprise and joy, they found the harbour almost intact. So swift had been the advance—over 200 miles in under four days —that the enemy had been run off their legs and given no time for their usual and thorough demolition.

But our ships could only reach Antwerp through the winding, difficult estuary of the Scheldt, and the Germans held both banks. Hard and costly operations were needed to expel them, and the task fell principally on General Crerar's First Canadian Army consisting of the I British and the II Canadian Corps. The latter included the Polish Armoured Division. Much depended on their success. By the 9th they had cleared all the Pas-de-Calais, with its flying bomb launching sites. The Channel ports,

Dieppe, Boulogne, Calais, Dunkerque, were either seized or invested. Le Havre, with a garrison over 11,000 strong, resisted fiercely, and in spite of bombardment from the sea by 15-inch guns, and more than 10,000 tons of bombs from the air, did not surrender till September 12. The Polish Armoured Division captured Ghent, only forty miles from Antwerp itself. Of course, this pace could not last. The forward leap was over and the check was evident before we sailed to Quebec.

But there was still the chance of crossing the lower Rhine. Eisenhower thought this prize so valuable that he gave it priority over clearing the shores of the Scheldt estuary and opening the port of Antwerp. To renew Montgomery's effort Eisenhower now gave him additional American transport and air supply. The First Airborne Army, under the American General Brereton, stood ready to strike from England and Montgomery resolved to seize a bridgehead at Arnhem. The 82nd U.S. Division was to capture the key bridges at Nijmegen and Grave, while the 101st U.S. Division made safe the road from Grave to Eindhoven. XXX Corps, led by the Guards Armoured Division, would force their way up the road to Eindhoven and thence to Arnhem along the "carpet" of airborne troops, hoping to find the bridges over the three major water obstacles already secured.

The preparations for this daring stroke, by far the greatest operation of its kind yet attempted, were complicated and urgent, because the enemy were growing stronger every day. It is remarkable that they were completed by the set date, September 17. There were not sufficient aircraft to carry the whole airborne force simultaneously, and the movement had to be spread over three days. However, on the 17th the leading elements of the three divisions were well and truly taken to their destinations by the fine work of the Allied air forces. The 101st U.S. Division accomplished most of their task, but a canal bridge on the road to Eindhoven was blown and they did not capture the town till the 18th. The 82nd U.S. Division also did well, but could not seize the main bridge at Nijmegen.

From Arnhem the news was scarce, but it seemed that some of our Parachute Regiment had established themselves at the north end of the bridge. The Guards Armoured Division began to advance in the afternoon up the Eindhoven road, preceded by an artillery barrage and rocket-firing planes, and protected by a Corps on either flank. The road was obstinately defended, and the Guards did not reach the Americans till the afternoon of the 18th. German attacks against the narrow salient began next day and grew in

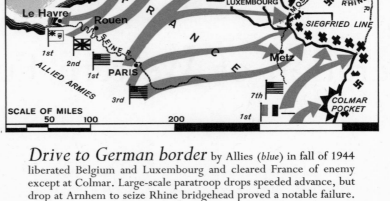

Drive to German border by Allies (*blue*) in fall of 1944 liberated Belgium and Luxembourg and cleared France of enemy except at Colmar. Large-scale paratroop drops speeded advance, but drop at Arnhem to seize Rhine bridgehead proved a notable failure.

strength. The 101st Division had great difficulty in keeping the road open. At times traffic had to be stopped until the enemy were beaten off. By now the news from Arnhem was bad. Our parachutists still held the northern end of the bridge, but the enemy remained in the town, and the rest of the 1st British Airborne Division, which had landed to the west, failed to break in and reinforce them.

The canal was bridged on the 18th, and early next morning the Guards had a clear run to Grave, where they found the 82nd U.S. Division. By nightfall they were close to the strongly defended Nijmegen bridge, and on the 20th there was a tremendous struggle for it. The Americans crossed the river west of the town, swung right, and seized the far end of the railway bridge. The Guards charged across the road bridge. The defenders were overwhelmed and both bridges were taken intact.

THERE remained the last lap to Arnhem, where bad weather had hampered the fly-in of reinforcements, food, and ammunition, and the 1st Airborne were in desperate straits. Unable to reach their bridge, the rest of the division was confined to a small perimeter on the northern bank and endured violent assaults. Every possible effort was made from the southern bank to rescue them, but the enemy were too strong. The Guards, the 43rd Division, the Polish Parachute Brigade, dropped near the road, all failed in gallant attempts at rescue. For four more days the struggle went on. Then, on the 25th Montgomery ordered the survivors of the gallant 1st Airborne back. They had to cross the fast-flowing river at night in small craft and under close-range fire. By daybreak about 2,400 men out of the original 10,000 were safely on our bank.

Heavy risks were taken in the Battle of Arnhem, but they were justified by the great prize so nearly in our grasp. Had we been more fortunate in the weather, which turned against us at critical moments and restricted our mastery in the air, it is probable that we should have succeeded. No risks daunted the brave men, including the Dutch Resistance, who fought for Arnhem.

Clearing the Scheldt estuary and opening the port of Antwerp was now given first priority. During the last fortnight of September a number of preliminary actions had set the stage. Breskens "island," defended by an experienced German division, proved tough, and there was heavy fighting to cross the Leopold Canal, but by the end of the month, after great exertions, the whole isthmus was captured. No fewer than 12,500 Germans who were anything but ready to surrender, were taken prisoner.

Walcheren Island, shaped like a saucer and rimmed by sand dunes, was garrisoned by nearly 10,000 men, installed in strong artificial defences, and supported by about thirty batteries of artillery. Antitank obstacles, mines, and wire abounded, for the enemy had had four years in which to fortify the gateway to Antwerp. Early in October the Royal Air Force struck the first blow. In a series of brilliant attacks they blew a great gap, nearly 400 yards across, in one of the dykes. Through it poured the sea, flooding all the center of the saucer and drowning such defences and batteries as lay within. But the most formidable emplacements and obstacles were on the saucer's rim. Our main stroke was launched by three Marine Commandos, supported by

a naval bombarding squadron and the whole artillery of the II Canadian Corps. In a few days the whole island was in our hands, with 8,000 prisoners. Mine sweeping began as soon as Flushing was secure, and in the next three weeks a hundred craft were used to clear the seventy-mile channel. On November 28 the first convoy arrived, and Antwerp was opened for the British and American Armies. Flying bombs and rockets plagued the city for some time, and caused many casualties, but interfered with the furtherance of the war no more than in London.

On our right flank the advance beyond Paris of the 12th American Army Group had been conducted with all the thrustful impulse of Bradley and his ardent officers. Charleroi, Mons, and Liège fell to their grasp. In a fortnight they freed all Luxembourg and Southern Belgium, and on September 12 they closed up to the German frontier on a sixty-mile front and pierced the Siegfried Line near Aachen. By the 16th bridgeheads over the Moselle were won at Nancy and just south of Metz. The Sixth Army Group under General Devers, coming up from their "Anvil"-"Dragoon" landing in southern France, met patrols from Patton's army west of Dijon five days before, and swinging to the east, drew level with the general advance. But here also was the end of the great pursuit. Everywhere enemy resistance was stiffening, and our supplies had been stretched to the limit. Aachen was attacked from three sides and surrendered on October 21. To the flank the Third Army were twenty miles east of the Moselle. The Seventh Army and the First French Army had drawn level and were probing towards the High Vosges and the Belfort Gap. The Americans had all but outrun their supplies in their lightning advances, and a pause was essential to build up stocks and prepare for large-scale operations in November.

THE Strategic Air Forces played a big part in the Allied advance to the frontiers of France and Belgium. In the autumn they reverted to their primary role of bombing Germany, with oil installations and the transportation systems as specific targets. The enemy's radar screen and early warning system had been thrust back behind his frontier, and our own navigation and bombing aids were correspondingly advanced. Our casualty rate decreased; the weight and accuracy of our attacks grew. The Allies' long-continued onslaught had forced the Germans to disperse their factories very widely. For this they now paid a heavy penalty, since they depended all the more on good communications. Urgently needed coal piled up at pitheads for lack of wagons to move it. Every day a thousand or more freight trains were halted for lack of fuel. Industry, electricity, and gas plants were beginning to close down. Oil production and reserves dropped drastically, affecting not only the mobility of the troops but also the activities and even the training of their air forces. In August Speer had warned Hitler that the entire chemical industry was being crippled through lack of by-products from the synthetic oil plants, and the position grew worse as time went on. In November he reported that if the decline in railway traffic continued it would result in "a production catastrophe of decisive significance," and in December he paid a tribute to our "far-reaching and clever planning." At long last our great bombing offensive was reaping its reward.

Paris and the Ardennes

IT was thought fitting that my first visit to Paris should be on Armistice Day, November 11, 1944, and this was publicly announced. There were many reports that collaborators would make attempts on my life and extreme precautions were taken. On the afternoon of November 10, I landed at Orly airfield, where de Gaulle received me with a guard of honour, and we drove together through the outskirts of Paris and into the city itself until we reached the Quai d'Orsay, where my wife and Mary and I were entertained in state. The building had long been occupied by the Germans, and I was assured I should sleep in the same bed and use the same bathroom as had Goering. Everything was mounted and serviced magnificently, and inside the palace it was difficult to believe that my last meeting there with Reynaud's Government and General Gamelin in May 1940 was anything but a bad dream.

At eleven o'clock on the morning of November 11th, de Gaulle conducted me in an open car across the Seine and through the Place de la Concorde, with a splendid escort of Gardes Républicains in full uniform with all their breastplates. They were several hundred strong, and provided a brilliant spectacle, on which the sun shone brightly. The whole of the famous avenue of the Champs Élysées was crowded with Parisians and lined with troops. Every window was filled with spectators and decorated with flags. We proceeded through wildly cheering multitudes to the Arc de Triomphe, where we both laid wreaths upon the tomb of the Unknown Warrior.

After this ceremony was over the General and I walked together, followed by a concourse of the leading figures of French public life, for half a mile down the highway I knew so well. We then took our places on a dais, and there was a splendid march past of French and British troops. Our Guards detachment was magnificent. When this was over I laid a wreath beneath the statue of Clemenceau, who was much in my thoughts on this moving occasion.

De Gaulle entertained me at a large luncheon at the Ministry of War, and made a most flattering speech about my war services, and on the night of the 12th after dinner at the Embassy we left for Besançon. The General was anxious for me to see the attack on a considerable scale which was planned for the French Army under General de Lattre de Tassigny. All the arrangements for the journey in a luxurious special train were most carefully made, and we arrived in plenty of time for the battle. We were to go to an observation point in the mountains, but owing to bitter cold and deep snow the roads were impassable and the whole operation had to be delayed.

I passed the day driving with de Gaulle, and we found plenty to talk about in a long and severe excursion, inspecting troops at intervals. The programme continued long after dark. The French soldiers seemed in the highest spirits. They marched past in great style and sang famous songs with moving enthusiasm. My personal party—my daughter Mary and my naval aide Tommy—feared that I should have another go of pneumonia, since we were out at least ten hours in terrible weather. But all went well, and

in the train the dinner was pleasant and interesting. I was struck by the awe, and even apprehension, with which half a dozen high generals treated de Gaulle in spite of the fact that he had only one star on his uniform and they had lots.

During the night our train divided. De Gaulle returned to Paris, and our half went on to Reims, arriving next morning, when I went to Ike's headquarters. In the afternoon I flew back to Northolt.

By now the situation on the Western Front was not nearly so agreeable. There had been much preparation for the advance to the Rhine, but the November rains were the worst for many years, flooding the rivers and streams, and making quagmires through which the infantry had to struggle. In the British sector Dempsey's Second Army drove the enemy back across the Meuse. Farther south we joined hands with the Ninth U.S. Army and toiled over saturated country towards the river Roer. It would have been rash as yet to cross it, because its level was controlled by massive dams which were still in enemy hands, and by opening the sluices he could have cut off our troops on the far bank. Heavy bombers tried to burst the dams and release the water, but in spite of several direct hits no gap was made, and on December 13 the First U.S. Army had to renew their advance to capture them.

South of the Ardennes, Patton had crossed the Moselle and thrust eastward to the German frontier. Here he confronted the strongest part of the Siegfried defences. Against formidable and obstinately held fortifications his Army came to a halt. On the right of the line General Devers's Sixth Army Group forced their way through the Vosges and the Belfort Gap. The French, after a week's battle, the opening of which I had hoped to see, captured Belfort on November 22 and reached the Rhine north of Bâle. Thence they swung down-river, turned the German flank in the Vosges and compelled the enemy to withdraw. Strasbourg was entered on the 23rd, and during the next few weeks the American Seventh Army cleared all Northern Alsace, wheeled up on the right of the Third Army, crossed the German frontier on a wide front, and penetrated the Siegfried Line near Wissembourg.

BUT these considerable successes could not mask the fact that the Western Allies had sustained a strategic reverse. Before this great movement was launched we placed on record our view that it was a mistake to attack against the whole front and that a far greater mass should have been gathered at the point of desired penetration. Montgomery's comments and predictions beforehand had in every way been borne out. "You must remember however," I cabled to Smuts, "that our armies are only about one-half the size of the American and will soon be little more than one-third. All is friendly and loyal in the military sphere in spite of the disappointment sustained. . . . But it is not so easy as it used to be for me to get things done. . . ."

I also recounted my forebodings to the President. "The time has come," I wrote on December 6, "for me to place before you the serious and disappointing war situation which faces us at the close of this year. Although many fine tactical victories have been gained . . . the fact remains that we have definitely failed to achieve the strategic object which we gave to our armies five weeks ago. We have not yet reached the Rhine in the northern part and most important sector of the front, and we shall have to continue the great battle for many weeks before we can hope to reach the Rhine and establish our bridgeheads. After that, again, we have to advance through Germany. . . .

"When we contrast these realities with the rosy expectations of our peoples, in spite of our joint efforts to damp them down, the question very definitely arises, 'What are we going to do about it?' My anxiety is increased by the destruction of all hopes of an early meeting between the three of us and the indefinite postponement of another meeting of you and me with our Staffs. Our British plans are dependent on yours, our Anglo-American problems at least must be surveyed as a whole, and the telegraph and the telephone more often than not only darken counsel. Therefore I feel that if you cannot come yourself before February I am bound to ask you whether you could not send your Chiefs of Staff over here as soon as practicable, where they all would be close to your main armies and to General Eisenhower and the whole stormy scene can be calmly and patiently studied with a view to action as closely concerted as that which signalised our campaigns of 1944."

Though sympathetic, Mr. Roosevelt did not appear to share my anxieties. "I always felt," he answered, "that the occupation of Germany up to the left bank of the Rhine would be a very stiff job. Because in the old days I bicycled over most of the Rhine terrain, I have never been as optimistic as to the ease of getting across the Rhine with our joint armies as many of the commanding officers have been.

"However, our agreed broad strategy is now developing according to plan. You and I are now in the position of Commanders-in-Chief who have prepared their plans, issued their orders, and committed their resources to battle according to those plans and orders. For the time being, even if a little behind schedule, it seems to me the prosecution and outcome of the battles lie with our Field Commanders, in whom I have every confidence. . . ."

A heavy blow now impended. Within six days of sending this telegram a crisis burst upon us. The Allied decision to strike hard from Aachen in the north as well as through Alsace in the south had left our centre very weak. In the Ardennes sector a single corps, the VIII American, of four

divisions, held a front of seventy-five miles. The risk was foreseen and deliberately accepted, but the consequences were grave and might have been graver. By a remarkable feat the enemy gathered about seventy divisions on their Western Front, of which fifteen were armoured. Many were under strength and needed rest and re-equipment, but one formation, the Sixth Panzer Army, was known to be strong and in good fettle. This potential spearhead had been carefully watched while it lay in reserve east of Aachen. When the fighting on that front died down in early December it vanished for a while from the ken of our Intelligence, and bad flying weather hindered our efforts to trace it. Eisenhower suspected that something was afoot, though its scope and violence came as a surprise.

The Germans had indeed a major plan. Rundstedt assembled two Panzer armies, the Fifth and Sixth, and the Seventh Army, a total of ten Panzer and fourteen infantry divisions. This great force, led by its armour, was intended to break through the Ardennes to the river Meuse, swing north and northwest, cut the Allied line in two, seize the port of Antwerp and sever the life line of all our northern armies. The stroke was planned by Hitler, who would brook no changes in it on the part of his doubting generals. The remnants of the German Air Force were assembled for a final effort, while paratroops, saboteurs, and agents in Allied uniforms were given their parts to play.

The attack began on December 16 under a heavy artillery barrage. At its northern flank the Sixth Panzer Army ran into the right of the First

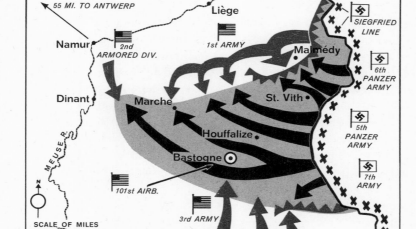
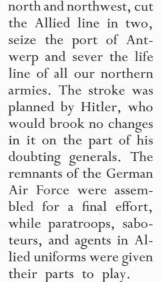

Battle of the Bulge began when Germans (*black*) tried to break through Allied lines (*brown*) to Antwerp. Bulge (*tan*) was contained along its north edge and Americans held out in encircled Bastogne. Finally U.S. thrusts from the south pushed enemy back.

U.S. Army in the act of advancing towards the Roer dams. After a swaying battle the enemy were held. Farther south the Germans broke through on a narrow front, but the determined defence of St. Vith, where the 7th U.S. Armoured Division specially distinguished itself, hindered them for several critical days. The Sixth Panzer Army launched a new spearhead to strike west and then northward at the Meuse above Liège. The Fifth Panzer Army cut through the centre of the American Corps, and penetrated deeply towards the Meuse. Although the time and weight of the attack surprised the Allied High Command its importance and purpose were quickly recognised. It was resolved to strengthen the "shoulders" of the breakthrough, hold the Meuse crossings both east and south of Namur, and mass mobile troops to crush the salient from north and south. Eisenhower acted speedily. He stopped all Allied attacks in progress and brought up four American divisions from reserve, and six more from the south. Two airborne divisions, one of them the 6th British, came from England. North of the salient, four divisions of the British XXX Corps, which had just come out of the line on the river Roer, were concentrated between Liège and Louvain behind the American First and Ninth Armies. These latter threw in all their reserves to extend a defensive flank westwards from Malmédy.

By severing the front of General Bradley's 12th Army Group the Germans had made it impossible for him to exercise effective command from his headquarters in Luxembourg over his two armies north of the Bulge. General Eisenhower therefore very wisely placed Montgomery in temporary command of all Allied troops in the north, while Bradley retained the Third U.S. Army and was charged with holding and counterattacking the enemy from the south. Corresponding arrangements were made for the tactical air forces.

Three of our reinforcing divisions lined the Meuse south of Namur. Bradley concentrated a corps at Arlon and sent the American 101st Airborne Division to secure the important road junctions at Bastogne. The German armour swung north and sought to break their way northwestward, leaving their infantry to capture the town. The 101st, with some armoured units, were isolated, and for a week beat off all attacks.

The wheel of the Fifth and Sixth Panzer Armies produced bitter fighting around Marche, which lasted till December 26. By then the German troops were exhausted, although at one time they were only four miles from the Meuse and had penetrated over sixty miles. Bad weather and low ground fogs had kept our air forces out of the first week of the battle, but on December 23 flying conditions got better and they intervened with tremendous effect. Heavy bombers attacked railways and centres of movement behind the enemy lines, and tactical air forces played havoc in his forward areas, starving him of reinforcements, fuel, food, and ammunition. Strategic raids on German refineries helped to deny him petrol and slacken the advance.

Baulked of their foremost objective, the Meuse, the Panzers turned savagely on Bastogne. The 101st Division, though reinforced, was vastly outnumbered. They held the town grimly for another week, and by the end of December the German High Command must have realised, however unwillingly, that the battle was lost. A counteroffensive by Patton was steadily if slowly progressing over the snow-choked countryside. The enemy made one last bid, this time in the air. On January 1, 1945, they made a violent low-level surprise attack on all our forward airfields. Our losses, though heavy, were promptly replaced, but the Luftwaffe lost more than they could afford in their final massed attack of the Second World War.

Three days later Montgomery launched a counterstroke from the north to join Patton's advance from the south. Two American corps, with the British on their western flank, pressed down upon the enemy. Struggling through snowstorms, the two wings of the Allied attack slowly drew closer and met at Houffalize on the 16th. The Germans were forced steadily eastwards and harassed continually from the air. By the end of the month they were back behind their frontiers, with nothing to show for their supreme effort except ruinous losses of matériel and casualties amounting to 120,000 men.

This was the final German offensive of the war. It caused us no little anxiety and postponed our own advance, but we benefited in the end. The Germans could not replace their losses, and our subsequent battles on the Rhine, though severe, were undoubtedly eased. Their High Command, and even Hitler himself, must have been disillusioned. Taken by surprise, Eisenhower and his commanders acted swiftly, but they will agree that the major credit lies elsewhere. In Montgomery's word, "The Battle of the Ardennes was won primarily by the staunch fighting qualities of the American soldier." The United States troops had indeed done almost all the fighting, and had suffered almost all the losses.

Yalta: Plans for World Peace

AT the end of January 1945, Hitler's armies were virtually compressed within their own territory, save for a brittle hold in Hungary and in Northern Italy, but the political situation, at any rate in Eastern Europe, was by no means so satisfactory. A precarious tranquillity had indeed been achieved in Greece, and it seemed that a free democratic Government, founded on universal suffrage and secret ballot, might be established there within a reasonable time. But Romania and Bulgaria had passed into the grip of Soviet military occupation, Hungary and Yugoslavia lay in the shadow of the battlefield, and Poland, though liberated from the Germans, had merely exchanged one conqueror for another. The informal and temporary arrangement which I had concluded with Stalin during my October visit to Moscow could not, and so far as I was concerned was never intended to, govern or affect the future of these wide regions once Germany was defeated.

The whole shape and structure of postwar Europe clamoured for review. When the Nazis were beaten, how was Germany to be treated? What aid could we expect from the Soviet Union in the final overthrow of Japan? And once our military aims were achieved what measures and what organisation could the three great Allied Powers provide for the future peace and good governance of the world? The discussions at Dumbarton Oaks had ended in partial disagreement. So, in a smaller but no less vital sphere, had the negotiations between the Soviet-sponsored "Lublin Poles" and their compatriots from London which Mr. Eden and I had with much difficulty promoted during our visit to the Kremlin in October 1944. An arid correspondence between the President and Stalin, of which Mr. Roosevelt had kept me informed, had accompanied the secession of M. Mikolajczyk from his colleagues in London, while on January 5, contrary to the wishes of both the United States and Great Britain, the Soviets had recognised the Lublin Committee as the Provisional Government of Poland.

The President was now fully convinced of the need for another meeting of "the Three," and after some urging on my part he also agreed that we should have a preliminary conference of our own at Malta. The reader will remember the anxieties which I had expressed about our operations in Northwest Europe in my telegram to the President of December 6. These still weighed with me. The British and American Chiefs of Staff had great need for discussions before we met the Soviets, and on January 29, 1945, I accordingly left Northolt in the Skymaster given to me by General Arnold. My daughter Sarah and the official party, together with Mr. Martin and Mr. Rowan, my private secretaries, and Commander Thompson, travelled with me. The rest of my personal staff and some departmental officials travelled in two other planes. We arrived at Malta just before dawn on January 30, and there I learnt that one of these two aircraft had crashed near Pantelleria. Only three of the crew and two passengers survived.

ON the morning of February 2 the Presidential party, on board the U.S.S. *Quincy*, steamed into Valletta harbour. It was a warm day, and under a cloudless sky I watched the scene from the deck of H.M.S. *Orion*. As the American cruiser steamed slowly past us towards her berth alongside the quay wall I could see the figure of the President seated on the bridge, and we waved to each other. With the escort of Spitfires overhead, the salutes, and the bands of the ships' companies in the harbour playing "The Star-spangled Banner," it was a splendid scene. I lunched on board the *Quincy*, and at six o'clock that evening we had our first formal meeting in the President's cabin. Here we reviewed the report of the Combined Chiefs of Staff and the military discussions which had been taking place in Malta during the previous three days. Our Staffs had done a remarkable piece of work. Their discussions had centred principally round Eisenhower's plans for carrying his forces up to and across the Rhine. There were differences of opinion on the subject. The opportunity was of course taken to review the whole span of the war, including the war against the U-boats, the future campaigns in Southeast Asia and the Pacific, and the Mediterranean situation. We reluctantly agreed to withdraw two divisions from Greece as soon as they could be spared, but I made it clear that we should not be obliged to do this until the Greek Government had built up its own military forces. Three divisions were also to be withdrawn from Italy to reinforce Northwest Europe, but I stressed that it would be unwise to make any significant withdrawal of amphibious forces. It was very important to follow up any German surrender in Italy, and I told the President that we ought to occupy as much of Austria as possible, as it was "undesirable that more of Western Europe than necessary should be occupied by the Russians." In all the military matters a large measure of agreement was reached, and the discussions had the useful result that the Combined Chiefs of Staff were aware of their respective points of view before engaging in talks with their Russian counterparts.

That night the exodus began. Transport planes took off at ten minute intervals to carry some 700 persons, forming the British and American delegations, over 1,400 miles to the airfield of Saki, in the Crimea. I boarded my plane after dinner, and went to bed. After a long and cold flight we landed on the airfield, which was under deep snow. My plane was ahead of Mr. Roosevelt's and we stood for a while awaiting him. When he was carried down the lift from the "Sacred Cow" he looked frail and ill. Together we inspected the guards of honour, the President sitting in an open car, while I walked beside him.

Presently we set off on a long drive from Saki to Yalta. Lord Moran and Mr. Martin, my private secretary, came with me in my car. The journey took us nearly eight hours, and the road was often lined by Russian soldiers, some of them women, standing shoulder to shoulder in the village streets and on the main bridges and mountain passes, and at other points in separate detachments. As we crossed the mountains and descended towards the Black Sea we suddenly passed into warm and brilliant sunshine and a most genial climate.

The Soviet headquarters at Yalta were in the Yusupov Palace, and from this centre Stalin and Molotov and their generals carried on the government of Russia and the control of their immense front, now in violent action. Mr. Roosevelt was given the even more splendid Livadia Palace, close at hand, and it was here, in order to spare him physical inconvenience, that all our plenary meetings were held. This exhausted the undamaged accommodation.

I and the principal members of the British delegation were assigned a very large villa about five miles away which had been built in the early nineteenth century by an English architect for a Russian Prince Vorontzov, one-time Imperial Ambassador to the Court of St. James. The rest of our delegation were put up in two resthouses about twenty minutes away, five or six people sleeping in a room, including high-ranking officers, but no one seemed to mind. The Germans had evacuated the neighbourhood only ten months earlier, and the surrounding buildings had been badly damaged. We were warned that the area had not been completely cleared of mines, except for the grounds of the villa, which were, as usual, heavily patrolled by Russian guards. Over a thousand men had been at work on the scene before our arrival. Windows and doors had been repaired, and furniture and stores brought down from Moscow.

THE setting of our abode was impressive. Behind the villa, half Gothic and half Moorish in style, rose the mountains, covered in snow, culminating in the highest peak in the Crimea. Before us lay the dark expanse of the Black Sea, severe, but still agreeable and warm even at this time of the year. Carved white lions guarded the entrance to the house, and beyond the courtyard lay a fine park with subtropical plants and cypresses. In the dining room I recognised the two paintings hanging each side of the fireplace as copies of family portraits of the Herberts at Wilton. It appeared that Prince Vorontzov had married a daughter of the family, and had brought these pictures back with him from England.

Every effort was made by our Russian hosts to ensure our comfort, and every chance remark was noted with kindly attention. On one occasion Portal had admired a large glass tank with plants growing in it, and remarked that it contained no fish. Two days later a consignment of goldfish arrived. Another time somebody said casually that there was no lemon peel in the cocktails. The next day a lemon tree loaded with fruit was growing in the hall. All must have come by air from far away.

The first plenary meeting of the Conference started at a quarter-past four on the afternoon of February 5. The discussion opened on the future of Germany. I had of course pondered this problem, and when Stalin now asked how Germany was to be dismembered, I said it was much too complicated to be settled in five or six days. It would require a very searching examination of the historical, ethnographical, and economic facts, and prolonged review by a special committee, which would go into the different proposals and advise on them. We then arranged to meet next day and consider two topics which were to dominate our future discussions, namely, the Dumbarton Oaks scheme for world security and Poland.

As has been recorded in an earlier chapter, the conference at Dumbarton Oaks had ended without reaching any complete agreement about the all-important question of voting rights in the Security Council, and space now forbids more than a reference to some of the salient points in our discussions. Stalin said he feared that, though the three Great Powers were allies to-day, and would none of them commit any act of aggression, in ten years or less the three leaders would disappear and a new generation would come into power which had not experienced the war and would forget what we had gone through.

"All of us," he declared, "want to secure peace for at least fifty years. The greatest danger is conflict among ourselves, because if we remain united the German menace is not very important. Therefore we must now think how to secure our unity in the future, and how to guarantee that the three Great Powers (and possibly China and France) will maintain a united front. Some system must be elaborated to prevent conflict between the main Great Powers." The Russians were accused of talking too much about voting. It was true they thought it was very important, because everything would be decided by vote and they would be greatly interested in the results. Suppose, for instance, that China as a permanent member of the Security Council demanded the return of Hong Kong, or Egypt demanded the return of the Suez Canal, he assumed they would not be alone and would have friends and perhaps protectors in the Assembly or in the Council, and he feared that such disputes might break the unity of the three Great Powers.

After much striving and explanation, we eventually persuaded him to accept an American scheme whereby the Security Council would be virtually powerless unless the "Big Four" were unanimous. If the United States, the U.S.S.R., Great Britain or China disagreed on any major topic, then any one of them could refuse their assent and stop the Council doing anything. Here was the Veto. Posterity may judge the results.

I myself have always held the view that the foundation of a World Instrument should be sought on a regional basis. Most of the principal regions suggest themselves—the United States, United Europe, the British Commonwealth and Empire, the Soviet Union, South America. Others are more difficult at present to define—like the Asian group or groups, or the African group—but could be developed with study. But the object would be to have many issues of fierce local controversy thrashed out in the Regional Council, which would then send three or four representatives to the Supreme Body, choosing men of the greatest eminence. This would make a Supreme Group of thirty or forty world statesmen, each responsible not only for representing their own region but for dealing with world causes, and primarily the prevention of war.

What we have now is not effective for that outstanding purpose. The summoning of all nations, great and small, powerful or powerless, on even terms to the central body may be compared with the organisation of an army without any division between the High Command and the divisional and brigade commanders. All are invited to the headquarters. Babel, tempered by skilful lobbying, is all that has resulted up to the present. But we must persevere.

Yalta: The Soviet Promise

POLAND was discussed at no fewer than seven out of the eight plenary meetings of the Yalta Conference, and the British record contains an interchange on this topic of nearly 18,000 words between Stalin, Roosevelt, and myself. The difficulties and the problems were ancient, multitudinous, and imperative.

The Soviet-sponsored Lublin Government of Poland, or the "Warsaw" Government as the Russians of all names preferred to call it, viewed the London Polish Government with bitter animosity. Feeling between them had got worse, not better, since our October meeting in Moscow. Soviet troops were flooding across Poland, and the Polish Underground Army was freely charged with the murder of Russian soldiers and with sabotage and attacks on their rear areas and their lines of communication. Both access and information were denied to the Western Powers. In Italy and on the Western Front over 150,000 Poles were now fighting valiantly for the final destruction of the Nazi armies. They and many others elsewhere in Europe were eagerly looking forward to the liberation of their country and a return to their homeland from voluntary and honourable exile. The large community of Poles in the United States were anxiously awaiting a settlement between the three Great Powers.

Poland had indeed been the most urgent reason for the Yalta Conference, and was to prove the first of the great causes which led to the breakdown of the Grand Alliance. I myself was sure that a strong, free, and independent Poland was much more important than particular territorial boundaries. I wanted the Poles to be able to live freely and live their own lives in their own way. It was for this that we had gone to war against Germany in 1939. It had nearly cost us our life, not only as an Empire but as a nation, and when we met on February 6, 1945, I posed the question as follows: Could we not create a Government or governmental instrument for Poland, pending full and free elections, which could be recognised by all? Such a Government could prepare for a free vote of the Polish people on their future constitution and administration. If this could be done we should have taken one great step forward towards the future peace and prosperity of Central Europe.

In the debate which followed, Stalin claimed to understand our attitude. For the British, he said, Poland was a question of honour, but for the Russians it was a question both of honour and security; of honour because they had had many conflicts with the Poles and they wished to eliminate the causes of such conflicts; of security, because Poland was on the frontiers of Russia, and throughout history Poland had been a corridor through which Russia's enemies had passed to attack her. The Germans had done this twice during the last thirty years and they had only been able to do it because Poland was weak. Russia wanted her to be strong and powerful so that she could shut this corridor of her own strength. Russia could not keep it shut from the outside. It could only be shut from the inside by Poland herself. This was a matter of life and death for the Soviet State.

As for her frontiers, Stalin went on to say that the President suggested some modification of the Curzon Line and that Lvov and perhaps certain other districts should be given to Poland, and I had just said that this would be a gesture of magnanimity. But the Curzon Line had not been invented by the Russians. It had been drawn up by Curzon and Clemenceau and representatives of the United States at the conference in 1918, to which Russia had not been invited. The Curzon Line had been accepted against the will of Russia on the basis of ethnographical data. Lenin had not agreed with it. The Russians had already withdrawn from Lenin's position, and now some people wanted Russia to take less than Curzon and Clemenceau had conceded. That would be shameful. When the Ukrainians came to Moscow they would say that Stalin and Molotov were less trustworthy defenders of Russia than Curzon or Clemenceau. It was better that the war should continue a little longer, although it would cost Russia much blood, so that Poland could be compensated at Germany's expense. When Mikolajczyk had been in Russia during October he had asked what frontier for Poland Russia would recognise in the west, and he had been delighted to hear that Russia thought that the western frontier of Poland should be extended to the Neisse. There were two rivers of that name, said Stalin, one near Breslau, and another farther west. It was the Western Neisse he had in mind.

When we met again on February 7, I reminded my hearers that I had always qualified the moving of the Polish frontier westward by saying that the Poles should be free to take territory in the west, but not more than they wished or could properly manage. It would be a great pity to stuff the Polish goose so full of German food that it died of indigestion. A large body of opinion in Great Britain was shocked at the idea of moving millions of people by force. Great success had been achieved in disentangling the Greek and Turkish populations after the last war, and the two countries had enjoyed good relations ever since; but in that case under a couple of millions of people had been moved. If Poland took East Prussia and Silesia up to the Oder that alone would mean moving six million Germans back to Germany. It might be managed, subject of course to the moral question, which I would have to settle with my own people. Stalin said there were no Germans in these areas, as they had all run away.

I replied that the question was whether there was really enough room for them in what was left of Germany. Six or seven millions of Germans had been killed and another million (Stalin suggested two millions) would most probably be killed before the end of the war. There should therefore be room for these migrant people up to a certain point. They would be needed to fill the vacancies. I was not afraid of the problem of transferring populations, so long as it was proportionate to what the Poles could manage and to what could be put into Germany. But it was a matter which required study, not as a question of principle, but of the numbers which would have to be handled.

In these general discussions maps were not used, and the distinction between the Eastern and Western Neisse did not emerge as clearly as it should have done. This was however soon to be made clear.

On the 8th Mr. Roosevelt agreed that the eastern boundary of Poland should be the Curzon Line, with modifications in favour of Poland in some areas of from five to eight kilometres. But he was firm and precise about the frontier in the west. Poland should certainly receive compensation at the expense of Germany, "but," he continued, "*there would appear to be little justification for extending it*

Frontiers of Poland before war are shown by two areas in brown; after war, by broken black line. Roosevelt and Churchill wanted border fixed at Eastern Neisse River, but Stalin fixed it on Western Neisse to make up for Russian seizure of area around Lvov.

up to the Western Neisse." This had always been my view, and I was to press it very hard when we met again at Potsdam five months later.

There remained the question of forming a Polish Government which we could all recognise and which the Polish nation would accept. Stalin began by pointing out that the Polish Government in London were hostile to the very idea of the Lublin Government, and described it as a company of bandits and criminals. The Lublin Government had paid them back in their own coin, and it was now very difficult to do anything about it. "Talk to the Lublin Government if you like," he said in effect. "I will get them to meet you here or in Moscow, but they are just as democratic as de Gaulle, and they can keep the peace in Poland and stop civil war and attacks on the Red Army." The London Government could not do this. Their agents had killed Russian soldiers and had raided supply dumps to get arms. Their radio stations were operating without permission and without being registered. It was vital for the Red Army to have safe rear areas, and as a military man he would only support the Government which could guarantee to provide them.

IT was now late in the evening and the President suggested adjourning till next day, but I thought it right to state that according to our information not more than one-third of the Polish people would support the Lublin Government if they were free to express their opinion. I assured Stalin that we had greatly feared a collision between the Polish Underground Army and the Lublin Government, which might lead to bitterness, bloodshed, arrests, and deportations, and that was why we had been so anxious for a joint arrangement. Attacks on the Red Army must of course be punished, but on the facts at my disposal I could not feel that the Lublin Government had a right to say that they represented the Polish nation.

Next day Stalin took up my complaint that I had no information and no way of getting it. "I have a certain amount," I replied. "It doesn't agree with mine," he answered, and proceeded to make a speech, in which he assured us that the Lublin Government was really very popular, particularly Bierut and others. What then was to be done? Perhaps the first thing was to call together the Poles from the different camps and hear what they had to say. The day was near when elections could be held. Until then we must deal with the Provisional Government, as we had dealt with General de Gaulle's Government in France, which also was not elected. If we approached the matter without prejudice we should be able to find a common ground. The situation was not as tragic as I thought, and the question could be settled if too much importance was not attached to secondary matters and if we concentrated on essentials.

"How soon," asked the President, "will it be possible to hold elections?"

"Within a month," Stalin replied, "unless there is some catastrophe on the front, which is improbable."

When we reassembled at four o'clock in the afternoon of February 9 Molotov produced a new formula, namely, that the Lublin Government should be "*reorganised* on a wider democratic basis, with the inclusion of democratic leaders from Poland itself, and also from those living abroad." He and the British and American Ambassadors should consult together in Moscow about how this would be done. Once "reorganised" the Lublin Government would be pledged to hold free elections as soon as possible, and we should then recognise whatever Government emerged.

This was a considerable advance, and I said so, but I felt it my duty to press Stalin on a final point. The opportunity presented itself next day, when Mr. Eden and I had a private conversation with him and Molotov at the Yusupov Villa. I once more explained how difficult it was for us to have no representatives in Poland who could report what was going on. The alternatives were either an Ambassador with an embassy staff or newspaper correspondents. The latter was less desirable, but I pointed out that I should be asked in Parliament about the Lublin Government and the elections and I must be able to say that I knew what was happening. "After the new Polish Government is recognised it would be open to you to send an Ambassador to Warsaw," Stalin answered. "Would he be free to move about the country?" I asked. "As far as the Red Army is concerned, there will be no interference with his movements, and I promise to give the necessary instructions, but you will have to make your own arrangements with the Polish Government." This was the best I could get.

Sunday, February 11, was the last day of our Crimean visit. As usual at these meetings many grave issues were left unsettled. The President was anxious to go home, and on his way to pay a visit to Egypt, where he could discuss the affairs of the Middle East with various potentates. Stalin and I lunched with him in the Czar's former billiard room at the Livadia Palace. During the meal we signed the final documents and official communiqués. All now depended upon the spirit in which they were carried out.

I HAD much looked forward to the sea voyage through the Dardanelles to Malta, but I felt it my duty to make a lightning trip to Athens and survey the Greek scene after the recent troubles. Early on February 14 accordingly we set off by car for Saki, where our aeroplane awaited us. We flew without incident to Athens, making a loop over the island of Skyros to pass over the tomb of Rupert Brooke, and were received at the airfield by the British Ambassador, Mr. Leeper, and General Scobie. Only seven weeks before I had left the Greek capital rent by street fighting. We now drove into it in an open car, where only a thin line of kilted Greek soldiers held back a vast mob, screaming with enthusiasm, in the very streets where hundreds of men had died in the Christmas days when I had last seen the city. That evening a huge crowd of about 50,000 people gathered in Constitution Square. The evening light was wonderful as it fell on these classic scenes. I had no time to prepare a speech. Our security services had thought it important that we should arrive with hardly any notice. I addressed them with a short harangue. That evening I dined at our shot-scarred Embassy, and in the early hours of February 15 we took off in my plane for Egypt.

Late that morning the American cruiser *Quincy* steamed into Alexandria harbour, and shortly before noon I went on board for what was to be my last talk with the President. We gathered afterwards in his cabin for an informal family luncheon. I was accompanied by Sarah and by Randolph. Mr. Roosevelt's daughter, Mrs. Boettiger, together with Harry Hopkins and Mr. Winant, joined us. The President seemed placid and frail. I felt that he had a slender contact with life. I was not to see him again. We bade affectionate farewells. That afternoon the Presidential party sailed for home. On February 19 I flew back to England, and at noon on the 27th I asked the House of Commons to approve the results of the Crimea Conference.

The general reaction was unqualified support for the attitude we had taken. There was however intense moral feeling about our obligations to the Poles, who had suffered so much at German hands and on whose behalf as a last resort we had gone to war. A group of about thirty Members felt so strongly on this matter that some of them spoke in opposition to the motion which I had moved. There was a sense of anguish lest we should have to face the enslavement of a heroic nation. Mr. Eden supported me. In the division on the second day we had an overwhelming majority, but twenty-five Members, most of them Conservatives, voted against the Government, and in addition eleven members of the Government abstained.

It is not permitted to those charged with dealing with events in times of war or crisis to confine themselves purely to the statement of broad general principles on which good people agree. They have to take definite decisions from day to day. They have to adopt postures which must be solidly maintained, otherwise how can any combinations for action be maintained? It is easy, after the Germans are beaten, to condemn those who did their best to hearten the Russian military effort and to keep in harmonious contact with our great Ally, who had suffered so frightfully. What would have happened if we had quarrelled with Russia while the Germans still had two or three hundred divisions on the fighting front? Our hopeful assumptions were soon to be falsified. Still, they were the only ones possible at the time.

Crossing the Rhine

DESPITE their defeat in the Ardennes, the Germans decided to give battle west of the Rhine, instead of withdrawing across it to gain a breathing space, and throughout February and most of March Field-Marshal Montgomery had conducted a long and arduous struggle in the north. The defences were strong and obstinately held, the ground was sodden, and both the Rhine and the Meuse had overflowed their banks. The Germans smashed open the valves of the great dams on the Roer and the river became uncrossable until the end of February, but on March 10 eighteen German divisions were all back across the Rhine. Farther south, General Bradley cleared the whole of the eighty-mile stretch between Düsseldorf and Koblenz in a brief, swift campaign.

On the 7th a stroke of fortune was boldly accepted. The 9th Armoured Division of the First U.S. Army found the railway bridge at Remagen partly destroyed but still usable. They promptly threw their advance guard across, other troops quickly followed, and soon over four divisions were on the far bank and a bridgehead several miles deep established. This was no part of Eisenhower's plan, but it proved an excellent adjunct, and the Germans had to divert considerable forces from farther north to hold the Americans in check. Patton cut off and crushed the last enemy salient around Trier. The defenders of the renowned and dreaded Siegfried Line were surrounded, and in a few days all organised resistance came to an end. As a by-product of victory the 5th U.S. Division made an unpremeditated crossing of the Rhine fifteen miles south of Mainz, which soon expanded into a deep bridgehead pointing towards Frankfurt.

Thus ended the last great German stand in the West. Six weeks of successive battles along a front of over 250 miles had driven the enemy across the Rhine with irreplaceable losses in men and matériel. The Allied Air Forces played a part of supreme importance. Constant attacks by the Tactical Air Forces aggravated the defeat and disorganisation and freed us from the dwindling Luftwaffe. Frequent patrols over the airfields containing the enemy's new jet-propelled fighters minimised a threat that had caused us anxiety. Continuing raids by our heavy bombers had reduced the German oil output to a critical point, ruined many of their airfields, and so heavily damaged their factories and transportation system as to bring them almost to a standstill.

I desired to be with our armies at the crossing, and Montgomery made me welcome. Taking only my secretary, Jock Colville, and Commander C. R. Thomson, R.N., my naval aide, with me, I flew in the afternoon of March 23 by Dakota from Northolt to the British headquarters near Venlo. The Commander-in-Chief conducted me to the caravan in which he lived and moved. I found myself in the comfortable wagon I had used before. We dined at seven o'clock, and an hour later we repaired with strict punctuality to Montgomery's map wagon. Here were displayed all the maps kept from hour to hour by a select group of officers. The whole plan of our deployment and attack was easily comprehended. We were to force a passage over the river at ten points on a twenty-mile front from Rheinsberg to Rees. All our resources were to be used. Eighty thousand men, the advance guard of armies a million strong, were to be hurled forward. Masses of boats and pontoons lay ready. On the far side stood the Germans, entrenched and organised in all the strength of modern firepower.

Everything I had seen or studied in war, or read, made me doubt that a river could be a good barrier of defence against superior force. In Hamley's *Operations of War*, on which I had pondered ever since Sandhurst days, he argues the truth that a river running parallel to the line of advance is a much more dangerous feature than one which lies squarely athwart it, and he illustrates this theory by Napoleon's marvellous campaign of 1814. I was therefore in good hopes of the battle even before the Field-Marshal explained his plans to me. Moreover, we had now the measureless advantage of mastery in the air. The episode which the Commander-in-Chief particularly wished me to see was the drop next morning of two airborne divisions, comprising 14,000 men, with artillery and much other offensive equipment, behind the enemy lines. Accordingly we all went to bed before ten o'clock.

The honour of leading the attack fell to our 51st and 15th Divisions and the American 30th and 79th. Four battalions of the 51st were the first to set forth, and a few minutes later they had reached the far side. Throughout the night the attacking divisions poured across, meeting little resistance at first, as the bank itself was lightly defended. At dawn bridgeheads, shallow as yet, were firmly held, and the Commandos were already at grips in Wesel.

In the morning Montgomery had arranged for me to witness from a hilltop amid rolling downland the great fly-in. It was full daylight before the subdued but intense roar and rumbling of swarms of aircraft stole upon us. After that in the course of half an hour over 2,000 aeroplanes streamed overhead in their formations. My viewpoint had been well chosen. The light was clear enough to enable one to see where the descent on the enemy took place. The aircraft faded from sight, and then almost immediately afterwards returned towards us at a different level. The parachutists were invisible even to the best field glasses. But now there was a double murmur and roar of reinforcements arriving and of those who had delivered their attacks returning. Soon one saw with a sense of tragedy aircraft in twos and threes coming back askew, asmoke, or even in flames. Also at this time tiny specks came floating to earth. Imagination built on a good deal of experience told a hard and painful tale. It seemed however that nineteen out of every twenty of the aircraft that had started came back in good order, having discharged their mission. This was confirmed by what we heard an hour later when we got back to headquarters.

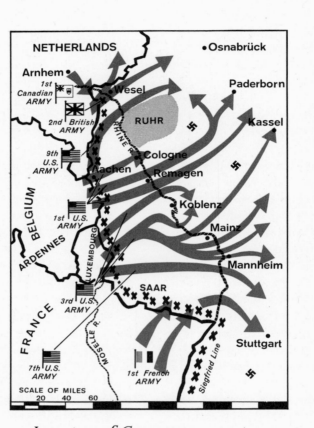

Invasion of Germany started as Allies (*red*) breached line on western border and drove to Rhine, taking a bridge at Remagen and then crossing at other points to push on into heartland.

The assault was now in progress along the whole front, and I was conducted by motor on a long tour from one point to another, and to the various corps headquarters. Things went well all that day. The four assaulting divisions were safely across and established in bridgeheads 5,000 yards deep. The airborne divisions were going strong and our air operations were most successful. The strike of the Allied Air Forces, second only to that of D-Day in Normandy, included not only the Strategic Air Forces in Britain but also heavy bombers from Italy, who made deep penetrations into Germany.

At 8 p.m. we repaired to the map wagon, and I now had an excellent opportunity of seeing Montgomery's methods of conducting a battle on this gigantic scale. For nearly two hours a succession of young officers, of about

the rank of major, presented themselves. Each had come back from a different sector of the front. They were the direct personal representatives of the Commander-in-Chief, and could go anywhere and see anything and ask any questions they liked of any commander. As in turn they made their reports and were searchingly questioned by their chief the whole story of the day's battle was unfolded. This gave Monty a complete account of what had happened by highly competent men whom he knew well and whose eyes he trusted. It afforded an invaluable cross-check to the reports from all the various headquarters and from the commanders, all of which had already been sifted and weighed by General de Guingand, his Chief of Staff, and were known to Montgomery. By this process he was able to form a more vivid, direct, and sometimes more accurate picture. The officers ran great risks, and of the seven or eight to whom I listened on this and succeeding nights two were killed in the next few weeks. I thought that the system was admirable, and indeed was the only way in which a modern Commander-in-Chief could see as well as read what was going on in every part of the front. This process having finished, Montgomery gave a series of directions to de Guingand, which were turned into immediate action by the Staff machine. And so to bed.

The next day, March 25, we went to meet Eisenhower. On our way I told Montgomery how his system resembled Marlborough's and the conduct of battles in the Eighteenth Century, where the Commander-in-Chief acted through his lieutenant-generals. Then the Commander-in-Chief sat on his horse and directed by word of mouth a battle on a five- or six-mile front, which ended in a day and settled the fortunes of great nations, sometimes for years or generations to come. In order to make his will effective he had four or five lieutenant-generals posted at different points on the front, who knew his whole mind and were concerned with the execution of his plan. These officers commanded no troops and were intended to be offshoots and expressions of the Supreme Commander. In modern times the general must sit in his office conducting a battle ranging over ten times the front and lasting often for a week or ten days. In these changed conditions Montgomery's method of personal eyewitnesses, who were naturally treated with the utmost consideration by the front-line commanders of every grade, was an interesting though partial revival of old days.

We met Eisenhower before noon. Here a number of American Generals were gathered. After various agreeable interchanges we had a brief lunch, in the course of which Eisenhower said that there was a house about ten miles away on our side of the Rhine, which the Americans had sandbagged, from which a fine view of the river and of the opposite bank could be obtained. He proposed that we should visit it, and conducted us there himself. The Rhine —here about four hundred yards broad—flowed at our feet. There was a smooth, flat expanse of meadows on the enemy's side. The officers told us that the far bank was unoccupied so far as they knew, and we gazed and gaped at it for a while. With appropriate precautions we were led into the building. Then the Supreme Commander had to depart on other business, and Montgomery and I were about to follow his example when I saw a small launch come close by to moor. So I said to Montgomery, "Why don't we go across and have a look at the other side?" Somewhat to my surprise he answered, "Why not?" After he had made some inquiries we started across the river with three or four American commanders and half a dozen armed men. We landed in brilliant sunshine and perfect peace on the German shore, and walked about for half an hour or so unmolested.

As we came back Montgomery said to the captain of the launch, "Can't we go down the river towards Wesel, where there is something going on?" The captain replied that there was a chain across the river half a mile away to prevent floating mines interfering with our operations, and several of these might be held up by it. Montgomery pressed him hard, but was at length satisfied that the risk was too great. As we landed he said to me, "Let's go down to the railway bridge at Wesel, where we can see what is going on on the spot." So we got into his car, and, accompanied by the Americans, who were delighted at the prospect, we went to the big iron-girder railway bridge, which was broken in the middle but whose twisted ironwork offered good perches. The Germans were replying to our fire, and their shells fell in salvos of four about a mile away. Presently they came nearer. Then one salvo came overhead and plunged in the water on our side of the bridge. The shells seemed to explode on impact with the bottom, and raised great fountains of spray about a hundred yards away. Several other shells fell among the motorcars which were concealed not far behind us, and it was decided we ought to depart. I clambered down and joined my adventurous host for our two hours' drive back to his headquarters.

DURING the next few days we continued to gain ground and by the end of the month we possessed a springboard east of the Rhine from which to launch major operations deep into Northern Germany. In the south, the American armies, though not opposed so strongly, had made astonishing progress. The two bridgeheads which were the reward of their boldness were being daily reinforced and enlarged, and more crossings were made south of Koblenz and at Worms. On March 29 the American Third Army was in Frankfurt. The Ruhr and its 325,000 defenders were encircled. Germany's Western Front had collapsed.

The question thus arose: Where should we go next? All kinds of rumours were rife about Hitler's future plans. It seemed possible that after losing Berlin and Northern Germany he might retire to the mountainous and wooded parts of Southern Germany and endeavour to prolong the fight there. The strange resistance he made at Budapest, and the retention of Kesselring's army in Italy so long, seemed in harmony with such an intention. Although nothing could be positive, the general conclusion of our Chiefs of Staff was that a prolonged German campaign, or even guerrilla, in the mountains was unlikely on any serious scale. The possibility was therefore relegated by us, as it proved rightly, to the shades. On this basis I inquired about the strategy for the advance of the Anglo-American armies as foreseen at Allied Headquarters.

"I PROPOSE," telegraphed General Eisenhower, "driving eastward to join hands with Russians or to attain general line of Elbe. Subject to Russian intentions, the axis Kassel-Leipzig is the best for the drive, as it will ensure the overrunning of that important industrial area, into which German Ministries are believed to be moving; it will cut the German forces approximately in half, and it will not involve us in crossing of Elbe. It is designed to divide and destroy the major part of remaining enemy forces in West. This will be my main thrust, and until it is quite clear that concentration of all our effort on it alone will not be necessary I am prepared to direct all my forces to ensuring its success. . . .

"Once the success of main thrust is assured I propose to take action to clear the northern ports, which in the case of Kiel will entail forcing the Elbe. Montgomery will be responsible for these tasks, and I propose to increase his forces if that should seem necessary for the purpose."

About the same time we learned that Eisenhower had announced his policy in a direct telegram to Stalin on March 28 in which he said that after isolating the Ruhr he proposed to make his main thrust along the axis Erfurt-Leipzig-Dresden, which, by joining hands with the Russians, would cut in two the remaining German forces. A secondary advance through Regensburg to Linz, where also he expected to meet the Russian armies, would prevent "the consolidation of German resistance in the redoubt in Southern Germany." Stalin agreed readily. He said that Eisenhower's proposal "entirely coincides with the plan of the Soviet High Command." "Berlin," he added, "has lost its former strategic importance. The Soviet High Command therefore plans to allot secondary forces in the direction of Berlin." This statement was not borne out by subsequent events.

This seemed so important that on April 1st I sent a personal telegram to President Roosevelt: ". . . Obviously, laying aside every impediment and shunning every diversion, the Allied armies of the North and Centre should now march at the highest speed towards the Elbe. Hitherto the axis has been upon Berlin. General Eisenhower, on his estimate of the enemy's resistance, to which I attach the greatest importance, now wishes to shift the axis somewhat to the southward and to strike through Leipzig, even perhaps as far south as Dresden. . . . I say quite frankly that Berlin remains of high strategic importance. Nothing will exert a psychological effect of despair upon all German forces of resistance equal to that of the fall of Berlin. It will be the supreme signal of defeat to the German people. On the other hand, if left to itself to maintain a siege by the Russians among its ruins, and as long as the German flag flies there, it will animate the resistance of all Germans under arms.

"There is moreover another aspect which it is proper for you and me to consider. The Russian armies will no doubt overrun all Austria and enter Vienna. If they also take Berlin will not their impression that they have been the overwhelming contributor to our common victory be unduly imprinted in their minds, and may this not lead them into a mood which will raise grave and formidable difficulties in the future? *I therefore consider that from a political standpoint we should march as far east into Germany as possible, and that should Berlin be in our grasp we should certainly take it. This also appears sound on military grounds.*"

ACTUALLY, though I did not realise it, the President's health was now so feeble that it was General Marshall who had to deal with these grave questions, and the United States Chiefs replied in substance that Eisenhower's plan appeared to accord with agreed strategy and with his directive. He was deploying across the Rhine in the north the maximum forces which could be used. The secondary effort in the south was achieving an outstanding success, and was being exploited as much as supplies would permit. They were confident that the Supreme Commander's action would secure the ports and everything else mentioned by the British more quickly and more decisively than the plan urged by them.

The Battle of Germany, they said, was at a point where it was for the Field Commander to judge the measures which should be taken. To turn away deliberately from the exploitation of the enemy's weakness did not appear sound. The single objective should be quick and complete victory. While recognising that there were factors not of direct concern to the Supreme Commander, the United States Chiefs considered his strategic concept was sound.

General Eisenhower himself assured me on April the 1st that he had never lost sight of the great importance of the drive to the northernmost coast, ". . . although your telegram did introduce a new idea respecting the political importance of the early attainment of particular objectives. I clearly see your point in this matter. The only difference between your suggestions and my plan is one of timing. . . . In order to assure the success of each of my planned efforts, I concentrate first in the Centre to gain the position I need. As it looks to me now, the next move thereafter should be to have Montgomery cross the Elbe, reinforced as necessary by American troops, and reach at least a line including Lübeck on the coast. If German resistance from now on should progressively and definitely crumble you can see that there would be little if any difference in time between gaining central position and crossing the Elbe. On the other hand, if resistance tends to stiffen at all I can see that it is vitally necessary that I concentrate for each effort, and do not allow myself to be dispersed by attempting to do all these projects at once. Quite naturally, if at any moment collapse should suddenly come about everywhere along the front we would rush forward, and Lübeck and Berlin would be included in our important targets." I answered, "Thank you again for your most kind telegram. I am however all the more impressed with the importance of entering Berlin, which may well be open to us, by the reply from Moscow to you, which . . . says, 'Berlin has lost its former strategic importance.' This should be read in the light of what I mentioned of the political aspects. I deem it highly important that we should shake hands with the Russians as far to the east as possible . . . Much may happen in the West before the date of Stalin's main offensive."

I thought it my duty to end this correspondence between friends, and the changes in the main plan, as I said to Roosevelt at the time, were much less than we at first supposed, but I must place on record my conviction that in Washington especially longer and wider views should have prevailed. As war waged by a coalition draws to its end political aspects have a mounting importance. It is true that American thought is at least disinterested in matters which seem to relate to territorial acquisitions, but when wolves are about the shepherd must guard his flock, even if he does not himself care for mutton. At this time the points of issue did not seem to the United States Chiefs of Staff to be of capital importance. They were of course unnoticed by and unknown to the public, and were all soon swamped, and for the time being effaced, by the flowing tide of victory. Nevertheless, as will not now be disputed, they played a dominating part in the destiny of Europe, and may well have denied us all the lasting peace for which we had fought so long and hard.

We can now see the deadly hiatus which existed between the fading of President Roosevelt's strength and the growth of President Truman's grip of the vast world problem. In this melancholy void one President could not act and the other could not know. Neither the military chiefs nor the State Department received the guidance they required. The former confined themselves to their professional sphere; the latter did not comprehend the issues involved. The indispensable political direction was lacking at the moment when it was most needed. The United States stood on the scene of victory, master of world fortunes, but without a true and coherent design.

Great Britain, though still very powerful, could not act decisively alone. I could at this stage only warn and plead. Thus this climax of apparently measureless success was to me a most unhappy time. I moved amid cheering crowds, or sat at a table adorned with congratulations and blessings from every part of the Grand Alliance, with an aching heart and a mind oppressed by forebodings.

THE destruction of German military power had now brought with it a fundamental change in the relations between Communist Russia and the Western democracies. They had lost their common enemy, which was almost their sole bond of union. Henceforward Russian imperialism and the Communist creed saw and set no bounds to their progress and ultimate dominion, and more than two years were to pass before they were confronted again with an equal will power. I should not tell this tale now when all is plain in glaring light if I had not known it and felt it when all was dim, and when abounding triumph only intensified the inner darkness of human affairs. Of this the reader must be the judge.

The Iron Curtain

As the weeks passed after Yalta it became clear that the Soviet Government was doing nothing to carry out our agreements about broadening the Polish Government to include all Polish parties and both sides. Molotov steadily refused to give an opinion about the Poles we mentioned, and not one of them was allowed to come even to a preliminary round-table discussion. He had offered to allow us to send observers to Poland, and had been disconcerted by the readiness and speed with which we had accepted, arguing, among other things, that it might affect the prestige of the Lublin Provisional Government. No progress of any kind was made in the talks at Moscow. Time was on the side of the Russians and their Polish adherents, who were fastening their grip upon the country by all kinds of severe measures, which they did not wish outside observers to see. Every day's delay was a gain to these hard forces.

On the very evening when I was speaking in the House of Commons upon the results of our labours at Yalta the first violation by the Russians both of the spirit and letter of our agreements took place in Romania. We were all committed by the Declaration on Liberated Europe, so recently signed, to see that both free elections and democratic Governments were established in the countries occupied by Allied armies. On February 27 Vyshinsky, who had appeared in Bucharest without warning on the previous day, demanded an audience of King Michael and insisted that he should dismiss the all-party Government which had been formed after the royal *coup d'état* of August 1944 and had led to the expulsion of the Germans from Romania.

The young monarch, backed by his Foreign Minister, Visoianu, resisted these demands until the following day. Vyshinsky called again, and, brushing aside the King's request at least to be allowed to consult the leaders of the political parties, banged his fist on the table, shouted for an immediate acquiescence, and walked out of the room, slamming the door. At the same time Soviet tanks and troops deployed in the streets of the capital, and on March 6 a Soviet-nominated Administration took office.

I was deeply disturbed by this news, which was to prove a pattern of things to come, but we were hampered in our protests because Eden and I during our October visit to Moscow had recognised that Russia should have a largely predominant voice in Romania and Bulgaria while we took the lead in Greece. Stalin had kept very strictly to this understanding during the six weeks' fighting against the Communists and E.L.A.S. in the city of Athens, in spite of the fact that all this was most disagreeable to him and those around him. Peace had now been restored, and, though many difficulties lay before us, I hoped that in a few months we should be able to hold free, unfettered elections, preferably under British, American, and Russian supervision, and that thereafter a constitution and Government would be erected on the indisputable will of the Greek people.

Meanwhile, the deadlock over Poland continued. All through March I was engaged in tense correspondence with Mr. Roosevelt, but although I had no exact information about his state of health I had the feeling that, except for occasional flashes of courage and insight, the telegrams he was sending us were not his own. The Soviet policy became daily more plain, as also did the use they were making of their unbridled and unobserved control of Poland. Molotov persisted that the Yalta communiqué merely meant adding a few other Poles to the existing Administration of Russian puppets, and that these puppets should be consulted first. It was as plain as a pikestaff that his tactics were to drag the business out while the Lublin Committee consolidated their power.

I was sure that the only way to stop Molotov was to send Stalin a personal message, and I therefore appealed to the President in the hope that we could address Stalin jointly on the highest level. But at this critical time Roosevelt's health and strength had faded. In my long telegrams I thought I was talking to my trusted friend and colleague as I had done all these years. I was no longer being fully heard by him. I did not know how ill he was, or I might have felt it cruel to press him. The President's devoted aides were anxious to keep their knowledge of his condition within the narrowest circle, and various hands drafted in combination the answers which were sent in his name. To these, as his life ebbed, Roosevelt could only give general guidance and approval. This was an heroic effort. The tendency of the State Department was naturally to avoid bringing matters to a head while the President was physically so frail and to leave the burden on the Ambassadors in Moscow. Harry Hopkins, who might have given personal help, was himself seriously ailing, and frequently absent or uninvited. These were costly weeks for all.

PRESIDENT Roosevelt died suddenly on Thursday, April 12, 1945, at Warm Springs, Georgia. He was sixty-three. While he was having his portrait painted, he suddenly collapsed, and died a few hours later without regaining consciousness. When I received these tidings early in the morning of Friday, the 13th, I felt as if I had been struck a physical blow. My relations with this shining personality had played so large a part in the long, terrible years we had worked together. Now they had come to an end, and I was overpowered by a sense of deep and irreparable loss. I went down to the House of Commons, which met at eleven o'clock, and in a few sentences proposed that we should pay our respects to the memory of our great friend by immediately adjourning. This unprecedented step on the occasion of the death of the head of a foreign State was in accordance with the unanimous wish of the Members, who filed slowly out of the chamber after a sitting which had lasted only eight minutes.

My first impulse was to fly over to the funeral, and I had already ordered an aeroplane. Lord Halifax telegraphed that both Hopkins and Stettinius were much moved by my thought of possibly coming over, and both warmly agreed with my judgment of the immense effect for good that would be produced. Mr. Truman had asked him to say how greatly he would personally value the opportunity of meeting me as early as possible. His idea was that after the funeral I might have had two or three days' talk with him.

Much pressure was however put on me not to leave the country at this most critical and difficult moment, and I yielded to the wishes of my friends. In the afterlight I regret that I did not adopt the new President's suggestion. I had never met him, and I feel that there were many points on which personal talks would have been of the greatest value, especially if they had been spread over several days and were not hurried or formalised. It seemed to me extraordinary, especially during the last few months, that Roosevelt had not made his deputy and potential successor thoroughly acquainted with the whole story and brought him into the decisions which were being taken. This proved of grave disadvantage to our affairs.

THERE is no comparison between reading about great events afterwards and living through them from hour to hour. In Mr. Eden I had a colleague who knew everything and could at any moment take over the entire direction, although I was myself in good health and full activity. But the Vice President of the United States steps at a bound from a position where he has little information and less power into supreme authority. How could Mr. Truman know and weigh the issues at stake at this climax of the war? Everything that we have learnt about him since shows him to be a resolute and fearless man, capable of taking the greatest decisions. In these early months his position was one of extreme difficulty, and did not enable him to bring his outstanding qualities fully into action.

Mr. Truman's first political act which concerned us was to take up the Polish question from the point where it stood when Roosevelt died, only forty-eight hours earlier. He proposed a joint declaration by us both to Stalin. The document in which this was set forth must of course have been far advanced in preparation by the State Department at the moment when the new President succeeded. Nevertheless it is remarkable that he felt able so promptly to commit himself to it amid the formalities of assuming office and the funeral of his predecessor.

Our joint message was sent on April the 15th. Meanwhile M. Mikolajczyk confirmed that he accepted the Crimea decision on Poland, including the establishment of Poland's eastern frontier on the Curzon Line, and I so informed Stalin. As I got no answer it may be assumed that the Dictator was for the moment content. Other points were open. Mr. Eden telegraphed from Washington that he and Mr. Stettinius agreed that we should renew our demand for the entry of observers into Poland, and that we should once more press the Soviet Government to hold up their negotiations for a treaty with the Lublin Poles. But shortly after deciding this, the news arrived that the treaty had been concluded.

On April 29, when it seemed evident we were getting nowhere, I put my whole case to Stalin in a lengthy telegram of which the following paragraphs may be deemed material: "It is quite true that about Poland we have reached a definite line of action with the Americans. This is because we agree naturally upon the subject, and both sincerely feel that we have been rather ill-treated . . . since the Crimea Conference. . . . Also, difficulties arise at the present moment because all sorts of stories are brought out of Poland which are eagerly listened to by many Members of Parliament, and which at any time may be violently raised in Parliament or the Press in spite of my deprecating such action, and on which M. Molotov will vouchsafe us no information at all in spite of repeated requests. *For instance, there is the talk of the fifteen Poles who were said to have met the Russian authorities for discussion over four weeks ago. . . and there are many other statements of deportations, etc.*

"How can I contradict such complaints when you give me no information whatever and when neither I nor the Americans are allowed to send anyone into Poland to find out for themselves the true state of affairs? There is no part of our occupied or liberated territory into which you are not free to send delegations, and people do not see why you should have any reasons against similar visits by British delegations to foreign countries liberated by you.

"There is not much comfort in looking into a future where you and the countries you dominate, plus the Communist Parties in many other States, are all drawn up on one side, and those who rally to the English-speaking nations and their associates or Dominions are on the other. It is quite obvious that their quarrel would tear the world to pieces and that all of us leading men on either side who had anything to do with that would be shamed before history. Even embarking on a long period of suspicions, of abuse and counterabuse, and of opposing policies would be a disaster hampering the great developments of world prosperity for the masses which are attainable only by our trinity. I hope there is no word or phrase in this outpouring of my heart to you which unwittingly gives offence. If so, let me know. But do not, I beg you, my friend Stalin, underrate the divergences which are opening about matters which you may think are small to us but which are symbolic of the way the English-speaking democracies look at life."

THE incident of the missing Poles mentioned in this telegram now requires to be recorded, although it carries us somewhat ahead of the general narrative. At the beginning of March 1945 the Polish Underground were invited by the Russian Political Police to send a delegation to Moscow to discuss the formation of a united Polish Government along the lines of the Yalta agreement. This was followed by a written guarantee of personal safety and it was understood that the party would later be allowed, if the negotiations were successful, to travel to London for talks with the Polish Government in exile.

On March 27 General Leopold Okulicki, the successor of General Bor-Komorowski in command of the Underground Army, two other leaders, and an interpreter had a meeting in the suburbs of Warsaw with a Soviet representative. They were joined the following day by eleven leaders representing the major political parties in Poland. One other Polish leader was already in Russian hands. No one returned from the rendezvous.

On April 6 the Polish Government in exile issued a statement in London giving the outline of this sinister episode. The most valuable representative of the Polish Underground had disappeared without a trace in spite of the formal

Russian offer of safe-conduct. Questions were asked in Parliament and stories have since spread of the shooting of local Polish leaders in the areas at this time occupied by the Soviet armies and particularly of one episode at Siedlce in Eastern Poland. It was not until May 4 that Molotov admitted at San Francisco that these men were being held in Russia, and an official Russian news agency stated next day that they were awaiting trial on charges of "diversionary tactics in the rear of the Red Army."

On May 18 Stalin publicly denied that the arrested Polish leaders had ever been invited to Moscow and asserted that they were mere "diversionists" who would be dealt with according to "a law similar to the British Defence of the Realm Act." The Soviet Government refused to move from this position. Nothing more was heard of the victims of the trap until the case against them opened on June 18. It was conducted in the usual Communist manner. The prisoners were accused of subversion, terrorism, and espionage, and

all except one admitted wholly or in part the charges against them. Thirteen were found guilty, and sentenced to terms of imprisonment ranging from four months to ten years, and three were acquitted. This was in fact the judicial liquidation of the leadership of the Polish Underground which had fought so heroically against Hitler. The rank and file had already died in the ruins of Warsaw.

Meanwhile, I received a most disheartening reply from Stalin to the appeal I had made to him on April 29. I repeated his forbidding message to President Truman, with the following comment: "It seems to me that matters can hardly be carried further by correspondence, and that as soon as possible there should be a meeting of the three heads of Governments. *Meanwhile we should hold firmly to the existing position obtained or being obtained by our armies in Yugoslavia, in Austria, in Czechoslovakia, on the main central United States front, and on the British front, reaching up to Lübeck, including Denmark. . . ."*

The German Surrender

GLEAMING successes marked the end of our campaigns in the Mediterranean. Alexander had succeeded Wilson as Supreme Commander in December, while Mark Clark took command of the 15th Army group. After their strenuous efforts of the autumn our armies in Italy needed a pause to reorganise.

The long, obstinate, and unexpected German resistance on all fronts had made us and the Americans very short of artillery ammunition, and our hard experiences of winter campaigning in Italy forced us to postpone a general offensive till the spring. But the Allied Air Forces, under General Eaker, and later under General Cannon, used their thirty-to-one superiority in merciless attacks on the supply lines which nourished the German armies. The most important one, from Verona to the Brenner Pass, where Hitler and Mussolini used to meet in their happier days, was blocked in many places for nearly the whole of March. Other mountain passes were often closed for weeks at a time, and two divisions being transferred to the Russian front were delayed almost a month.

The enemy had enough ammunition and supplies, but lacked fuel. Units were generally up to strength, and their spirit was high in spite of Hitler's reverses on the Rhine and the Oder. The German High Command might have had little to fear had it not been for the dominance of our Air Forces, the fact that we had the initiative and could strike where we pleased, and their own ill-chosen defensive position, with the broad Po at their backs. They would have done better to yield Northern Italy and withdraw to the strong defences of the Adige, where they could have held us with much smaller forces, and sent troops to help their overmatched armies elsewhere, or have made a firm southern face for the National Redoubt in the Tyrol mountains, which Hitler may have had in mind as his "last ditch."

But defeat south of the Po spelt disaster. This must have been obvious to Kesselring. Hitler was of course the stumbling block and when General Vietinghoff, who

succeeded Kesserling, proposed a tactical withdrawal he was thus rebuffed: "The Fuehrer expects, now as before, the utmost steadiness in the fulfillment of your present mission to defend every inch of the Northern Italian areas entrusted to your command."

In the evening of April 9, after a day of mass air attacks and artillery bombardment, the Eighth Army attacked. By the 14th there was good news all along the front. The Fifth Army, after a week of hard fighting, backed by the full weight of the Allied Air Forces, broke out from the mountains, crossed the main road west of Bologna, and struck north. On the 20th Vietinghoff, despite Hitler's commands, ordered a withdrawal. It was too late. The Fifth Army pressed towards the Po, with the Tactical Air Force making havoc along the roads ahead. Trapped behind them were many thousand Germans, cut off from retreat, pouring into prisoners' cages or being marched to the rear.

We crossed the Po on a broad front at the heels of the enemy. All the permanent bridges had been destroyed by our Air Forces, and the ferries and temporary crossings were attacked with such effect that the enemy were thrown into confusion. The remnants who struggled across, leaving all their heavy equipment behind, were unable to reorganise on the far bank. The Allies armies pursued them to the Adige. Italian Partisans had long harassed the enemy in the mountains and their back areas. On April 25 the signal was given for a general rising and they made widespread attacks. In many cities and towns, notably Milan and Venice, they seized control. Surrenders in Northwest Italy became wholesale. The garrison of Genoa, 4,000 strong, gave themselves up to a British liaison officer and the Partisans.

There was a pause before the force of facts overcame German hesitancies, but on April 24 General Karl Wolff, the commander of the SS in Italy, appeared in Switzerland with full powers from Vietinghoff. Two plenipotentiaries were brought to Alexander's headquarters, and on April 29 they signed the instrument of unconditional surrender in the presence of high British, American, and Russian officers. On May 2 nearly a million Germans surrendered as prisoners of war, and the war in Italy ended.

For Mussolini also the end had come. Like Hitler the Duce seems to have kept his illusions until almost the last moment. Late in March he had paid a final visit to his German partner, and returned to his headquarters on Lake Garda buoyed up with the thought of the secret weapons which could still lead to victory. But the rapid Allied advance from the Apennines made these hopes vain. There was hectic talk of a last stand in the mountainous areas of the Italo-Swiss frontier. But there was no will to fight left in the Italian Socialist Republic.

ON April 25 Mussolini decided to disband the remnants of his armed forces and to ask the Cardinal Archbishop of Milan to arrange a meeting with the underground Military Committee of the Italian National Liberation Movement. That afternoon talks took place in the Archbishop's palace, but with a last furious gesture of independence Mussolini walked out. In the evening, followed by a convoy of thirty vehicles, containing most of the surviving leaders of Italian Fascism, he drove to the prefecture at Como. He had no coherent plan, and as discussion became useless it was each man for himself. Accompanied by a handful of supporters, he attached himself to a small German convoy heading towards the Swiss frontier. The commander of the column was not anxious for trouble with Italian Partisans. The Duce was persuaded to put on a German greatcoat and helmet. But the little party was stopped by Partisan patrols; Mussolini was recognised and taken into custody. Other members, including his mistress, Signorina Petacci, were also arrested.

On Communist instructions, the Duce and his mistress were taken out in a car next day and shot. Their bodies, together with others, were sent to Milan and strung up head downwards on meathooks in a petrol station on the Piazzale Loreto, where a group of Italian Partisans had lately been shot in public. Such was the fate of the Italian dictator. A photograph of the final scene was sent to me, and I was profoundly shocked. But at least the world was spared an Italian Nürnberg.

In Germany the invading armies drove onward in their might and the space between them narrowed daily. By early April Eisenhower was across the Rhine and thrusting deep into Germany and Central Europe against an enemy who in places resisted fiercely but was quite unable to stem our triumphant onrush. Many political and military prizes still hung in the balance. Poland was beyond our succour. So also was Vienna, where our opportunity of forestalling the Russians by an advance from Italy had been abandoned eight months earlier when Alexander's forces had been stripped for the landing in the south of France. The Russians moved on the city from east and south, and by April 13 were in full possession.

But there seemed nothing to stop the Western Allies from taking Berlin. The Russians were only thirty-five miles away, but the Germans were entrenched on the Oder and much hard fighting was to take place before the Soviet troops could force a crossing and resume their advance. The Ninth U.S. Army, on the other hand, had moved so speedily that on April 12 they had crossed the Elbe near Magdeburg and were about sixty miles from the capital. But here they halted. Four days later the Russians started their attack and surrounded Berlin on the 25th. Stalin had told Eisenhower that his main blow against Germany would be made in "approximately the second half of May," but he was able to advance a whole month earlier. Perhaps our swift approach to the Elbe had something to do with it.

On this same 25th day of April, 1945, spearheads of the United States First Army from Leipzig met the Russians near Torgau, on the Elbe. Germany was cut in two. The German Army was disintegrating before our eyes. Over a million prisoners were taken in the first three weeks of April, but Eisenhower believed that fanatical Nazis would attempt to establish themselves in the mountains of Bavaria and Western Austria, and he swung the Third U.S. Army southward. Its left penetrated into Czechoslovakia as far as Budejovice, Pilsen, and Carlsbad.

Prague was still within our reach and there was no agreement to debar him from occupying it if it were militarily feasible. On April 30 I suggested to the President that he should do so, but Mr. Truman seemed adverse. A week later I also telegraphed personally to Eisenhower, but his plan was to halt his advance generally on the west bank of the Elbe and along the 1937 boundary of Czechoslovakia. If the situation warranted he would cross it to the general line Carlsbad-Pilsen-Budejovice. The Russians agreed to this and the movement was made. But on May 4 they reacted strongly to a fresh proposal to continue the advance of the Third U.S. Army to the river Vltava, which flows through Prague. This would not have suited them at all. So, as Eisenhower reported to the Combined Chiefs of Staff, the Americans "halted while the Red Army cleared the east and west banks of the Moldau River and occupied Prague." The city fell on May 9, two days after the general surrender was signed at Reims.

AT this point a retrospect is necessary. The occupation of Germany by the principal Allies had long been studied. In mid-1943 a Cabinet Committee which I had set up under Mr. Attlee, in agreement with the Chiefs of Staff, recommended that the whole country should be occupied if Germany was to be effectively disarmed, and that our forces should be disposed in three main zones of roughly equal size, the British in the northwest, the Americans in the south and southwest, and the Russians in the east. Berlin should be a separate joint zone, occupied by each of the three major Allies. These recommendations were approved and forwarded to the European Advisory Council, which then consisted of M. Gousev, the Soviet Ambassador, Mr. Winant, the American Ambassador, and Sir William Strang of the Foreign Office.

At this time the subject seemed to be purely theoretical. No one could foresee when or how the end of the war would come. The German armies held immense areas of European Russia. A year was yet to pass before British or American troops set foot in Western Europe, and nearly two years before they entered Germany. The proposals of the European Advisory Council were not thought sufficiently pressing or practical to be brought before the War Cabinet. Like many praiseworthy efforts to make plans for the future, they lay upon the shelves while the war crashed on. In those days a common opinion about Soviet Russia was that she would not continue the war once she had regained her frontiers, and that when the time came the Western Allies might well have to try to persuade her not to relax her efforts. The question of the Russian zone of occupation in Germany therefore did not bulk in our thoughts or in Anglo-American discussions, nor was it raised by any of the leaders at Tehran.

At the Quebec Conference in September 1944 we had reached a firm agreement between us. The President had a large map unfolded on his knees. One afternoon, most of the Combined Chiefs of Staff being present, he agreed

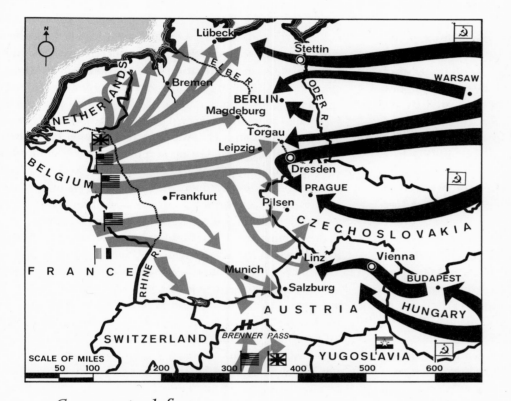

Germany in defeat was overrun by Allies from west (*blue*) and east (*black*). Russian and U.S. forces had met at Torgau (*center*) and at Linz in Austria. Other Russian units were closing pincers on Berlin and Prague. Meanwhile U.S. Fifth Army from Italy was pushing up from the south toward the Brenner Pass.

verbally with me that the existing arrangement should stand subject to the United States armies having a nearby direct outlet to the sea across the British zone. Bremen and its subsidiary Bremerhaven seemed to meet the American needs, and their control over this zone was adopted. We all felt it was too early as yet to provide for a French zone in Germany, and no one as much as mentioned Russia.

At Yalta in February 1945 the Quebec plan was accepted without further consideration as the working basis for the inconclusive discussions about the future eastern frontier of Germany. This was reserved for the Peace Treaty. The Soviet Armies were at this very moment swarming over the prewar frontiers, and we wished them all success. We proposed an agreement about the zones of occupation in Austria. Stalin, after some persuasion, agreed to my strong appeal that the French should be allotted part of the American and British zones and given a seat on the Allied Control Commission. It was well understood by everyone that the

agreed occupational zones must not hamper the operational movements of the armies. Berlin, Prague, and Vienna could be taken by whoever got there first. We separated in the Crimea not only as Allies but as friends facing a still mighty foe with whom all our armies were struggling in fierce and ceaseless battle.

The two months that had passed since then had seen tremendous changes cutting to the very roots of thought. Hitler's Germany was doomed and he himself about to perish. The Russians were fighting in Berlin. Vienna and most of Austria was in their hands. The whole relationship of Russia with the Western Allies was in flux. Every question about the future was unsettled between us. The agreements and understandings of Yalta, such as they were, had already been broken or brushed aside by the triumphant Kremlin. New perils, perhaps as terrible as those we had surmounted, loomed and glared upon the torn and harassed world.

My concern at all these ominous developments was apparent even before the President's death. He himself was also anxious and disturbed. In spite of the victorious advance of General Eisenhower's armies, President Truman found himself faced in the last half of April with a formidable crisis. I had for some time past tried my utmost to impress the United States Government with the vast changes which were taking place both in the military and in the political spheres. Our Western armies would soon be carried well beyond the boundaries of our occupation zones, as both the Western and Eastern Allied fronts approached one another penning the Germans between them.

Telegrams which I have published elsewhere show that I never suggested going back on our word over the agreed zones provided other agreements were also respected. I became convinced however that before we halted, or still more withdrew, our troops, we ought to seek a meeting with Stalin face to face and make sure that an agreement was reached about the whole front. It would indeed be a disaster if we kept all our agreements in strict good faith while the Soviets laid their hands upon all they could get without the slightest regard for the obligations into which they had entered.

On April 18 I addressed myself to the new President. Mr. Truman was of course only newly aware at second hand of all the complications that faced us, and had to lean heavily on his advisers. His reply carried us little further. He proposed that all the Allied troops should retire to their agreed zones of occupation in Germany and Austria as soon as the military situation allowed.

Hitler had meanwhile pondered where to make his last stand. As late as April 20 he still thought of leaving Berlin for the "Southern Redoubt" in the Bavarian Alps. That day he held a meeting of the principal Nazi leaders. As the German double front, east and west, was in imminent danger of being cut in twain by the spearpoint thrust of the Allies, he agreed to set up two separate commands. Admiral Doenitz was to take charge in the north both of the military and civil authorities, with the particular task of bringing back to German soil nearly two million refugees from the east. In the south General Kesselring was to command the remaining German armies. These arrangements were to take effect if Berlin fell.

Two days later, on April 22, Hitler made his final and supreme decision to stay in Berlin to the end. The capital was soon completely encircled by the Russians and the Fuehrer had lost all power to control events. It remained for him to organise his own death amid the ruins of the city. He announced to the Nazi leaders who remained with him that he would die in Berlin. Goering and Himmler had both left after the conference of the 20th, with thoughts of peace negotiations in their minds. Goering, who had gone south, assumed that Hitler had in fact abdicated by his resolve to stay in Berlin, and asked for confirmation that he should act formally as the successor to the Fuehrer. The reply was his instant dismissal from all his offices. In a remote mountain village of the Tyrol he and nearly a hundred of the more senior officers of the Luftwaffe were taken prisoner by the Americans. Retribution had come at last.

THE last scenes at Hitler's headquarters have been described elsewhere in much detail. Of the personalities of his regime only Goebbels and Bormann remained with him to the end. The Russian troops were now fighting in the streets of Berlin. In the early hours of April 29 Hitler made his will. The day opened with the normal routine of work in the air raid shelter under the Chancellery. News arrived of Mussolini's end. The timing was grimly appropriate. On the 30th Hitler lunched quietly with his suite, and at the end of the meal shook hands with those present and retired to his private room. At half-past three a shot was heard, and members of his personal staff entered the room to find him lying on the sofa with a revolver by his side. He had shot himself through the mouth. Eva Braun, whom he had married secretly during these last days, lay dead beside him. She had taken poison. The bodies were burnt in the courtyard, and Hitler's funeral pyre, with the din of the Russian guns growing ever louder, made a lurid end to the Third Reich.

The leaders who were left held a final conference. Last-minute attempts were made to negotiate with the Russians, but Zhukov demanded unconditional surrender. Bormann tried to break through the Russian lines, and disappeared without a trace. Goebbels poisoned his six children and then ordered an SS guard to shoot his wife and himself. The remaining staff of Hitler's headquarters fell into Russian hands.

For Himmler a less spectacular end was reserved. He had gone to the Eastern Front and for some months had been urged to make personal contact with the Western Allies on his own initiative in the hope of negotiating a separate surrender. He now tried to do so through Count Bernadotte, the head of the Swedish Red Cross, but we repulsed his offers. No more was heard of him till May 21, when he was arrested by a British control post at Bremervörde. He was disguised and was not recognised, but his papers made the sentries suspicious and he was taken to a camp near Second Army Headquarters. He then told the commandant who he was. He was put under armed guard, stripped, and searched for poison by a doctor. During the final stage of the examination he bit open a phial of cyanide, which he had apparently hidden in his mouth for some hours. He died almost instantly, just after eleven o'clock at night on Wednesday, May 23.

IN the northwest the drama closed less sensationally. On May 2 news arrived of the surrender in Italy. On the same day our troops reached Lübeck, on the Baltic, making contact with the Russians and cutting off all the Germans in Denmark and Norway. On the 3rd we entered Hamburg without opposition and the garrison surrendered unconditionally. A German delegation came to Montgomery's headquarters on Lüneburg Heath. It was headed by Admiral Friedeburg, Doenitz's emissary, who sought a surrender agreement to include German troops in the north who were facing the Russians. This was rejected as being beyond the authority of an Army Group commander, who could deal only with his own front. Next day, having received fresh instructions from his superiors, Friedeburg signed the surrender of all German forces in Northwest Germany, Holland, the Islands, Schleswig-Holstein, and Denmark.

Friedeburg went on to Eisenhower's headquarters at Reims, where he was joined by General Jodl on May 6. They played for time to allow as many soldiers and refugees as possible to disentangle themselves from the Russians and come over to the Western Allies and they tried to surrender the Western Front separately. Eisenhower imposed a time limit and insisted on a general capitulation. Jodl reported to Doenitz: "General Eisenhower insists that we sign to-day. If not, the Allied fronts will be closed to persons seeking to surrender individually. I see no alternative—chaos or signature. I ask you to confirm to me immediately by wireless that I have full powers to sign capitulation."

The instrument of total, unconditional surrender was signed by Lieut.-General Bedell Smith and General Jodl, with French and Russian officers as witnesses, at 2:41 a.m., on May 7. Thereby all hostilities ceased at midnight on May 8. The formal ratification by the German High Command took place in Berlin, under Russian arrangements, in the early hours of May 9. Air Chief Marshal Tedder signed on behalf of Eisenhower, Marshal Zhukov for the Russians, and Field-Marshal Keitel for Germany.

The unconditional surrender of our enemies was the signal for the greatest outburst of joy in the history of mankind. The Second World War had indeed been fought to the bitter end in Europe. The vanquished as well as the victors felt inexpressible relief. But for us in Britain and the British Empire, who had alone been in the struggle from the first day to the last and staked our existence on the result, there was a meaning beyond what even our most powerful and most valiant Allies could feel. Weary and worn, impoverished but undaunted and now triumphant, we had a moment that was sublime. We gave thanks to God for the noblest of all His blessings, the sense that we had done our duty.

Battling toward Germany, an American paratrooper dashes through enemy shellbursts as he crosses a field near Arnhem in The Netherlands

THE CRACK-UP

The Battle Comes to German Soil

In August of 1944, as the German armies in France disintegrated, the speed of the Allied advance was so great that air drops repeatedly had to be cancelled because ground troops had already overrun the objectives. In the heady air of victory, commanders were expecting to burst into Germany, strike at its undefended heart and end the war then and there. But at this crucial moment of history, the Allied armies ran out of gas.

While planes and trucks rushed up fuel and ammunition, a few precious weeks were lost. In that time, the Germans managed to rearrange the remnants of their armies and bring up new formations that included boys, old men and semi-invalids. They settled down in old fortifications on both sides of the German frontier, and there, in the middle of September, the Allies came to a halt.

In eastern France, the Germans used French forts which they had stormed in the Franco-Prussian War of 1870. Inside Germany, they held the Siegfried Line which Hitler had begun in 1936. The Allies tried an outflanking move with a paratroop attack at Arnhem, but when that failed they had no choice but to hit head on at these old but still formidable fortifications.

The U.S. First Army finally cracked the Siegfried Line in October, capturing Aachen, but the advance soon bogged down in Huertgen Forest a few miles beyond. All through the cold and muddy autumn, American, British, Canadian and French troops hammered forward yard by painful yard. The German Army was bleeding to death—4,000 casualties a day and no replacements—but it went on fighting blindly. Hitler assured his soldiers that if they held on a little longer he had new secret weapons which could still win the war.

Truckload of corpses (*left*), the American casualties of a quiet day when there was little action but sniping and strafing, are driven back through a muddy shell-shattered village near the German frontier.

Mantle of debris lies about broken Siegfried Line where artillery has blown a bunker to pieces and killed the Germans in their foxholes before it. The vaunted Siegfried Line was made up of hundreds of strong fortifications like this, located to give each other maximum fire support. Between and around them extended miles of the antitank obstacles that appear in the left background of this painting by Aaron Bohrod.

539

Allied Setback in the Ardennes

As winter dragged on, Allied armies were still chipping at the German line in the north and south. In the center was a lightly held front where nobody was fighting much. General Eisenhower, recalling a similar situation two years earlier in Tunisia, speculated that the enemy might try a "nasty little Kasserine" again. But he decided to take the risk. Hitler, on the other hand, decided to send 28 of his best remaining divisions against the weak center, smash through the Ardennes and on to Antwerp, surround the bulk of the Anglo-American armies and "bring about a decisive turning point . . . in the war as a whole."

On December 16 the Germans attacked down twisting roads. Surprise was complete, and in 10 days they drove a bulge some 60 miles deep into the Allied line. A few more miles and they would be running loose in the unprotected Allied rear, just as they had done to the French in May 1940. But they could not keep it up. Their armored columns shortly began to run out of supplies. Stiff American resistance at St. Vith and Bastogne upset the Wehrmacht timetable. Then, after seven days of fog, the Allied air forces flew again and made a shambles of every road leading into the bulge. In a month of battle in the snow, the Allies cleared it out entirely. Hitler's last bolt was shot.

Solitary tank (*below*) moves down a tree-lined road as the U.S. counterattack in the Ardennes gains momentum. When the battle was over, the Germans left behind 600 irreplaceable tanks and assault guns.

Snowbound column of American armor (*above*), moving up to meet the German offensive in the Ardennes, comes to a halt on the icy road. One gun carriage at the right has slid off the road into the fir trees.

Cold soldiers warm themselves at a roadside fire. Bitter weather was often as great an enemy as the Germans. In five weeks of fighting in the Bulge, there were 12,000 cases of trenchfoot among U.S. soldiers.

Confident German signals to his comrades to follow him down a road in the Ardennes. The Germans picked their best troops and gambled their best remaining equipment on this do-or-die offensive.

Wounded German, taken prisoner while his unit was trying to capture an American fuel depot at the opening of the Battle of the Bulge, lies in pain on a stretcher near the Belgian village of La Gleize.

Murdered Americans lie in the snow near Malmedy where Nazis shot them in cold blood. They had been overrun by German tanks and surrendered. Instead of sending them to a POW camp, the Germans

On the attack, two U.S. soldiers run through a Belgian village whose walls are collapsing under artillery fire. Speed with which the Americans went over to the attack surprised the German command.

herded them into a field and sprayed them with small-arms fire. Then they walked among them, shooting any who moaned. They killed 129, but a handful of wounded kept quiet and later escaped to the woods.

Captured Germans, ragged and worn from exposure after weeks of marching and fighting in the snow under frequent attack from the air, are marched off to a prison enclosure by an American soldier.

543

Wintry Interludes in the Bulge

Snowy landscape in a valley on the German frontier, at the base of the Bulge, suggests a Christmas card scene except for the bursts of German shellfire. The paintings on these pages are by Aaron Bohrod.

Roadside meal of K rations (*below*) is shared by Americans in the ruins of Bastogne. At the left a woman who has survived all the days of battle pushes a cart containing what is left of her worldly goods.

Moment of repose before returning to the battle is found by cold and weary Americans in a church in the little Luxembourg town of Berdorf. These were Third Army men who had been inching their way across the German frontier in the sector below Luxembourg. They were hurriedly turned north to beat in the southern side of the Ardennes bulge and helped drive the Germans back where they had started from.

Crossing the Rivers of Germany

Every river in Germany was an obstacle, and worst of all was the muddy little Roer where the Germans could inundate the valley by opening the dams. The Americans got to the Roer in November, but could not cross it until February 23, when they finally bridged the flood created by the Germans (*below*). Once over, they joined the general sweep of the Allied armies forward to the Rhine.

The first crossing of the Rhine was made by accident, at Remagen to the south (*pages 548-49*). The second was scheduled to be made by Montgomery's 21st Army Group in the north, to the accompaniment of violent bombardments, huge smoke screens and an airborne assault. But Patton wanted to beat Montgomery across, so he loaded a spearhead of his Third Army into boats one dark night and —with no preparation whatever—sent it to the eastern bank. This operation was successful, so was Montgomery's, and Germany's last defense line in the west was breached.

At the shore of the Rhine (*below*), an LCM for the crossing is hauled by a Ninth Army truck. Some landing craft were so long that buildings in towns had to be partly demolished to let them through.

On a footbridge, put up in smoke screen on the morning of the assault, U.S. Ninth Army men dash across the Roer. The soldier in the foreground was killed when he was only 50 feet from the east bank.

On the Rhine (*above*), Third Army men crouch in an amphibious truck as it heads for the terraced slopes on the eastern bank, after the surprise night attack which had gotten over the river at very little cost.

In a tree, a paratrooper dangles a few miles east of the Rhine crossing he has come to help. Some paratroopers were shot as they hung like this, but most landed safely and quickly cleared up their sector.

Rhine bridge at Remagen lies in ruins after days of shelling by Germans. On March 7, U.S. soldiers had reached it and crossed while it was still intact. The American bridgehead held against repeated counterattacks and served as a springboard for the encirclement of the Ruhr. By March 17 when the German fire finally knocked the bridge down—and Ogden Pleissner painted this picture—boats and pontoon bridges were sending steady streams of U.S. reinforcements across the Rhine.

The Grisly Mark of Nazi Barbarism

"We Germans," said Heinrich Himmler, boss of the SS and of the German police, "we Germans, who are the only people in the world who have a decent attitude toward animals, will also assume a decent attitude toward these human animals but it is a crime against our own blood to worry about them." The "human animals" were the non-German men, women and children who fell into Nazi hands during the war; and the "decent attitude" found its expression in enslavement and mass murder.

When the gates of Germany cracked open in 1945, the Allied armies discovered that the Third Reich was an immense jail. Among the inmates, the prisoners of war from the U.S. and the British Empire were the best off, being kept in life if not in health by Red Cross packages. Russian POWs were worked like cattle and died like flies. Worst off was the mass of miserable humanity herded into the concentration camps: Jews, political prisoners, underground fighters, gypsies, hostages, black-market dealers and miscellaneous thousands who ran afoul of Himmler's police. Flogged and starved behind the barbed wire of scores of camps, they worked in quarries and mines and underground factories making V-bombs for Hitler. Six million and more of them went up in black smoke in the tall crematorium chimneys that clouded the skies of Germany.

Gaunt American, taken prisoner in the Battle of the Bulge, stares up uncomprehendingly at the U.S. troops who have come to rescue him after three months of near-starvation in a German prison camp.

Gross Germans, SS guards in the Belsen concentration camp where some 80,000 people died, are put to work by the Allies stacking starved bodies of their victims after the arrival of the invading armies.

Field of prisoners, gathered in western Germany, awaits disposition by the Allies. There are something like 160,000 Germans in this open field, setting up pup tents given to them by the American army after one of the mass surrenders that marked the last two weeks of the war when seven million soldiers on the western front in Germany and in what was left of the occupied countries laid down their arms.

Tumbling Walls of the Third Reich

In the spring of 1945, with the Rhine breached by the British and Americans in the west and the Oder by the Russians in the east, all the shrinking Germany between was prey for the bombers. One by one the factories that enabled Germany to make war were overrun. Transportation broke down and refugees clogged the roads. Despite Hitler's command to shoot any officer who ordered retreat, whole armies were in flight, and hordes of German soldiers were pouring into prisoner compounds with a feeling of relief that for them the war was over.

In the 30-room shelter 50 feet below the Reich Chancellery in the center of Berlin, the belief in German victory kept obstinately and irrationally alive. Here Hitler had his headquarters, cut off from his troops, when the Russians surrounded Berlin on April 25. By now he was a stooped, palsied, gray-faced old man doddering into imbecility. Once he shouted, "Shoot them all!" and his startled entourage did not know whom he was referring to. But he was still the undisputed master of Germany, and as long as he lived no one had the authority to surrender.

Even back in July 1944 Hitler had been led to lament, "I am beginning to doubt whether the German people is worthy of my great ideals." Now, in the ruins of Berlin, his despair was complete. On April 29 he married his mistress and made his will. Next day he blew his brains out.

Dispirited Fuehrer, in one of his last appearances (*right*), walks through rubble. "I can't understand why everything has gone wrong for the past two years," he said plaintively to his Chief of Staff.

The End of the War against Germany

After Hitler killed himself, Germans no longer felt bound by an oath of allegiance to a madman. As their world came crumbling down around them, they began looking for a way to end the futile fight. But illusions died hard—Himmler had an idea he could negotiate for an independent state in Schleswig-Holstein, and some generals thought they could give up to the western Allies alone. They soon learned there was no alternative to total and unconditional surrender.

The thunder of Allied gun and bomb went on as the Reich disintegrated. Russian armies pounded Berlin to ruins and then pushed on to the River Elbe, where the Americans—who had been waiting there for two weeks—greeted them in a spirit of jovial fraternity on April 25. The Nazi warlords took poison or went to jail. Mass surrenders of Germans began—a million men in Italy on May 2, a million and a half more in northwest Germany on May 5. When the final capitulation was signed at Reims on May 7 (*below*), only isolated units, spread haphazardly from Brittany to Latvia and the North Cape to the Aegean Sea, remained of the monstrous machine that had blighted Europe.

Unconditional surrender of the German armed forces is offered to the Allies in Reims by Colonel-General Alfred Jodl (*center*), of the German General Staff, who was later hanged for war crimes.

Russian and American officers (right) meet in a bearhug at the Elbe

554

Dead for the Emperor, a Japanese soldier—painted by Frede Vidar
—lies on the battlefield where he fell in one of the many "banzai" suicide
charges which the enemy ordered in a last-ditch effort to turn defeat into victory.

22

DEFEAT OF JAPAN

The Chasm Opens

APPREHENSION for the future and many perplexities filled my mind as I moved about among the cheering crowds of Londoners in their hour of well-won rejoicing after all they had gone through. The Hitler peril, with its ordeals and privations, seemed to most of them to have vanished in a blaze of glory. The tremendous foe they had fought for more than five years had surrendered unconditionally. All that remained for the three victorious Powers was to make a just and durable peace, guarded by a World Instrument, to bring the soldiers home to their longing loved ones, and to enter upon a Golden Age of prosperity and progress. No more, and surely, thought their peoples, no less.

However, there was another side to the picture. Japan was still unconquered. The atomic bomb was still unborn. The world was in confusion. The main bond of common danger which had united the Great Allies had vanished overnight. The Soviet menace, to my eyes, had already replaced the Nazi foe. But no comradeship against it existed. At home the foundations of national unity, upon which the wartime Government had stood so firmly, were also gone. Our strength, which had overcome so many storms, would no longer continue in the sunshine. How then could we reach that final settlement which alone could reward the toils and sufferings of the struggle? I could not rid my mind

of the fear that the victorious armies of democracy would soon disperse and that the real and hardest test still lay before us. I had seen it all before. I remembered that other joy-day nearly thirty years before, when I had driven with my wife from the Ministry of Munitions through similar multitudes convulsed with enthusiasm to Downing Street to congratulate the Prime Minister. Then, as at this time, I understood the world situation as a whole. But then at least there was no mighty army that we need fear.

My prime thought was a meeting of the three Great Powers and I hoped that President Truman would come through London on his way. Instead, very different ideas were being pressed upon the new President from influential quarters in Washington. The sort of mood and outlook which had been noticed at Yalta had been strengthened. The United States, it was argued, must be careful not to let herself be drawn into any antagonism with Soviet Russia. This, it was thought, would stimulate British ambition and would make a new gulf in Europe. The right policy, on the other hand, should be for the United States to stand between Britain and Russia as a friendly mediator, or even arbiter, trying to reduce their differences about Poland or Austria and make things settle down into a quiet and happy peace, enabling American forces to be concentrated against Japan. These pressures must have been very strong upon

Truman. His natural instinct, as his historic actions have shown, may well have been different. I could not of course measure the forces at work in the brain-centre of our closest Ally, though I was soon conscious of them. I could only feel the vast manifestation of Soviet and Russian imperialism rolling forward over helpless lands.

Obviously the first aim must be a conference with Stalin. Within three days of the German surrender I cabled the President that we should now invite him to a conference. *"Meanwhile I earnestly hope that the American front will not recede from the now agreed tactical lines."* He replied at once that he would rather have Stalin propose the meeting, and he hoped our Ambassadors would induce him to suggest it. Mr. Truman then declared that he and I ought to go to the meeting separately, so as to avoid any suspicion of "ganging up." When the Conference ended he hoped to visit England if his duties in America permitted. I did not fail to notice the difference of view which this telegram conveyed, but I accepted the procedure he proposed.

During these same days President Truman asked Harry Hopkins to go as his special envoy to Moscow to make another attempt to reach a working agreement on the Polish question. Although far from well, Hopkins set out gallantly for Moscow. His friendship for Russia was well known, and he received a most friendly welcome. Certainly for the first time some progress was made. Stalin agreed to invite Mikolajczyk and two of his colleagues to Moscow from London for consultation, in conformity with our interpretation of the Yalta agreement. He also agreed to invite some important non-Lublin Poles from inside Poland.

In a telegram to me the President said he felt this was a very encouraging, positive stage in the negotiations. Most of the arrested Polish leaders were apparently only charged with operating illegal radio transmitters, and Hopkins was pressing Stalin to grant them an amnesty so that consultations could be conducted in the most favourable atmosphere possible. He asked me to urge Mikolajczyk to accept Stalin's invitation. I persuaded Mikolajczyk to go to Moscow, and in the upshot a new Polish Provisional Government was set up. At Truman's request this was recognised by both Britain and the United States on July 5.

I T is difficult to see what more we could have done. For five months the Soviets had fought every inch of the road. They had gained their object by delay. During all this time the Lublin Administration, under Bierut, sustained by the might of the Russian armies, had given them a complete control of Poland, enforced by the usual deportations and liquidations. They had denied us all the access for our observers which they had promised. All the Polish parties, except their own Communist puppets, were in a hopeless minority in the new recognised Polish Provisional Government. We were as far as ever from any real and fair attempt to obtain the will of the Polish nation by free elections. There was still a hope—and it was the only hope—that the meeting of "the Three," now impending, would achieve a genuine settlement. So far only dust and ashes have been gathered, and these are all that remain to us to-day of Polish national freedom.

On June 1 President Truman told me that Marshal Stalin was agreeable to a meeting of what he called "the Three" in Berlin about July 15. I replied at once that I would gladly go to Berlin with a British delegation, but I thought that July 15, which Truman had suggested, was much too late for the urgent questions demanding attention between us, and that we should do an injury to world hopes and unity if we allowed personal or national requirements to stand in the way of an earlier meeting. "Although," I cabled, "I am in the midst of a hotly contested election I would not consider my tasks here as comparable to a meeting between the three of us. If June 15 is not possible why not July 1, 2, or 3?" Mr. Truman replied that after full consideration July 15 was the earliest for him, and that arrangements were being made accordingly. Stalin did not wish to hasten the date. I could not press the matter further.

T HE main reason why I had been anxious to hasten the date of the meeting was of course the impending retirement of the American Army from the line which it had gained in the fighting to the zone prescribed in the occupation agreement. The story of the agreement about the zones is recorded in the previous section. I feared that any day a decision might be taken in Washington to yield up this enormous area—400 miles long and 120 at its greatest depth. It contained many millions of Germans and Czechs. Its abandonment would place a broader gulf of territory between us and Poland, and practically end our power to influence her fate. The changed demeanour of Russia towards us, the constant breaches of the understandings reached at Yalta, the dart for Denmark, happily frustrated by Montgomery's timely action, the encroachments in Austria, Marshal Tito's menacing pressure at Trieste, all seemed to me and my advisers to create an entirely different situation from that in which the zones of occupation had been prescribed two years earlier. Surely all these issues should be considered as a whole, and *now* was the time. Now, while the British and American Armies and Air Forces were still a mighty armed power, and before they melted away under demobilisation and the heavy claims of the Japanese war—now, at the very latest, was the time for a general settlement.

A month earlier would have been better. But it was not yet too late. On the other hand, to give up the whole centre and heart of Germany—nay, the centre and keystone of Europe—as an isolated act seemed to me to be a grave and improvident decision. If it were done at all it could only be as part of a general and lasting settlement. We should go to Potsdam with nothing to bargain with, and all prospects of the future peace of Europe might well go by default. The matter however did not rest with me. Our own retirement to the occupation frontier was inconsiderable. The American Army was three millions to our one. All I could do was to plead, first, for advancing the date of the meeting of "the Three," and, then, when that failed, to postpone the withdrawal until we could confront all our problems as a whole, together, face to face, and on equal terms.

How stands the scene after eight years have passed? The Russian occupation line in Europe runs from Lübeck to Linz. Czechoslovakia has been engulfed. The Baltic states, Poland, Romania, and Bulgaria have been reduced to satellite States under totalitarian Communist rule. Yugoslavia has broken loose. Greece alone is saved. Our armies are gone, and it will be a long time before even sixty divisions can be once again assembled opposite Russian forces, which in armour and manpower are in overwhelming strength. This also takes no account of all that has happened in the Far East. The danger of a third World War under conditions at the outset of grave disadvantage, casts its lurid shadow over the free nations of the world. Thus in the moment of victory was our best, and what might prove to have been our last, chance of durable world peace allowed composedly to fade away. On June 4th I cabled to the President these words, which few would now dispute:

"I am sure you understand the reason why I am anxious for an earlier date, say the 3rd or 4th [of July]. I view with profound misgivings the retreat of the American Army to our line of occupation in the central sector, thus bringing Soviet Russian power into the heart of Western Europe and the descent of an iron curtain between us and everything to the eastward. I hoped that this retreat, if it has to be made, would be accompanied by the settlement of many great things which would be the true foundation of world peace. Nothing really important has been settled yet, and you and I will have to bear great responsibility for the future. I still hope therefore that the date will be advanced."

Mr. Truman replied on June 12. He said the tripartite agreement about the occupation of Germany approved by President Roosevelt after "long consideration and detailed discussion" with me, made it impossible to delay the withdrawal of American troops from the Soviet Zone in order to press the settlement of other problems. The Allied Control Council could not begin to function until they left, and the military government wielded by the Supreme Commander should be terminated without delay and divided between Eisenhower and Montgomery. He had been advised, he said, that it would harm our relations with the Soviet to postpone action until our meeting in July, and he accordingly proposed sending a message to Stalin. This document suggested that we should at once instruct our armies to occupy their respective zones. He was ready to order all American troops to begin their withdrawal in Germany on June 21. The military commanders should arrange for the simultaneous occupation of Berlin and for free access thereto by road, rail, and air from Frankfurt and Bremen for the United States forces. In Austria arrangements could be completed more quickly and satisfactorily by making the local commanders responsible for defining the zones both there and in Vienna, only referring to their Governments such matters as they were unable to resolve themselves.

Withdrawal in Europe of British and U.S. forces (*blue arrows*) to zones agreed on for postwar occupation added 20,000 square miles (*light blue*) to area (*grey*) already held by Russians.

This struck a knell in my breast. But I had no choice but to submit. "Obviously," I telegraphed to Mr. Truman on the 14th of June, "we are obliged to conform to your decision, and the necessary instructions will be issued.

"It is not correct to state that the tripartite agreement about zones of occupation in Germany was the subject of 'long consideration and detailed discussion' between me and President Roosevelt. References made to them at Quebec were brief, and concerned only the Anglo-American arrangements which the President did not wish to raise by correspondence beforehand. These were remitted to the Combined Chiefs of Staff, and were certainly acceptable to them. . . . I sincerely hope that your action will in the long run make for a lasting peace in Europe." There was nothing more that I could do.

It must not be overlooked that Mr. Truman had not been concerned or consulted in the original fixing of the zones. The case as presented to him so soon after his accession to power was whether or not to depart from and in a sense repudiate the policy of the American and British Governments agreed to under his illustrious predecessor. He was, I have no doubt, supported in his action by his advisers, military and civil. His responsibility at this point was limited to deciding whether circumstances had changed so fundamentally that an entirely different procedure should be adopted, with the likelihood of having to face accusations of breach of faith. Those who are only wise after the event should hold their peace.

On July 1 the United States and British Armies began their withdrawal to their allotted zones, followed by masses of refugees. Soviet Russia was established in the heart of Europe. This was a fateful milestone for mankind.

While all this was passing I was plunged into the turmoil of the General Election, which began in earnest in the first week of June. This month was therefore hard to live through. Strenuous motor tours to the greatest cities of England and Scotland, with three or four speeches a day to enormous and, it seemed, enthusiastic crowds, and, above all, four laboriously prepared broadcasts, consumed my time and strength. All the while I felt that much we had fought for in our long struggle in Europe was slipping away and that the hopes of an early and lasting peace were receding. The days were passed amid the clamour of multitudes, and when at night, tired out, I got back to my headquarters train, where a considerable staff and all the incoming telegrams awaited me, I had to toil for many hours. The incongruity of party excitement and clatter with the sombre background which filled my mind was in itself an affront to reality and proportion. I was glad indeed when polling day at last arrived and the ballot papers were safely sealed for three weeks in their boxes.

I was resolved to have a week of sunshine to myself before the Conference. On July 7, two days after polling day, I flew to Bordeaux with Mrs. Churchill and Mary, and found myself agreeably installed at General Brutinel's villa near the Spanish frontier at Hendaye, with lovely bathing and beautiful surroundings. I spent most of the mornings in bed reading a very good account, by an excellent French writer, of the Bordeaux armistice and its tragic sequel at Oran. It was strange to revive my own memories of five years before and to learn of many things which I had not known at that time. In the afternoons I even sallied forth with my elaborate painting outfit, and found attractive subjects on the river Nive and in the Bay of St. Jean de Luz. I found a gifted companion of the brush in Mrs. Nairn, the wife of the British Counsul at Bordeaux, with whom I had made friends at Marrakech a year before. I dealt only with a few telegrams about the impending Conference, and strove to put party politics out of my head. And yet I must confess the mystery of the ballot boxes and their contents had an ugly trick of knocking on the door and peering in at the windows. When the palette was spread and I had a paintbrush in my hand it was easy to drive these intruders away.

The Basque people were everywhere warm in their welcome. They had endured a long spell of German occupation and were joyful to breathe freely again. I did not need to prepare myself for the Conference, for I carried so much of it in my head, and was happy to cast it off, if only for these few fleeting days. The President was at sea in the United States cruiser *Augusta*, the same ship which had carried Roosevelt to our Atlantic meeting in 1941. On the 15th I motored through the forests to the Bordeaux airfield, and my Skymaster took me to Berlin.

The Atomic Bomb

THE struggle in the Pacific had moved swiftly to its climax. The time at last had come to strike at the homeland of Japan. On February 19 Admiral Spruance attacked Iwo Jima, in the Bonin Islands, whence American fighters would be able to escort bombers from the Marianas in attacking Honshu. The struggle was severe and lasted over a month, but victory was won. Meanwhile the British Fleet, now known as Task Force 57, comprising the battleships *King George V* and *Howe*, four fleet carriers mustering nearly 250 aircraft, five cruisers, and eleven destroyers, reached its battle area east of Formosa on March 26. That day its bombers made their first strike at airfields and installations among the islands south of Okinawa. The task of the British was to stop the enemy using the airfields in the islands to the south and in northern Formosa. In the meantime Spruance himself was engaged in full-scale air operations as a prelude to the amphibious attack on Okinawa itself, due to be launched on April 1.

The capture of Okinawa Island was the largest and most prolonged amphibious operation of the Pacific war. Four American divisions made the first landings. The rugged island provided ample facilities for defence and the Japanese garrison of over 100,000 fought desperately. The whole of Japan's remaining sea and air power was committed. Her last surviving modern battleship, the *Yamato*, supported by cruisers and destroyers, tried to intervene on April 7, but the expedition was intercepted by Spruance's air carrier fleet and almost annihilated. Only a few destroyers survived.

Attacks by suicide bombers reached astonishing proportions. No fewer than 1,900 were made before the island was conquered, and according to Admiral King thirty-four destroyers and small craft were sunk and about 200 other ships were hit. These attacks and several thousand ordinary sorties constituted the most furious onslaught ever launched by the Japanese. But all was in vain. On June 22, after nearly three months' fighting, the island was subdued. The battle had occupied the full strength of Admiral Nimitz's Central Pacific forces, including an army of 450,000 men.

In the midst of my election and other preoccupations I had followed these moving struggles with day-to-day interest, and I realised at once the magnitude of the American achievement. "The strength of will power, devotion, and technical resources applied by the United States to this task," I cabled at the time to Mr. Truman, "joined with the death struggle of the enemy, of whom 90,000 are reported to be killed, places this battle among the most intense and famous in military history."

Farther south the liberation of the East Indies was proceeding. On May 1 the 9th Australian Division, supported by United States and Australian naval and air forces, landed at Tarakan, in Dutch Borneo. In June the Australians recaptured Brunei and Sarawak. On July 1 the 7th Australian Division landed at Balikpapan, supported by Dutch, American, and Australian naval forces. But these heartening events were soon to be overshadowed by the climax of the Far Eastern war, which was now approaching.

PRESIDENT Truman arrived in Berlin the same day as I did. I was eager to meet a potentate with whom my cordial relations, in spite of differences, had already been established by correspondence. I called on him the morning after our arrival, and was impressed with his gay, precise, sparkling manner and obvious power of decision.

On July 16 both the President and I made separate tours of Berlin. The city was nothing but a chaos of ruins. No notice had of course been given of our visit and the streets had only the ordinary passers-by. In the square in front of the Chancellery there was however a considerable crowd. When I got out of the car and walked about among them, except for one old man who shook his head disapprovingly, they all began to cheer. My hate had died with their surrender and I was much moved by their demonstrations, and also by their haggard looks and threadbare clothes. Then we entered the Chancellery, and for quite a long time walked through its shattered galleries and halls. Our Russian guides then took us to Hitler's air raid shelter. I went down to the bottom and saw the room in which he and his wife had committed suicide, and when we came up again they showed us the place where his body had been burned. We were given the best firsthand accounts available at that time of what had happened in these final scenes.

The course Hitler had taken was much more convenient for us than the one I had feared. At any time in the last few months of the war he could have flown to England and surrendered himself, saying, "Do what you will with me, but spare my misguided people." I have no doubt that he would have shared the fate of the Nürnberg criminals. The moral principles of modern civilisation seem to prescribe that the leaders of a nation defeated in war shall be put to death by the victors. This will certainly stir them to fight to the bitter end in any future war, and no matter how many lives are needlessly sacrificed it costs them no more. It is the masses of the people, who have so little to say about the starting or ending of wars, who pay the additional cost. The Romans followed the opposite principle, and their conquests were due almost as much to their clemency as to their military prowess.

World-shaking news arrived on the 17th day of July, 1945. In the afternoon Mr. Henry Stimson called at my private abode and laid before me a sheet of paper on which was written, "Babies satisfactorily born." By his manner I saw something extraordinary had happened. "It means," he said, "that the experiment in the New Mexico desert has come off. The atomic bomb is a reality." Although we had followed this dire quest with every scrap of information imparted to us, we had not been told beforehand, or at any rate I did not know, the date of the decisive trial. No responsible scientist would predict what would happen when the first full-scale atomic explosion was tried. Were these bombs useless or were they annihilating? Now we knew. The "babies" had been "satisfactorily born." No one could yet measure the immediate military consequences of the discovery, and no one has yet measured anything else about it.

Next morning a plane arrived with a full description of this tremendous event in the human story. Stimson brought me the report. I tell the tale as I recall it. The bomb, or its equivalent, had been detonated at the top of a pylon 100 feet high. Everyone had been cleared away for ten miles round, and the scientists and their staffs crouched behind massive concrete shields and shelters at about that distance. The blast had been terrific. An enormous column of flame and smoke shot up to the fringe of the atmosphere of our poor earth. Devastation inside a one-mile circle was absolute. Here then was a speedy end to the Second World War, and perhaps to much else besides.

The President invited me to confer with him forthwith. He had with him General Marshall and Admiral Leahy. Up to this moment we had shaped our ideas towards an assault upon the homeland of Japan by terrific air bombing and by the invasion of very large armies. We had contemplated the desperate resistance of the Japanese fighting to the death with Samurai devotion, not only in pitched battles, but in every cave and dugout. I had in my mind the spectacle of Okinawa Island, where many thousands of Japanese, rather than surrender, had drawn up in line and destroyed themselves by hand grenades after their leaders had solemnly performed the rite of hara-kiri. To quell the Japanese resistance man by man and to conquer the country yard by yard might well require the loss of a million American lives and half that number of British—or more if we could get them there: for we were resolved to share the agony. This nightmare picture had now all vanished. In its place was the vision—fair and bright it seemed—of the end of the whole war in one or two violent shocks. I thought immediately myself of how the Japanese people, whose courage I had always admired, might find in the apparition of this almost supernatural weapon an excuse which would save their honour and release them from the obligation of being killed to the last fighting man.

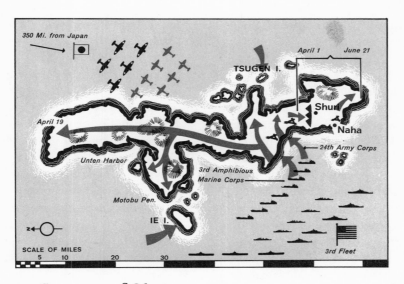

Conquest of Okinawa, made possible by biggest Allied amphibious operation of Pacific war, proceeded from U.S. landings (*brown*) as naval support fought off kamikazes. Fighting in north of island ended after three weeks but in south it lasted three months.

Moreover, we should not need the Russians. The end of the Japanese war no longer depended upon the pouring in of their armies for the final and perhaps protracted slaughter. We had no need to ask favours of them. The array of European problems could therefore be faced on their merits and according to the broad principles of the United Nations. We seemed suddenly to have become possessed of a merciful abridgment of the slaughter in the East and of a far happier prospect in Europe. I have no doubt that these thoughts were present in the minds of my American friends. At any rate, there never was a moment's discussion as to whether the atomic bomb should be used or not. To avert a vast, indefinite butchery, to bring the war to an end, to give peace to the world, to lay healing hands upon its tortured peoples by a manifestation of overwhelming power at the cost of a few explosions, seemed, after all our toils and perils, a miracle of deliverance.

British consent in principle to the use of the weapon had been given on July 4, before the test had taken place. The final decision now lay in the main with President Truman, who had the weapon; but I never doubted what it would be, nor have I ever doubted since that he was right. The historic fact remains, and must be judged in the after-time, that the decision whether or not to use the atomic bomb to compel the surrender of Japan was never even an issue. There was unanimous, automatic, unquestioned agreement around our table; nor did I ever hear the slightest suggestion that we should do otherwise.

A more intricate question was what to tell Stalin. The President and I no longer felt that we needed his aid to conquer Japan. His word had been given at Tehran and Yalta that Soviet Russia would attack Japan as soon as the German Army was defeated, and in fulfillment of this a continuous movement of Russian troops to the Far East had been in progress over the Siberian Railway since the beginning of May. In our opinion they were not likely to be needed, and Stalin's bargaining power, which he had used with effect upon the Americans at Yalta, was therefore gone. Still, he had been a magnificent ally in the war against Hitler, and we both felt that he must be informed of the great New Fact which now dominated the scene, but not of any particulars.

How should this news be imparted to him? Should it be in writing or by word of mouth? Should it be at a formal and special meeting, or in the course of our daily conferences, or after one of them? The conclusion which the President came to was the last of these alternatives. "I think," he said, "I had best just tell him after one of our meetings that we have an entirely novel form of bomb, something quite out of the ordinary, which we think will have decisive effects upon the Japanese will to continue the war." I agreed to this procedure.

MEANWHILE the devastating attack on Japan had continued from the air and the sea. By the end of July the Japanese Navy had virtually ceased to exist. The homeland was in chaos and on the verge of collapse. The professional diplomats were convinced that only immediate surrender under the authority of the Emperor could save Japan from complete disintegration, but power still lay almost entirely in the hands of a military clique determined to commit the nation to mass suicide rather than accept defeat. The appalling destruction confronting them made no impression on this fanatical hierarchy, who continued to profess belief in some miracle which would turn the scale in their favour.

In several lengthy talks with the President alone, or with his advisers present, I discussed what to do. I dwelt upon the tremendous cost in American and to a smaller extent in British life if we enforced "unconditional surrender" upon the Japanese. It was for him to consider whether this might not be expressed in some other way, so that we got all the essentials for future peace and security and yet left them some show of saving their military honour and some assurance of their national existence, after they had complied with all safeguards necessary for the conqueror. The President replied bluntly that he did not think the Japanese had any military honour after Pearl Harbor. I contented myself with saying that at any rate they had something for which they were ready to face certain death in very large numbers, and this might not be so important to us as it was to them. He then became quite sympathetic, and spoke, as

had Mr. Stimson, of the terrible responsibilities that rested upon him for the unlimited effusion of American blood.

Eventually it was decided to send an ultimatum calling for an immediate unconditional surrender of the armed forces of Japan. This document was published on July 26. Its terms were rejected by the military rulers of Japan, and the United States Air Force made its plans accordingly to cast one atomic bomb on Hiroshima and one on Nagasaki. We agreed to give every chance to the inhabitants. The procedure was developed in detail. In order to minimise the loss of life, eleven Japanese cities were warned by leaflets on July 27 that they would be subjected to intensive air bombardment. Next day six of them were attacked. Twelve more were warned on July 31, and four were bombed on August 1. The last warning was given on August 5. By then the Superfortresses claimed to have dropped a million and a half leaflets every day and three million copies of the ultimatum. The first atomic bomb was not cast till August 6.

On August 9 the Hiroshima bomb was followed by a second, this time on the city of Nagasaki. Next day, despite an insurrection by some military extremists, the Japanese Government agreed to accept the ultimatum, provided this did not prejudice the prerogative of the Emperor as a sovereign ruler. The Allied Fleets entered Tokyo Bay, and on the morning of September 2 the formal instrument of surrender was signed on board the United States battleship *Missouri*. Russia had declared war on August 8, only a week before the enemy's collapse. None the less she claimed her full rights as a belligerent.

It would be a mistake to suppose that the fate of Japan was settled by the atomic bomb. Her defeat was certain before the first bomb fell, and was brought about by overwhelming maritime power. This alone had made it possible to seize ocean bases from which to launch the final attack and force her metropolitan Army to capitulate without striking a blow. Her shipping had been destroyed. She had entered the war with over five and a half million tons, later much augmented by captures and new construction, but her convoy system and escorts were inadequate and ill-organised. Over eight and a half million tons of Japanese shipping were sunk, of which five million fell to submarines. We, an island Power, equally dependent on the sea, can read the lesson and understand our own fate had we failed to master the U-boats.

FRUSTRATION was the fate of the final Conference of "the Three." I shall not attempt to describe all the questions which were raised though not settled at our various Potsdam meetings. I content myself with telling the tale, so far as I was then aware of it, of the atomic bomb and outlining the terrible issue of the German-Polish frontiers. These events dwell with us to-day. During the course of the Conference I allowed differences that could not be adjusted either round the table or by the Foreign Ministers at their daily meetings to stand over. A formidable body of questions on which there was disagreement was in consequence piled upon the shelves. I intended, if I were returned by the electorate, as was generally expected, to come to grips with the Soviet Government on this catalogue of decisions. For instance, neither I nor Mr. Eden would ever have agreed to the Western Neisse being the frontier line. The line of the Oder and the Eastern Neisse had already been recognised as the Polish compensation for retiring to the Curzon Line, but the overrunning by the Russian armies of the territory up to and even beyond the Western Neisse was never and would never have been agreed to by any Government of which I was the head. Here was no point of principle only but rather an enormous matter of fact affecting about three additional millions of displaced people.

There were many other matters on which it was right to confront the Soviet Government, and also the Poles, who, gulping down immense chunks of German territory, had obviously become their ardent puppets. All this negotiation was cut in twain and brought to an untimely conclusion by the result of the General Election. To say this is not to blame the Ministers of the Labour Socialist Government, who were forced to go over without any serious preparation, and who were unacquainted naturally with the ideas and plans I had in view, namely to have a showdown at the end of the Conference, and, if necessary, to have a public break rather than allow anything beyond the River Oder and the Eastern Neisse to go to Poland.

The real time to deal with these issues was, however, as has been explained in earlier chapters, when the fronts of the mighty Allies faced each other in the field, and before the Americans, and to a lesser extent the British, made their vast retirement on a 400-mile front to a depth in some places of 120 miles, thus giving the heart and a great mass of Germany over to the Russians. At that time I desired to have the matter settled before we had made this tremendous retirement and while the Allied armies were still in being.

The American view was that we were committed to a definite line of occupation, and I on the other hand held strongly that this line of occupation could only be taken up when we were satisfied that the whole front, from north to south, was being settled in accordance with the desires and spirit in which our engagements had been made. However, it was impossible to gather American support for this, and the Russians, pushing the Poles in front of them, wended on, driving the Germans before them and depopulating large areas of Germany, whose food supplies they had seized, while chasing a multitude of mouths into the

Air attack on Japan was made by Allies (*blue*) from air bases on newly won islands and from carriers. Meanwhile invasion threatened the Ryukyus (*broken blue arrow*) and Russia had attacked Manchuria (*grey*). Finally A-bombs fell on Hiroshima and Nagasaki.

overcrowded British and American zones. Even at Potsdam the matter might perhaps have been recovered, but the destruction of the British National Government and my removal from the scene at the time when I still had much influence and power rendered it impossible for satisfactory solutions to be reached.

It remains for me only to mention some of the social and personal contacts which relieved our sombre debates. Each of the three great delegations entertained the other two. First was the United States. When it came to my turn I proposed the toast of "The Leader of the Opposition," adding, "whoever he may be." Mr. Attlee, whom I had invited to the Conference in accordance with my conviction that every head of Government in periods of crisis should have a deputy who knows everything and can thus help preserve continuity should accidents occur, was very much amused by this. So indeed were the company. The Soviets' dinner was equally agreeable, and a very fine concert, at which leading Russian artistes performed, carried the proceedings so late that I slipped away.

It fell to me to give the final banquet on the night of July the 23rd. I planned this on a larger scale, inviting the chief commanders as well as the delegates. I placed President Truman on my right and Stalin on my left. There were very many speeches, and Stalin, without even ensuring that all the waiters and orderlies had left the room, proposed that our next meeting should be in Tokyo. There was no doubt that the Russian declaration of war upon Japan would come at any moment, and already their large armies were massed upon the frontier ready to overrun the much weaker Japanese front line in Manchuria. To lighten the proceedings we changed places from time to time, and the President sat opposite me. I had another very friendly talk with Stalin, who was in the best of tempers and seemed to have no inkling of the momentous information about the new bomb the President had given me. He spoke with enthusiasm about the Russian intervention against Japan, and seemed to expect a good many months of war, which Russia would wage on an ever-increasing scale, governed only by the Trans-Siberian Railway.

Then a very odd thing happened. My formidable guest got up from his seat with the bill-of-fare card in his hand and went round the table collecting the signatures of many of those who were present. I never thought to see him as an autograph hunter! When he came back to me I wrote my name as he desired, and we both looked at each other and laughed. Stalin's eyes twinkled with mirth and good humour. I have mentioned before how the toasts at these banquets were always drunk by the Soviet representatives out of tiny glasses, and Stalin had never varied from this practice. But now I thought I would take him on a step. So I filled a small-sized claret glass with brandy for him and another for myself. I looked at him significantly. We both drained our glasses at a stroke and gazed approvingly at one another. After a pause Stalin said, "If you find it impossible to give us a fortified position in the Marmara, could we not have a base at Dedeagach?" I contented myself with saying, "I will always support Russia in her claim to the freedom of the seas all the year round."

Next day, July 24, after our plenary meeting had ended and we all got up from the round table and stood about in twos and threes before dispersing, I saw the President go up to Stalin, and the two conversed alone with only their interpreters. I was perhaps five yards away, and I watched with the closest attention the momentous talk. I knew what the President was going to do. What was vital to measure was its effect on Stalin.

I can see it all as if it were yesterday. He seemed to be delighted. A new bomb! Of extraordinary power! Probably decisive on the whole Japanese war! What a bit of luck! This was my impression at the moment, and I was sure he had no idea of the significance of what he was being told. Evidently in his intense toils and stresses the atomic bomb had played no part. If he had had the slightest idea of the revolution in world affairs which was in progress his reactions would have been obvious. Nothing would have been easier than for him to say, "Thank you so much for telling me about your new bomb. I of course have no technical knowledge. May I send my expert in these nuclear sciences to see your expert to-morrow morning?" But his face remained gay and genial and the talk between these two potentates soon came to an end. As we were waiting for our cars I found myself near Truman. "How did it go?" I asked. "He never asked a question," he replied.

ON the morning of the 25th the Conference met again. This was the last meeting I attended. I urged once more that Poland's western frontier could not be settled without taking into account the million and a quarter Germans who were still in the area, and the President emphasised that any Peace Treaty could only be ratified with the advice and consent of the Senate. We must, he said, find a solution which he could honestly recommend to the American people. I said that if the Poles were allowed to assume the position of a fifth occupying Power without arrangements being made for spreading the food produced in Germany equally over the whole German population, and without our agreeing about reparations or war booty, the Conference would have failed.

I flew home that afternoon. My wife met me at Northolt, and we all dined quietly together. Excellent arrangements had been made by Captain Pim and the staff of the Map Room to present a continuous tale of election results as they came in next day. The latest view of the Conservative Central Office was that we should retain a substantial majority. I had not burdened myself unduly with the subject while occupied with the grave business of the Conference. On the whole I accepted the view of the party managers, and went to bed in the belief that the British people would wish me to continue my work. My hope was that it would be possible to reconstitute the National Coalition Government in the proportions of the new House of Commons. Thus slumber.

However, just before dawn I woke suddenly with a sharp stab of almost physical pain. A hitherto subconscious conviction that we were beaten broke forth and dominated my mind. All the pressure of great events, on and against which I had mentally so long maintained my "flying speed," would cease and I should fall. The power to shape the future would be denied me. The knowledge and experience I had gathered, the authority and goodwill I had gained in so many countries, would vanish. I was discontented at the prospect, and turned over at once to sleep again. I did not wake till nine o'clock, and when I went into the Map Room the first results had begun to come in. They were, as I now expected, unfavourable. By noon it was clear that the Socialists would have a majority. At luncheon my wife said to me, "It may well be a blessing in disguise." I replied, "At the moment it seems quite effectively disguised."

IN ordinary circumstances I should have felt free to take a few days to wind up the affairs of the Government in the usual manner. Constitutionally I could have awaited the meeting of Parliament in a few days' time, and taken my dismissal from the House of Commons. This would have enabled me to present before resignation the unconditional surrender of Japan to the nation. The need for Britain being immediately represented with proper authority at the Conference, where all the great issues we had discussed were now to come to a head, made all delay contrary to the public interest. Moreover, the verdict of the electors had been so overwhelmingly expressed that I did not wish to remain even for an hour responsible for their affairs. At seven o'clock therefore, having asked for an audience, I drove to the Palace, tendered my resignation to the King, and advised His Majesty to send for Mr. Attlee.

I issued to the nation the following message, with which this account may close:

26 July 45

The decision of the British people has been recorded in the votes counted to-day. I have therefore laid down the charge which was placed upon me in darker times. I regret that I have not been permitted to finish the work against Japan. For this however all plans and preparations have been made, and the results may come much quicker than we have hitherto been entitled to expect. Immense responsibilities abroad and at home fall upon the new Government, and we must all hope that they will be successful in bearing them. It only remains for me to express to the British people, for whom I have acted in these perilous years, my profound gratitude for the unflinching, unswerving support which they have given me during my task, and for the many expressions of kindness which they have shown towards their servant.

Finis

On the flaming battlefield of Iwo Jima, painted by a Japanese artist, enemy soldiers fire on Americans from behind a wrecked U.S. plane

THE LAST ACT

The Black and Bloody Sands of Iwo Jima

To Iwo Jima, a desolate rock 758 miles from Tokyo, came another great American armada on February 19, 1945. At the beaches, 30,000 Marines found little opposition —their chief obstacle was the coarse black volcanic sand into which they sank to the ankles and in which wheels could get little traction. Men, tanks and bulldozers got ashore in good order, and it began to look as if, for once, the pre-invasion bombardment—72 consecutive days of it from air and sea—had knocked out a Japanese island.

Then the firing began. The Japanese were snug in bomb-proof shelters amid the network of underground forts, tunnels and trenches they had been digging into the soft black rock for many months. When the Marines captured a blockhouse and advanced beyond it, they might find out later that the Japanese had slipped back in by underground passages and were firing into their rear. Men might dig in for the night and be wakened by blasts beneath them as the Japanese fired heavy guns or blew themselves up in hollowed-out hills.

The U.S. needed Iwo because its airfields could support the B-29 raids from the Marianas on Japan. The Japanese could not afford to lose it for the same reason. Both sides had to fight it out with mortar, grenade, flame thrower and bayonet until one side was annihilated. Of 21,000 Japanese all but 1,083 committed suicide or were killed. Of 84,000 Americans, 26,038 were killed or wounded.

Flag raising atop Mount Suribachi, the highest point on Iwo, is recorded in this picture by Joe Rosenthal, which was widely published around the world and has since been reproduced in stamps and statuary.

Iwo from the air is here seen in its entirety: Mount Suribachi (*foreground*), the beaches, the airfields and the rising ground beyond, where Japanese soldiers were still fighting when this picture was taken.

Demolition team (*opposite*) crouches as it detonates a charge to blast the Japanese out of a cave. It was terrain like this that held up the Americans for 26 days before they could mop up Iwo Jima.

The High Cost of the Final Island

Blinded and bloodstained on Okinawa, the soldier praying below was one of the 49,000 Americans killed or wounded in what proved to be the last major land battle of the Pacific war. When LIFE Photographer W. Eugene Smith took this picture, U.S. troops were on soil which was part of the enemy homeland—only 350 miles from the main islands of Japan. There a Japanese army of more than 100,000

men was dug in with plenty of weapons and all the lessons learned from all the previous disasters in the Pacific war.

On April 1, 1945, in the biggest amphibious military operation in the Pacific, 542,000 Americans converged on Okinawa. Suicide planes damaged but did not cripple the invasion fleet. On shore, the enemy made no attempt to defend the beaches. But throughout the southern half of the island, they had built a massive defense system of a now familiar design, using every ridge, gully, cave and ancient Okinawan tomb as fortresses. The Americans took almost three months to wipe out the Japanese and clear the island. The U.S. thereupon began making arrangements for the invasion of Japan itself which was scheduled for November and would cost, it was believed, a million men.

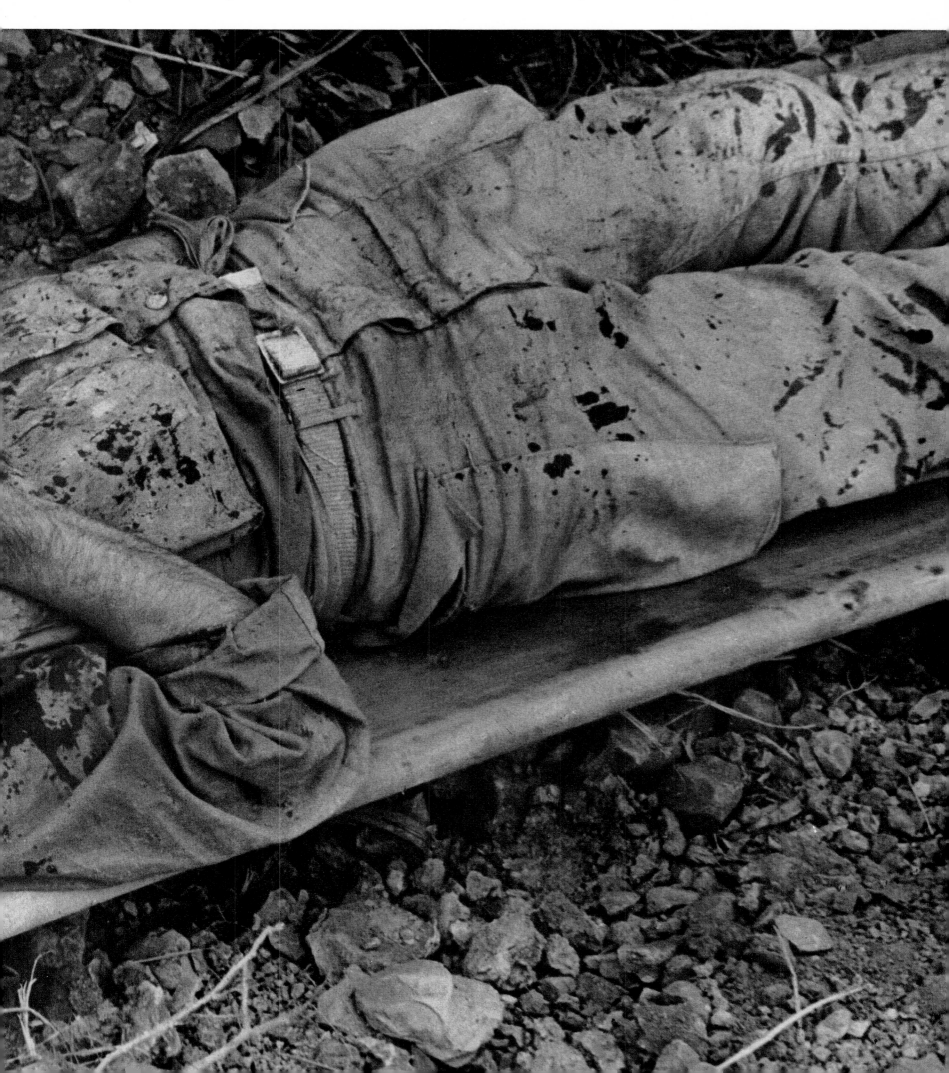

The Massive Blow
from the Sea

While its army was being broken piecemeal on a dozen scattered islands, Japan's home front was throttled by the U.S. Navy. The two mighty forces illustrated here—submarines and fast carrier groups—between them cut all the supply lines on which the island empire depended. They sank 8,900,000 tons of shipping—the equivalent of everything Japan possessed before the war and three-fourths of what she had built or captured since.

By the summer of 1945, Japanese supplies had been cut dangerously low. When they sent out the 45,000-ton *Yamato*—the biggest battleship in the world—to break up the U.S. invasion fleet off Okinawa, the Japanese could load it with only enough oil for a one-way journey. As it turned out, this was too much. The *Yamato* was sunk by carrier planes before it had gone half the distance to Okinawa.

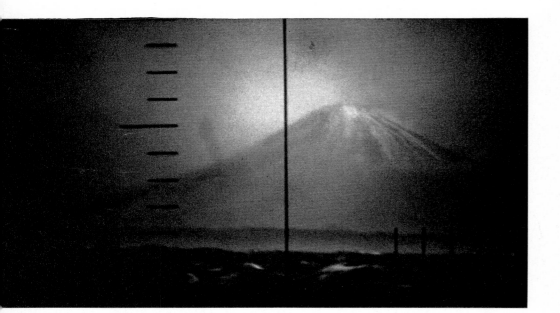

Periscope views of Mount Fuji (*top*) and a sinking Japanese destroyer (*bottom*) recall the far-ranging activities of the 226 big, hardy American submarines which harried the Japanese throughout the war.

Battle line of the U.S. Navy heads menacingly for Japan. The task forces that roamed the Pacific were formed around carriers of the light *Independence* class (*foreground*), built on cruiser hulls, and the heavier

Essex class (*second in line*), designed as carriers from the outset. They were made virtually immune from enemy attack by their own fighters and the antiaircraft barrage put up by their escorting battleships (*rear*).

They fueled at sea from tankers, and floating workshops repaired damage, so they could spend months on the ocean, switching from target to target before the Japanese had time to recover from the last blow.

A kamikaze plane, its pilot seeking honor in death, heads for the deck of the new U.S. carrier *Hornet*. This plane missed, as did every other that attacked the *Hornet* during its 52 days of action. The kamikaze (divine wind) units were Japan's last attempt to win the war, by exploiting her only remaining resource: the willingness of her young men to kill themselves for their country. They were enrolled by the

thousands, received rudimentary flight training and, in obsolete planes with a 550-pound bomb aboard, took off to attack the enemy. Less than one in five kamikazes got through the screen of fighters and antiaircraft fire around the Allied fleets, but the 475 that did caused tremendous damage. At Okinawa alone, 42 ships were sunk and 216 damaged— the greatest losses ever suffered by the U.S. Navy in a single battle.

573

Doom in the Skies over Japan

The U.S. Air Force first tried, with not much success, to bomb Japan from Chinese bases. When Guam and Saipan fell, the B-29s moved there. But the great distance (1,500 miles to Tokyo), bad weather and inaccurate bombing kept the attacks from doing much damage until the night of March 9, 1945. Then, in a bold new tactic, 334 B-29s came in at low level and set fire to a fourth of all the wood-and-paper buildings of Tokyo. Steadily thereafter the bombers roamed through Japanese skies. The statistics of destruction were as fearful as those in Germany: 330,-000 civilians dead, 40 per cent of 66 cities turned to ashes. Japan's rulers could no longer pretend that victory was

possible. High officials began to plan for surrender. But the fanatical militarists who had led Japan into war still thought they could win a decisive battle in the homeland. They were preparing 9,000 kamikaze planes to meet any Allied invasion fleet. "Even though we may have to eat grass, swallow dirt and lie in the fields," said the War Ministry, "we shall fight on to the bitter end."

The debate was still raging in Tokyo when on the morning of August 6, an American B-29, nicknamed *Enola Gay* after the pilot's mother, appeared in the clear summer sky over Hiroshima. At 8:15 it released a device which in a few seconds destroyed the city and abruptly closed the debate.

Shower of incendiaries falls from B-29s over Yokohama. By spring of 1945, U.S. air supremacy was so complete that most B-29s were stripped of guns and ammunition to give more space for bombs.

Mushroom over Nagasaki (*opposite*) is left by the second atomic bomb to be used in war. Like the first one, dropped three days before at Hiroshima, it had the explosive force of 20,000 tons of TNT.

'One thing was common to everyone I saw— complete silence'

So wrote a doctor in Hiroshima of the hour or so after the blast of the atom bomb, when he was stumbling, half-naked and bleeding, to his hospital. Among the dazed survivors was a Japanese photographer who—within 10 minutes after the explosion—took the remarkable picture at the left, which he shot on inferior wartime film and washed in a creek near the city. The people of Hiroshima did not know what had hit them: they called it simply *pikadon* (flash-boom). All they saw was their city destroyed in the twinkling of an eye and the dead and dying spread on the ground "like so many codfish spread for drying." Days passed before they learned that their tragedy, which shocked the Japanese government at long last into surrender, marked the opening of the atomic age of mankind.

The surrender of General Yoshijiro Umezu, the Japanese Chief of Staff, on board the U.S. battleship *Missouri* in Tokyo Bay, under the eyes of General MacArthur and a line of admirals and generals representing all the Allies who had fought in the war against Japan. Thus, at 9:08 on the morning of September 2, ended the Second World War.

Her Majesty's First Minister, 1953

EPILOGUE

The Postwar Years

THE publication of my War Memoirs in an abridged form gives me an opportunity to look back and express my views on some of the major events of the postwar years. When I left Potsdam on the 25th of July, 1945, I certainly expected that the election figures would leave me a reasonable majority, and it was startling to be confronted with the facts. Entirely absorbed as I had been in the prosecution of the war and the situation at its victorious close, I did not understand what had taken place in the British Isles. Otherwise, I thought and still think I could have arranged things differently. Above all, the opinion in the mass of the Army, after so many signs of good will, was a great surprise to me. The election results were an even greater surprise to Europe and America, and indeed to the U.S.S.R. They naturally thought that the steadfastness of the British peoples, having survived the grim ordeals of 1940 and having come triumphantly through the five years' struggle, would remain unshaken, and that there would be no change of Government.

During the course of the Conference at Potsdam I had not so far sought to come to grips with Russia. Since Yalta she had behaved in an astonishing fashion. I had earnestly hoped that the Americans would not withdraw from the wide territories in Central Europe they had conquered before we met. This was the one card that the Allies held when the fighting stopped by which to arrange a level settlement. Britain sought nothing for herself, but I was sure she would view the vast advance which Russia was making in all directions as far exceeding what was fair. The Americans seemed quite unconscious of the situation, and the satellite states, as they came to be called, were occupied by Russian troops.

Berlin was already in their hands, though Montgomery could have taken it had he been permitted. Vienna was Russian-held, and representatives of the Allies, even as individuals, were denied access to this key capital. As for the Balkans, Bulgaria and Romania had already been conquered. Yugoslavia quivered under Tito, her famous patriotic leader. The Russians had occupied Prague with, as it seemed, the approval of the Americans. They held Poland, whose western boundary, it was agreed, should be moved into the heart of Europe at the expense of Germany. All these steps had in fact been taken by the Russians while their armies were still advancing. Yet the American view seemed to be that all this was a necessary part of the process of holding down Germany, and that the great national object of the United States was not to get drawn into siding too closely with Britain against Russia.

When the winter came along I went to the United States and remained in that country for several months. I visited the White House and the State Department. While there I received an invitation to address the Westminster College in Fulton, Missouri, in March 1946. Mr. Truman had said he would himself preside. This was several months ahead, and I kept myself as fully informed as was possible. I made inquiries at the White House and the State Department in order to learn whether certain topics would cause embarrassment, and having been assured that I could say what I liked I devoted myself to the careful preparation of a speech.

Meanwhile the dire situation with which the insatiable appetites of Russia and of international Communism were confronting us was beginning at last to make a strong impression in American circles. I now showed the notes I had prepared to Mr. Byrnes, then Secretary of State, and found that he was very much in agreement with me. The President invited me to travel with him in his train the long night's journey to Fulton. We had an enjoyable game of poker. That was the only topic which I remember. However, as I was quite sure that his Secretary of State had imparted my general line of thought to Mr. Truman, and he himself seemed quite happy about it, I decided to go ahead. One always has to be very careful about speeches one makes in other people's countries. This is from what I said: "A shadow has fallen upon the scenes so lately lighted by the Allied victory. Nobody knows what Soviet Russia and its Communist international organisation intends to do. . . . From Stettin in the Baltic to Trieste in the Adriatic, an iron curtain has descended across the Continent. Behind that line lie all the capitals of the ancient states of Central and Eastern Europe. Warsaw, Berlin, Prague, Vienna, Budapest, Belgrade, Bucharest and Sofiya, all these famous cities and the populations around them lie in what I must call the Soviet Sphere, and all are subject, in one form or another, not only to Soviet influence but to a very high and, in many cases, increasing measure of control from Moscow. Athens alone—Greece with its immortal glories—is free to decide its future at an election under British, American and French observation. The Russian-dominated Polish Government has been encouraged to make enormous and wrongful inroads upon Germany, and mass expulsions of millions of Germans on a scale grievous and undreamed-of are now taking place. The Communist parties, which were very small in all these Eastern States of Europe, have been raised to pre-eminence

Iron Curtain dropped between victorious Allies after war as Russians—disregarding wartime agreements—gradually replaced coalition governments with Communist cliques in the areas they occupied (*brown*). East Austria later rejoined west Austria to form a free state.

and power far beyond their numbers and are seeking everywhere to obtain totalitarian control. Police governments are prevailing in nearly every case, and so far, except in Czechoslovakia, there is no true democracy.

"Whatever conclusions may be drawn from these facts —and facts they are—this is certainly not the Liberated Europe we fought to build up. Nor is it one which contains the essentials of permanent peace."

The audience listened with great attention, and the President and Mr. Byrnes both expressed their approval. The newspapers, however, were very varied in their comments. When the news reached Russia, it was ill received, and both Stalin and the *Pravda* reacted as might be expected. The *Pravda* denounced me as "an anti-Soviet warmonger," and said I was trying to destroy the United Nations. And Stalin in a newspaper interview accused me of calling for a war against the Soviet Union and compared me with Hitler. Questions were also asked in the House of Commons, to which Mr. Attlee, now Prime Minister, replied that the Government was not called upon to express any opinion on a speech delivered in another country by a private individual.

I spent the early autumn of 1946 painting in a lovely villa by the Lake of Geneva with Mont Blanc over the water in the background. I paid a very pleasant visit to Zurich University, and made them a speech about the tragedy of Europe and the plight to which she had been reduced, and I urged the foundation of a kind of United States of Europe.

"I was very glad to read in the newspapers two days ago that my friend President Truman had expressed his interest and sympathy with this great design. There is no reason why a regional organisation should in any way conflict with the world organisation of the United Nations. On the contrary, I believe that the larger synthesis will only survive if it is founded upon coherent natural groupings. . . .

"I am now going to say something that will astonish you. The first step in the re-creation of the European family must be a partnership between France and Germany. In this way only can France recover the moral leadership of Europe. There can be no revival of Europe without a spiritually great France and a spiritually great Germany. The structure of the United States of Europe, if well and truly built, will be such as to make the material strength of a single state less important. Small nations will count as much as large ones and gain their honour by their contribution to the common cause. . . . But I must give you a warning. Time may be short. At present there is a breathing space. The cannon have ceased firing. The fighting has stopped; but the dangers have not stopped. If we are to form the United States of Europe or whatever name or form it may take, we must begin now."

Thus ran my thoughts in 1946. To tortured France, lately occupied and humiliated, the spectacle of close association with her finally vanquished executioner seemed at first unthinkable. By degrees, however, the flow of European fraternity was restored in French veins, and natural Gallic pliant good sense overcame the bitterness of the past.

I HAVE always held, and hold, the valiant Russian people in high regard. But their shadow loomed disastrously over the postwar scene. There was no visible limit to the harm they might do. Intent on victory over the Axis Powers, Britain and America had laid no sufficient plans for the fate and future of Occupied Europe. We had gone to war in defence not only of the independence of smaller countries but to proclaim and endorse the individual rights and freedoms on which this greater morality is based. Soviet Russia had other and less disinterested aims. Her grip tightened on the territories her armies had overrun.

In all the satellite states behind the Iron Curtain, coalition governments had been set up, including Communists. It was hoped that democracy in some form would be preserved. But in one country after another the Communists seized the key posts, harried and suppressed the other political parties, and drove their leaders into exile. There were trials and purges. Romania, Hungary, and Bulgaria were soon engulfed. At Yalta and Potsdam I had fought hard for Poland, but it was in vain. In Czechoslovakia a sudden coup was carried out by the Communist Ministers, which sharply alerted world opinion. Freedom was crushed within and free intercourse with the West was forbidden. Thanks largely to Britain, Greece remained precariously independent. With British and later American aid, she fought a long civil war against the insurgent Communists. When all had been said and done, and after the long agonies and efforts of the Second World War, it seemed that half Europe had merely exchanged one despot for another.

Today, these points seem commonplace. The prolonged and not altogether unsuccessful struggle to halt the all-destroying tide of Russian and Russian-inspired incursion has become part of our daily lives. Indeed, as always with a good cause, it has sometimes been necessary to temper enthusiasm and to disregard opportunism. But it was not easy at the time to turn from the contemplation of a great and exhausting victory over one tyranny to the prospect of a tedious and expensive campaign against another.

The United Nations Organisation was still very young, but already it was clear that its defects might prove grave enough to vitiate the purposes for which it was created. At any rate it could not provide quickly and effectively the union and armed forces which Free Europe and the United States needed for self-preservation. At Fulton, Missouri, I had suggested that the United Nations Organisation should forthwith be equipped with an international armed force. But for the immediate future and the long term I had urged

the continuation of the special Anglo-American relationship which has been one of the main themes of my political life. The next three years were to see the unfolding of a design that approached but has not yet attained this ideal.

I do not wish to claim a monopoly of credit for these conceptions. One of the advantages of being in Opposition is that one can outdistance in imagination those whose fortune it is to put plans into practical effect. The British Government, much inspired by the stouthearted and wise Mr. Ernest Bevin, took the lead in rebuilding something of the Concert of Europe, at least in what was left of Europe. Initial thoughts were mainly of the dangers of a resurrected Germany. In 1947 Great Britain and France signed the Treaty of Dunkerque binding each to come to the other's assistance if there was another German attack. But already the grim realities of the present were overshadowing the fears of the past.

After months of diplomatic activity the Brussels Treaty was signed in 1948. France, Britain, the Netherlands, Belgium and Luxembourg undertook to assist one another against aggression, from whatever quarter it might come. Germany was not mentioned. Moreover, the beginnings of a military organisation were set up under the chairmanship of Field-Marshal Montgomery to assess the resources available for defence and to draw up a plan with what little was available. This became known as the Western Union. All this I endorsed, but vehemently hoped that the United States, without whose aid they would be woefully incomplete, could soon be brought into the association. We were fortunate at the time to have in the American Secretary of State the far-sighted and devoted General Marshall, with whom we had worked in closest comradeship and confidence in the war years. Within the limits imposed by Congressional and public opinion, Mr. Truman and he sought to add weight to what was being done in Europe.

THE efforts on both sides of the Atlantic bore fruit, and in April 1949 the North Atlantic Treaty was signed, in which for the first time in history the United States bound herself, subject always to the constitutional prerogative of Congress, to aid her allies if they were attacked. The European signatories, besides the Brussels Treaty Powers, included Norway, Denmark, Iceland, Italy and Portugal. Canada also acceded to the Treaty, and thereby gave additional proof to the faith we in Britain have always entertained of her friendship and loyalty.

The work that followed was complex and it resulted in the setting up of the North Atlantic Treaty Organisation, headed by a military planning staff under General Eisenhower at Versailles. From the efforts of the Supreme Headquarters Atlantic Powers Europe, or SHAPE as it was called, there gradually grew a sober confidence that invasion from the East could be met by an effective resistance. Certainly in its early stages the Atlantic Treaty achieved more by being than by doing. It gave renewed confidence to Europe, particularly to the territories near Soviet Russia and the satellites. This was marked by a recession in the Communist parties in the threatened countries, and by a resurgence of healthy national vigour in Western Germany.

The association of Germany with the Atlantic Treaty remained in the forefront of Western plans. But it was very difficult to overcome French fears of a revived German army, and the topic was a fruitful one for the misguided as well as the mischievous. Within the space of seventy years the French had been invaded three times from across the Rhine. It was hard to forget Sedan, the agonies at Verdun, the collapse in 1940, the long, grinding occupation of the Second World War, which had sundered so many loyalties, and in which Frenchman had fought Frenchman. In Britain I was conscious of a wide hostility to giving weapons, even under the strictest safeguards, to the new German Republic. But it was unlikely that a Soviet invasion of Western Europe could ever be repulsed without German help.

Many schemes were tried and failed. The French had taken the lead in the closer integration of Western Europe in civil matters, and they sponsored a scheme for a European army with a common uniform, into which German units would be merged without risk to their neighbours. I did not care for this idea. A sludgy amalgam of half a dozen nationalities would find it difficult to share common loyalties and the trust which is essential among comrades in battle. It was not for some years that the final simplicity of a direct German contribution through a national army to the strength of the West was achieved. But even today little has been done to put it into effect. I myself have never seen the disadvantage of making friends with your enemy when the war is over, with all that that implies in co-operation against an outside menace.

Side by side with these developments, many of them lying only in the paper sphere, the United States continued to manifest her determination to assist Europe, and thus herself. Long before the Atlantic Treaty was signed American aircraft were stationed in East Anglia in substantial numbers. Here was a most practical deterrent. Alas, the splendid structure of the Anglo-American Combined Chiefs of Staff, who had been the architects of so much of our victorious war planning, had been dismantled at American instigation. Nothing has subsequently equalled it, and the best of the NATO arrangements are but a poor shadow of the fraternal and closely knit organisation that formerly existed.

THE crucial test came in June 1948 when the Russians cut off Berlin from the outside world. Their object was to incorporate the whole of Berlin in the Communist state which they had promoted in Eastern Germany. It seemed that Britain, France and America must either abandon the city or try to force supply convoys in from Western Germany, as was their legitimate right. Fortunately a solution was found which avoided many perils. The Airlift began, and by February 1949 over a million tons of supplies had been flown in by American and British aircraft. This original conception was highly successful. In due course the Russians had to yield, and they were forced to abandon the blockade entirely.

Economic assistance to the allies was also vital. We in Britain had spent so much money in the war that, even if the greatest skill and economy had been exercised, we would have been very hard pressed. In spite of a huge American loan the position was getting ever more serious. The rest of Europe was also suffering in varying degrees. General Marshall gave his name to a remarkable plan for economic aid and mutual co-operation among sixteen free European countries. The benefits were offered to the Soviet bloc, but were refused. The Organisation for European and Economic Co-operation has rendered the greatest service to us all. But without the massive dollar aid provided by the American administration, in spite of some hostility on the part of Congress, Europe might well have foundered into ruin and misery in which the seeds of Communism would have grown at a deadly pace. General Marshall's decision was on the highest level of statesmanship, and it was a source of great pleasure, but not surprise, to me that my old friend should have presided in America over the two great enterprises of the Marshall Plan and the Atlantic Treaty.

AS the stark and glaring background to all our cogitations on defence lay man's final possession of the perfected means of human destruction: the atomic weapon and its monstrous child, the hydrogen bomb. In the early days of the war Britain and the United States had agreed to pool their knowledge and experiments in nuclear research, and the fruits of years of discovery by the English pioneer physicists were offered as a priceless contribution to the vast and most secret joint enterprise set on foot in the United States and Canada. Those who created the weapons possessed for a few years the monopoly of a power which might in less scrupulous hands have been used to dominate and enslave the entire world. They proved themselves worthy of their responsibilities, but secrets were soon disclosed to the Soviet Union which greatly helped Russian scientists in their researches. Henceforward most of the accepted theories of strategy were seen to be out of date, and a new undreamed-of balance of power was created, a balance based on the ownership of the means of mutual extermination.

At the end of the war I felt reasonably content that the best possible arrangement had been made in the agreement which I concluded with President Roosevelt in Quebec in 1943. Therein Britain and America affirmed that they would never use the weapon against each other, that they would not use it against third parties without each other's approval, that they would not communicate information on the subject to third parties except by mutual consent, and that they would exchange information on technical developments. I do not think that one could have asked for more.

However, in 1946 a measure was passed by the American Congress which most severely curtailed any chance of the United States providing us with information. Senator McMahon, who sponsored the Bill, was at the time unaware of the Quebec Agreement, and he informed me in 1952 that if he had seen it there would have been no McMahon Act. The British Socialist Government certainly made some sort of a protest, but they felt unable to press it home and they did not insist on the revelation of the Quebec Agreement, at least to the McMahon Committee, which would have vindicated our position and perhaps saved us many years of wearisome and expensive research and development. Thus, deprived of our share of the knowledge to which we had a most certain right, Britain had to fall back on her own resources. The Socialist Government thereupon devoted vast sums to research, but it was not until 1952 that we were able to explode our first atomic bomb. The relative stages of research and development remain unknown, but experimental explosions are not the sole criterion, and we may perhaps in some ways claim to have outdistanced even the United States. But research is one thing, production and possession another.

It was in this, then, the American possession or preponderance of nuclear weapons, that the surest foundation of our hopes for peace lay. The armies of the Western Powers were of comparative insignificance when faced with the innumerable Russian divisions that could be deployed from the Baltic to the Yugoslav frontier. But the certain knowledge that an advance on land would unleash the devouring destruction of strategic air attack was and is the most certain of deterrents.

For a time, when the United States was the sole effective possessor of nuclear weapons, there had been a chance of a general and permanent settlement with the Soviet Union. But it is not the nature of democracies to use their advantages in threatening or dictatorial ways. Certainly the state of opinion that prevailed in those years would not have tolerated anything in the way of rough words to our late ally, though this might well have forestalled many unpleasant developments. Instead the United States, with our support, chose a most reasonable and liberal attitude to the problems of controlling the use of nuclear weapons. Soviet opposition to efficient methods of supervision brought this to nothing. In former days no country could hope to build up in secret military forces vast enough to overwhelm a neighbour. Now the means of destruction of many millions can be concealed in the space of a few cubic yards.

EVERY aspect of military and political planning was altered by these developments. The vast bases needed to sustain the armies of the two world wars have become the most vulnerable of targets. All the workshops and stores on the Suez Canal, which had fed the Eighth Army in the desert, could vanish in a flash at the stroke of a single aircraft. Harbours, even when guarded by anti-aircraft guns and fighter planes, could become the grave-yard of the fleets they had once protected. The evacuation of noncombatants from the cities was a practical proposition even in the days of highly developed bombing methods in the last war. Now, desirable though they may be, such measures are a mere palliative to the flaring ruin of nuclear attack. The whole structure of defence had to be altered to meet the new situation. Conventional forces were still needed to keep order in our possessions, and to fight what people call the small wars, but we could not afford enough of them because nuclear weapons and the means of delivering them were so expensive.

The nuclear age transformed the relations between the Great Powers. For a time I doubted whether the Kremlin accurately realised what would happen to their country in the event of war. It seemed possible that they neither knew the full effect of the atomic missiles nor how efficient were the means of delivering them. It even occurred to me that an announced but peaceful aerial demonstration over the main Soviet cities, coupled with the outlining to the Soviet leaders of some of our newest inventions, would produce in them a more friendly and sober attitude. Of course such a gesture could not have been accompanied by any formal demands, or it would have taken on the appearance of a threat and ultimatum. But Russian production of these weapons and the remarkable strides of their air force have long since removed the point of this idea. Their military and political leaders must now be well aware of what each of us could do to the other.

HOPES of more friendly contacts with the Soviet Union remained much in my mind, and the death of Stalin in March 1953 seemed to bring a chance. I was again Prime Minister. I regarded Stalin's death as a milestone in Russian history. His tyranny had brought fearful suffering to his own country and to much else of the world. In their fight against Hitler, the Russian peoples had built up an immense good will in the West, not least of all in the United States. All this had been impaired. In the dark politics of the Kremlin, none could tell who would take Stalin's place. Fourteen men and 180,000,000 people lost their master.

The Soviet leaders must not be judged too harshly. Three times in the space of just over a century Russia has been invaded by Europe. Borodino, Tannenberg and Stalingrad are not to be forgotten easily. Napoleon's onslaught is still remembered. Imperial and Nazi Germany were not forgiven. But security can never be achieved in isolation. Stalin tried not only to shield the Soviet Republics behind an iron curtain, military, political and cultural. He also attempted to construct an outpost line of satellite states, deep in Central Europe, harshly controlled from Moscow, subservient to the economic needs of the Soviet Union and forbidden all contact or communion with the free world, or even with each other. No one can believe that this will last for ever. Hungary has paid a terrible forfeit. But to all thinking men, certain hopeful features of the present situation must surely be clear. The doctrine of Communism is slowly being separated from the Russian military machine. Nations will continue to rebel against the Soviet Colonial Empire, not because it is Communist, but because it is alien and oppressive.

An arms race, even conducted with nuclear weapons and guided missiles, will bring no security or even peace of mind to the great powers which dominate the land masses of Asia and North America, or to the countries which lie between them. I make no plea for disarmament. Disarmament is a consequence and a manifestation of free intercourse between free peoples. It is the mind which controls the weapon, and it is to the minds of the peoples of Russia and her associates that the free nations should address themselves.

But after Stalin's death it seemed that a milder climate might prevail. At all events it merited investigating, and I so expressed myself in the House of Commons on the 11th of May, 1953. An entirely informal conference between the heads of the leading powers might succeed where repeated acrimonious exchanges at lower levels had failed. I made it plain that this could not be accompanied by any relaxation of the comradeship and preparations of the free nations, for any slackening of our defence efforts would paralyse every beneficial tendency towards peace. This is true today. What I sought was never fully accomplished. Nevertheless for a time a gentler breeze seemed to blow upon our affairs. Further opportunities will doubtless present themselves, and they must not be neglected.

It is not my purpose to attempt to assign blame in any quarter for the many disagreeable things that have occurred since 1945. Certainly those who were responsible in Great Britain for the direction of our affairs in the years that followed the war were beset by the most complex and malignant problems both at home and abroad. The methods by which they chose to solve them were often forced upon them by circumstances or by pre-determined doctrinaire policies, and their results were not always felicitous either for Britain or for the free world.

THE granting of independence to the Indian subcontinent had long been in the forefront of British political thought. I had contributed a good deal to the subject in the years between the wars. Supported by seventy Conservative members, I had fought it in its early stages with all my strength. When I was at the head of the Coalition Government I was induced to modify my former views. Undoubtedly we came out of the desperate world struggle committed to Dominion status for India, including the right to secede from the Commonwealth.

I thought however that the method of setting up the new Government should have given the great majority of the Indian people the power and the right to choose freely for themselves. I believed that a constitutional conference in which all the real elements of strength in India could participate would have shown us the way to produce a truly representative self-governing India which would adhere to the British Empire. The "untouchables," the Rajahs, the loyalists, of whom hundreds of millions existed, and many other different, vital, living interests, would all have had their share in the new scheme. It must be remembered that in the last year of the war we had had a revolt of the extremists in the Indian Congress Party which was put down without difficulty, and with very little loss of life. The British Socialist Party took a violently factional view. They believed that the advantage lay in the granting of self-government within the shortest space of time. And they gave it without hesitation—almost identifiably—to the forces which we had vanquished so easily. Within two years of the end of the war they had achieved their purpose. On August 18, 1947, Indian independence was declared.

All efforts to preserve the unity of India had broken down, and Pakistan became a separate state. Four hundred million inhabitants of the subcontinent, mainly divided between Moslem and Hindu, flung themselves at one another. Two centuries of British rule in India were followed by greater bloodshed and loss of life than had ever occurred during our ameliorating tenure. In spite of the efforts of the Boundary Commission, the lines drawn between India and Pakistan were inevitably and devastatingly cruel to the areas through which the new frontiers passed. The result was a series of massacres arising out of the interchange of Moslem and Hindu population which may have run into four or five hundred thousand men, women and children. The vast majority of these were harmless people whose only fault lay in their religion.

Fortunately, at the head of the larger of the two new states erected on this bloody foundation was a man of singular qualities. Nehru had languished for years in jail or other forms of confinement. He now emerged as the leader of a tiny minority of the foes of British rule, largely free alike from two of the worst faults of human nature, Hate and Fear. Gandhi, who had so long led the cause of Indian independence, was murdered by a fanatic shortly after Nehru's installation as head of the Government. Jinnah presided over the Moslem state, Pakistan. We are on easy terms with the two Republics which have come into being. Their leaders attend the meetings of the Commonwealth, and their power for good or evil in Asia and the world is undeniable. I will not attempt to prejudge the future.

In the year of Indian independence Burma was also severed from the Commonwealth. It had been the main theatre of land operations in the war in the Far East, and we had put forward a major effort to recover it from the Japanese, who had driven us out in 1942. The Nationalist elements, most of whom at some stage in the war to achieve their aims had collaborated with the Japanese invaders against the Allies, were established in the government of the country. Their control was far from full, and to this day the Burmese Government's writ runs but incompletely through its territories. They too, however, are a firmly established entity with whom our relations are friendly, and where the long and honourable tradition of British authority and its legacies of justice and order have borne fruit.

Both in India and Burma the conflict between Communism and the Free World was of relative unimportance in the immediate postwar years. Certainly Russia rejoiced at every sign of the diminution of our influence in the world and sought by all the means in her power to expedite and bedevil the birth of the new nations. She did great mischief in Indochina and Malaya. On the whole, however, her interest was more concentrated on China, where amid confusion and slaughter a new pattern was emerging. The regime of Chiang Kai-shek, our friend and ally in the war, was gradually losing its hold. The United States attempted by every means short of armed intervention to halt the advance of Communism.

BUT the Chinese Government carried within it the seeds of its own destruction. In spite of many years of resistance to the Japanese, the corruption and inefficiency of its sprawling system encouraged and supported the advance of the Communist armies. The process was slow, but by the end of 1949 all was over. The "People's Government," as it is called, henceforth ruled in Peking, and controlled the whole Chinese mainland. Chiang Kai-shek fled to Formosa, where his independence was secured by the American fleet and Air Force. Thus the world's most populous state passed into Communist hands and it will no doubt wield an effective force in world affairs. In this period the influence of China was mainly exerted in Korea, and in Indochina. The wrangles over her admission to the United Nations have demonstrated one of the many weaknesses of that organisation, and China's traditional friendship with America has been suspended.

Communist attempts to harass the West, to exploit Nationalist feeling in Asia and to seize upon exposed salients culminated in the peninsula of Korea. Previously their efforts had been less direct. In Indochina the principal opponent of the French, Ho Chi Minh, had indeed been Moscow-trained, but material support for his guerrillas had not been on a large scale. In Malaya comparatively few terrorists, by murdering planters and loyal Malays and Chinese, had tied down disproportionate forces to restore order. But they, too, in general owed only their training, ideology and moral support to the Communist States.

At Cairo, in 1943, President Roosevelt, Chiang Kai-shek and I had recorded our determination that Korea should be free and independent. At the end of the war the country had been liberated from the Japanese and occupied by American troops to the south and Russian to the north. Two separate Korean states were set up, and relations between them became increasingly strained and embittered. The 38th parallel formed an uneasy frontier, and the two States were very much like Eastern and Western Germany. Efforts by the United Nations to reunite the country had been frustrated by Soviet opposition. Tension and border incidents grew.

On June 25, 1950, North Korean forces invaded South Korea and advanced with great rapidity. The United Nations called on the aggressors to withdraw, and asked all member states to help. That the Soviet veto in the Security Council did not on this occasion render impotent the United Nations' intentions was due to good fortune. The faults of the system remained to be exploited again and again in later years. On this occasion the United Nations merely provided the framework in which the effective action of the United States was cast.

These bare facts encompass a momentous and historic decision by President Truman. Within the briefest interval of the news of the invasion, he had reached the conclusion that only immediate intervention by the armed forces of the United States could meet the situation. They were the nearest to the scene as well as by far the most numerous, but this was not the point. As he has said in his memoirs, "I felt certain that if South Korea was allowed to fall, Communist leaders would be emboldened to override nations closer to our own shores. If this were allowed to go unchallenged it would mean a third world war." His celerity, wisdom and courage in this crisis make him worthy, in my estimation, to be numbered among the greatest of American Presidents.

In Britain the Government endorsed and sustained the Americans, and made offer of naval units. By December British ground forces were also in Korea. In the House of Commons on the 5th of July the Opposition supported Mr. Attlee, then Prime Minister, and I myself as its leader said that I was "fully able to associate myself with . . . his broad conclusion that the action which had been taken by the United States gives on the whole the best chance of maintaining the peace of the world." The Left Wing of the Socialist Party, true to their traditions, alone stood out from the courage and wisdom of what was being done. I

From "The Aftermath"

by Winston S. Churchill, 1929

Mankind . . . has got into its hands for the first time the tools by which it can unfailingly accomplish its own extermination. . . . Death stands at attention, obedient, expectant, ready to serve, ready to shear away the peoples *en masse*; ready, if called on, to pulverise, without hope of repair, what is left of civilisation. He awaits only the word of command. He awaits it from a frail, bewildered being, long his victim, now—for one occasion only—his Master.

---

will not dwell on the pendulum of military success and failure in Korea. The outcome can scarcely be thought of as satisfactory. However, South Korea remained independent and free, the aggressor suffered a costly repulse and, most important of all, the United States showed that she was not afraid to use armed force in defence of freedom, even in so remote an outpost.

Elsewhere in the continent of Asia the Western empires crumbled. Our allies the Dutch had been hustled out of the East Indies, which they had made a model of effective administration. The French endured years of frustrating and debilitating warfare in Indochina, where casualties absorbed more officers in each year than the output of their military college at St. Cyr. Communist armies, mightily reinforced from China, gradually won control of the north of the country. In spite of heroic episodes of resistance, the French were compelled to abandon this great and populous area. After long and painstaking negotiation something was saved from the wreckage of their hopes. Three states, South Vietnam, Laos and Cambodia, came into existence, their independence assured, their future uncertain. North Vietnam, like North Korea, maintained a Communist Government. Partition was once more the answer in the conflict of Communist and Western interests. All these new countries were rent by factions within and overshadowed by their gigantic neighbour to the north.

The changes in Asia are immeasurable. Perhaps they were inevitable. If a note of regret is to be found in this brief account, let it not be supposed that it is in hostility to the right of Asian peoples to self-determination, or a reflection on their present standing and integrity. But the means by which the present situation was reached give pause. Was so much bloodshed necessary? Without the haste engendered by foreign pressure and the loss of influence inherent in our early defeats in the Far Eastern war, might progress to the same end have been happier, and the end itself more stable?

† † †

A great part of the Second World War had run its course to defend the land bridge where Africa and Asia meet, to maintain our oil supplies and guard the Suez Canal. In the process the Middle Eastern countries, and notably Egypt, had enjoyed the advantage of protection from German and Italian invasion at no cost to themselves. There followed a further increase in the number of independent states that existed in the former domains of the Ottoman Empire. The departure of the French from Syria and the Lebanon was bitter to them but inevitable. No one can claim that we ourselves have derived any advantage there. Throughout this region the world has witnessed a surge of nationalist feeling, the consequences of which have yet to run their course. From Indonesia to Morocco the Moslem peoples are in ferment. Their assertiveness has confronted the Western powers, and especially those with overseas responsibilities, with problems of peculiar difficulty. Amid jubilant cries for self-government and independence, it is easy to forget the many substantial benefits that have been conferred by Western rule. It is also hard to replace the orderliness which the Colonial powers exercised over these large areas by a stable new system of sovereign states.

The most intractable of all the difficulties that faced Great Britain in these regions was Palestine. Ever since the Balfour Declaration of 1917 I have been a faithful supporter of the Zionist cause. I never felt that the Arab countries had had anything from us but fair play. To Britain, and Britain alone, they owed their very existence as nations. We created them; British money and British advisers set the pace of their advance; British arms protected them. We had, and I hope have, many loyal and courageous friends in the area. The late King Abdullah was a most wise ruler. His assassination removed a chance of a peaceful settlement of the Palestinian tumult. King Ibn Saud was a most staunch ally. In Iraq I followed with admiration the sagacious and brave conduct of Nuri es-Said, who most faithfully served his monarch and led his country on a path of wisdom, unaffected by threats from without or foreign-bought clamour at home. Unfortunately these men were exceptions.

As mandatory power Great Britain was confronted with the tortuous problem of combining Jewish immigration to their national home and safeguarding the rights of the Arab inhabitants. Few of us could blame the Jewish people for their violent views on the subject. A race that has suffered the virtual extermination of its national existence cannot be expected to be entirely reasonable. But the activities of terrorists, who tried to gain their ends by the assassination of British officials and soldiers, were an odious act of ingratitude that left a profound impression.

THERE is no country in the world less fit for a conflict with terrorism than Britain. This is not because of weakness or cowardice; it is because of restraint and virtue, and the way of life which we have lived in our successfully defended island. Stung by the murders in Palestine, abused by the Middle Eastern countries, and even by our allies, it was not unnatural that the British Government of the day should finally wash its hands of the problem and in 1948 leave the Jews to find their own salvation. The brief war that ensued dramatically dispelled the confidence of the Arab countries who closed in for an easy kill.

The infective violence of the birth of the State of Israel has sharpened the difficulties of the Middle East ever since. I look with admiration on the work done there in building up a nation, reclaiming the desert and receiving so many unfortunates from Jewish communities all over the world. But the outlook is sombre. The position of the hundreds of thousands of Arabs driven from their homes and existing precariously in the no man's land created round Israel's frontiers is cruel and dangerous. The frontiers of Israel flicker with murder and armed raids, and the Arab countries profess irreconcilable hostility to the new State. The more far-sighted Arab leaders cannot voice counsels of moderation without being howled down and threatened with assassination. It is a black and threatening scene of unlimited violence and folly. One thing is clear. Both honour and wisdom demand that the State of Israel should be preserved, and that this brave, dynamic and complex race should be allowed to live in peace with its neighbours. They can bring to the area an invaluable contribution of scientific knowledge, of industriousness and productivity. They must be given an opportunity of doing so in the interest of the whole Middle East.

BEFORE I complete this brief survey of the things that have struck me since the war, let us have a look at the United Nations. The machinery of international government may easily fail in its purpose. My idea as the end of the war approached was that the greatest minds and the greatest thoughts possessed by men should govern the world. This entailed, if all countries great and small were to be represented, that they must be graded. The spectacle presented by the United Nations is no more than a vain assertion of equality of influence and power which has no relation to the actual facts. The result is that a process of ingenious lobbying has attempted to take possession of the government of the world. I say attempted, because the vote of a country of a million or two inhabitants cannot decide or even sway the actions of powerful states.

The United Nations in its present form has to cringe to dictatorships and bully the weak. Small states have no right to speak for the whole of mankind. They must accept, and they would accept, a more intimate but lower rank. The world should be ruled by the leading men of groups of countries formed geographically. The mere process of letting the groups shape themselves and not judging by their power or their numbers would tell its own tale.

I do not intend to suggest that all the efforts and sacrifices of Britain and her Allies recorded in my War Memoirs have come to nothing and led only to a state of affairs more dangerous and gloomy than at the beginning. On the contrary, I hold strongly to the belief that we have not tried in vain. Russia is becoming a great commercial country. Her people experience every day in growing vigour those complications and palliatives of human life that will render the schemes of Karl Marx more out of date and smaller in relation to world problems than they have ever been before. The natural forces are working with greater freedom and greater opportunity to fertilise and vary the thoughts and the power of individual men and women. They are far bigger and more pliant in the vast structure of a mighty empire than could ever have been conceived by Marx in his hovel. And when war is itself fenced about with mutual extermination it seems likely that it will be increasingly postponed. Quarrels between nations, or continents, or combinations of nations there will no doubt continually be. But in the main human society will grow in many forms not comprehended by a party machine. As long therefore as the free world holds together, and especially Britain and the United States, and maintains its strength, Russia will find that Peace and Plenty have more to offer than exterminatory war. The broadening of thought is a process which acquires momentum by seeking Opportunity-for-All who claim it. And it may well be if wisdom and patience are practised that Opportunity-for-All will conquer the minds and restrain the passions of Mankind.

"When war is itself fenced about with mutual extermination . . .

. . . it seems likely that it will be increasingly postponed.''

BIKINI, 1946

PICTURE CREDITS

This list shows the sources from which the illustrations were gathered. Credits are separated from left to right by commas and semicolons, from top to bottom by dashes

Volume I

x Copyright Karsh, Ottawa from Combine
xi Studio Sun Ltd.
xii Painting by Sir William Orpen, R. A. photographed by Larry Burrows courtesy Imperial War Museum, London
4,5 Maps by K.C.&S. Studios
7 Culver Service
8,9 Wide World, The Bettmann Archive
10 Hugo Jaeger
14 Map by K.C.&S. Studios
19 through 25 Hugo Jaeger
26 Paramount Pictures
28,31 Maps by K.C.&S. Studios
32,33 Diagrams by Seymour Robins
35 through 40 Maps by K.C.&S. Studios
45 Wide World from Paramount Pictures
46 Wide World—Text and Bilder
47 Dever from Black Star
48,49 United Press International—Carl Mydans
50,51 European Picture Service; (c) Imperial War Museum, London; Dever from Black Star
52 From a painting by Richard Eurich photographed by Walter A. Curtin courtesy The Massey Collection of English Painting, The National Gallery of Canada
60 through 71 Maps by K.C.&S. Studios
73 Wide World
74 Heinrich Hoffmann—Wide World
75 Wide World
76,77 European Picture Service, Wide World—(c) The Times, London
78,79 Painting by Richard Eurich photographed by Larry Burrows by permission of The Trustees of the National Maritime Museum, Greenwich
80 Hugo Jaeger
85,87 Maps by K.C.&S. Studios
91 Diagram by K.C.&S. Studios
93 European Picture Service
94,95 Heinrich Hoffmann—Dever from Black Star
96,97 Hugo Jaeger
98 Mauritius from Black Star
99 United Press International—Heinrich Hoffmann
100 Dever from Black Star—Pix
101,102 United Press International

103 Movietone News
104 Frank Scherschel
112 Map by K.C.&S. Studios
118 Graph by K.C.&S. Studios
123 Map by K.C.&S. Studios
125 Douglas Miller
126 United Press International—Wide World
127 British Official
128 William Vandivert—British Official
129 William Vandivert
130,131 Painting by Richard Eurich photographed by Larry Burrows courtesy Imperial War Museum, London
132,133 William Vandivert, Mirrorpic from Combine
134 Wide World
135 United Press International
136,137 William Vandivert, Mirrorpic from Combine—Mirrorpic from Combine
138,139 From a painting by Leonard Rosoman photographed by Studio Sun Ltd. courtesy Imperial War Museum, London; painting by Henry Moore photographed by Larry Burrows courtesy The Trustees of the Tate Gallery, War Artists Commission Collection
140 Hugo Jaeger
147 Graph by K.C.&S. Studios
150,151 Diagrams by Seymour Robins
153 William Vandivert
154,155 Painting by Richard Eurich photographed by Larry Burrows, Crown Copyright reserved, courtesy of The Trustees of the Tate Gallery
156,157 William L. White, United Press International
158 Charles Steinheimer from Black Star
159 Margaret Bourke-White
160 Hugo Jaeger
162 through 175 Maps by K.C.&S. Studios
177 From a painting by John Berry photographed by Larry Burrows courtesy Imperial War Museum, London
178,179 Painting by Edward Ardizzone photographed by Zoltan Wegner courtesy Imperial War Museum, London; painting by Edward Ardizzone photographed by Larry Burrows courtesy Im-

perial War Museum, London—painting by Anthony Gross photographed by Larry Burrows courtesy Imperial War Museum, London; painting by Anthony Gross photographed by Zoltan Wegner, Crown Copyright reserved, by permission of The Controller of H.M. Stationery Office and of The City Museum and Art Gallery, Birmingham
180,181 Left, W. Bosshard from Black Star—Wide World; right, Dever from Black Star
182,183 British Official
184 From a painting by Roman J. Feldmeyer photographed by Herbert Orth courtesy Office of Military History, Department of the Army
189 through 195 Maps by K.C.&S. Studios
197 Dever from Black Star
198,199 Wide World
200 From a painting by Willfried Nagel photographed by Herbert Orth courtesy Office of Military History, Department of the Army
201 From a painting by Walter Preis photographed by Herbert Orth courtesy Office of Military History, Department of the Army—painting by Roman J. Feldmeyer photographed by Herbert Orth courtesy Office of Military History, Department of the Army
202,203 Painting by Max Ohmayer photographed by Herbert Orth courtesy Office of Military History, Department of the Army
204 Official U.S. Marine Corps
207 through 219 Maps by K.C.&S. Studios
221 Movietone News
222,223 Right, Official U.S. Navy
224,225 Movietone News
226,227 Painting by Saburo Miyamoto photographed by Herbert Orth courtesy Office of Military History, Department of the Army; painting by Hoshun Yamaguchi photographed by Horace Bristol courtesy Office of Military History, Department of the Army
228,229 Painting by Saburo Miyamoto photographed by Horace Bristol courtesy Office of Military History, Department of the Army
230 Painting by Kehei Ezaki photo-

graphed by Horace Bristol courtesy Office of Military History, Department of the Army
231 Painting by Chosei Miwa photographed by Horace Bristol courtesy Office of Military History, Department of the Army
232,233 Left, Official U.S. Army; center and right, Melville Jacoby
234 Wide World—Official U.S. Army
235 Wide World
236 Painting by Tom Lea photographed by Robert Crandall Associates
238 through 243 Maps by K.C.&S. Studios
245 Dmitri Kessel
246,247 Painting by Anton Otto Fischer photographed by Robert Crandall Associates courtesy U.S. Coast Guard Academy
248,249 Official U.S. Coast Guard
250,251 Wide World—Official U.S. Navy, Wide World, United Press International
252 through 255 Official U.S. Navy
256 Ullstein Bilderdienst
258,261 Maps by K.C.&S. Studios
273 Ullstein Bilderdienst
274,275 Wide World—European Picture Service, Ullstein Bilderdienst
276 Painting by Leslie Cole photographed by Larry Burrows, British Crown Copyright reserved, courtesy The City Art Gallery, Manchester
277 Paintings by Leslie Cole photographed by Larry Burrows courtesy Imperial War Museum, London
278,279 From a painting by Richard Eurich photographed by Walter A. Curtin courtesy Imperial War Museum, London; painting by Richard Eurich photographed by Walter A. Curtin courtesy The Trustees of the Tate Gallery
280 Frank Scherschel
282 through 291 Maps by K.C.&S. Studios
293 British Official courtesy Imperial War Museum, London
294,295 European Picture Service, Wide World—Twentieth Century Fox
296,297 British Official Newsreel from Pathe News
298,299 Painting by Richard Eurich

Continued Next Page

photographed by Larry Burrows by permission of The Trustees of the National Maritime Museum, Greenwich
300,301 British Official courtesy Imperial War Museum, London; Official U.S. Army; Official U.S. Army Signal Corps—British Official courtesy Imperial War Museum, London
302 Wide World
303 United Press International
304,305 United Press International, Pathe News
306,307 Eliot Elisofon
308,309 Painting by Fletcher Martin photographed by Robert Crandall Associates
310,311 Eliot Elisofon

Volume II

viii Artkino-Sovfoto
314,315 Maps by K.C.&S. Studios
317 News of the Day Newsreel
318,319 bottom center, Artkino-Sovfoto
320,321 Sovfoto
322,323 Top, Sovfoto
324 Painting by Aaron Bohrod photographed by Robert Crandall Associates
327 Map by K.C.&S. Studios
329 United Press International
330 Official U.S. Marine Corps from Pathe News
331 Ralph Morse
332,333 Painting by Aaron Bohrod photographed by Robert Crandall Associates, painting by Aaron Bohrod photographed by Herbert Orth
334,335 Painting by Tom Lea photographed by Herbert Orth
336 through 339 Paintings by Tom Lea photographed by Robert Crandall Associates
340,341 George Strock
342,343 Painting by Edward Laning photographed by Robert Crandall Associates, painting by Ogden Pleissner photographed by Robert Crandall Associates
344 From a painting by Mitchell Jamieson photographed by Henry Beville courtesy U.S. Navy
346,349 Maps by K.C.&S. Studios
352 Diagram by Seymour Robins
356 through 359 Maps by K.C.&S. Studios

361 From a painting by Mitchell Jamieson photographed by Henry Beville courtesy U.S. Navy
362,363 Painting by Mitchell Jamieson photographed by Henry Beville courtesy U.S. Navy
364,365 Robert Capa, United Press International
366,367 Robert Capa
368 Painting by Tom Craig photographed by Robert Crandall Associates
372,386 Maps by K.C.&S. Studios
389 through 393 Robert Capa
394,395 George Rodger, George Silk
396 through 398 George Silk
399 John Phillips
400 Painting by Floyd Davis photographed by Robert Crandall Associates
409,412 Maps by K.C.&S. Studios
415 Diagram by K.C.&S. Studios
417 British Official
418 Painting by Georg Brütting photographed by De Venny-Wood Studio courtesy Air Force Museum, Wright-Patterson Air Force Base, Dayton, Ohio—painting by Lothar Van Helden photographed by Henry Beville courtesy Office of Military History, Department of the Army
419 From a painting by Karl Raible courtesy Office of Military History, Department of the Army
420,421 Painting by Peter Hurd photographed by Robert Crandall Associates
422,423 Black Star, Official U.S. Air Force—Combine, Official U.S. Air Force (2)
424,425 Painting by Floyd Davis photographed by Robert Crandall Associates
426,427 Official U.S. Air Force
428 Royal Canadian Navy
430 through 439 Maps by K.C.&S. Studios
441 Official U.S. Army
442,443 Painting by Ogden Pleissner photographed by Robert Crandall Associates; from a painting by Richard Eurich photographed by Larry Burrows courtesy Imperial War Museum, London
444,445 Official U.S. Coast Guard
446,447 Robert Capa
448 Official U.S. Army—Official U.S. Coast Guard
449 Robert Capa
450,451 Painting by Aaron Bohrod

photographed by Robert Crandall Associates
452,453 Official U.S. Army, United Press International
454,455 Painting by Ogden Pleissner photographed by Herbert Orth courtesy City of Detroit Civic Center Commission
456 Painting by Aaron Bohrod photographed by Robert Crandall Associates—painting by Aaron Bohrod photographed by Herbert Orth
457 Painting by Aaron Bohrod photographed by Herbert Orth
458 Bob Landry
459 Ralph Morse
460 Painting by Tom Lea photographed by Robert Crandall Associates
462 through 471 Maps by K.C.&S. Studios
473 Painting by Aaron Bohrod photographed by Robert Crandall Associates
474,475 Painting by Kerr Eby photographed by Henry Beville courtesy U.S. Navy and Abbott Collection
476,477 Paintings by David Fredenthal photographed by Robert Crandall Associates
478,479 George Strock, Official U.S. Marine Corps
480,481 W. Eugene Smith
482,483 Upper right, George Rodger—Official U.S. Air Force
484 through 487 Paintings by Tom Lea photographed by Robert Crandall Associates
488 Painting by Dwight C. Shepler photographed by Henry Beville courtesy U.S. Navy
489 Painting by James Turnbull photographed by Henry Beville courtesy U.S. Navy
490,491 Carl Mydans
492 From a painting by Zygmunt Menkes photographed by Robert Crandall Associates
494 through 504 Maps by K.C.&S. Studios
509 Painting by Bernard Perlin
510,511 Paintings by Bernard Perlin photographed by Robert Crandall Associates
512 From the Archives of The Polish Underground Movement Study Trust—Ullstein Bilderdienst
513 European Picture Service
514,515 Paintings by David Fredenthal photographed by Robert

Crandall Associates
516 Official U.S. Army from Wide World
518 through 535 Maps by K.C.&S. Studios
537 Official U.S. Army
538,539 Paintings by Aaron Bohrod photographed by Robert Crandall Associates
540,541 George Silk
542,543 Left, Official U.S. Army Signal Corps—Johnny Florea; center, Johnny Florea; right, Official U.S. Army Signal Corps
544,545 Paintings by Aaron Bohrod photographed by Herbert Orth
546,547 Left, George Silk; center, Official U.S. Army—William Vandivert; right, Robert Capa
548,549 Painting by Ogden Pleissner photographed by Robert Crandall Associates
550 Johnny Florea
551 George Rodger
552,553 Official U.S. Army, Official U.S. Army from Wide World
554,555 Official U.S. Army Signal Corps, Free Lance Photographers Guild
556 Painting by Frede Vidar photographed by Henry Beville courtesy Office of Military History, Department of the Army
559 through 563 Maps by K.C.&S. Studios
565 From a painting by Takaeo Terada photographed by Henry Beville courtesy Office of Military History, Department of the Army
566 © Associated Press—W. Eugene Smith
567 through 569 W. Eugene Smith
570,571 Left, Official U.S. Navy; right, Wide World
572,573 From a painting by Dwight C. Shepler photographed by Henry Beville courtesy U.S. Navy
574 Official 21st Bomber Command
575 Official U.S. Air Force
576,577 Yoshito Matsushige
578,579 Official U.S. Navy
580 Drawing by Feliks Topolski
582 Map by K.C.&S. Studios
589 Joint Task Force
590,591 Official U.S. Air Force

Acknowledgement
Page 164 "We're off to See the Wizard," lyric by E. Y. Harburg, music by Harold Arlen, copyright 1939 Leo Feist Inc. Used by permission.

INDEX

601

608

615

The type face used in this book is Perpetua,

designed by Eric Gill and cut by Monotype Corporation Ltd., London, England

Engravings by R. R. Donnelley & Sons Company, Chicago, Illinois

and Graphic Color Plate, Inc., Stamford, Connecticut

Printed and bound by R. R. Donnelley & Sons Company,

Chicago, Illinois and Crawfordsville, Indiana

Paper by the Mead Corporation, Dayton, Ohio